The 50 Greatest Professional Wrestlers of All Time

The Definitive Shoot

by Larry Matysik

Published by ECW Press
2120 Queen Street East, Suite 200, Toronto, Ontario, Canada M4E 1E2
416-694-3348 / info@ecwpress.com

LIBRARY AND ARCHIVES CANADA CATALOGUING IN PUBLICATION

Matysik, Larry
The 50 greatest professional wrestlers of all time : the definitive shoot / Larry Matysik.

ISBN 978-1-77041-104-3
ALSO ISSUED AS: 978-1-77090-304-3 (PDF); 978-1-77090-305-0 (EPUB)

1. Wrestlers--Biography. 2. Wrestling. I. Title.

II. Title: Fifty greatest professional wrestlers of all time.

GV1196.A1M37 2013   796.812092'2   C2012-902747-2

Editor for the press: Michael Holmes
Cover design: Ellissa Glad
Cover images: (left to right) George Napolitano, Napolitano, Napolitano, Courtesy Special Collections of the University Libraries of Notre Dame. Back Cover: Courtesy Barbara Goodish
Text Design: David Gee
Typesetting & Production: Carolyn McNeillie
Printing: Edwards Brothers Malloy

Printed and Bound in the United States of America

For Pat and Kelly,
each of whom scores
at the top of her category.

"Some are born great, some achieve greatness, and some have greatness thrust upon them."

William Shakespeare, *Twelfth Night*

Contents

The 50 Greatest

CHAPTER 1
The Truth

The best. The finest. The greatest ever . . . baseball players, movies, presidents, rock 'n' roll tunes, actors, books, pizzas . . . No matter how specialized the interest, list-making almost always ignites passions.

Why should professional wrestling be any different? A colorful, chaotic, and thoroughly engrossing mix of athletics, theater, and excitement, since 1900 professional wrestling has lured countless fans and thousands of unique and supremely talented performers who have driven the industry in different and variously successful directions.

So, who *is* the best ever?

It's a great question, one fueled by Vince McMahon and World Wrestling Entertainment. National cable television and an omnipresent website are the perfect way for a mammoth marketing company to exploit the concept.

WWE is the twenty-first-century version of a national wrestling promotion, indeed a mammoth marketing operation, but it doesn't generally call what it produces *wrestling* because it fears being sneered at by some corporate type. And then the company and its leader berate that very disdain as being unfair to fans of wrestling, or does WWE want it called sports entertainment . . . Forget it, fans who follow WWE. Talk about wanting to have it both ways!

But that isn't the point. Late in 2010, Vince and WWE released a DVD celebrating what they called the "Top 50 Superstars of All Time." Of course they didn't call them wrestlers — it's as if Vince K. McMahon (or VKM as he likes to be called) and his minions are embarrassed to be involved in the very endeavor that has made the McMahon family filthy rich. Wasn't it professional wrestling, by whatever title Vince wishes to give it, that allowed his wife Linda to reportedly spend $100 million in two failed attempts to become a United States senator?

Why be ashamed of a business that stuffs your pockets full of money while entertaining millions of people from all walks of life? McMahon and his company slap every fan who ever spent a penny on them in the face — they can claim their tactics are just marketing, or television production, but it's mostly about ego.

Certainly he has the right, perhaps even the obligation to his shareholders, to expand the company into other areas. To pretend, however, that the removal of *wrestling* from the business' vocabulary will increase the odds of success in other promotional fields is absurd.

I want to spend the greater part of this opening chapter saying good things about Vince and WWE. Really, that is my intention. Make no mistake; Vince McMahon himself is one of a kind. Love him or hate him, but always respect him and his accomplishments while noting his failures.

After all, his company is a monopoly and a global enterprise, so how many bad decisions could he have made? Energy, imagination, ambition, need for complete control, understanding of television's all-powerful role, little regard for either ethics or individuals when it comes to business . . . all that and much more describe Vince.

He revolutionized professional wrestling at a time when television was changing. Somebody was going to do it. If the timing had been right, Sam Muchnick might have promoted pay-per-view shows, Fritz

Von Erich (Jack Adkisson) might have produced a seven-camera live television show, or Jim Barnett might have gone high-def.

Vince McMahon happened to be the right guy at the right time in the right place. He was very smart. And he was very, *very* driven.

See how difficult it is to write something praising Vince without adding "except" or "but"?

Let's try again.

Vince can certainly broadcast his list of the 50 greatest wrestlers (performers? entertainers? superstars?) to step into the revered squared circle. Nobody else enjoys his wrestling lineage, following his father and grandfather as a mover and shaker. Think of the stories he must have heard, the education he would have received, growing up in the McMahon family's highly profitable promotion.

Admittedly, with the overall wrestling business at the time fragmented geographically into numerous smaller territories, Vince may have overlooked the true value of certain headliners, since his attention would have been focused on Dad's little corner of the business.

Still, Vince watched many of the stars from the early 1970s on, and once in command he *made* a high percentage of the stars from the late 1980s on. Of course, having the playing field basically to himself (except for Ted Turner's World Championship Wrestling in the 1990s) helped. McMahon should have a legitimate grasp on the warriors who made this sport what it is today.

So, we have a right to expect a lot.

But we did not get what we expected.

Here is the list that WWE and Vince McMahon authored of the best 50 superstars to ever answer the opening bell . . .

1. Shawn Michaels
2. The Undertaker
3. Stone Cold Steve Austin
4. Bret Hart
5. Dwayne "The Rock" Johnson

6. Harley Race

7. Ricky Steamboat

8. Andre the Giant

9. Rey Mysterio

10. "Rowdy" Roddy Piper

11. Eddie Guerrero

12. Triple H

13. Gorgeous George

14. Randy Savage

15. Curt Hennig

16. John Cena

17. Ric Flair and Dusty Rhodes (tie)

19. Edge

20. Jerry Lawler

21. Lou Thesz

22. Terry Funk

23. Hulk Hogan

24. Bruno Sammartino

25. Chris Jericho

26. Ted DiBiase

27. Fabulous Moolah

28. "Classy" Freddie Blassie

29. Randy Orton

30. Pat Patterson

31. Iron Sheik

32. Jimmy Snuka

33. Mick Foley

34. Kurt Angle

35. Buddy Rogers

36. Gorilla Monsoon

37. Junkyard Dog

38. "Superstar" Billy Graham

39. Jake "The Snake" Roberts

40. "Big Show" Paul Wight
41. Jack Brisco
42. Sgt. Slaughter
43. Kane
44. Nick Bockwinkel
45. Jeff Hardy
46. Dory Funk Jr.
47. Bob Backlund
48. "Ravishing" Rick Rude
49. Batista
50. Killer Kowalski

Well now, imagine a professional baseball equivalent. The list's author would be skewered by the national media and the public alike for his abuse and ignorance of the legends who built the game — not to mention the total lack of comprehension about how past and present fit together.

Professional wrestling, too, has a true and real history, one that should be celebrated, not trashed in favor of the almighty dollar and the ego of a corporation that will not even admit that what it promotes is *wrestling*.

Call it what it is. Professional wrestling at its highest level requires an indefinable mix of hard work, showmanship, drawing power, and, like it or not, toughness and skill. By designating these 50 as the best *professional wrestlers* of all time, the wrestlers on this list would by definition have to embody the concept of being a superstar, a great worker, and having a magnetic personality.

When the WWE list became public, many in the industry — those not tied in some way to WWE — began to grumble. Even a rookie could scan the list and realize that many stars were included only to promote the current product and the alleged history belonging to WWE. Anyone could grasp what a large role personal politics played.

But really, was anyone surprised? This was marketing, with a tinge of politics. It's what Vince does, how he's always been. Get attention and turn a profit. WWE exists to make money, so why let truth get in the way?

How else does Kane end up among the 50 finest talents in the history of the game? How else could The Undertaker be selected as the second greatest ever to step through the ropes?

Yet WWE putting Harley Race sixth makes you blink because it's not far off the truth. Race is part of a generation to which McMahon has shown little respect. The answer to the riddle of why Race was selected over others from the old school elite is also more the result of politics and personality than anything else.

Overall, WWE's "greatest ever" package fits right in with McMahon's never-ending quest to rewrite the history of wrestling. Vince wants to run everything, control every thought, make every decision. Why not alter the past enough so that it supports the present?

This strategy works to a degree because such a high percentage of the current WWE audience is young and, understandably, knows little about the *true* history of wrestling. An entire generation of followers has grown up aware of wrestling only as a McMahon product. Sadly, some of the Internet voices who should celebrate a diversity of opinion and deeper knowledge are easily manipulated — so it is as if the past never counted.

This also explains how some of the goofiest ideas for booking in the WWE pass. The team responsible for creating the television shows, more and more, is made up of people who have no background in wrestling . . . and this is because of a conscious decision on Vince's part. To most of the creative team, WWE is just a silly stunt show with comedic undertones. In other words, Vince is happy to allow these limited booking minds to believe the history he has woven. It's a shock to some of these writers when Vince alters a plot, and the result looks at least a little like valid wrestling booking. Imagine what it's like when they discover wrestling existed *before* WWE — and that it was successful. The WWE list is an indictment of the business itself, and of those who watch it. Many griped, but not enough people did. And not enough to help new followers realize there *was* a Babe Ruth in wrestling, and there *was* a Wilt Chamberlain, and there *was* a Johnny Unitas — and someone comparable to Elvis Presley too.

Some truly important characters made their way onto WWE's top 50, but their lowly positions seem to display McMahon's personal distaste or disregard. It's politics as usual, no matter what WWE calls it. Only the most naïve could fail to see that the entire enterprise was corrupt.

But there are still a few of us who give a damn.

And maybe some of the young and the new are intrigued enough to delve a little deeper, to ask the right questions, to discover the rich heritage that professional wrestling has always brought to the table. The argument is not about whether those on the WWE list are good, and in some cases great, wrestlers. Of course, all are superb performers at some level. This is about who is *not* there; it is about where some have been buried when they unquestionably belong at the top.

The WWE list says that fans do not *care* to get it right. Once again, Vince and WWE *should* be ashamed about insulting the intelligence of their supporters.

It's time to get serious about this business. What are the parameters? What do we mean by the "best" wrestler? (You can bet your last dime that being the toughest certainly did matter into the late 1970s.) What part does charisma play? Who drew the money, the crowds? Who made an impact on popular culture?

Recognizing all the potential flaws, realizing that the end result is always subjective . . . this is the antidote to WWE and its flawed version of the 50 greatest professional wrestlers of all time. In the language of the business: this is a shoot.

Vince, I really did try to be nice and balanced. But your list is tainted by profit, politics, and personality.

It stinks.

CHAPTER 2

How to Choose

Vince McMahon and WWE had it easy. "Who can sell some DVDs for us?" was the only question that mattered to them.

The answer, naturally, was Shawn Michaels — because Michaels was headlining WWE's Hall of Marketing 2011. (Why call it anything else? Their own people openly describe their Hall of Fame as nothing but a marketing tool.) For the greater part of the 2000s, Michaels had been pushed by WWE as its premier worker, even though Michaels himself cleverly worked the system to get plenty of time off while protecting his position in the pecking order.

The deification of Michaels also fit nicely with the way WWE booked toward *WrestleMania*: the 2010 edition was highlighted by a truly tremendous duel between Michaels and The Undertaker. That titanic tussle was fresh in everyone's mind, and Michaels' name generated good buzz. Tying the massive promotional effort that always accompanies *WrestleMania* to pushing WWE's "greatest ever" DVD made business sense.

Michaels was going into the Hall the night before the 2011 *WrestleMania*, the show in which The Undertaker was making a comeback from a complicated shoulder surgery, so once more the marketing plan made sense — that's a compliment, not a complaint.

As for The Undertaker, his career is winding down in the wake of age and injury, but he has always been a major player, often the focus of spotlighted *WrestleMania* matches that put his long winning streak at stake. In fact, opening opposite The Undertaker in 2011 proved to be the perfect platform for the return of Vince's son-in-law, Triple H. No other match-up looked like it would draw much more than a hill of beans, so it was time to save the show by headlining older, proven names.

The trend continued in 2012, even with a pair of blockbuster draws like The Rock and John Cena topping the lineup. After surgery, recovery, and another year out of action, The Undertaker returned for a rematch with none other than Triple H, whose buddy Michaels was thrown into the mix as the special referee.

The others billed near the top of *WrestleMania* unfortunately were seen only as glorified supporting acts. The stars who made the show unique were The Rock, The Undertaker, Triple H, and Shawn Michaels.

And make no mistake, it was The Rock — in action, actually wrestling an opponent who meant something — who made *WrestleMania XXVIII* special.

According to the WWE version of the best of all time, clearly and obviously, Shawn Michaels is the greatest *superstar* of all time. He was their leading box-office draw at the time that list was issued. The Undertaker is listed at number two, because, like Michaels, he heads the group most likely to sell merchandise and pay-per-view buys.

They are the two greatest wrestlers in history — according to the gospel of Vince.

Oh, and Gorgeous George gets a slot in the top fifteen because WWE was bankrolling a movie about the erstwhile George Wagner turned bleached-blond bad guy in the hope of anointing him the father of modern sports entertainment (the McMahon rendition of wrestling today). If that movie hadn't been scheduled (and it has since slipped to documentary DVD status), poor George's stock would have sunk like a rock in the ocean. But, it made sense for WWE at the time.

For what WWE is and the goals that it has, this was without question the correct way to go. Vince made the right choice.

And any controversy only serves to boost awareness of the WWE project.

I'm helping them with this very book by calling attention to their list, and they helped me by starting the discussion. Those who agree with the selections of McMahon will be incensed by my arguments. Those insulted by McMahon's list will be more kindly inclined toward my choices.

This demonstrates excellent marketing as usual by McMahon and crew; WWE is right in the middle of every discussion, pro or con.

But let's get on with the real, serious business of deciding who the 50 best really are. WWE only dealt with professional wrestling from its rise in TV popularity. In fact, many of the big names from the early days of TV got short shrift.

Is that fair? If baseball created a comparable list, Babe Ruth and Ty Cobb would be eliminated because both were pre-television. In boxing, Jack Dempsey and Joe Louis would disappear. Think of football and Bronko Nagurski. Yet when those icons of culture, not just of sports, were prominent, so were Frank Gotch, Ed "Strangler" Lewis, and Jim Londos in wrestling.

Moreover, the public awareness of Lewis, Londos, and others was not all that far from what Ruth and Dempsey enjoyed. In some cases, certain historians would consider them comparable. Dig back through the old newspaper copies: the wrestlers often got as many column inches and headlines as the baseball players and boxers did. Additionally, the huge crowds for wrestling stars in the era compared favorably to the attendance figures for the stars from other sports.

What about the period of time, in television's infancy, dominated by Joe DiMaggio, Willie Mays, Mickey Mantle, and Rocky Marciano? Consider the wrestling equivalents of Lou Thesz and Verne Gagne (yes, and perhaps Gorgeous George to some extent). The entire country talked about wrestlers as much as the others, all thanks to their early television appearances. WWE television today, as slick as it is, is not the only television there ever was or that mattered.

Is Shawn Michaels today equal to Kobe Bryant when it comes to public profile? Hardly. How much did Mike Tyson being involved in a *WrestleMania* angle help Stone Cold Steve Austin? Who got the rub? And remember, Tyson was already well on his downslide.

Despite the modern marketing efforts of WWE, did their stars mean any more to the general public than Thesz or Londos, Lewis or Sammartino? In fact, with the proliferation of television cable outlets as well as the growth of the Internet, today there are many more ways for wrestlers to gain exposure. In the past, wrestling's stars had to compete for attention without corporate assistance in order to be recognized by the overall media and public. It was much more difficult to reach or even find the core audience of dedicated fans. But they did it and did it well.

Without the trailblazers — from Ruth to Lewis, from Dempsey to Londos, from Mantle to Thesz — their sports would have never become the mainstays of television that they are today. To ignore their contributions is just wrong.

Therefore, just on public awareness alone, just as it's possible to compare Ruth to Pujols and Howe to Crosby, it is also possible to compare Lewis and Thesz to Undertaker and Michaels.

Have the events changed over time? Of course. In baseball, more relief pitchers and more home runs. In football, less reliance on grind-it-out ground games and more on wide-open passing tactics. Hockey, basketball, *and* pro wrestling changed as well. On the mat, less concentration on the stiff, psychological work and more flying with a faster pace. More talk, less ring action, except on the biggest of the big shows.

But a home run is still a home run. A touchdown is still a touchdown. A pin is still a pin. A sellout crowd is still a sellout crowd. Measures and comparisons between eras are difficult, but possible and — truthfully — fun to do.

Thus, it's quite reasonable, with some serious thinking, to devise a rational and intelligent ranking of the greatest ever in each field —

including professional wrestling. In the end, the goal of pro wrestling has not changed one iota in more than a century . . . make money, hook the audience, entertain everyone.

This list celebrates those incomparable performers who were able to rise above their peers. The tough part is picking only 50 — *only 50* — from all those incredible talents over the decades . . . and then matching one against the other. But that's our goal: taking advantage of numerous different equations, qualities, and accomplishments to decide who belongs and who doesn't.

Maybe the most critical part of deciding who is here and is in what order really comes down to something very simple.

Common sense.

CHAPTER 3
And Common Sense Is . . .

Common sense is *not* easy to come by in a venture like this. It's certainly simplest to create a list the way WWE did, in which the primary consideration is marketing.

Common sense may be the hard way — but it is the *correct* way. Contradictions, inconsistencies, and controversies are bound to pop up despite the best effort to be fair and reasonable. No matter how much I struggle to be objective, in the end the creation of this list is subjective, an inexact science.

Nonetheless, without the *legitimate* greats, whether old school or new, Vince McMahon and WWE wouldn't have had a foundation to build upon.

There's a little wiggle room, of course, should Vince want to defend some pretty drastic missteps in his inventory of the greatest. According to Dave Meltzer and his superb website and newsletter *Wrestling Observer,* several WWE wrestlers with long histories (Dusty Rhodes, Ricky Steamboat, Michael Hayes, Gerald Brisco, surely Triple H, and likely more) took part in the balloting. The results were allegedly "tweaked" by an employee to satisfy Vince and Kevin Dunn, McMahon's longtime television production guru.

Meltzer was told Vince himself did not change the list but that there were indeed alterations made. For instance, supposedly Rey Mysterio was bumped much higher than his original slot to help sell his character to kids. What does that say about the seriousness of the WWE version?

Allegedly, some popular 1960–70s World Wide Wrestling Federation aces not as well known outside the WWWF boundaries were deleted for a more national name or two. Reportedly, Triple H is a serious student of the game and a huge fan of Harley Race. Add that to Trips's politically powerful position as Vince's son-in-law, and it may explain Race's surprisingly high position compared to others of his era.

Doesn't it seem odd, with the community of full-time wrestlers significantly smaller than it has ever been, that 11 of the top 20 who WWE claims are the best in history are current or very recent employees of WWE? And that Race is essentially the only outsider (despite more than 100 years and who-knows-how-many first-class wrestlers) qualified to land in the top 20 candidates, according to WWE?

Nonetheless, everyone involved clearly recognized that the likes of Michaels, The Undertaker, The Rock, Triple H, Hart, Austin, and Cena needed to be prominent. Of course, everyone involved felt the obligation to satisfy Vince first, which skewed the entire effort. Getting it right to satisfy the true history was obviously a much lesser consideration.

With all due respect to the effort Meltzer always makes to get the right story, does anyone truly believe that a micro-managing ruler like Vince McMahon didn't make sure, by quiet manipulation if not by specific direction, that the end result was what he wanted?

Whatever criteria WWE did or did not use, is there actually a better way to decide who are really, honestly, truly the 50 finest professional wrestling talents in history?

To make my results more accessible, my parameters are the English-speaking territories, where so many of the superstars have built notable reputations. Working within the English-speaking world alone is an overwhelming, almost insurmountable, task. And yet it leaves out the stars from Japan, Mexico, and even Europe. Realistically, no matter how much I respect many of them, few could have dealt with the language and custom barriers in order to become big names in the English-speaking world, and the promotions would not have supported them as big names. It's a long shot that the public would have accepted them as stars.

Japan is the country I'm most uncomfortable ignoring, since so many major stars in the United States and Canada also headlined there. In their heyday, All Japan and New Japan were meeting grounds for many of North America's leading names. The style in Japan was even more physically demanding, and the Japanese stars were tough and talented. So wrestlers who did big business in both America and Japan get extra points in this tabulation.

Unfortunately, the native Japanese names hardly ever crossed the Pacific except early in their careers when they were learning. No matter how good they were in the ring, North American promoters emphasized charisma and talking. The cultural and language obstacles eliminated these performers from getting the "big push." Only Antonio Inoki and perhaps Rikidozan or Baba have name recognition with the general North American fan. Trying to include those three plus the likes of Misawa, Tsuruta, Kawada, and Muta would confuse a system already overwhelmed by the number of entrants.

In Mexico, performers who are typically smaller than their North American counterparts and have a radically different style make comparison virtually impossible. The reality, which might sadly reflect prejudice, is that American names were big deals when they went to Japan or Mexico. But without major buildup, Japanese or Mexican names generally meant zero to audiences when they came to North America. It's for someone else to decide how that diverse group of wrestlers might figure into this kind of catalog.

And then there's the steroid issue. You can't change history, and I question if anyone has the right to claim moral superiority here. Guys are what they are, or were, and must be judged accordingly. Probably the only way to talk about steroid use is to compare how someone who benefited from enhancement drugs would have done without them in another period. That's tricky too — but what isn't in a project like this?

Still, it ties into another concern. Athletes train differently today, and they're bigger, stronger, and faster than ever before. Some people wonder if Lou Thesz or "Strangler" Lewis or Buddy Rogers would make today's WWE. Really? If these superb athletes were provided with the same modern training opportunities and advancements, none of them would be any good? That's ridiculous. They would shine because they started with more natural ability than anyone else. If Thesz had been born in 1968 like Kurt Angle, his inherent talent plus updated diet and training regimens would make him every bit the equal of the gold medal winner.

The other side is whether some of today's leading lights, without benefit of modern training or perhaps artificial help in some form, would have had the natural stuff to make it when the ride was a good deal rougher. If Angle had been born in 1916 like Thesz and had to learn and train as Thesz did, would he have reached the level he attained? For that matter, how much hard training did Shawn Michaels really do?

The quantity of talent in professional wrestling is so much smaller today than it ever has been, so how many of these performers really deserve to be in a legitimate Hall of Fame or, even less likely, on a selective index of the greatest wrestlers of all time?

As one prominent insider, who requested anonymity for fear of reprisal, openly admitted to me, the level of working ability is lower than it has ever been in wrestling history. The acrobatics are better, but that's about it. He is in the majority with this opinion. "It's not their fault," he said, alluding to those in WWE's employ, especially the newer players. "Most of them are terrific athletes, but they have nowhere to develop well-rounded skills and psychology anymore. Some of the bumps they take are spectacular, mind-boggling. But so much of the rest is missing.

"An advantage of the territory system was that, in addition to working constantly, you worked in the same towns regularly. So you had to think, change up your match, try new things, and become versatile," he added.

"Now the crew works the same town maybe twice a year, maybe three times. And the television is mostly all talk and skits or stunts. You don't have to think, and you don't have to sharpen your working skills. That means the quality of most matches slips, except for those big bumps or one high spot after another with no flow."

Anyone who says there is a clear-cut, black-and-white answer is not looking at all aspects of the problem. To just say the newer guys are better because they are newer is taking the easy way out.

One idea about how to choose the 50 finest came from serious fan Paul Fontaine. He would poll so-called historians. (Some of whom are excellent, some of whom aren't, just like sportswriters. Some have done oodles of research and are indeed knowledgeable. Others are more off-the-cuff opinion, without actual experience.) These historians would vote on a predetermined list of current and possible future Hall of Fame members. The Hall of Fame in question would be an unbiased one, such as the *Wrestling Observer's*. The historians would rank each candidate in certain areas, determine and add up point totals, and see who the Top 50 point-getters were.

The recipe, unfortunately, involves far too many cooks for the entrée to be successful. Additionally, few if any of the historians were personally involved deeply enough in the business to be aware of the politics that played such a part in who did or didn't get pushes and why. This study cannot all be about numbers.

A list like this can turn into a popularity contest. The good historians understand that meaningful results from any research on a subject that provokes as much heat as professional wrestling depend on a number of factors, including the context, promotions, talents, personalities, and politics of the time period being considered. And how many really were deep enough in the business themselves to grasp all the nuances?

So my decision was to go with my gut after some quiet, private input from a few keen and discerning wrestling intellects.

Some of those wise folks put the biggest emphasis on whether the wrestler in question was a great worker, regularly providing an exciting match no matter who the opponent was. Others were all about the box office, looking at who drew money consistently, because in this theory a fine match means nothing if nobody sees it. Finally, some felt it all came down to shooting, because if most of the other factors were in place, the shooter can make happen what *has* to happen for the good of the business — even if it is him losing.

At this point, I realized trusting my instincts meant finding the perfect balance between all these factors.

I began by listing all those names that stood out, regardless of era. Lewis, Londos, Stecher, Cena, The Rock, Austin, Flair, Thesz, Bruno, Funks, Hogan, and so on. Then, with more contemplation, I added other stars who deserved an invitation to this dance. (No, sorry, The Ultimate Warrior's attendance was never requested.) A little more study and digging through notes I'd made working for Sam Muchnick put some more names in play. I included those whom Vince trumpeted as the best ever, for many honestly deserve consideration.

Now I was fiddling with around 100 major performers from across the pro wrestling spectrum. Thus began the effort to work backward, eliminating some who just didn't make the cut whether by achievement, reputation within the industry, legitimate talent, or comparison against one another. Who stays? Who goes? Who had lasting power?

Finally, after a private Texas Death Match of epic proportions, I got the group down to around 60. Rather than continue with an unmanageable Battle Royal, it made sense to put them in order from very best to just best. After all, that's the goal. Actually, the first few were fairly easy, though some critics will disagree.

After going over everyone again and again, certain clusters of stars seemed to come together. That didn't make putting one ahead of the other any easier, but it became easier to see who belonged together, and which groups were superior to others, superior being a relative term considering the huge level of play involved.

The two most difficult choices were, first, ranking those from about number 20 on up, since they were all extremely close when considered objectively, and, second, deciding on who got the final spot. Who got number 50? Who got left out? I'll never be confident the correct selection was made. Even without voting from outside, Paul Fontaine inadvertently helped me in his suggestions of the qualities that had to be evaluated. His categories were *working ability, charisma, mic work, drawing ability,* and *legacy.* Only one attribute needed to be added.

First, I had to figure out the most inclusive and useful definition for each category. Then, notably, I had to add that one missing category, which is quite possibly *the most important.*

Real.

Reality. Legitimacy. Believability. The real deal. A true tough guy. A wrestler who can wrestle. And, before anyone squawks that everyone now knows professional wrestling isn't real, I add this proviso: the great wrestler has the ability to project reality. Pro wrestling has been built on great personalities, because the business is in fact a mesmerizing illusion; isn't it critical, then, that part of creating and sustaining the great personality is projecting reality? The perception of reality bleeds over into every category considered.

Eventually the great personality must deliver when it counts, when the paying public comes to see him perform in person or on a pay-per-view. If Joe Namath's Jets don't win the Super Bowl, he is not a great personality. The great personality in any field — *even* professional wrestling — must have something more than everyone else, or nobody will care about or pay to see him for very long.

At this point, I grant the careful reader an important point. Pro wrestling has a long and sordid history of paying homage to its carnival roots — yes, Vince, you too (remember Hulk versus *Zeus?*) — by developing one-dimensional, absurd personalities to steal a single house. These personalities are then tossed in the trash with no guilt.

But to be one of the truly finest 50 pro wrestlers in history — to be one of the guys who possessed more than a pretty face, a pumped-up physique, or a quirky delivery, and who met head-on the test of time and performance — a hell of a lot more is required. The *real* is pretty damn important to the final result.

Actors, directors, and writers move heaven and earth to make their characters in TV shows or movies seem *real,* even when a character is larger than life. It is the capacity to draw in the audience, make them care, and create the spectacle that has always hooked fans.

That moment when everyone suspends disbelief can only be created by a performer whom fans believe is real. Whether an athlete has the goods or has convinced the crowd that he does, *real* has *always* been a critical part of the "greatest" equation.

And, wait one moment for all the newer followers of this grand phenomenon who say *real* doesn't matter anymore, that it's all about catch phrases, sophomoric promos, stunt bumps, and subversive characters . . . The truth now is the same truth as it has always been. After all the highly polished baloney is finished, when the stakes are the biggest, what gets sold — lo and behold — is the flash of REAL.

For proof, look at the February 27, 2012, edition of *Raw,* when The Rock and John Cena were trying to clinch the audience for *WrestleMania.* Of course, everything was basically choreographed in detail as it always is today, improv having been shoved aside for the most part. But there came one moment . . . one brilliant instance . . . when tempers flashed, when the trigger was pushed right up to the point of no return.

Whether it was scripted (which by far would have surpassed the general writing of promos) or manipulation by the crafty McMahon (placing two proud and volatile personalities in a situation that became more intense than the performers anticipated) is not the point of this discussion.

What exploded was a moment of REAL. Or certainly what looked like real. Either way, the point is that this succeeded. Was Cena truly angry? Was Rock really upset? My goodness, those two do dislike each other, and they're ready to smack the snot out of each other — for real.

They sold REAL, which helped sell *WrestleMania XXVIII.* The general audience was buzzing about it the next day. Different place, different time . . . Lou Thesz could sell *real* with a glare and an elbow jammed in a vulnerable and highly visible place on an opponent. Skeptics would gasp, "Was a line crossed?" The crowd leaving would be talking: "Did you see how mad Thesz was? Don't know about the rest of that card, but that Thesz . . . wow, that match with Thesz was the real deal." And they'd pay to see it again, bringing along their friends who heard about it from them.

When everyone is all in and the time is at hand to draw the big money for the giant show, the ability to project real is critical. Always was, is now, always will be. In this case, it demonstrated why Rock and Cena belong with Thesz among the 50 greatest of all time.

So *is* professional wrestling real? The physical, mental, emotional, professional, and business demands on a meaningful performer show that this business is often all too real, at least for those within it.

Roddy Piper made an insightful observation at a legends convention in St. Louis in 2010. Looking over a head table that included Dory and Terry Funk, Ted DiBiase, Jimmy Snuka, Paul Orndorff, Ken Patera, and many others, Piper noted the crowd's emotional response. "You believed in us, because we were real!" Piper said. "What we did wasn't scripted or choreographed; it was a part of us coming out. Our personalities were our own. Whatever wrestling is now or was then, whether you booed or cheered, it was because you could feel how real we were. And you loved us!"

Projecting the aura of real is much easier when you *are* real — in fact, being real is often required. Something in the presence projected by Lou Thesz, Jack Brisco, Dan Hodge, and Kurt Angle shouted out that these were athletes that nobody, absolutely nobody, should ever mess with. The same was true of "Strangler" Lewis, Frank Gotch, Ray Steele, and Jim Londos, though in their time wrestling had a much stronger image, so it may have been easier for them.

These guys were tremendous entertainers with strong personalities. Brisco and Hodge were national collegiate champions (Brisco for Oklahoma State and Hodge for Oklahoma University), and Hodge was the only wrestler ever to be on the cover of *Sports Illustrated* until Hulk Hogan. In the play-for-pay wrestling world, Hodge was most famous for being the longtime junior heavyweight champion for the National

Wrestling Alliance. He also captured the Chicago Golden Gloves boxing title and had several victories as a pro boxer. In short, he was a monster, if one of smaller proportions than most professional grapplers at the time.

Brisco, who *looked* like a prime athlete, was the heavyweight king for the NWA from 1973 through almost all of 1975, not to mention NCAA champ in 1965 when he was a junior. He lost only one bout as an amateur.

The respect Brisco had within the industry as a professional was exemplified by a letter that Portland promoter Don Owen sent to then-NWA president Sam Muchnick. Complaining that the business was changing, Owen praised Brisco and called him a champion who could take care of trouble — for real. If Brisco had ever found himself double-crossed, a sudden shoot inside the squared circle, no doubt he would have solved the problem.

Angle, also an amateur titleholder (for Clarion University), earned an Olympic gold medal in freestyle wrestling in 1996. Despite being scripted into some of the goofiest interludes this side of John Cena, Angle took to the pro game like a duck to water. Even when the promotion diverted attention from his ring skills, his history and the smoothness of his work showed spectators that Angle was the real deal. He simply wasn't allowed to display it to the fullest extent.

As for Thesz, he was already a salty professional at the age that Hodge, Brisco, and Angle were beginning their college careers. Originally trained by legendary hooker George Tragos (a true tough guy who taught Thesz how to hurt uncooperative foes in a variety of ways), as a young stud Thesz came under the influence of Ad Santel, who furthered Tragos' teaching, and then particularly "Strangler" Lewis. Thesz's knowledge of how to handle an opponent was polished by the dangerous Lewis. And Ray Steele, also an adept shooter, educated Thesz in making money in the business. For years, Thesz dominated the professional wrestling game because he drew big gates on cards he topped and because nobody wanted to test him if the game got nasty. Thesz's reputation of legitimacy elevated any bout far above the usual drama; paying customers instinctively knew Lou's skills were on a higher plane than the vast majority.

In other words, the fact that Thesz could cast the spell that he was real made his work that much more effective. Being real today is much more difficult because most of wrestling's magic has been divulged to the public. Furthermore, the talent who can display that kind of dexterity are now often lured to Mixed Martial Arts.

But there is another kind of real. Consider Dick the Bruiser. A football player for the Green Bay Packers before he became a wrestler, Bruiser's claim to reality fame may have come on November 19, 1957. Bruiser and Dr. Jerry Graham sparked a riot at New York's Madison Square Garden as they battled Antonio "Argentina" Rocca and Edouard Carpentier. According to most accounts, while the other three wrestlers found cover or guarded Dick's back, Bruiser clobbered numerous fans who jumped into the ring. Dick had a wonderful time.

In 1963, Bruiser was in a feud with suspended pro football star Alex Karras, who had taken up wrestling in the interim. Bruiser invaded a Detroit bar owned by Karras, resulting in a back-alley donnybrook that ended with Bruiser injuring several police officers and getting arrested. Lawsuits from the brawl lasted for years. This was not an angle. It wasn't scripted by anyone. Dick just went to the dive looking for trouble, quite real on his own terms. And one look made every fan understand that fact.

By the same token, Harley Race, Bruiser Brody, and Stan Hansen were tough guys in the ring *and* out. With them, the *feel* of danger was always present. Whether or not Andre the Giant actually was 7'4", was there any doubt he truly was a *giant* who could hurt someone *for real*? The huge face and immense hands alone were enough to terrify most folks.

Isn't this the formula that Stone Cold Steve Austin also successfully tapped into? While the in-ring business had changed notably from the days of Bruiser, didn't Austin convey that edge of real danger? True, Vince McMahon and his creative crew drew from what Austin brought to the table, but fans screamed for him because they believed that for at least one moment in time Stone Cold might actually be just as mean as he acted.

Did this factor actually help Hulk Hogan, of all people? Nobody would question his incredible physique and those bulging biceps. Yet, when he was really on fire, the idea that Hulk might in truth be unbeatable played in his favor. He was incredibly powerful — and fans wondered what would happen if he actually did snap, *for real.*

At Hogan's peak in the 1980s I was working for the World Wrestling Federation. Big John Studd, often a rival of the Hulkster, was a buddy of mine from my St. Louis days, and we shared the common thread of a friendship with Bruiser Brody. We often discussed the business, particularly when Brody talked about coming into the WWF to deal with Hogan and Vince.

How Brody, the last real independent, would interact in a corporate environment and with Hogan in particular had me curious. Admittedly, I was less than impressed with Hulk as a wrestler when the chips were down. As Thesz told me, "Hogan doesn't know a wristwatch from a wristlock. A wrestler would tear him apart."

Of course, Brody was not a wrestler per se, not like Brisco or Pat O'Connor. He was a marvelous athlete, a street brawler who was tough as nails. Brody was not a shooter in the vein of Thesz, though he certainly was able to shoot. Brody was nonetheless a volatile personality who had his moments. I thought there was the chance something in the ring might get out of control between him and Hogan, though that seldom happened anymore. I asked Big John for his thoughts, because I knew Brody would go to war: how would Hulk do if that moment occurred?

"Let me tell you," said the easygoing Studd, "Hulk is for real. He's strong as a bull. Those muscles are real. He'll fight. I know him. Hulk's a tough son of a bitch. He's worked too hard to get to this point, and he'll fight anyone."

Somehow, fans understood that reality — whatever it was — about Hulk Hogan. Maybe it wasn't the same reality that they sensed about Thesz, Brisco, or Angle, but it was a reality that made believing even easier.

Want another version of real? How about Bruno Sammartino? In a time before most competitors were gassed, Bruno was a powerhouse who made sense. While his ethnic appeal in parts of the Northeast helped, what helped much more was how he came across: a class act, a no-nonsense scrapper, a competitor. Willing to fight for what he had earned. A *good* guy, more than just a "babyface." His followers *cared* what happened to Sammartino.

How many stars of today come across as real? Once upon a time, John Cena could have delivered in that area. In fact, he does more charitable work for WWE than is called for. He goes the extra mile for his boss, never ducking a public relations outing. But so much of his wrestling persona is scripted and clearly fiction that he fails to connect with a large part of the potential audience. Bruno made that connection.

Even in this so-called modern period, when so many of wrestling's secrets have been made public, McMahon occasionally reverts to a time when the reputation of being a "real" tough guy made a difference. For example, when Booker T got the better of muscular Dave Batista in a personal squabble, Vince reportedly changed the way he booked Batista for a time to keep the public from becoming aware that a potential champion had lost a real fight.

Now, for this exclusive list, just being a terrific wrestler is not enough. Plenty of solid performers who raised the quality of any show they were on would never be considered for this list. They might have been superb wrestlers but they lacked in other areas. Being rugged either in the ring or in an alley is also not enough. But add being real, or at least being perceived as real, to any of the other vital traits and you'll have someone who might well belong in that unique class of the best ever.

The air of legitimacy adds to every other attribute that a wrestler must possess in order to make the greatest ever lineup. Legitimacy permeates the entire discussion. This is just common sense.

Let's examine working ability. Working is required, but "being a good worker" alone is not enough, just as being a fine technical wrestler is not enough. There is a broader and much more valuable definition of what working at *this level* is.

Many currently define working as flying, executing inventive aerial moves, and incorporating acrobatics into a smooth exhibition that to the uninitiated would appear totally choreographed. Stunt bumping becomes the sizzle. Those whose knowledge of the sport is limited to the last decade will be massively impressed by this style because that is how they've been educated by television wrestling.

On *Tough Enough* in 2011, Austin — as the coach — called one candidate "a good mechanic" who lacked that extra something to set himself apart from the herd.

In a St. Louis dressing room, I once heard Hulk describe "up-and-down guys." He said, "Really need them on a good card, brother." John Studd, who was also there, added, "They're valuable, make the show better. But they don't draw money."

Sam Muchnick, while never failing to respect what good performers could accomplish, was quick to point out that stars, who come in unique packages, draw money. In the quiet of the wrestling office, or behind the closed door of a dressing room at Kiel Auditorium, I often heard some of the smartest people (not just Muchnick) ever involved in the business say, "He's a great worker, but . . ."

What followed the "but" was always the same: "He can't draw money."

Thus, working is much more than just going "up-and-down" efficiently, particularly when competing for a spot among the greatest who ever stepped through the ropes.

Foremost, a great worker must draw the fans into every aspect of the battle. He must create the roller coaster of emotions that comes from wanting one combatant to win, one to lose. It might be done with acrobatics, superior wrestling, perhaps even brawling. Psychology is the real key, even if it's not recognized as such today. Every great worker discovered how to use his unique talents to build to the climax. There is more than one way to achieve the goal.

To that end, I vehemently argue for widening the definition of *working* and *worker*. It's face and pace, context and content and connection with the crowd. If he can succeed at that complete form of working, a true superstar really gets over as more than just inspiring noise; he can sell tickets (or PPVs) on his own strength, whatever modern branding is attached to him.

Lou Thesz built his crowning moments from a chess battle, a test of wills. Often he would use his mat skills against a brawler, overwhelmed by the brute force and then coming back with sharp back body drops and drop kicks. His facial expression, his seriousness, and even his anger all played into the development of a great match: psychology. Once in a while in a title battle Thesz would deliver a hard elbow to the jaw of a foe, or a sudden twist of the neck, and because he was so in control even those subtle movements would elicit an "ooh" from the crowd.

Thesz had the reputation of being legitimate, so no matter what some critics said about wrestling, the matches he engineered often reached a crescendo equal to anything aided by fireworks and music today. There's nothing wrong with the latter, but individuals are not as responsible for the response. Yet when The Undertaker and Triple H trade finishing maneuvers that the crowd believes in, the reaction is deafening.

Thesz understood that a performer sold differently when he was meeting Pat O'Connor or Wilbur Snyder than when he was dueling Dick the Bruiser or "Wild Bill" Longson. A so-called rest hold was never a rest hold to a great worker in the classic scientific mold. The grappler applying the hold had to add an expression, move his body, give an extra twist. The recipient had to squirm and groan and show his pain visually, to demonstrate to the audience why it mattered. For a master such as Thesz or Brisco, if his opponent was *not* selling sufficiently, a few more degrees of tension might make it easier for the victim to yell in pain.

For a heel like Longson, Bruiser, or Fritz Von Erich, the key was to make the good guy suffer — to sell that suffering — from the kicks, punches, and punishment they unleashed. The bad guy had to lay those shots in, and the good guy had to sell. Thus, when the comeback finally got going, fans were ready to roar. Guess whose selling mattered then?

Terry Funk has said this to me often: "Nobody today knows how to sell. They don't understand how important it is to get the crowd on your side. Babyfaces sell, then heels sell. Sell for each other, but so few of them now understand how. And nobody knows how to punch right either."

Bob Orton Jr., Randy's father, noted that the focus isn't on the ring nearly as much anymore: "The agenda is different. It's all about characters and how they are written."

And virtually every wise heel decries the loss of that art, how to really *be* a heel. Ah, there is that word again — real. Heels don't do enough heel stuff. Everybody works pretty much the same, similar bumps and high spots, except when the never-ending angles begin, and a lot of wrestlers — good guy and bad guy — look pretty much alike and do pretty much the same moves!

Considering his lengthy experience in wrestling, one would not be surprised to hear Vince McMahon — if he were relaxed and off-guard — agree that working is a lost art. New talent doesn't have the benefit of years of experience against different rivals before smaller crowds. The learning curve is mostly flat. Much of the psychology has disappeared. Once, wrestling was accused of being scripted, but it was all improvisation. Now, due to a perceived need, it becomes highly scripted and often choreographed.

In the long run, scripted fights may not detract from what today's talent does. After all, they can only perform within the boundaries of what the owner wants. The point is, though, that having to call your own shots and build your own story was perhaps a more challenging scenario for those wrestlers from the early twentieth century through the '80s.

Yes, they knew the destination. They knew the finish. They knew where they were going. But how they got there was *their* challenge and the big unknown. The true greats made the journey to "get there" nothing short of fascinating.

Many big stars had different philosophies of what worked for them. Johnny Valentine was certainly like that. At times, the legitimate tough guy was criticized for being slow or even plodding, though physically he was often stiff and punishing. But when he directed the action toward the finish, suddenly explosions happened everywhere and the crowd, every man and woman and child, was on their feet. Suddenly the roof was rattling. Valentine had everyone hooked.

"I remember how guys in a territory were when Valentine first arrived," Terry Funk recalled. "At first, they'd gripe about his style. The second time around, and after Valentine had some television, all of them would be trying to work like Johnny Valentine. His success would make everyone rethink the best way to work."

But that was Valentine's style. Rey Mysterio, having been raised in the acrobatic culture of Lucha Libre in Mexico, had a totally different approach. When he finally got the opportunity to work with bigger foes, Mysterio made it all fit. Of course, with regard to his small stature (is he even 5'4"?), whether he would have gotten that chance in earlier times when the number of active wrestlers was larger, and many were much bigger, is questionable.

And yet another method to get over was used by Gene Kiniski, a whirlwind who never took a backward step and never stopped moving, much like Killer Kowalski. "Wild Bill" Longson, the first all-out heel to have the championship, established the parameters for a bad guy sitting on the throne. He made the piledriver a famous and dreaded finishing maneuver. Nick Bockwinkel, meanwhile, made the fans care; he made them want to see the erudite Bockwinkel get smacked around. Probably Joe Stecher and Ray Steele had specific strategies to hook the customers psychologically too.

Would it work now? Well, consider that the likes of The Undertaker, Shawn Michaels, and even Triple H borrow useful pieces from many of the past greats. Moves are often rewarded by being called "new" and "inventive" even when they were bombshell finishes in perhaps 1960. But that trio has some political strength within the WWE boardroom, which allows them more room to lay out their bouts. How much leeway do John Cena and CM Punk have in calling their matches?

And up pops a current criticism. Could the old-school heroes do the high-flying antics executed today? And similarly, could modern stars perform the stiffer, more psychological material of their predecessors? What likely matters most is whether either could dominate in the style that was or is prevalent for them.

Everybody today, or so it feels, wants smooth, seamless action with one spot following another. Of course, that's because television shows have educated one group of followers to like only that style. Yet there are criticisms when the crowd doesn't react as expected. Seamless action without emotion is not great work. Flip-flop, flip-flop = a cheerleading competition.

Great workers had and have rough edges.

Maybe the closest in recent years to that so-called perfect match was Randy Savage against Ricky Steamboat at *WrestleMania III*, although some would argue for Michaels versus Undertaker. But that was one test, one night in either case. Go back a few or more years to Dory Funk Jr. against Jack Brisco, a series of who-knows-how-many highly athletic, one-hour duels. Each outing told a different story, usually with a different crowd favorite, and eventually with a different titleholder. Rather than gearing all the training, strategy, and thinking toward one single event in the year, every outing for Brisco and Dory Jr. was *the* big match in that specific market, and most of those matches sold out. They had to deliver over and over, and they did. What a challenge!

How comparable was that to Pat O'Connor against Lou Thesz, or Thesz against Longson? Or even "Strangler" Lewis against Joe Stecher? Maybe Gotch versus Hackenschmidt?

The point is all of the greats — whether 100 years ago or 50 years ago or today — found a way to elevate the art of working higher than it had ever been.

CHAPTER 4
From Charisma to Box Office

Consider the mysterious issue of charisma. Who's got it? Who doesn't? And what in the world is it really? It's not a straightforward issue. Many promoters and bookers have believed they've spotted some performer who had that indefinable something, that gift of magnetism that will draw in the dollars. Then they booked that particular wrestler as if he were a star. And . . . nothing. People just didn't buy the guy in a top position.

Even those with a reputation for uncovering wrestlers who have the rare gift of charisma have guessed wrong — even before the late 1980s, when the equation of big muscles with charisma reached its apex under Vince and what was then called the World Wrestling Federation. Some really poor performers were hyped but then failed at the box office. Too many promoters thought that a wrestler who looked like "Superstar" Billy Graham would automatically generate charisma. How wrong they were.

Charisma is tricky enough without artificial enhancement. Physique — whether brought about by genetics, weights, or drugs — can help a wrestler. But by themselves, muscles do not make a star.

Size is something anyone can spot when searching for that break-out performer. Particularly today, WWE seems fixated on finding someone 6'2" or taller, someone 240 in-shape pounds or heavier. That might make sense, until both this book's list and the WWE's are compared. The sizes of the entrants are all over the map.

Thus, there's something more to consider. Is it being handsome? What exactly does *handsome* look like, since different people may have different tastes? The need for a larger casual audience demands a need to hook female followers. Does that mean the guys have to be good looking? Sex appeal definitely is part of it. But good looks cannot be forced. Spectators see right through that, which is why so many a gimmick performer has failed, whether he's an independent matman trying to be bizarre or an eager youngster reading the lines and wearing the costume as scripted.

Perhaps personality is the added ingredient. Intensity is part of it too. The fans have to "buy into" the particular quest of the individual wrestler. If his look is bland, if the sincerity of his enthusiasm is suspect, a performer is not going to reach that special plateau. And I'm not talking about being one of the 50 greatest, but rather earning a spot on the big stage at all. And what an accomplishment that is.

Charisma can be as simple as the twinkle in the performer's eye. Spectators and promoters alike can see when someone is having fun doing what he's doing. He's not there only for a payday; it's not just a job. He is there because this is his dream, his passion, what he wants to do more than anything else.

You can see it. You can feel it. You can sense it.

This is what the true superstars have always had, along with all the other gifts. On my list of the 50 best, every single one has an ineffable presence.

Once upon a time, the word *showmanship* was freely substituted for charisma. It's not the same, though showmanship is probably part of the quality of a performer's charisma. A wrestler can dress himself up, bleach his hair, or dance to music. Many did. Is that charisma? For the most part, the guys who were in preliminaries before their makeovers are *still* in preliminaries.

Over the years, Vince McMahon actually formalized showmanship. His theory is that adding the fireworks, the video screen, and the ear-splitting music, along with a touch of choreography, can emphasize whatever charisma the performer has. All the noise and sizzle did add to the fun of going to a wrestling show for a certain portion of the audience.

But let's look at the Ultimate Warrior, always a polarizing figure. The music blaring and the fireworks blasting, he sprints into the ring in St. Louis for a battle with Andre the Giant. He flexes his muscles, shakes the ropes, and snarls. Criss-cross, he bounces from one side of the ring to the other. Then the bell rings. And there is no noise. Why are the fans silent? Everyone is waiting for . . . nothing. The ability to lead a match, to work with different opponents, to get into the heads and hearts of many fans, just wasn't present for Warrior.

As Ted DiBiase said, "We had to lead him around by the nose." That's harsh, because Warrior had some athleticism. Jim Hellwig was a product of his time, a muscle monster with explosive energy who busted his tail for a promotion that convinced its audience this made a star. He had a memorable *WrestleMania* duel with Hulk (kudos for Hogan) in 1990 and did draw generally strong houses during his stardom. But Warrior required a strong hand who grasped what needed to be done in order to have a decent match. Showmanship wasn't enough.

Finding the potential break-out star is much more than difficult. John Cena is a perfect example. Jim Ross was deeply involved with finding talent for WWE when he and Bruce Prichard found Cena, at Rick Bassman's UPW operation in Southern California. Ross's group signed Cena (a huge wrestling fan who had also been an offensive lineman at a small college in Massachusetts) and sent him to Ohio Valley Wrestling in Louisville, which was then WWE's training facility.

The late Jim Barnett was working for McMahon at the time. A brilliant albeit controversial operator, Barnett had a reputation for spotting potential stars that dated back to the early 1960s, when he promoted

Detroit and later had a tremendously successful operation in Australia. Eventually he landed in Atlanta during the early days of cable before gravitating to the WWF/WWE.

Barnett was big on Cena from day one and reputedly repeated to Vince that Cena was a potential star. Paul Heyman was also pushing for Cena, though maybe before Cena had all the experience he needed on the mat. Cena got the reputation that he couldn't work, which often happens to new talent that WWE brings aboard. Before Barnett passed away, he told a couple of friends that he'd called Vince and told him not to bury Cena — that Cena had the goods. At least, that was Barnett's story!

Then Stephanie McMahon, Vince's daughter and a huge influence on the creative and talent side of WWE, spotted Cena doing a rap. She was smitten with the character, so Cena zoomed to the top.

All that drama for someone who definitely has charisma! And it has always been that difficult for the performer to be seen by the right people, to land the most advantageous chances, and finally to get the opportunity to shine. As much as professional wrestling has always sought out new and invigorating talent, finding it is so difficult that even the sharpest eyes often struggle to recognize exactly what they are looking for.

"Mic work," as it's now known, helps display a performer's charisma. This certainly was easier when wrestlers did their interviews off-the-cuff, with minimum planning and maximum personality. "Easier," that is, for a promoter or booker to discover what the wrestler had to offer. More of the real person was on display because he had to come up with both the words and the presentation himself.

In theory, the recent practice of scripting interviews allows the wrestler to stay consistent with the character a promoter has assigned to him and to follow up directly on angles that involve him.

In the past 20 years, more attention has been focused on outspoken and colorful characters. More time is spent talking, not wrestling. In the context of a "50 greatest" list, should these newer verbal pyrotechnics give someone from the modern era a leg up on those who did interviews in the 1970s or 1960s? Because these wrestlers are on national cable television, exposed to a larger audience, are they better than those who had to get over in market after market, with subtle changes in emphasis and nuance? Which is the bigger achievement?

Well, part of the answer naturally leads to another question — are the wrestlers who do that type of promotion drawing bigger crowds? It's a difficult calculation, considering the change in emphasis from drawing at arena cards to obtaining PPV buys and television ratings.

The general consensus is that the total national audience for professional wrestling (or "sports entertainment") is not as big as it once was, even though it still reaches huge numbers of fans and, with only one major promotion, is easier to see for the mainstream media.

The question of whether today's version of mic work deserves more points, so to speak, cannot be clearly answered. Consider this: many observers would say Shawn Michaels, John Cena, or Edge are better with a mic than Jack Brisco, Lou Thesz, or Bruno Sammartino because they're more explosive, more controversial.

But there's the point: the world was different for Brisco, Thesz, and Sammartino. The line between so-called good guys and bad guys was more clearly defined. That is what the audience wanted and expected.

To say that Brisco or Verne Gagne or the babyface version of Ted DiBiase were not comparable with their mic work to Michaels, Triple H, or Stone Cold Steve Austin is flat-out wrong. The audience of the time expected their heroes to sound like Tom Seaver, John Havlicek, and Bobby Orr: serious, smart, knowledgeable, and determined to be the best. Top-of-the-line professional athletes. Always projecting intensity, not bizarreness: comic-book characters need not apply. This was a natural and real part of these wrestling heroes' personalities and charisma. This is not to say that one time period in wrestling was better than the other, but rather that you *can't* choose between the two. Wrestlers of each era were equally effective in gaining attention and making money for both themselves and the business.

And the bad guys? Were the promos of the likes of Harley Race, Gene Kiniski, and even "Superstar" Billy Graham any less productive or entertaining than what The Miz or Alberto Del Rio do?

I mentioned DiBiase, and he's an interesting case study. He excelled as a babyface interview when he was a rising young territorial star; he excelled as a heel interview as the evil Million Dollar Man. That speaks to what charisma is.

Telling the difference between good and bad is much more difficult today, especially when the same writers are generating material for both parties. Individual personalities don't sound as varied as they once did, and that is to the detriment of pro wrestling. Anyone who ever heard Terry Funk, Dick Murdoch, Fred Blassie, or The Crusher in their primes, cutting loose with the full force of their personalities, has probably realized that the stars of that time could play the game with anyone from today.

Step back a few more years and consider Buddy Rogers, giving incredible interviews oozing with presence, arrogance, and disdain — and drawing money! Or Johnny Valentine, so intense and serious and plain mean. All of them did what the time required, and they did it beautifully.

Now, complicate the mic-work issue even further. Consider the media as it was confronted by "Strangler" Lewis, Jim Londos, "Wild Bill" Longson, Frank Gotch, Joe Stecher, and even Lou Thesz in his early days. Just because these wrestlers weren't promoting their product on television doesn't mean they weren't doing public relations. They were, and it required hard work, lots of imagination, and the ability to talk and get themselves over with editors and writers. They still needed bigger-than-life personalities. Indeed, that kind of PR was just another version of mic work.

Newspapers were the key. And by all accounts "Strangler" Lewis was one of the best at using his reach. In every town where he headlined (and he was on top *everywhere*, from coast to coast), the local newspaper would herald whatever main event he was in. He could be charming or controversial, always someone who generated a story to read. In fact, Lewis was so good that the NWA used him *after* he retired, having him go into towns ahead of Thesz to stir up interest.

Still, all of the charisma in the world cannot get a pro wrestler into a top position if he cannot work. Even if his charisma snags opportunities for him, he won't stay long if his matches are lousy. Charisma and an ability for mic work may help the performer connect with fans, but not without at least an element of credibility in his athletic execution. Face it — Harrison Ford made viewers believe in Indiana Jones, at least while they were watching the movies. Of course, Harrison had the advantage of special effects in making movies.

Pro wrestlers have to do it alone and nearly naked in the ring.

The point is that none of the areas to be considered when choosing the 50 greatest pro wrestlers of all time stands alone. Charisma is critical. Alone it's not enough. Talking is important. Alone it's not enough. Working is necessary. Alone it's not enough.

So how else do we determine which performers put all the pieces of this complex puzzle together? One obvious indicator might be found in attendance numbers. But we can't just look at gross money figures because inflation has changed things too much for reasonable comparison across the eras. We can't rely on turnstile numbers either, because even the best formulas are not perfect.

And while the ability to draw fans may not be enough to secure a spot among the 50 greatest performers ever, it still should be part of the equation. Every finalist had to draw a significant amount of money. Making money is the point of the entire exercise, whether it is called professional wrestling or sports entertainment.

Who connected well enough to make people spend their hard-earned dollars to see the pro wrestler in action? In the decades before pay-per-view, there were many more "big" house shows, more opportunities to crack what was generally considered the magic mark of 10,000 in attendance. This meant more chances to either pack the joint or to fail. Advantage: old school or territorial stars.

Today, because the big pay-per-view events set up shop in a large building, the attendance is virtually guaranteed to be more than 10,000. Larger lineups and more headline matches mean more wrestlers who get credit for busting the 10,000 ceiling. Advantage: new school or monopoly promotion stars.

Maybe in the end it evens out, which makes research such as that done by hard-working Matt Farmer all the more meaningful. While Farmer doesn't claim to have written the complete gospel of attendance, his study gives a well-rounded picture of those who, over time, generally drew fans. It may not be perfect, but it is pretty doggone good.

For example, when calculating the territorial period, there were a lot of strong markets that had buildings with 6,000– or 7,000-seat capacities. Selling them out was profitable; over time huge numbers of fans added up because they wanted to see a certain wrestler. This unfortunately doesn't count in Farmer's equation, but he had to set a standard somewhere. Ten thousand people it is.

After digging through countless files, clippings, and accounts of arena shows, Farmer developed a formula to determine who is among the best drawing cards of all time. The following list is updated through the end of 2010. The position of each wrestler is based on the number of shows each headlined that drew 10,000 or more, with added points for those who dominated in drawing customers in a particular year. Please note that Farmer also included Mexico and Japan in his computations.

The results, geared to the 50 best ever, are eye-opening:

1. Jim Londos
2. Bruno Sammartino
3. Lou Thesz
4. "Wild Bill" Longson
5. Hulk Hogan
6. Ed "Strangler" Lewis
7. Argentina Rocca
8. Ric Flair
9. Buddy Rogers
10. Joe Stecher
11. Dick the Bruiser

12. The Sheik

13. Triple H

14. Killer Kowalski

15. Bob Backlund

15. Andre the Giant

17. "Whipper" Billy Watson

17. Stanislaus Zbyszko

19. Yvon Robert

20. John Pesek

21. The Rock

22. The Undertaker

23. Frank Gotch

23. Konnan

25. Mistico (now Sin Cara in WWE)

26. Everett Marshall

27. Gene Kiniski

29. Ed Don George

29. Harley Race

29. Dick Shikat

29. Gus Sonnenberg

29. Stone Cold Steve Austin

29. Antonio Inoki

34. John Cena

35. Danno O'Mahoney

35. Randy Savage

35. Johnny Valentine

38. Shawn Michaels

38. Perro Aguayo Sr.

38. Gorgeous George

41. "Classy" Freddie Blassie

41. The Crusher

43. "Superstar" Billy Graham

43. Shinya Hashimoto

45. Ray Steele

45. Dory Funk Jr.

47. Ray Stevens

47. Verne Gagne

49. Pat O'Connor

50. Keiji Mutoh

50. Rikidozan

50. Dusty Rhodes

50. Sandor Szabo

Antonio "Argentina" Rocca jumps out. Although he had a strong run due to what was in the early days of television a style totally different from other grapplers, most critical observers would maintain that Rocca's main popularity was in the Northeast, a narrow geographical area but one that was densely populated and therefore had larger auditoriums in which to work. Risking political correctness, some would also say that his appeal was ethnically limited. And Rocca never duplicated that drawing power for any length of time elsewhere.

Furthermore, many would call Rocca's in-ring skills mediocre, although he was a dynamic acrobat. In the same vein, some might respond, "What about Andre the Giant? He was just a giant."

But Andre drew *everywhere* he appeared, filling both the buildings that held greater than 10,000 and the many that seated fewer. He did so for many years and still had enough juice left in his career to entice gigantic national television ratings when the WWF was on NBC, along with an incredible attendance at *WrestleMania III*. Everyone, no matter age or sex or race, wanted to see Andre. Moreover, what he could do once the bell rang garnered much more respect than anything Rocca could do, even if both were essentially limited to their gimmick.

When the comparisons and the contradictions and the contrasts have been weighed, when the judgments and evaluations have been completed, each performer who belongs on this treasured roster should leave a legacy. Fans, promoters, and other wrestlers will always remember these performers for what they brought to the table, for the unique talents that energized the crazy wrestling world.

Add and appraise how much each candidate has to offer when it comes to being real, to working, to having and displaying charisma, to being able to project his personality by whatever media avenue was available at the time, to consistently draw a big paying audience . . .

After *all* of that, who is special? Really, truly *distinctive?* These are the men who belong among the 50 greatest pro wrestlers of all time.

CHAPTER 5
The Championship Play

As difficult as it is to choose a group of the top pro wrestlers of all time, rating them within that group presents an even bigger dilemma.

In making that ultimate determination, I was inclined to play the championship card, to look at those who have been in command of major championships. Not surprisingly, how long someone was the king is valuable information.

With one wild card: Verne Gagne. Down the road we'll see if it's a trump card or not.

Those who consider this project from only the modern outlook might claim that being champion doesn't matter much. Understandable, since titles do *not* mean all that much as 2012 rolls into 2013. Lip service is paid, but more often than not the crowns are bounced around like marbles on a tile floor, at least until *WrestleMania* pops up each year. Then Vince McMahon's brain trust, likely at his instruction, puts more emphasis on championships: who has them and who wants them.

But the sudden attention is often too little, too late. Thus, at *WrestleMania* in 2012, the main spotlight was on iconic performers including The

Undertaker versus Triple H, or The Rock and John Cena yapping at each other. In fact, the buildup on Taker and Trips was as expertly executed as any in wrestling history. All of those involved, of course, had title reigns as a strong part of their legacies. At the same time, those who had held current championships, like The Miz, were mostly meaningless because those titles had been so devalued in that particular reign.

Of course, as the buildup began for the alleged penultimate confrontation between The Rock and Cena at the 2012 *WrestleMania*, the title became a worthwhile bargaining chip and booking tool once more. After *Mania*, WWE thinkers seemed willing to attach the rocket to CM Punk by giving him the championship and working strong angles around Punk and his possession.

In computing the best ever wrestlers, the only title I considered is *the* title, the world championship, the crown that comes with the name of the company. In the case of the WWE, it is the WWE prize that has precedence over the world crown. I didn't consider the Intercontinental, the United States, the Interstate, any state, the Brass Knucks, the television, the Gizmo, or any other of the infinite number of so-called titles that clutter a lineup with junk. Those "titles" add nothing to the impact or drawing power of a show.

Think about one fact: whoever has the World or company championship is paid significantly more than everyone who has lesser titles, in essence nothing more than preliminary laurels. In fact, the guy on top, particularly for the NWA and usually the WWF, gets a healthy percentage of the net receipts. All those other fellows running around with belts get paid exactly what they would have been paid for being in the second or third preliminary anyhow. Those titles often were and still are ego-placating political moves: "See, guys, we're giving you a push — doing something with you." And promoters paid this talent the same money as they would pay someone without the titles!

So, does a list of world championship owners mean anything when selecting the 50 greatest in history? The big titles almost always go to those performers who stand a little taller than the rest of the pack and are known as such by the true power brokers.

Perhaps that philosophy changed a bit when WWE became such an audience-drawing brand by name alone. The qualifications may not have been as strict in certain cases. Many fans buy WWE because of what they have been taught the company is, through television and marketing. In a pinch, Vince wants the big gun on top. Even a quick look at the record demonstrates that it matters in the long run who has the *main* honor in WWE, just as it has always mattered to the companies that were prominent in the industry. After all, John Cena has been WWE champion the fourth longest amount of time — and is moving up fast — in the nearly five-decade history of WWE. Cena, obviously, has been Vince's golden boy in recent years.

For the greater part of wrestling history — and thus the major focus of a study of the top 50 of all time — it mattered who the champion was, big time. While the reasons a certain warrior was made kingpin might vary depending on politics and circumstance, the world champion could truly be considered the best (or very close) at that moment in time. Therefore, someone who occupied the throne regularly, consistently, and for a meaningful length of time can lay claim to a primary position on the gilded list of 50. Surely being successful for many years in the most stressful and publicized position in the industry counts for something — even if the industry itself was different in 2011 than it was in 1981 or 1951 or 1921.

Just because wrestling has changed does not make what happened before this era any less meaningful. Different or new is not necessarily better . . . or worse.

This logic makes a few prominent names jump to the head of the class. Bruno Sammartino. Lou Thesz. A quiet surprise in Nick Bockwinkel. Ric Flair. Frank Gotch. Hulk Hogan. And, loudly, Verne Gagne.

Put aside, for the moment, charisma, drawing power, working skill, and legitimate toughness. Agree to this premise: no promoters, with their money at stake, would allow anyone to remain champion unless that champion had the goods to deliver a busy box office. They would lose money. Vince McMahon Sr. would not do it. Sam Muchnick would not do it. The Bowsers, the Curleys, the Packs, the Sandows, the Mondts, and all the rest of the power brokers throughout history would not do it. Gagne would not do it either, right?

Consider these statistics. Sammartino was a champion for 4,040 days. Bruno started a reign in 1963 and ended very early in 1971. A second tour of duty began late in 1973 and stretched into 1977. In total, Sammartino was the king of what was then the World Wide Wrestling Federation roughly 11 of 14 years.

Even more mind-boggling, Thesz was on a throne for 4,293 days. He had captured the most widely recognized world championship four times prior to becoming the NWA standard bearer on November 27, 1949. In fact, he was in the midst of his fourth reign following a win over "Wild Bill" Longson when the NWA became the preeminent organization and Lou its champion in 1948. From 1937 until 1966, Thesz was a champion for all or part of 16 of those 29 years.

Even more impressive, remember that this was a time when stars worked 300 or more matches every year. The WWE champion seldom came near to 200 outings in a year, nor did any of the company's main-event names, although Punk as champion might come close.

Remember the earlier comparison of today's championships to marbles that just get bounced around? Don't be distracted by how often a performer won a title. While naturally that is something to brag about, context determines its true worth. A perfect example is Triple H, who seldom fails to include that he has snared laurels 13 times (though some objective sources show only 8 such triumphs). Yet Triple H held the titles involved only 539 days, which certainly pales in comparison to Bruno winning twice but retaining for 4,040 days or Thesz for 4,293 days. That's something like just over two years for all H's reigns added together! Quite a difference from Thesz and Sammartino's individual tenures of roughly seven *years*.

Dory Funk Jr. owned the title for 1,502 days. Gene Kiniski was in charge for 1,131 days, Pat O'Connor for 903, and Jack Brisco for 866. Pedro Morales was on top in the WWWF for 1,027 days, and Pedro is widely ignored.

Furthermore, within those 539 days that he dominated, Triple H did not have nearly as many actual defenses because the schedule is now lighter. Make no mistake, the slate is still strenuous, but not like it once was in earlier eras. Regardless, the gap between 539 days and 4,293 is insurmountable.

For Thesz and Sammartino, along with their peers, every bout was *the* main event in whatever city they appeared. A certain level of expertise, skill, and intensity was required, in every single match, every single night, against every style of opponent. On a nearly daily basis, they were in the most important position on the card and routinely expected to go a hard, exhausting 20 minutes, all the way up to an hour for NWA champions.

Arguing about different styles, whether bumps were bigger or smaller or more numerous, how strenuous a stiffer regimen of more matches was . . . that all pales against the sheer quantity *and* quality of what Thesz and Sammartino did.

Alone, that puts Lou Thesz and Bruno Sammartino a notch above most of the rest.

Yet the gap isn't too big. Nick Bockwinkel was a major titleholder for 2,990 days, no small feat considering it was Gagne's AWA belt he wore. Ric Flair was on top with the NWA for 3,101 days, although that number could vary by a bit. Unfortunately, Flair caught the peak of "lose it, win it, lose it, win it" several times within a week or two, so most records are unreliable. Nevertheless, Flair was the champion for one hell of a long time too. Add to that 501 days with World Championship Wrestling (the Ted Turner-WTBS operation), which had a grueling schedule, and another 118 for WWF/WWE.

In total, Flair had the major championship where he worked for 3,720 days.

Hulk Hogan was the ruler for 2,184 days, not much more than Bob Backlund's 2,138 days. No matter how much some modern observers want to denigrate Backlund, he did have something where it really counted. You have to be bringing in money and having terrific bouts for the powers-that-be to keep you on top for that long. Harley Race had 1,801 with a big-time crown (not the cartoon WWF version of "king") when the NWA was *the* wrestling company.

Prior to the formation of the NWA, "Wild Bill" Longson was a champion for 1,930 days. Go back even further, before the National Wrestling Alliance (but certainly when wrestling was every bit as popular as it is now). In particular, think about "Strangler" Lewis. He was in command of various versions of the world title from 1920 into 1932. Figuring out how many days is virtually impossible due to the lack of accurate records and even more the explanations of why things happened and when. Lewis was in the middle of many reputed shoots, or at least promotional battles, all of which involved lucrative towns or promotional wars where being the champion meant the difference between success and failure.

Step back further in time. From 1906 until 1913, Frank Gotch was a champion more recognized than we realize today. Many later versions of the world championship spun off from what Gotch did. Some records name Gotch as champion from 1908, some from 1906. Gotch was in control for somewhere between 1,825 days and 3,255 days, give or take a few hundred.

When devising a list of the greatest ever, how can names like those be ignored or given less-than-serious consideration?

And Verne Gagne was the American Wrestling Association titleholder for 4,677 days. In all of wrestling, *nobody* held a major championship longer than Verne. While there is an argument to make about the strength of this claim, the sheer amount of time spent on the highest rung of the ladder is worth something. The AWA was a thriving territory with major towns and top-notch talent, and in the early part of Gagne's career, he was always a major professional star with the athletic credentials to make him more than just a performer.

So why pick on Gagne? Well, there is only one reason, which may or may not make a difference in the ultimate position Gagne deserves among the 50 best of all time. He does belong there.

But still, he owned the AWA . . . so does that wild card trump anyone else, or not?

In deciding who rates where among the finest ever, we must look at who had a truly meaningful championship for the longest period of time. Wrestling, being the animal that it is, has always been plagued with far too many titles, most of which are worth zero. But certain trophies became special because of who controlled them politically and who won them in the ring, where and against whom, the quality of the matches involved, and the history that evolved around them.

Clearly, the two that stand out the most are the World Wrestling Federation/World Wrestling Entertainment prize and the National Wrestling Alliance, which naturally loses some luster since the NWA no longer exists in any worthwhile form and time takes its toll.

Yet consider how strong the American Wrestling Association (AWA) was for approximately two and a half decades. While the AWA didn't run in as many locations as the NWA, nor in towns as large as the WWF/WWE, the spots in which it did operate were good-sized markets (Chicago was more than that obviously) in the middle of the United States, with some useful forays into Canada and contacts in Japan. It was a major league territory (and with all due respect, Memphis was not considered in that realm).

The schedule in the AWA was less back-breaking, particularly when compared to that carried by the NWA champion. Many critics, a large percentage of whom never even saw an AWA card, felt that the promotion was stodgy and rigid, though most newcomers make that complaint about any organization prior to 2000. Put that gripe to bed.

The talent that passed through the AWA was absolutely excellent. Its key performers headlined main events in all the primary markets run by both the NWA and the WWF. Just look at who held AWA laurels in addition to Gagne: Mad Dog Vachon, The Crusher, Big Bill Miller under the mask, Gene Kiniski, Fritz Von Erich, Dick the Bruiser, Hulk Hogan, Larry Zbyszko, Rick Martel, Curt Hennig, Jumbo Tsuruta, and very notably Nick Bockwinkel.

The key, naturally, is that Verne Gagne owned the AWA. After all, I pick on Jerry Lawler for his ownership position in Memphis. And plenty of big stars sooner or later gained ownership in their territories.

In the AWA, Gagne decided who would be champion, and he usually chose himself. He must have been at least partially correct in doing so because the company was always tremendously profitable. Gagne could perform, wrestle, and draw money. In AWA locales, his name remained bigger than Sammartino or Thesz.

Regardless, current critics scoff, claiming AWA success occurred because no other wrestling product existed in AWA markets to compete against. Yet how is that different from today, when WWE has no real competition? (Please, let's agree TNA has posed no threat thus far.)

Almost all of the names listed as AWA titleholders should be in the discussion of leading wrestlers for their time period, if not for the 50 greatest consideration. And that doesn't touch the many who were main-event stars but never held the crown, such as Ray Stevens. Expand that list to 100, or 200, and AWA headliners would be heavily represented.

Still, it was obviously more difficult for Sammartino or Thesz to get the belt. And Flair in WCW was always in some sort of political struggle to keep the crown. Vince Sr. had the final say on when and how long Sammartino's reign would last. Is there any question today who chooses the champion for WWE? Fortunately for Bruno, McMahon's father was never as mercurial or explosive as his son. Senior fit into the pattern of having a champion (if he continued to draw money and have terrific bouts) as an established kingpin.

Again, certain modern observers would gripe that this wouldn't work today. First, nobody has tried it, so who can say for certain? Second, it worked wonderfully with the *right* performer in the lengthy stretch of years dominated by Sammartino in the WWWF. Naturally, as proven with

Thesz and Gagne, this philosophy made the titles *much* more valuable as drawing tools than they are today.

One criticism of Bruno has been that the ethnic appeal of an Italian superstar on top in the Northeast garnered him more credit than he deserved. Early on, there might have been some truth to this. Again, the total dimension of Sammartino's body of work over the years surpasses that tacky complaint.

Thesz had it tougher than anyone, because he had to navigate the board of directors of the NWA. Annually, Lou had a lot of bosses to please, most of whom were stubborn and opinionated, with different ideas about how wrestling should be.

The National Wrestling Alliance was not owned by one person but rather was a cooperative of different promoters from all over North America, with a few foreign members at different points. Getting everyone to agree, much less behave legally, was always a challenge. Nonetheless, during its heyday the NWA was by far the largest and most powerful force in recognizing a champion. Getting such a diverse group to agree — for years — on who was *the* man to hold the gold belt required more than just political acumen.

Even though Muchnick, the supreme political force in the NWA, was solidly in Thesz's corner as the champion, the truth was that Thesz's strength as a wrestler, performer, and drawing card was demonstrated by the fact that he seldom was in danger of being removed from the throne — unless he himself made the decision.

And that is a key point. Thesz was the one making the decisions not only about when he would lose but also about who would follow in his footsteps. Though he might have been influenced by people like Muchnick, as long as he was strong, Thesz actually called his own shots.

Another key point: who was asked to guard the title when problems erupted with Buddy Rogers and Vince Sr. in 1963? Who did the promoters trust to regain the prize if it came to an actual shoot in the ring? Who was the athlete and personality that everyone felt could restore credibility and stability to the NWA honor?

It was Lou Thesz.

Dealing with the wrestling barons in those days was a knock-down, drag-out brawl in itself. For Thesz to be as strong as he was demonstrates just how dominant he was both behind closed doors and in the squared circle. Everyone knew he was the man — for real. What other stars at their peak (and whose peak was as long?) were saluted in the same manner?

Keep in mind too that when Thesz was anointed as the champion in 1937 (the youngest wrestler to ever have a title of that sort), the industry's politics were a bigger quagmire. Yet Thesz ended up with the most recognized laurel of the time again in 1939 (when he was still a baby!) and in 1947. Think of the crusty, clever competitors Thesz had to deal with both in the ring and in the boardroom to land the honor he did.

The situation into which Thesz stepped as a rookie champion was convoluted, to say the least. While there was some structure because certain promoters in key markets stuck together, they all stepped on each other's toes often enough trying to steal a profitable venue or national recognition of who the true champion was.

Thus, those on top of the mountain during the early to mid 1900s get a boost when it comes to considering the 50 best ever. "Strangler" Lewis in particular pops up after considering the early contributions of Frank Gotch.

Modern fans may scoff, but do baseball critics ignore Cy Young, Christy Mathewson, Ty Cobb, or Babe Ruth? As close to impossible as the task may be, finding a method to include those building blocks of the sport is essential. How serious is the list going to be? Just a marketing venture or a current popularity trending discussion of who gets the most hits on Yahoo? Or a serious effort to truly "get it right," or at least come close and spark serious discussion?

As the NWA became the most powerful organization in wrestling (check out Tim Hornbaker's excellent book *National Wrestling Alliance: The Untold Story of the Monopoly That Strangled Pro Wrestling*), Sam Muchnick had his friend Ray Gillespie do some detailed research on the history of the world championship. Gillespie showed how a line could be drawn connecting the honor from the time of Frank Gotch to the title held by Lou Thesz. Of course, the idea was to legitimize the crown recognized by the NWA. Gillespie took it seriously, as any true journalist would and as Muchnick expected.

Gillespie was an associate editor for the *Sporting News* when that publication was nicknamed the "Bible of Baseball" and was extremely influential on the national sports scene. Gillespie had been a longtime sportswriter in St. Louis, where Muchnick covered baseball before going into wrestling promotion under the guidance of Tom Packs.

What Gillespie uncovered was a hornet's nest of wins, losses, claims, and counter-claims. Between the two of them, they shunted some bouts to the side and emphasized those they felt were more important. Names like Joe Stecher, Gus Sonnenberg, Stanislaus Zbyszko, Jim Londos, Ray Steele, and even Bronko Nagurski fit into the storyline most prominently — and accurately, within the confines of the objective.

This was around 1960, and the goal was to establish a link between wrestling's past and present. Ironically, the work Gillespie did, and Muchnick helped edit, is still used as the basis of title claims and lineage by, of all people, WWE!

Now, just because someone won a version of the championship does not mean he should automatically be included in the group of the 50 finest pro wrestlers ever. To the contrary. There were a few pretenders who sneaked in the back door as part of political and business warfare. Some were stronger, some weaker. Many who never held the belt have far greater claim to be in the best of all time. This chapter, however, does remind us of a few amazing talents.

Jim Londos was a special character, one who belongs among the elite for his drawing power, charisma, and ability. Londos, famed as the "Golden Greek" while regularly packing buildings nationwide, made a mark in society as a whole, giving wrestling the unique place that decades later Vince Jr. sought with a corporate approach.

And what about Bronko Nagurski? An incredible athlete always listed among the greatest ever to play football, does Bronko fit into the same position for wrestling? Speaking of gridiron players moving onto the mat, what about the mostly forgotten Gus Sonnenberg? He introduced the flying tackle to the game, along with other tactics that opened up the action. Maybe his skill set wasn't the best, but his contributions *at the time* surely made a difference.

Ray Steele did not have the crown for long, but in the dressing room all the boys realized Steele was at the top of the totem pole. Though his title reign was brief, most everyone from that era who knew the truth felt that Steele was the "policeman," the one who kept troublemakers in line and forced any potential champion to prove his mettle. Steele was a shooter. Like Thesz and Lewis, Ray Steele was the real deal. In fact, based on interviews and discussions with Lewis and Thesz, if they could vote, Ray Steele would reside among the 50 greatest.

Yet maybe another shooter, almost a generation before Steele but just as dangerous and reputedly unbeatable in a real battle, is John Pesek.

To say none of that matters now is incorrect. It mattered then and decided the pecking order in a dog-eat-dog business. We must at least discuss counting among the best these gladiators who had the top championships and why they did for however long. Each wrestler/ performer/athlete brought *something* to the table.

The point of all this is that, no matter how inclusive we attempt to be, someone deserving is almost guaranteed to be left out because the sands of time simply wash away true accomplishments and superior ability in favor of grapplers from recent years who might get credit. At least by considering championship achievements, we add another layer of accuracy to a devilish chore.

As for Verne Gagne, was he the best just because he defended a major championship for the longest amount of time? No, of course not.

But is championship longevity one vital card, an ace or at least a king, in the winning hand of those who are the greatest?

The champs are here! That surely means something for each and every one.

CHAPTER 6
Why Not These Superstars?

Turn a negative into a positive . . . What a wonderful philosophy, both professionally and personally. If something's wrong, make it right. Figure out what the problem is, then make the changes needed to cure the headache. Vince McMahon has often, perhaps in different words, preached the same sermon.

So, let's try to correct the errors on WWE's all-time greatest roster. In many cases, to do this calls for an eraser — another phrase I first heard from Vince, who at the time was talking about a wrestler being paid more than McMahon thought he deserved.

This seems so terribly negative, to point out the flaws and failures of accomplished wrestlers and to explain why they are not among the 50 best ever. Think about this, though. The 50 finest talents ever to perform in more than 100 years! The standards must be impossibly high to mean something to those who know the business. A lot of very good pro wrestlers, unique characters in their own right, will not make the cut.

Everyone listed by WWE has plenty of good points, but that doesn't mean they *all* had *enough* genuine credentials to convince a reasonable and unprejudiced observer that each of them truly belonged. Sadly, it looks like I'm scoffing at a few pretty good hands by bumping them, but that's not the intent. In fact, some are actually pretty close to deserving such an award. Others are far enough away from the list that they would need binoculars to find number 50.

I don't mean to disrespect the efforts of solid performers, but in explaining why certain grapplers are not among the 50 best, I will also spotlight the qualities others who deserve to be in the elite 50 do have.

The *why not* for one person often helps explain the *why* for someone else.

Sometimes the line between yes and no can be pretty thin. Sometimes that border can be as wide as the Atlantic Ocean.

Wait, this was originally the section that would house the argument *against* including John Cena! But, in the end, Cena has gained admission to the unparalleled company.

Take a look at the chapter on Cena for the reasons why he made it at the finish after it looked like he wouldn't cut it. As far as I'm concerned, his stock keeps inching upward. Cena earned this acclaim the hard way, with consistently excellent and reliable work. I'm not saying Cena can wrestle like Lou Thesz or perform like Ric Flair. He *cannot*. But face it, Cena does what he has to do in today's environment. And he does it well. Look at the numbers and the history he's had as top dog with the dominant company. Take in the entire picture and you'll see John Cena belongs in the mix with the best there have ever been.

The Cena conundrum helps explain the difficulty in trying to choose among so many special talents over periods of time so agonizingly different. And some of the names WWE put on their marketing roster as the best ever do indeed have important gifts, but not important enough to grab a spot in a legitimate consideration of the 50 greatest pro wrestlers ever.

It's a juggling act, once the contexts are understood and compared objectively.

For instance . . .

Make the hard call on potential hot-button characters like Rey Mysterio and Eddie Guerrero. Surely nobody with wrestling knowledge would think that Mysterio is the ninth and Guerrero the eleventh best ever, as WWE would have the world believe. At the risk of sounding cynical and politically incorrect, I say it's obvious that the placements of Mysterio and Guerrero have more to do with marketing (and trying to make headway in Mexico for WWE promotions) and selling gimmicks to the very young than being accurate and fair.

Prior to the specialized situations created by WWE, the hard fact is that someone like Guerrero, though truly talented, would have been doing jobs for Race, The Bruiser, or Kowalski. While Guerrero would have had main events in smaller territories, in average or large markets he would have been that fabulous undercard guy putting over the big money headliners.

Mysterio, without the shrinking talent pool, would never have gotten a regular job outside of Mexico or Japan, despite his ability to fly in admittedly spectacular fashion. That is a hard, likely unpopular, fact. While the junior heavyweight ranks have always been highly respected in Japan, the odds of Rey being a main-event headliner on major shows in Japan are slim indeed. In the USA or Canada? A valuable part of the lineup? At best, maybe. The headliner? No.

The irony is that both Mysterio and Guerrero come from wrestling families. As such, they share a basic understanding of so-called old-school psychology, which pops up in their work.

This is especially true for Eddie, whose father Gory was a major player in the Southwest — where Gory came under the influence of Dory Funk Sr. — and in Mexico, where he displayed a most independent nature. Gory invented many in-ring maneuvers. His sons, including Eddie, have a deep understanding of both ring psychology and wrestling politics.

After a strong run in Mexico, where Eddie was particularly noted for his tag team with Art Barr, he had a nice tenure in Japan, where he clicked as the new Black Tiger in the juniors division. Like Mysterio, though, Eddie was never at the head of the card there. Someone ranking ninth or eleventh in the history of wrestling *had* to have been in major main events in wrestling-crazy Japan.

The original Extreme Championship Wrestling and the imaginative booking of Paul Heyman opened a door to another level for both Mysterio and Guerrero in North America. The fact that the dysfunctional World Championship Wrestling was re-energized to some degree provided another step for both. Moving to WWE at the right time was clearly the biggest leap of all. Although neither was ever *the* man to build a major pay-per-view show around, both Guerrero and Mysterio were vital ingredients on numerous productions.

Nobody, especially not me, wants to disrespect the accomplishments of either wrestler, both of whom clawed and scrapped and fought to prove they could get over on the biggest stage of all in their time period.

I applaud what Rey Mysterio and Eddie Guerrero have done, especially in proving that smaller performers are valuable and can be sold to the general public. Nonetheless, neither belongs in the top 50 of all time. In the long run, size does matter. Guerrero is closer by one set of standards, but Mysterio might be closer due to the novelty of what he accomplished despite his diminutive stature. Rey's size is both a blessing and a curse in a competition like this. Being able to make an impact when so small is unique and helps secure a space on the list I've designed. Expecting a suspension of disbelief at his size, however, is difficult and therefore a hindrance. More than novelty is required. Does Abdullah the Butcher belong because of the novelty of spilling more blood than anyone else? On various versions of my list I've fooled with placing Eddie or Rey in that number 50 slot. To put them there in the end, however, would be patronizing. I look at who this would mean leaving out, make the logical comparisons, and find that I can't let a list stand like that.

Many fabulous stars are not going to be among the "Fab 50." That's why it is supposed to be the best of the best. That's why *real* Halls of Fame exist. Not every single scintillating performer will make it — only 50 among the thousands who performed in more than 100 years. A true

Hall of Fame is more inclusive, opening its doors for larger numbers who deserve special recognition for various reasons.

So, neither Mysterio nor Guerrero makes it into the exclusive club of the 50. And neither do Vachon, Orndorff, Murdoch, Koloff, Robinson, Ladd, Sonnenberg, Zbyszko (Stanislaus or Larry), and so on. Think about booking Mysterio against Dick Murdoch or Billy Robinson. Think about putting Guerrero against Ivan Koloff or Ernie Ladd. Who goes over in most, if not all, contexts? Who gets the push from the promoter who intends to turn a profit? They back the big guy, like it or not, especially if he can go.

To make it even more decisive, pit either one against Jim Londos. Who do you build a promotion around that has credibility and makes money? Guerrero or Buddy Rogers? Mysterio or Bruno Sammartino?

When the dust settles, that is not only fair but, to most knowledgeable observers, obvious!

Putting it all into some kind of perspective makes it much easier to explain why the likes of Curt Hennig, Edge, Jerry Lawler, and Chris Jericho aren't on my list either.

Curt Hennig is an interesting case. Everyone has always agreed that Curt was a superb worker, most notably as a bump-taker. During his tenure as Mr. Perfect and a lengthy feud with Hulk Hogan, many insiders told this joke but meant it seriously: "Hulk puts a quarter in and Hennig bumps, bumps, bumps. Curt is a bump machine." In fact, Hennig was a perfect complement for Hogan's style and was honestly too generous. Of course, that was smart politics at the time. Additionally, he was part of a red-hot period for the WWF and thus received a genuine boost to his reputation.

Hennig was a remarkable all-around performer. His best individual performance is generally forgotten now because it was aired on a little-viewed AWA television show on ESPN. On December 31, 1986, Hennig had a brilliant one-hour draw with Nick Bockwinkel. It helped to be battling a legitimate top 50 hand, but Hennig certainly proved he could play in the same ring with Bockwinkel in that duel. The action was sharp, smooth, and stiff enough to support the story they told.

Unfortunately, for all the solid work he did, Hennig generally falls a notch below the big guns. Curt brought a semblance of respect to WWE's intercontinental title. He had generally excellent matches, although a subsequent run with World Championship Wrestling fell short of expectations.

Injuries and personal demons took their toll on this son of Larry "The Axe" Hennig. Claimed by a lethal combination of cocaine, painkillers, and steroids at age 44, the closing chapter of Hennig's career is sad, just as Guerrero's is. Ironically, those shocking deaths probably boosted the stock of Guerrero and did nothing for Hennig.

As far as the WWE list, would anyone realistically put Hennig ahead of Flair, Thesz, Sammartino, "Strangler" Lewis, and so on, if marketing or altering historical fact weren't the goal?

Edge is not unlike Hennig. Adam Copeland created an interesting character, plus he was a good worker. Better as a heel than as a babyface, Edge lost some quality time due to injury, including more than a year thanks to a broken neck. He stole a few big shows and laid some new ground with his work in three-way tag matches and ladder bouts — of course, the ladder bouts could be critiqued for relying more on stunts and props than on personal abilities.

He definitely grasped how to fit what he did into the WWF/WWE philosophy. The benefits of being on television with a national platform certainly are evident with Edge, whom many new observers tend to overrate because they aren't aware of a century's worth of superior talent. That his career ended sadly and abruptly due to neck injuries also gives him, like Guerrero, a sympathy vote from a few quarters.

WWE's placement of him is, however, silly. Edge doesn't fit at the level (nineteenth) he's assigned by WWE in a best-ever congregation. Ahead of Thesz, Hogan, and Sammartino? Or compare Edge to the many who are not in the final entourage. Is Edge better than Jonathan, Murdoch, Orndorff, Slaughter, Robinson, and Nagurski? Or, for that matter, better than Jericho? No. The result could not be clearer.

Edge does fit well into a large group of impressive talents vying for a limited number of positions in the final product. Good, solid worker. Charisma and personality. Got himself over to the important extent that fans cared about what happened to him. Where would Edge have fit in territorial days? Generally a regular main-eventer but not necessarily in the big-money places. Lots of minor titles, but check the discussion of championships in Chapter Five. As they say, close, but no cigar.

Now Jerry Lawler is going to be trickier, even though he shouldn't be. If the top 50 list was geared to the greatest manipulators/operators/survivors, Lawler would belong. He was given the idea of billing himself as "The King" by the late, imaginative Bobby Shane in the early 1970s and still rides that gimmick today. His 1982 skit with comedian Andy Kaufman earned him national attention far surpassing what his wrestling talent had earned him. Few recall how poorly the actual matches springing from the angle drew in Lawler's beloved base of Memphis.

"The King" was often part-owner, booker, and always in-ring star for the Memphis territory, which lasted longer than others did when the World Wrestling Federation expansion put most everyone else out of business. On the other hand, some critics claim Memphis survived that long only because the area included many small southern towns and that Vince and crew were too busy taking over bigger markets at the time, leaving Memphis near the end of the "to do" list. Nonetheless, Memphis survived, and Jerry took personal advantage of it better than anyone else.

For one thing, in the early-to-mid 1980s, he began importing known national stars including Nick Bockwinkel, Ken Patera, Terry Funk, and Curt Hennig for main events that, naturally, put himself over. Part-owner Lawler was admittedly a smart worker. The outsiders made good money for their efforts, something surprising in a territory known for its pitifully lousy payoffs, and it all gave a bump to Lawler's reputation.

When Lawler booked a fight with Bruiser Brody in Memphis, Brody told me that Lawler wanted to win the first match but then promised he'd do something to even it up in the second bout. "He doesn't trust me to come back if I win, which really is the right thing to do to set up the comeback against the new heel," explained Brody. "But I don't trust him either. He'll never return the favor. So I'll do a tag match or a DQ or something. Otherwise, I don't need the headache."

Before wrestling began to change, Lawler was too small and not outstanding enough as a worker to be invited as a headliner in New York, Toronto, Tampa, Atlanta, Minneapolis, St. Louis, Dallas, Los Angeles, or Japan (by either Giant Baba or Antonio Inoki in the two primary promotions). Except for doing jobs, he was never in any of those territories or towns.

While finishing college and working part-time writing publicity for Muchnick, I was in the control room of KPLR-TV for a taping of *Wrestling at the Chase* on March 14, 1970. Sam and director Jim Herd were going over the planned lineup. Herd, of course, later became the ill-fated first chief of World Championship Wrestling owned by Ted Turner, but this was long before WCW and just prior to Herd becoming general manager of KPLR.

Carrying several large pieces of paper in his hands, Pat O'Connor, then Sam's booker, came into the control room. "Look at these!" Pat said as he spread the sheets on the desk before Muchnick and Herd. On each paper was a sketch, detailed and accurate, of the various wrestlers in the dressing room upstairs.

"That little Lawler kid drew these!" exclaimed O'Connor. "He's terrific. He should be a cartoonist." It turned out that Lawler, at the time 20 and only a couple years younger than me, did some writing and drawing for various wrestling publications. Jerry also earned a commercial art scholarship to Memphis State University.

Muchnick and Herd were impressed. "Where did he come in from again? Memphis? The kid is an artist. I hope he can wrestle a little bit, too," Muchnick said as he and Herd chuckled.

Lawler was in St. Louis for some of his earliest bouts, two of only three he had in the fabled days of Chase wrestling. For what it's worth, Lawler lost to Bennie Ramirez and then was pinned by Harley Race in a tag-team match. Maybe that artistic mentality played into the career he would go on to build.

Jerry was bright, personable, clever between the ropes, talented enough — but not a main-eventer anywhere except Memphis and territory towns where he had major influence. In fact, the way Lawler kept his town and name alive impressed Vince enough that he worked angles himself with Lawler in Memphis in the early 1990s (thus allowing the then-ravaged territory to stumble on a bit longer). This set the stage for what has been a generally comfortable long-term relationship.

We give Lawler special attention because of his WWF/WWE run, which he continues today as a television commentator. He also survived a heart attack on-air late in 2012. Lawler has been very good at what he does, and his wrestling reputation grew larger than he really deserved.

But to confuse Lawler's modern role as a television personality (and a good one) with what it takes to be among the 50 finest pro wrestlers of all time is an insult to many amazing ring gladiators. For WWE purposes, it makes sense. For any serious study of the issue, it does not. Jerry Lawler deserves plaudits and praise for what he has done in many different roles in wrestling; he does not, however, belong anywhere near the best wrestlers there ever were.

Regarding Chris Jericho . . . he *is* good, very good. His varied background has made Chris a well-rounded performer. The son of former National Hockey League player Ted Irvine, Jericho's early training was at the dungeon run by Stu Hart and his family in Calgary. Despite the character he has often portrayed in WWE, Jericho is indeed a pretty tough guy.

Jericho spent a couple of years in Mexico, picking up the high-flying acrobatic tactics of the luchadores. It was an interesting contrast to the stiff, physical style he had learned from the Harts. Then Jericho had a terrific run in Japan, providing him with yet another layer of ring knowledge. He returned to North America by way of the original ECW with Paul Heyman, to World Championship Wrestling, and finally to WWE.

For all he offered stylistically, the reputation of great junior heavyweight worked against him. He got the same rap as Guerrero and Mysterio — he was too little. In WWE, the opportunity to work with larger foes on a grander scale arose because the talent base dwindled. The emphasis on cartoon muscles had also slipped at least a bit and that too helped. Jericho excelled both as one of the top three or four features for pay-per-view and as an important regular cast member of *Raw* on cable. When it comes to projecting his personality, Jericho is right there — when he is interested.

All of this brings him close to consideration, but comparisons to others in that league hurt Jericho. For instance, Jericho or Jack Brisco? It's not close; Brisco wins. How about Jericho versus Bruiser Brody? Brody gets every main event around the world, while Jericho slides into a supporting bout. Jericho or Randy Savage? Savage headlined by himself and did it a lot.

Figure this one: Jericho or Dusty Rhodes? Rhodes made himself a superstar who drew big money everywhere. Jericho made himself a name, but even if he has the athletic edge, Dusty wins the race because he leaves the bigger impact, the stronger legacy.

If Jericho, as entertaining as he is, tackled Killer Kowalski or Big Bill Miller, is there any doubt who would do the job and who would get his hand raised — likely after a sensational big-man-versus-little-man duel? How about Ray Stevens? He is the closest to Jericho in size, but Stevens was on top for so many cards that drew sellouts and Jericho doesn't have that credit.

Or Superstar Graham against Jericho? Who goes over? The Undertaker, Bret Hart, or either of the Funks and Jericho? Who would go on in main events, and who would stay just a place below, having great matches and putting over main-event regulars?

Now, and this is trickier than I first anticipated, how would Jericho fit in with the likes of Ray Steele or Joe Stecher? He loses, but consider this: with his athleticism and also his acceptance of the early grinding training, at a time when size wasn't quite as big a consideration, if Jericho came along in that era with that background, could he have adapted to the demands better than some other moderns would have? Edge and

Lawler would have been eaten alive. Jericho might well have been more competitive, but . . .

Once more, Jericho's position is a statement about *how* extraordinary someone has to be to fit into the 50 greatest ever. Chris Jericho is very, very good, but he's not good enough for an invitation to the ball.

And what about The Fabulous Moolah (Lillian Ellison), the token female on the WWE greatest list?

Is a token girl wrestler even necessary? Lady grappling has been a novelty throughout the industry's history. When McMahon began the giant wrestling war in 1984, one of his goals was to use Wendi Richter to make the ladies more of a drawing card than they had been. Even with the help and cross-marketing of pop singer Cyndi Lauper, it didn't work too well.

As colorful and interesting as the history of female wrestling is, finding one woman who belongs in the list of 50 greatest ever simply isn't realistic. And why in the world choose Moolah over the likes of Mildred Burke or June Byers or even Penny Banner, legitimate athletic studs who knew the nuts and bolts of what to do in the ring, not to mention often serving as part of the co-feature or special attraction on major national cards? That said, Moolah certainly belongs in any legitimate Hall of Fame. She was a top and talented performer for many years, even if never equal to Byers or Burke. As Moolah's career wound down, she was smart enough in the ring to entertain. She trained a stable of skilled girl wrestlers that from the mid 1970s on supplied lady wrestling in North America. And that is probably why she was included on the WWE roster of greatest ever.

Since Moolah was called by most promoters (who were looking to book ladies) when the business was divided into numerous smaller, regional businesses, she became privy to many secrets and rumors. She loved to talk and was easy to talk to, becoming a close friend of Vince McMahon Sr. early in her career.

Any time Moolah picked up on news or gossip that might benefit an operator like Vince's father, she was on the telephone to brief Daddy.

Sam Muchnick always cautioned me to be careful what I told Moolah. "She's a great gal," Sam said, "but anything you say is going right back to McMahon."

Somehow eliminating Bruiser Brody or Johnny Valentine or Jim Londos just to include The Fabulous Moolah because she was Vince's father's buddy seems a major injustice.

Ironically, WWE places Moolah ahead of one of wrestling's truly gifted workers in Pat Patterson, who has been a close buddy of the younger Vince for decades. The two worked together as television commentators after Patterson slowed and then ended his in-ring career. Patterson has generally had Vince Junior's ear as an advisor and booker in WWE's gigantic run to the top. While that shouldn't boost Patterson's standing among the greatest, an observer might expect that the respect Vince has for Patterson would help his standing on the best-ever roster.

My list of the greatest contains Ray Stevens but not Patterson. The WWE group has Patterson but not Stevens. Not only were the two comparable in size and pure skill (ask any Cauliflower Alley member — both will be described as "great workers"), they formed one of the best tag teams on both the West Coast and in the AWA. Stevens was incredible on top for promoter Roy Shires in the old San Francisco territory.

While Patterson was a major component on many WWF lineups in the 1970s. Not much to decide between them, is there? So, why Stevens and not Patterson? Stevens was *the* man in a major promotion for a longer period of time, whereas Patterson fell into that second spot, most notably with Vince Sr. Important, but not the guy who would get the blame if a show didn't draw. That said, he often was lauded by outsiders for selling tickets when Backlund was the champion, a premise that's hard to prove because Backlund drew on cards without Patterson.

The bottom line, in my mind, is that Stevens was simply better. Patterson was a fine performer who deserves praise, but Stevens set the standard for that era. Not taking into account marketing or personal considerations, how much did WWE really feel certain wrestlers deserved to be in their top 50 group? What was the company's definition of the word *deserved*?

As Clint Eastwood said in the movie *Unforgiven*, "Deserve's got nothin' to do with it." Maybe that describes WWE's philosophy.

CHAPTER 7
Those *Other* WWE Selections

Everyone under consideration has earned his moment in the spotlight. Every nominee merits a discussion of why he does or doesn't belong in that final tally of the 50 finest pro wrestlers in history. So let's look at those WWE honored who have not earned a position on this hopefully more justifiable list.

Here's a softball: does Kane *really* belong?

Poor Glen Jacobs. To suggest that his character Kane is one of the 50 finest wrestlers ever must make even him squirm a little. Thousands of wrestlers over more than 100 years, and Kane is one of the 50 best ever? According to WWE marketing? Why yes, of course.

The funny thing is, from an athletic standpoint, if Jacobs had developed in a different environment, he could have rivaled smooth-moving big men. He might not have attained the lofty level of Don Leo Jonathan or Gene Kiniski, but he did share some of the gifts those legitimate greats possessed. He was, however, seldom if ever asked to provide that type of action in WWE.

An English literature major at Truman State University in Missouri, Jacobs also played basketball and football. He was an athlete, not just a bodybuilder, and he made the difficult trek from independent promotions to the "big time." Vince McMahon maintains that he tries to incorporate some part of the wrestler's personality into the final version of the gimmick identity he gives to the wrestler. That theory gets a test with Glen Jacobs.

First, he was Isaac Yankem, a mad dentist. Then he was the imitator of Diesel after Kevin Nash left that part to jump to WCW. Finally, Jacobs became Kane, the mad brother of The Undertaker. Exactly what portion of all this is really Jacobs might be difficult to ascertain.

At least Kane gave Jacobs the opportunity for many lucrative battles with leading WWF/WWE stars. Some of the storylines, such as his interaction with the diva Lita, were ridiculous. Over time, Kane seemed to settle at a plateau. Injuries likely took a toll. The agenda of much WWE booking has to do with character instead of in-ring skill, and Kane never really took those next few steps like The Undertaker did. Or maybe he simply topped out, like just another .240 hitter in baseball.

Decent performer, okay gimmick under the circumstances, but not special. When all was said and done, Kane became a one-note player trapped within the rigid confines of a cartoon character. Top 50? No. Top 100? No.

But he could have been more than he was.

WWE's ranking of the Iron Sheik should raise a few eyebrows as well, placing him right behind Pat Patterson. This makes little sense, even for WWE. Of course, Iron Sheik is part of WWE history in that he won the title from Bob Backlund and lost it to Hulk Hogan. Incorporating Iron Sheik apparently helps from both a historical and a marketing standpoint. Really, though, how many Iron Sheik dolls can the company sell?

Kosrow "Ali" Vaziri was someone I got to know before he was christened the Iron Sheik. Muchnick liked to book Vaziri in St. Louis for prelims in the mid 1970s when he began with Verne Gagne's AWA. Even though he was still green, Vaziri's reputation as a legitimate wrestler appealed to Sam. Some of the publicity was hogwash, some was accurate, but he was acceptable on the undercard.

Without the gimmick of the Iron Sheik, Vaziri might never have landed main events. Nor would he have had the half-comedy tag-team run with Nikolai Volkoff. He was a legitimate tough guy, an athlete who could wrestle. Yet apart from his few weeks on top between Backlund and Hogan, he was never a consistent main event guy in major markets. The smoothness that typified workers like Patterson and Stevens was never there for the Iron Sheik. His performances were less than dynamic.

How in the world can WWE place Iron Sheik ahead of Jimmy Snuka, Mick Foley, "Superstar" Graham, and Jake Roberts? Or, for that matter, Ivan Koloff, who didn't get a sniff. A far superior worker who headlined in many major territories, Koloff also ended the legendary first title reign of Bruno Sammartino. The truth is that the Iron Sheik isn't close to belonging.

There are certainly arguments to be made on behalf of Mick Foley. But when the serious comparisons are made with other contenders, Mick, like the last kid trying out for a high school basketball team, fails to make the cut. But he was entertaining and, in particular, made a big impact with the casual audience.

The neatest item on Foley's resume might well be that he became known nationally under his real name, not just Mankind in his WWF/WWE incarnation, or Cactus Jack or even Dude Love. All were personalities Foley has displayed, but the real Foley somehow overwhelmed them all. Perhaps more than anyone, Mick has taken advantage of greater openness to pro wrestling personalities and also utilized his fame to help others. He has written wrestling memoirs and also well-received adult and children's fiction.

Foley also deserves plaudits for his charitable work with causes such as early childhood education, even in remote parts of the world, and continuing efforts with the U.S. Military. Most recently, Foley became involved with RAINN (Rape, Abuse, and Incest National Network), an organization dedicated to helping victims of sexual abuse.

In the real world, those efforts surpass the blood and guts and battered body parts that Foley gave to the wrestling world. Though never a great athlete, Foley was a gritty performer who was either crazy or especially courageous. He did what he had to do to become famous in pro wrestling, becoming a hardcore legend both through his explosive outings in Japan (literally, one duel featured *bombs* that burned Foley during the bout) and the original Extreme Championship Wrestling. Taking ridiculous body-jarring bumps, squirting his own blood repeatedly over rings around the world, ripping his body on barbed-wire ropes, and being hit with everything from baseball bats to canes to cattle prods, Foley became a walking advertisement for violence in pro wrestling.

Somehow Foley managed to move his character into the mainstream stateside with his first World Championship Wrestling run and then WWE, where the tortured soul of Mankind was born. Eventually, Foley showed all parts of his ring persona in WWE until he was accepted as Mick Foley. His many comedic moments both helped and hindered him. Still, as Foley writes, some of his stunts were so extreme, Vince McMahon made him promise "never to do anything like that again."

From a wrestling standpoint, Foley was a trooper, never failing to do the right thing for the business. Established as a major figure who had no false ego, Foley put over The Rock. He did the job for Triple H. And Randy Orton. And Edge. We should forget and forgive his stumbling around with what has generally been a dysfunctional TNA promotion.

Foley has made an argument for joining the top 50 from a totally unexpected direction. The case can be made that he took what monsters like Bruiser Brody and Dick the Bruiser did, even though he wasn't blessed with either wrestler's athleticism, to radical new levels. His body surely has paid the price.

How much should self-abuse in pursuit of fame and fortune count as an athletic gift? Foley gave what he had. He was a brawler, pure and simple, and a daredevil, not a take-down-and-submit wrestler. And he was one smart cookie. Foley got everything out of himself there was to give, but his all-around game lacked enough to keep Mankind/Cactus/

Dude/Mick off the top 50 ever. Who comes closer to grabbing that fiftieth slot? Foley or Jimmy Snuka, Junkyard Dog, Big Show, Sgt. Slaughter, Rick Rude, or Jake Roberts?

Every single one of those performers was a solid main event attraction, yet none is exceptional enough to be included in the 50 best ever. Each has something to pin a candidacy on, and deserves consideration, but once again the fine lines of acceptance keep them all out, some farther away than others.

Wrestling has been overwhelmed by "characters." Everybody has or wants a gimmick, so being some off-the-wall weirdo who qualifies as a box-office draw is not enough for the best of the best. It takes more. Though, as Terry Funk has stated, when it's done correctly, "Less is more." Gimmicks only go so far.

At any rate, Superfly Snuka certainly did plenty correctly, not the least of which was to introduce an explosive high-flying style into the WWF in the 1970s. He was his own gimmick. From the Fiji Islands, Snuka gained a superb reputation in territories like Oregon, Texas, and the Carolinas, where he faced skilled foes and gained much of the polish that was so prevalent in those days.

When Snuka hit the WWF in 1982, he was ready for prime time. Fans still talk about Superfly's legendary leap from the top of a 15-foot steel cage at Madison Square Garden on June 28, 1982, because he *missed* titleholder Bob Backlund. What a mind-boggling crash that was! When Snuka made the same jump from the top of a cage over a year later and connected with Don Muraco, a generation of young fans was totally hooked by the intensity of both moves.

Originally a heel, he was made into a babyface almost immediately because the fans cheered his athletic high-flying before the promotion actually booked him to be a favorite. Snuka was a strong babyface when he was later involved in one of McMahon's wildest early angles, during the start of the wrestling war in 1984. "Rowdy" Roddy Piper went on a verbal tirade against Snuka before blasting Jimmy in the head with a coconut. The feud was a showstopper for the WWF and also led to the first *WrestleMania* main event in 1985, when Snuka was in the corner with Hulk Hogan and Mr. T as they battled Piper and Paul Orndorff, who had Bob Orton Jr. in their corner.

Of course, that placement also demonstrates exactly where in the pecking order Vince had Snuka at the time — just a notch below the big attractions. Valuable support, but support nonetheless.

Speaking of Orton, for pure working ability he belongs in a conversation about the best, though Bob is usually forgotten because he was not a great talker. And, truthfully, Snuka has the same reputation. Though more spectacular than Orton, Snuka was not as good an all-around worker. Neither wrestler was spellbinding with a microphone.

The point is to consider how many truly gifted performers were involved at the time. Snuka more than held his own due to his phenomenal aerial offensive. Superfly was also a major attraction in Japanese rings, where business was thriving. He often teamed with Bruiser Brody, who loved Snuka and called him "a man's man," adding, "You can count on him, and he'll fight."

All of that boosts Snuka, but not enough to break into the sacred top 50 circle. For all the dangerous acrobatics, Snuka lacks some of the wrestling versatility and definitely the verbal dexterity that distinguishes those in the top 50.

What about Jake Roberts? Truly a gifted thinker, Jake was imaginative and clever. His personality had a tasty dark side. He could put himself across in an interview and knew how psychology worked inside the ring. Like Snuka and so many others of the time, his fame came from working for Vince and the WWF during the 1980s promotional conflict as Jake "The Snake." With Vince, Jake really did carry a snake, a gimmick that put him a step ahead of the game. Pretty much forgotten was the effective work Roberts had done before the WWF for Bill Watts in the Mid-South promotion.

Ironically, for all his sinister angles with Ricky Steamboat, Rick Rude, Randy Savage, and The Undertaker, Roberts never got an expected run with Hulk Hogan when Hulk was on top. Some in the business blamed it on fan reaction, which seemed to make Jake the good guy. He would have gotten the cheers instead of Hogan, which supposedly made Hulk and Vince back away.

Sadly, the dark side of Jake Roberts is all too real. Not only did injuries take a toll, but the effects of drugs and alcohol chopped away at his ring efforts and perhaps even cost him spots on the booking side of promotions. Nobody was confident Jake could go the distance. He has been in and out of rehab. Too bad, for Roberts had a brain for the business.

From a time when the quantity of top-level performers was possibly at its highest, Roberts may have a case. But he also has as many quirks that disqualify him from the position. His smarts were better than his athleticism. In addition, plenty of bright folks think he was overrated, that carrying the snake made a bigger impression for him than he could have earned as a wrestler.

Sgt. Slaughter is yet another wrestler whose credentials, while good, aren't quite enough for him to burrow his way into the top 50. He was a strong character, powerful in both build and voice, as would befit a Marine drill sergeant. Trained by Verne Gagne, Bob Remus had solid fundamentals. Probably his biggest attribute as a performer, especially in youth and his prime, was that he was a nimble big man, one who could take impressive bumps and make them believable. It was easy to believe Slaughter hurt someone or that he got hurt himself.

Main events? You bet. From a successful run in the Carolinas when that territory started smoking in the 1970s, to a tour of duty with a mask as Super Destroyer Mark II in the AWA, Slaughter got attention with hard-hitting action. He saved his best, though, for the WWF/WWE. When he hit that circuit in 1980, Slaughter had terrific scraps with titleholder Bob Backlund and what many consider to be historic duels against Pat Patterson. The Marine gimmick made a difference for Bob Remus.

When Hulk Hogan came in at the beginning of Vince's wrestling invasion in 1984, Slaughter became a fan favorite during his conflict with the Iron Sheik. Some felt that Sarge enjoyed the same level of popularity as Hogan, which allegedly made for some backroom tension. Slaughter was always a stubborn sort, willing to stand up for his rights. Apparently, whether the dispute was about money or time off, things between McMahon and Slaughter turned sour, so Sarge flew the WWF coop.

The independent market, though, was tough in those days. Bruiser Brody was one of the only ones who had learned how to work it in a profitable manner, and Brody had Japan in his hip pocket for the big bucks. Slaughter based his operations out of the AWA, which was struggling for its own survival. He also was part of the group trying to form a new national promotion out of Chicago, but the effort flopped. Critics contend he was just floating, relying on his name.

Thus, by 1990 Slaughter was back with McMahon. Except he worked again as a heel, the frustrated Marine complaining that America had gone soft. Slaughter captured the WWF crown from the Ultimate Warrior and lost it to Hulk. He was the main character in a *WrestleMania* that inflamed some legitimate patriotic passions because of how his character was portrayed.

After that, Slaughter slid back into his comfortable role as pro-America, ex-Marine butt-kicker. That led to the middle of the card and then to a dressing room position as an agent (or *producer*, as agents have come to be called). A bump or two with the main office was smoothed over, with Slaughter becoming a reliable "ambassador" for WWE.

Sgt. Slaughter was, like many from his well-rounded generation, very good in all facets of performing. His talents as an agile big man put him a cut above many, but not above those who compete for a spot in the upper echelon. Gene Kiniski, Killer Kowalski, Bruiser Brody, Big Bill Miller, and Don Leo Jonathan all had a more serious, and thus dangerous, edge over Slaughter, whose Marine gimmick verged at times on cartoonish.

Fortunately, it is an easier verdict when looking at Junkyard Dog, Big Show, and Rick Rude after weighing the unique gifts of Snuka, Foley, and Roberts, as well as the dependable service of Slaughter.

Junkyard Dog, in real life former pro football player Sylvester Ritter, got the most out of a lot of charisma and a little athleticism. He had nothing else to offer. Buck Robley, who was working and booking for

Watts when JYD got his break in Mid-South, said, "The Dog couldn't do a thing. All he had was a steroid body, although he really did have charisma. He was so stiff."

Watts was actually ready to fire Dog, who was working as a heel originally, because so many of the boys griped to Watts how bad JYD was. But Robley stuck up for Dog, who had been touted by none other than Jake Roberts, offering to work for a week with Dog to see if there was anything there. That's when Robley suggested making JYD a babyface, telling Watts that he really did have that indefinable quality of charisma. "Let the heels worry about working with him," Robley says he instructed.

And JYD started to click. "He had no clue how to work," recalls Robley, "but he had that huge body and a wicked power slam." In turn, Robley's booking led to one of wrestling's famous angles involving the Dog and the Fabulous Freebirds. In a hair-versus-hair match between Robley and Freebird leader Michael Hayes (now a key component of WWE's creative team), the Freebirds hoped to use a "magic potion" on Robley to remove his hair.

By then, JYD was allied with Robley as babyfaces against the Freebirds. In an emotional television shoot, Dog came charging in to save Robley from the potion. During the mayhem, Hayes "accidentally" put the stinky goop into JYD's eyes, "blinding" him. As they read this, longtime fans will likely recall the Los Angeles blinding angle involving Fred Blassie and John Tolos. In this case, though, Robley designed a heart-breaking scene for the Mid-South television program where he went to the now-blind Dog's house. In the scene, Dog wanted to show Robley his new baby daughter.

But JYD, unable to see thanks to the dastardly Freebirds, pointed to the wall instead. Robley sadly took Dog's arm, moved it to his baby daughter, and said, "Dog, I'm sorry. But your daughter is here. This is her."

As Junkyard Dog "miraculously" recovered his sight, he also drew fantastic crowds all over the Mid-South territory for his epic duels with the Freebirds, including Hayes, Buddy Roberts, and tremendous worker Terry Gordy. With Gordy, a big man who could move, JYD had a foe who was adept at making an opponent look much, much better than he really was. Gordy could flat-out work. The story of the new star drawing these big houses spread like wildfire, with most of the credit going to, naturally, Junkyard Dog.

When the promotional conflict of the 1980s began, Vince was thrilled to land JYD as one of his stars when McMahon stripped the territories of their best box-office draws. "But he still couldn't work a lick!" laughed Robley. Protected in booking, doing angles with masters like Terry Funk, Junkyard Dog was an important part of WWF lineups in those days.

Using that as a reason, though, to put JYD among the greatest pro wrestlers of all time is a big stretch for any reasonable observer. This brings up another touchy subject: if WWE named JYD specifically to highlight an African-American wrestler, what about Bobo Brazil, Ernie Ladd, or Rocky Johnson? When the final call is made, all of them should be thrown into the mix and only the greatest — white, black, Hispanic, whatever — should survive. That leaves Junkyard Dog out.

Also left out are Big Show and Rick Rude, who both should have accomplished more. Rude in particular is a tragic case. But just because they did their best work for WWE, should either be named best ever?

Paul Wight, aptly named The Big Show due to his gigantic size, was once touted by WCW as the next Andre the Giant. That was most unfair to Wight, who debuted in 1995 as a rookie fresh from a career in college basketball. When Andre the Giant became ANDRE THE GIANT, he already had several years of important experience and knew how to maximize his size. Wight was a kid trying to figure out how it all worked, employed by a company that was renowned for being incompetent and knee-deep in personal politics.

Billed as The Giant, Wight had his moments in WCW, but the entire episode was loaded with disappointments. Even when he supposedly won the world heavyweight championship twice (from Hulk Hogan and from Ric Flair), the lifelong fan's career in the ring wasn't really ignited. It's understandable that he allowed his WCW contract to expire in 1999. He had to be as frustrated as anyone else.

Landing with WWE was fortuitous for Wight because McMahon has a fondness for the biggest of the big. He could reward Wight with a fat contract and repeated pushes at the top.

A new name and good money surely helped Wight feel better about his athletic career. Obviously, being a key figure in *WrestleMania XXIV* for a duel with boxing star Floyd Mayweather was good for the ego. Show continues to battle injuries that are often caused by his girth, but he is normally pushed in meaningful, if not headline, roles by WWE creative. In fact, during 2012, Big Show got lots of attention messing with John Cena and CM Punk, doing a nice job in the heel role.

There's no way, however, to get around one fact: The Big Show is not Andre the Giant, nor is he close to being among the 50 best ever.

Where Show had one gift in his enormous size, Rick Rude had many gifts. An eye-catching physique, strong verbal delivery, and solid working skills (skills often found in Minnesota natives who grew up watching Verne Gagne's AWA) were all attributes of "Ravishing Rick."

He had a strong early burst with WWF in the late 1980s; of course, having Bobby Heenan as his manager and Jake Roberts as his rival didn't hurt Rude's performances one bit.

Rude then had a series of bouts with the Ultimate Warrior, keeping intact his reputation of being able to work. Bravo for Rude! But Rick was gone from the WWF pretty quickly. He got some mileage with WCW before being sidelined by injury, bounced back and forth between the big promotions of the time without ever really stepping into the ring, and — boom! It was over.

His death at age 40 was another reminder of how ruthless the business could be to its performers during that time. With all due respect, placing Rude in the WWE top 50 minimizes, almost buries, the disasters that cut short many a promising career. Was that the idea? If Rude is in the top 50, fans will forget everything that went wrong with him and others?

Next, let's be blunt as we consider Jeff Hardy. He simply does not belong in the top 50 pro wrestlers of all time. Yes, I hear the squeals of disagreement from certain fans. But this is a no-brainer. Even WWE in hyper-marketing mode should accept that Hardy doesn't fit ahead of luminaries like Valentine, Kiniski, Brody, Carpentier . . .

The hope for Hardy's future is that he gets his life in order, successfully deals with his personal issues, and finds a flow that works for him so he can enjoy his eclectic pursuits in art and such.

Maybe consistent success in pro wrestling will come along for the ride. His problems after leaving the strict structure of WWE for TNA raise a warning flag, and Jeff struggled at times in WWE. The last thing anyone wants is for him to be classified with Guerrero, Benoit, Rude, or, for that matter, with David and Kerry Von Erich.

Ironically, Hardy and his brother Matt were trained by, among others, Dory Funk Jr., long considered one of the more straight personalities in a business that draws oddballs. But this also shows that Jeff learned those good fundamentals and knows another side of working, even if that doesn't rank too high on the list of skills he displays.

Having a knack for a rather narrow version of pro wrestling and displaying a willingness to execute some risky stunt bumps does not qualify anyone to be ranked among the greatest ever, any more than it means a person will have a comfortable, healthy life. Getting a couple-year run near the top with a national promotion with much "big favorite in the middle-of-the-card" booking is not enough for Hardy to make the list. Likewise, some independent-level cult status is not the stuff of a legend.

Hardy definitely went over with a certain portion of WWE fans who reacted loudly and skewed young. Whether that by itself sold tickets or made PPV views go up is arguable. Hardy does get points for the time he tackled Triple H (a significant draw himself) on a Royal Rumble slate, and that promotion did draw better than expected. A one-time blip, or could it have been something more? After that, there was no appreciable difference.

Emphasizing the counter-culture, rebellious look can work for the right personality, and Hardy has often flaunted it. Generally, good performance outweighs bad in WWE. But there were behavior concerns to go along with the injuries that his high-flying, risk-taking style caused.

When he moved over to TNA, he took a disastrous turn to heel that fans rejected, and he ended up in legal difficulties before appearing in unable-to-perform mode at some shows. The jury is out on whether Hardy can put all the pieces back together. The verdict regarding the top 50 is in. A consistent body of reliable top-flight work and results are not at all present.

Why WWE wanted him on the all-time-greatest roster was to make the company appeal to youngsters who liked Hardy, as well as to cross-market and sell some more DVDs and action figures. His inclusion also has the scent of politics and manipulation. Unfortunately, Jeff's inclusion on the list says it all about the WWE version of best 50 superstars ever. And that's not meant as a slap at Hardy, who has doggedly chased his dream as hard as he can under the circumstances.

Dave Batista is also the stuff of dreams — both his own visions of conquering the wrestling world and WWE's. The company dreams of him as the most successful in a long line of jacked-up bodybuilder types rushed to the national arena based on their looks, before they're ready to perform at that level.

Actually, Batista had originally tried out with the feeder system for World Championship Wrestling, only to be rudely rejected. WWE liked his look, which isn't surprising given those bulging muscles and the bodybuilder background. They hustled him from their OVW farm to the big leagues.

With a unique look (from his Filipino-Greek background) and a feel for what goes on when the bell rings, Batista did better than most. He'd been a bouncer before trying wrestling, and that gave him an aura of being someone not to mess with; augmented with some showmanship, Batista got over quickly with the fans despite obvious green spots. The monster Batista: a beast unchained. Getting locked in with the likes of Flair and Triple H didn't hurt either. In retrospect, suffering the first of many muscle injuries may actually have helped Batista by giving the newcomer a chance to survey the landscape.

Essentially, except for significant injury down time, Batista was in the mix at the top of PPVs for roughly six years. He was over, part of the play, and he was meaningful if limited in his repertoire. Batista really did seem to have part of the idea. He was quoted in the British newspaper *The Sun,* criticizing TNA and their ace A.J. Styles for "car wreck matches [and] . . . doing his stunts. That's not wrestling. Wrestling is storytelling."

He is correct on some level. It also sparked a retort from Styles, who said, "I think it's funny that a guy who takes a bump and tears his back tells me that I don't know how to wrestle." Ouch. As exciting as Batista was, especially with his bells and whistles, he was hardly a good wrestler. Yet he showed a passion for the business, and the blood ran hot when he got in with opponents who could complement him. When he made the inevitable flip to heel, Batista actually clicked better than expected and was effective as a bad-guy personality. The energy was there, when he was able to go.

Did he go enough to make the top 50? No. Maybe if he had lasted longer, stayed healthier, and proven himself a top-notch worker by breaking out of the protective cocoon, this would be a harder question to answer.

And, finally, as far as Gorilla Monsoon is concerned, Monsoon definitely belongs in the WWE Hall of Fame but *not* in the top 50 pro wrestlers in history.

Certainly Gino Marella, who had finished second in the NCAA wrestling tourney in 1959 before turning pro, made a wonderful decision when he became Gorilla Monsoon, the 400-pound wildman from Manchuria who became one of Bruno Sammartino's best foes in pursuit of the World Wide Wrestling Federation laurels.

Bruno and Gorilla battled on pretty much even terms in bruising brawls (including some one-hour draws) around the territory, beginning in 1963, after which Monsoon was established as a headliner in the area. For a huge man, he was athletic and could move. Monsoon understood how to play his part. And he could wrestle, though he seldom displayed it.

But Marella made an even better decision behind the scenes when he became a stockholder in Capitol Wrestling Corporation, which was the legal name of the WWWF. The majority owner, naturally, was Vince McMahon Sr. It was a strong and profitable relationship for many years. Monsoon was a smart man who also bought a minority position in Carlos Colón's Puerto Rico promotion.

His business acumen, dollars and cents, was excellent. He played the stock market, much like Angelo Poffo (Randy Savage's dad). Gino also liked to visit Atlantic City. Monsoon did have some giant moments in the squared circle. One of the most memorable, however, was not actually a bout. During the run-up in 1976 to the mixed match between boxing great Muhammad Ali and Japanese wrestling star Antonio Inoki, which McMahon promoted as a closed-circuit event around the United States, Ali squared off with matman "Baron" Mikel Scicluna on ABC's *Wide World of Sports*.

Monsoon leaped into the ring, snatched up Ali, and gave him the airplane spin. The message was supposed to be that a wrestler like Inoki could whip the boxing king.

The actual struggle was something different, as we all know, but the angle obviously put Monsoon in the spotlight at the time. Ironically, it was Vince Jr. who was the television commentator for this scuffle.

Gorilla had become a babyface on the WWWF circuit prior to that moment with Ali, but was scaling back his in-ring exploits to concentrate on the business side. He did, however, play an interesting role on June 16, 1980, when Hulk Hogan made his then-WWF debut as a bad guy. Hogan's victim in his first outing? It was Monsoon. And Hulk whipped Gorilla in less than a minute at Madison Square Garden, where the faithful were stunned and enraged.

Only three years later, things changed. Vince Sr.'s son was buying out everyone at Capitol Wrestling, including his dad, in order to begin the march across the wrestling landscape. Marella struck an excellent deal, which reportedly guaranteed him lifetime employment and strong income. Vince Jr. apparently had learned he could rely on Monsoon, so it was a worthwhile bargain for all involved.

In addition to his chores in the dressing room (the spot from which he directed traffic at television tapings was dubbed the "Gorilla position"), Gorilla became the noted play-by-play television commentator for what was now World Wrestling Federation television and PPVs. His fabulous on-air chemistry with first Jesse Ventura and then Bobby Heenan played a big part in getting the entire production over with the larger general audience.

He was a strong personality in the operation. His passing in 1999 was truly a sad moment.

His background tells the tale. Gorilla Monsoon was a major player in the development of what has become WWE. He was a doggone good performer. Was he one of the 50 best ever to lace up boots? Well, no. But he deserves the consideration, and his inclusion in WWE annals at least makes sense.

By this point the trend is certainly clear that the McMahon top 50 catalog includes a number of standouts who are good, but benefit from their connections with the WWF/WWE. In a real analysis to determine the 50 finest, they miss grabbing pro wrestling's brass ring.

In fact, there are other remarkable talents and characters who deserve closer scrutiny to decide . . . is he in? Or is he out? The quest to finalize who are the 50 greatest of all time can become even more deliciously complex.

CHAPTER 8
What About . . . ?

At this point, many of you have to be wondering, "What about this guy . . . ?"

It's part of the beauty of the beast that is professional wrestling. Everyone has a favorite, some particularly memorable character whom he or she thinks deserves to be considered for the leading 50 performers of wrestling history.

Even when the number of warriors in the business shrank but became more nationally recognizable within one or two dominant promotions, fans found different stars that appealed to their particular tastes.

While it is nearly impossible to look at every potential finalist, let's review some of the more worthy prospects who missed the cut. Keep in mind that a few of those who appeared on WWE's worked list were given strong consideration before being bumped.

Begin with the wildest of the wild cards . . .

Chris Benoit. He is not on the final roster, and it's not because of his horrible crimes. In 2007, Benoit murdered his wife and young son before killing himself. The WWE quickly removed any reference to Benoit from its archives thanks to that inexplicable tragedy. But that couldn't erase the many stellar matches Benoit had from the annals of the industry.

Fortunately, removing Benoit from consideration to be included in the greatest 50 due to his atrocity was unnecessary after a serious evaluation of Benoit's wrestling credentials, impressive though they were. Benoit fits into the category of Eddie Guerrero: he simply didn't have enough all-around credentials to slip into the elite gathering despite the many skills he possessed.

Look, I get it. Benoit was a superior worker who had absolutely no fear of risking his body to make a match tremendous. He was driven, knew he was on the small side, and probably used his size as motivation for his gut-wrenching style. Japanese fans, promoters, and talent alike were enthralled with Benoit's intense skills. After a frustrating tenure with WCW, he moved far higher on WWE lineups than expected, considering his size and the politics of the company.

On the other hand, he never was *the* man at the top of a major program. His interviews were below average. Benoit was in matches and angles that mattered and helped make an attractive package for potential buyers, but he did not individually drive the branded shows. By Vince's design, the success or failure of a production seldom rested on any one wrestler.

Imagining the performer in another era to get a look at his overall value, how would Benoit have fared? He would have topped cards for smaller territories and been a good addition, but he wouldn't have been in main events in the major markets. He would have been a favorite internationally, but again not as the number one stud. Sadly, the question that always arises is "How would he have appeared and performed without steroids? Would he have been big enough to get a serious look by the major promotions?"

His extreme competitive nature might have served him better in the Lewis-Stecher era, since size also was not as defining a quality as it would come to be. Benoit definitely could have been a shooter if he'd had the right background. But he is not one of the 50 greatest pros in history.

The Sheik. Eddie Farhat, the original Sheik, belongs on any collection of the greatest heels ever. In addition, he likely should reside in most wrestling Halls of Fame. Unfortunately for his supporters, though, he does not get into the 50 greatest pro wrestlers ever.

Yes, The Sheik got phenomenal heat. More than one disturbance was sparked by The Sheik's antics, though smart promoters who didn't care for liability lawsuits might not have found that so wonderful. He wasn't a particularly good wrestler, though he obviously did his gimmick well. Still, when he controlled the main events as promoter or booker, most of his matches were short, eerily violent and bloody, ending with no decision, a disqualification, or a victory stolen by The Sheik. Finding jobs done by The Sheik would be challenging. As a worker, did he make lesser foes look better? Were it not for the blood, few, if any, of his bouts would be considered classics.

As the promoter in Detroit, he was involved in one of wrestling's more nasty promotional battles with Dick the Bruiser. When he got involved behind the scenes with promoter Frank Tunney in Toronto, he guided the town through a dizzying ride up and down. Up, way up, but then down . . . down . . . down.

Aside from the heel character, the biggest case usually cited in his favor is The Sheik as a drawing card. That, however, has to be disputed. His two most successful spots were Detroit and Toronto, where he had either total or partial control of booking. Where else was he in main events that drew consistent money? In Detroit and Toronto, after fabulous runs of a couple years, the towns were left dead. Neither drew flies until the clientele had been regained. Detroit didn't recover until WWF came in during the 1980s war.

That was not good for the pro wrestling business, nor was the impression his booking and performances left with the mainstream. A true top drawing card not only pulls in the public when he is in main events, he also leaves business in good shape for whoever follows him — and for himself if he returns. The Sheik failed on those critical points, and, despite a remarkable heel persona, his wrestling or tough-guy talents aren't nearly enough to put him in the top 50 of all time.

Dick Murdoch. If it were up to his peers, the athletes who were in the ring with him night after night or who saw his antics on a regular basis, Dick Murdoch would have an outstanding chance of being selected. They know, without any question, what a gifted worker Murdoch was, able to elevate a poor performer into a decent match and to lift a good opponent into a terrific bout. When worked with at his level, the results were amazing. Stan Hansen, who knows the territory, called Murdoch "one of the greatest talents . . . the best big man ever."

What made him special, though, was the fact that Murdoch was much more than a brilliant technician. He was flat-out a character. He had personality, charisma, showmanship — you name it, Murdoch had it. He was also a comedian and a joker who was occasionally moody and undisciplined. Nobody could get more heat, honest chuckles, or ear-splitting roars. By any standard, Dick Murdoch was a free spirit, not a political player. And those latter qualities work against his ability to climb into the highest echelon.

There certainly is a disconnect between Murdoch and what wrestling historians, some bright and some not, think about Dick. For example, when Dave Meltzer runs the yearly voting for his highly respected *Wrestling Observer* Hall of Fame, Murdoch always falls a little bit short. Wrestlers who know him almost unanimously vote for him. Historians, on the other hand, instead cast their ballots for preliminary guys who made up exciting tag teams or standouts who didn't offer what Murdoch did. Few of these voters were fortunate enough to see Murdoch at his best. He was in Japan so often that territories hesitated to give him that all-out push, so he didn't have the regional titles that historians seem to like. Murdoch narrowly misses the cut.

I understand why he is in the position he is. While he headlined over most of North America and was a huge star in Japan's best promotions Murdoch is only at the entrance to a Hall of Fame.

He was a good drawing card, but not great. He was a legitimate tough guy, not someone to provoke. He could be inconsistent, stiffing an opponent he didn't like or shutting down the action if a promoter had aggravated him (though that didn't occur nearly as often as Dick's detractors would have others believe). He had fantastic matches against a who's who of wrestling, many of whom are on our top 50 roster. He was a fabulous interview, but he could go off on tangents, entertaining though they were. He did not suck up or pretend he liked people he didn't, including fans. But he'd go out to dinner with a family he enjoyed and have the kids in stitches all night long. He'd just shake his head in disgust at the politics of wrestling.

He knew why he never got serious consideration for the NWA title. "They don't trust me," Murdoch told me once. "They don't know if I can stay serious or not." Funny, but he never explained himself or disputed that claim. Maybe he didn't know either.

Hopefully, Dick Murdoch will understand why he's guarding the door but not in the top 50. Maybe I'm wrong leaving him out and should give a little favoritism to a friend. Plus, the talent is all there whether someone likes him personally or not. But it's almost like why Murdoch knew he'd never be chosen as the NWA champion — just too rambunctious, a few too many quirks. Regardless, every single person in the final 50 will know that if you wanted a real barn-burner of a match, one that blows the roof off, the man to have it with was Dick Murdoch.

Paul Orndorff. Doesn't it seem odd that Paul Orndorff is not on the WWE list, considering some of the others who are? Who did he aggravate in that office? After all, Orndorff was one of the best, if not maybe *the* best, challengers that Hulk Hogan ever had.

Orndorff, a terrific college football player at the University of Tampa, had been catching attention throughout pro wrestling circles when he was an early signee with WWF. This was in late 1983 as McMahon was gearing up to take on the world. Orndorff had been featured both on the

WTBS national show and in Bill Watts's Mid-South promotion, and he invaded New Japan. He was hot and new.

With Roddy Piper as his manager, Orndorff was blessed by Vince with a terrific nickname: Mr. Wonderful. He tangled with Hulk, then the new WWF king, around the country and drew many sellouts. Their matches were excellent because Orndorff understood his role, was extremely athletic, and was able to make spectators believe that he might well be able to defeat Hulk — more so than Curt Hennig.

This made Orndorff an essential element in the first *WrestleMania* main event, where he and Roddy Piper tackled Hulk and Mr. T. After that mega-success for WWF, Orndorff was also right in the middle of some well-rated *Saturday Night's Main Event* shows on NBC. After a turn as a good guy, even teaming with Hulk at one point, Orndorff was again thrown into a feud with Hogan. The highlight of that time was a showdown between Hogan and Orndorff that drew 76,000 fans outdoors in Toronto. And once again, Mr. Wonderful was back on NBC and working a memorable cage match with Hogan.

Hulk and Orndorff brought big money, along with many of Hogan's best outings, into WWF/WWE coffers. At some point during those years, Orndorff suffered a serious neck and shoulder injury that led to atrophy of his right arm. This was a crisis because physiques meant so much to the company. Orndorff took no time off, until finally he could go no longer and retired.

Of course, retirements in wrestling are an iffy thing. Mr. Wonderful fiddled around on the independent circuits. He eventually rebuilt his body enough to take another run at the big time with World Championship Wrestling when the Atlanta-based organization competed with the WWF. Maybe that's why Paul isn't included on the WWE dream list.

Things really didn't click in WCW for Orndorff. He was mid-card, and his body broke down from all the abuse and the original injury. So Orndorff helped train some young talent, made personal appearances, and was inducted into the WWE Hall of Fame. For our more serious purposes, Orndorff is a borderline performer who was excellent in the ring and played a major role in the early success of WWF. It would also be unfair to make it sound like Paul only had eye-catching bouts with Hulk. He helped execute dandy duels with Ricky Steamboat, Mick Foley as Cactus Jack, Rick Rude, "Cowboy" Bob Orton, and Roddy Piper. The injuries, however, did take the edge off as his career wound down.

Maybe Orndorff, Murdoch, and Chris Jericho come up a little short of making the best 50 ever, but if I were starting a new promotion, then or now, I could do a lot worse than those three at their peaks.

Billy Robinson and Karl Gotch and . . . Just as Kurt Angle, Dan Hodge, Pat O'Connor, and Jack Brisco would all move near the top of the list, Billy Robinson would most assuredly be included among the greatest 50 if the only consideration was pure wrestling ability. In fact, even considering all the other necessary qualities, Robinson was one who came very, very close to joining the party.

A couple of vexing decisions had to be made regarding variations of style and approach. Stan Hansen is a legendary brawler, Randy Orton personifies new school, and Billy Robinson could twist an opponent into a pretzel 1,000 different ways. His beautiful bridge after a double arm suplex really was something to see.

As an amateur, Robinson was the British national champion and the European open champion. Then he connected with fabled trainer Billy Riley, who ran a gym called the Snake Pit in Wigan, England. The place was a haven for learning catch wrestling, turning out some very nasty shooters who understood submission holds. Robinson was one of Riley's finest graduates.

After he turned pro, the best thing Robinson did was connect with Verne Gagne and the AWA in 1970. Gagne appreciated a great wrestler, and Robinson was one. Some promoters had been skeptical whether Robinson had the personality to succeed as a main event star despite his obvious wrestling skills, but Gagne had no hesitation about using Robinson on top.

He was rewarded with a performer who made outsiders respect the business, lured in crowds in the correct context, and provided a terrific challenger for Gagne himself. Robinson and Gagne had some incredible matches together, proving that a base of wrestling skills mixed with modern moves and sharp psychology could make money and thrill an audience.

Despite the plaudits for his talent, a perception always existed that Robinson lacked charisma and was not a particularly good interview. All things are relative, of course, but it is true that Robinson never got the big push in different areas that some others got. I saw him several times in St. Louis, including in one super match with Harley Race, and I always found him an entertaining performer. What he did in the ring was never duplicated by anyone else.

He was a star in Canada, where one of his biggest moments was a one-hour draw with WWF king Bob Backlund in Montreal in 1982. Critics might crab, "See, just like against Gagne, a scientific match." What's wrong with that? Done correctly and with the right promotional development, a tight, psychological, exhausting scientific battle is every bit as exciting as a knock-down, drag-out, back-alley donnybrook, but for different reasons.

Japan became a home away from home for Robinson, where he was recognized as a legitimate wrestler with excellent submission skills. When he squared off with Antonio Inoki, the Japanese press gleefully pushed the confrontation as a test between the world's two best wrestling technicians.

As Robinson aged, he became deeply involved with training shoot wrestling and mixed martial arts in Japan. His finest students included Kazushi Sakuraba and Josh Barnett. In many ways, he followed in Karl Gotch's footsteps.

And what about Karl Gotch? When it comes to technique, athleticism, and a touch of controversy, Gotch surely would qualify for a position among the finest ever. Judging just wrestling and not charisma or box office appeal, Gotch is most likely in the best 20.

Under his real name Charles Istaz, Gotch competed for Belgium in both Greco-Roman and freestyle wrestling at the 1948 Olympics. Like Robinson, he trained to be a professional at Billy Riley's Snake Pit and became a hooker of high caliber. After working carnivals and tournaments in Europe, Gotch came to the attention of Edouard Carpentier, who put Gotch with Montreal promoter Eddie Quinn. That didn't pan out because Quinn thought he was colorless and stuck him in openers under the name Karl Krauser. In 1960, Gotch caught the eye of promoter Al Haft in Columbus, Ohio. A wily assessor of talent, Haft loved shooters and thought Gotch had the potential to become a good worker and then a star. Haft changed the newcomer's last name to Gotch, in honor of Frank Gotch, and worked with Karl's interview and presentation. Those lessons clicked and everyone discovered just how dangerously good Karl Gotch really was.

Gotch was a physical fitness freak who felt wrestlers needed flexibility rather than the bulkiness brought on by weightlifting, so he stuck to a regimen of Indian calisthenics that began with a warm-up of 300 Hindu squats. Does that say it all? He was stubborn and not generally interested in the opinions of others. His wrestling reflected his personality in that he was incredibly skilled with swift, hard maneuvers that left mere workers gasping. His atomic suplex made casual fans squirm because it obviously could break a foe in two.

Although he became a main event performer, or close, in most of North America, not all promoters would book him, and most were careful about selecting his opponents. His unyielding personality, his skill set, and his reputation inspired caution. Yet some, like Dominic DeNucci, Bruno Sammartino, and Big Bill Miller, liked and learned from him.

Gotch once asked DeNucci, quite sincerely, about why he wasn't clicking with more of the fans. A gentleman and a class act, DeNucci told Gotch that there was more to pro wrestling than knowing the holds, that selling the action and telling the story were every bit as important. Gotch never quite absorbed that lesson.

Controversy came in 1962 during the reign of Buddy Rogers as NWA champion. Apparently, Rogers said that Gotch couldn't be trusted as a shooter. Rogers also included Big Bill Miller in his diatribe. In Columbus, Ohio, Gotch and Miller confronted the cocky kingpin. Rogers not only admitted that he'd made those claims but that he also couldn't make any money facing Gotch. Gotch allegedly attacked Rogers. Rogers ended up bloody and with an injured hand or elbow that caused him to cancel several dates, which furthered an NWA member uprising that only ended when Rogers lost the title. The incident cemented American promoters' belief that Gotch's strict style wasn't good for box office.

As a kid, I saw a duel between Gotch and Lou Thesz, then the champion, at Kiel Auditorium in St. Louis on December 27, 1963. I remember it being stiff, with sporadic action that jolted you in its ferocity in between cautious interludes. It was a work, and Thesz won cleanly. I was too young to realize that the shoot mentality was alive and well, if only for scattered moments within the work, whenever two hookers like Thesz and Gotch went against each other.

Gotch ended up in Japan, where he is now a god of wrestling. His so-called strong style went over immediately with the more serious Japanese crowds. With a status on par with Inoki, Thesz, and Rikidozan, Gotch found a new wrestling home in Japan. As his in-ring career wound down, Gotch trained countless Japanese standouts, including those who helped bring shoot wrestling to the forefront in that country.

What is the difference between Karl Gotch, Billy Robinson, and Lou Thesz, all great *wrestlers* by any definition? Robinson and Gotch were both confident, efficient, and cool, perhaps even cold or arrogant.

The difference? Emotion.

Within Thesz, a fire burned quite visibly, accompanying all those technical tools. Fans could feel it. Not that Gotch or Robinson didn't care, but that heat, for whatever reason, always stayed just under the surface, out of reach of the fans who wanted it most. Thesz's passion boiled and everyone knew it, which is why he is the best of all time.

Now look at **Dick Hutton**, whom Thesz chose as his own replacement as champion in 1957. Once again, if this compilation of the 50 greatest ever was based strictly on wrestling, Hutton would go from not being on the list right into the top 20. He was that good.

Hutton was a three-time national collegiate champion. He might have won four titles, but lost his final try by decision to Verne Gagne. Tulsa promoter Leroy McGuirk, who was a major influence on Dan Hodge, brought Hutton into the professional ranks, and none other than "Strangler" Lewis helped train Hutton. Thesz has often called Hutton the best wrestler he ever knew when the action went down on the mat.

While Hutton brought a high degree of credibility to the oft-criticized business, and he was a main event performer almost from the beginning, he was seen as impassive, without color or showmanship. There were no physical tricks or maneuvers Hutton could not do, but he wasn't outgoing and that worked against him. After he took the championship from Thesz, business stayed flat and Hutton's title matches did not spark any rise. This led to O'Connor's reign starting in 1959.

Nonetheless, Hutton was every bit the grappling talent that Gotch and Robinson were, probably even the equal of Thesz and Angle, or Brisco. Despite legitimate genius skills as a wrestler, Hutton failed to meet all the unique demands that professional wrestling requires to create an unforgettable superstar.

Yvon Robert and . . . Strong sentiment is always present for someone like Robert, who gets plaudits for helping to make Montreal one of wrestling's hottest cities in the 1940s and laying the groundwork for long thereafter. But he isn't the only standout from pre-television who deserves consideration.

Think about **John Pesek** or **Bronko Nagurski**. If Nagurski gets a look, how about **Gus Sonnenberg**? And then the scope widens to include **Earl McCready, Everett Marshall, Dick Shikat, Stanislaus Zbyszko**, maybe **George Hackenschmidt**, and look at the Pandora's box that has been opened.

Robert was a fantastic drawing card in the province of Quebec, along with Boston, some Northeastern locales, and Texas. He had a brief run as the world champion in 1942, beating "Wild Bill" Longson and losing to Bobby Managoff (and wasn't Managoff a sturdy competitor in retrospect?). While not a spectacular performer, Robert was someone who immediately captured the respect of the audience, which meant so much at the time. And everyone in Montreal knew who he was. Even today, many folks have stories about their parents or grandparents who lived and died with what Yvon Robert did. Unfortunately for Robert, while impressive, it's not quite enough to nudge him onto the top 50.

Pesek's only claim to the championship came in the late 1930s when he had slowed down and the claimant list was lengthy. He had long been saluted by his fellow tough guys as a shooter whom nobody wanted to cross. "Strangler" Lewis and Billy Sandow often used Pesek as a "policeman" in shoot situations. He had trained with Joe Stecher and had a short fuse, at one point getting banned from New York for eye gouging — for real! The temper kept some of the promotional big shots in the 1920s from giving Pesek a push, so Pesek joined yet another independent group of promoters. He often ruffled feathers with his public challenges to name stars of the time. Had he handled the politics better, perhaps he would have received better opportunities that would have boosted his stock in the search for the 50 finest.

Nagurski is most famous as an all-time-great football player (check the greatest ever gridiron lists and note that Nagurski is right there with stars from every era). And the powerhouse had a terrific record for his ring work. With the aura of a sports celebrity, Nagurski gave a boost to pro wrestling that wasn't available from just anyone. Plus, he was a terrific athlete and the top stars loved working with him.

Sonnenberg was also a football star and, like Bronko, was the world champion for a while. But he was often caught in the middle of double-crosses. Greedy promoters would hire shooters because while Sonnenberg was a fine athlete and performer, he was not much of a wrestler. Sonnenberg's contribution to pro wrestling came from adding credibility as a famous football player and in his flying tackles, which helped open up the product and set the stage for fast, hard-hitting action.

Can you see how each age offers a set of unique and spellbinding talents that should at least be looked at when putting together the overall package? Of course, the deep pool of talented performers made each other work harder and perform better, even in the time before World War II.

Don Leo Jonathan and The Crusher and . . . I anticipate squawks because the deeply respected Jonathan is not included in this remarkable 50. Jonathan was a terrific worker who always lands high in any evaluation. Few big men (he was billed at 6'6" and 320 pounds) could move as smoothly and gracefully as Jonathan.

He had terrific brawls with Killer Kowalski in Montreal, where on May 31, 1972 he defeated by disqualification none other than Jean Ferré before that Giant became Andre. Jonathan gave NWA titleholders Gene Kiniski (with whom he also formed a dynamite tag team), Dory Funk Jr., and Jack Brisco spectacular tests in Vancouver and the Pacific Northwest, where Jonathan made his longest and strongest claim to fame. I still remember as a kid watching two of Jonathan's tremendous struggles in 1962 because they looked so real and hard. One was with Lou Thesz, the other with Johnny Valentine. No wonder I fondly recall those names going at it!

Jonathan falls into that ticklish position of oh so close, but not close enough. After studying his career and finding out the high regard other stars of the day held for him, who would argue if he had been slotted among the 50 finest?

And then here comes a growling complaint about Reggie Lisowski, known far and wide to AWA loyalists as The Crusher. In a city like Milwaukee, The Crusher probably still enjoys as much fame as any of the old Milwaukee Braves do (including Hank Aaron, Eddie Mathews, and Warren Spahn). Talk about a character! At least, the argument can be made that in their respective primes, The Crusher was not as athletic as Dick the Bruiser, his partner in crime. But The Crusher had that natural ability to get himself over.

What about **"Cowboy" Bob Ellis?** Or **Wilbur Snyder?** It's hard to believe that these two don't get more recognition, for they were the hugely popular prototypical babyfaces of the 1950s and 1960s. The cowboy character fit Ellis perfectly, with his aw-shucks, humble yet sincere interviews. Ellis popularized the bulldog headlock, a great finishing maneuver, and truly knew how to project a temper-tantrum comeback. More to the point, Ellis was the main event good guy, drawing sellouts at the Cow Palace in San Francisco, at Kiel Auditorium in St. Louis, and at Madison Square Garden in New York. What a diverse set of accomplishments. The guy definitely had something special to offer the discussion.

Snyder was the long, lean super athlete whose good-guy personality made sinister, snarling, vicious heels like Fritz Von Erich and Dick the Bruiser who they were. It's amazing that Snyder is usually overlooked considering he also beat Verne Gagne on national television on April 7, 1956, ending Gagne's five-year reign as the United States champion. Snyder also thrilled audiences during a nearly one-hour draw with Lou Thesz in 1954 that was nationally televised. The rivalry with Thesz went everywhere and included one 90-minute — that's right, *90-minute* — stalemate.

His name always popped up when potential NWA titleholders were considered from the 1950s into the early 1960s. Like Ellis, Snyder was a superb drawing card whenever he headlined against other stars.

The possibilities seem endless. One generation offers Sting, another complains that Mad Dog Vachon cannot be ignored, nor Ernie Ladd, and a little further back they conjure up thoughts of Enrique Torres and Pepper Gomez. Ponder Ken Patera and Wahoo McDaniel. Where are Rocca and Bobo Brazil? Shouldn't one of them be number 50?

Is the picture clear now? Isn't it obvious after all this discussion what a disservice WWE did to the tradition of professional wrestling with their account of who is the greatest talent in the history of this glorious, ridiculous, crazy business — or who isn't?

Not that the people WWE named didn't deserve consideration. They all did. But there is such a wealth of unparalleled characters and performers that mere marketing tactics fail to do justice to the final document. Look at all the names brought up, considered, and compared. How many did I miss? What a struggle it is to slot everyone, and frustrating that it never seems perfect.

Who will make their mark in the near future and challenge the top 50 for an esteemed position? How close is someone like CM Punk to vaulting over those like Edge or Eddie Guerrero and seeking a seat with the all-time greats? Is Punk the harbinger of what's to come, an underdog fighting his way from dinky independent shows to the big time? In fact, as the criteria apply to Punk, the self-styled rebel and seriously determined performer has had a red-hot 18 months as this book goes to print. Now he needs to add another four or so years just like it to match what Randy Orton has accomplished, or another 20 years to challenge what Ric Flair did.

Is there some young lightning bolt poised to break out in TNA or Ring of Honor and rattle the entire business? Perhaps a polished and hungry amateur stud might pick pro wrestling as his career and explode on the scene.

Just because a star is new doesn't mean he is better. And just because a star is old doesn't make him better either. You must weigh each against the other, consider time and circumstances, and make a final decision.

And you know what? How much fun is this, having an excuse to dig into the chronicles of the business and the characters who have inspired it all. To anticipate the future and reevaluate the ghosts of the past. Who am I kidding? This is a gold mine of enjoyment.

CHAPTER 9
Who Is Taro Myaki?

Before Vince McMahon was unintentionally kind enough to drop an idea in our laps, my editor Michael Holmes and I were bouncing around thoughts for my fourth book with ECW Press. Of course, Michael has embraced this bizarre world as passionately as anyone I know. The fact that he tolerates my occasional rants about the good and bad of professional wrestling proves that beyond any question!

At any rate, one of my rambling topics would have been entitled something like *Who Is Taro Myaki?* or *What Happened to Taro Myaki? Unraveling the Mysteries of Wrestling Mystique.* The plan was to work through the hundreds, maybe thousands, of performers who laced up boots and use something from their experiences to connect the past and present of wrestling in an entertaining way.

So who was Taro Myaki? As it turned out, Myaki fit in with the purpose to uncover the best 50 of all time. In the late 1950s and early 1960s, the Myaki I remember was a roly-poly, sinister, totally entertaining heel who often teamed with Kinji Shibuya for tag-team bouts in my hometown of St. Louis. I can remember the duo joining announcer Joe Garagiola to do a commercial for Busch Bavarian Beer on Channel 11's *Wrestling at the Chase* show.

"Ah so! Buschie Bavarian. Ichiban! Icihiban! Buschie Bavarian, number one!" Myaki and Shibuya would proclaim, happy smiles on their faces as they hoisted a glass of the beverage in front of the camera. Garagiola, whose remarkable career ranged from hosting the *Today Show* to commentating for Major League Baseball on national television, still calls the commercial one of the most fun spots he ever did.

Myaki was a workman who "judo-chopped" and tossed salt and made great facial expressions through many solid matches in St. Louis. He and Shibuya beat George and Sandy Scott but lost to "Whipper" Billy Watson and Bobby Managoff. Taro lost to Dan Hodge, Wilbur Snyder, Johnny Valentine, and Pat O'Connor and got disqualified a few times. But he beat John Paul Henning, Ron Reed (who later became Buddy Colt), Bill Dromo, and Farmer Marlin and had draws with Joe Blanchard and Gory Guerrero. That's just the tip of his iceberg in one town, and all were enjoyable to watch. Think of how many more outings elsewhere that Myaki had in his career, how many more newcomers learned from working with this sturdy journeyman.

And he *was* a journeyman, part of the guts of the wrestling business in its heyday. Clever and never boring, talented and versatile. Someone who could have a terrific battle with the main event guys, provide quality time in a preliminary, or impart knowledge by osmosis working with a rookie. Sadly, though, Myaki has disappeared in the fog of history. I had a difficult time trying to find out about his background and what happened to him, even enlisting researchers like Matt Farmer and Joe Svinth to help me. Finally I was able to put together a few pieces of his puzzle.

Taro was a native of Hawaii who started as a sumo wrestler in Japan, where he trained with the legendary Rikidozan. When Rikidozan moved from sumo to pro wrestling with the help of Bobby Bruns, Myaki also made the switch. Originally an accomplished wrestler himself, Bruns was making a transition from wrestler to booker, eventually landing with Sam Muchnick in St. Louis in the late 1950s. Bruns helped to get Taro booked in the Pacific Northwest, several Southern territories, Kansas City, and notably St. Louis.

Myaki's real name was George Kahaumia. Sam Muchnick and Bill Longson told me that George was quite successful in real estate in his native Hawaii, leaving wrestling to move back home in the late 1960s. As a sumo, George used the name Kongozan. He became Taro Myaki in the pro ranks. He died in Hawaii on November 7, 2010, at the age of 89, and was noted as a professional wrestler in the obituary.

Now, you might ask what exactly Taro Myaki has to do with the list of the greatest 50 professional wrestlers ever and for all time.

Lou Thesz described the pro wrestlers, when they were much greater in number than they are now, as forming a pyramid. In *Hooker*, the engrossing book he wrote with Kit Bauman, Lou noted that the largest group was composed of journeymen. Thesz said, "These were the boys who had proven themselves as good performers and dedicated players . . . they took their profession seriously . . . served as its backbone." In Thesz's firm opinion, without the Taro Myakis, there could be no stars.

In something that added to the same thought, when Terry Funk was inducted into the St. Louis Wrestling Hall of Fame in 2010, he wrote me a heartfelt thank-you note. He praised the standouts with whom he had worked, and he saluted those who helped train and hone him. And Terry added, "I also thank those who were marred by blood, sweat, dust, and dirt; those who strived valiantly and came up short again and again." Again, like Taro Myaki and all of those similar to him.

Like Thesz, Terry Funk understood there could be no attempt to name the 50 greatest ever if there weren't those who laid the building blocks of that greatness. Each made his or her contribution; they were at those levels simply because their ability had been stretched as far as it could go. The titans of wrestling needed people like Taro Myaki, who had the respect of both the fans and the other performers, to do the jobs in a meaningful fashion that would elevate the stars.

Only the finest can reach the zenith, but it also takes a genuine level of skill to lay bricks and mortar. Not being chosen is not a slight; being selected in any forum is an honor. In some form, all contributed to a list like this one.

Good hands like Myaki made up the cast that allows us to determine who the best 50 ever are. They formed a basis from which to work, setting a high standard for what was supposedly the average. The very best had to surpass that and every plateau above it. Unfortunately, this once-solid hunk of good talent has disappeared, and that has hindered the development of both current and likely future great performers. Their fading has made judgments about who really is top of the line even more difficult. Those considerations, Taro Myaki and all, blended with the lovely opportunity to present an honest and serious analysis of who have been the greatest in the long history of professional wrestling. This project became all too enticing for me.

Obviously, when the decision was made to write about this particular subject, Michael and I knew there would be mixed reactions. Newer followers of wrestling, because they have been brainwashed by the WWE machine or simply don't know any better, will struggle to accept anything that is not part of the style in which they have been educated. Some others will have their own method to figure out who they think are the most worthy stars of all time, and perhaps they won't enjoy getting into a deep discussion of why or why not, who versus who, how and context. Sadly, in certain cases, some will fail to recognize how tightly woven the past and present are in professional wrestling.

But there are those who will get it. I like to think what I'm doing here achieves two purposes. One, this is a discussion that stands strong and alone and proud, documenting what I believe is an honest assessment of who the absolute finest 50 pro wrestlers ever are as of 2012. Two, it should start a realistic discussion that acknowledges the true impact of what some performers did, whether in 1920, 1970, or 2010.

Naturally, this material will not get the benefit of national television and monumental marketing like WWE's list received. Still, somebody — somebody who does understand this business — had to at least start a meaningful debate because the WWE version, no matter how widely it is disseminated, is a flawed document.

The WWE tabulation is disrespectful of their own culture and actually harms the company's own best interests by insulting both fans who fondly recall the glory days and young enthusiasts who want to know the genuine heritage of their newfound interest. Maybe Vince and crew believe they are too big to feel it, but nonetheless . . . Viewer surveys in the past few years have actually shown that the highest percentage of those watching WWE television shows are 50 and older! Doesn't Vince think they'll buy PPVs too?

Look at every other sport or form of entertainment. In every case, those who write, talk, or produce video pay homage to the stars of the past. They recognize the equality of then versus now.

Baseball broadcasters spin yarns about Mickey Mantle, Stan Musial, Sandy Koufax, Babe Ruth, Rogers Hornsby, and Ty Cobb. Rock 'n' roll critics talk about the greatness of Elvis Presley, Chuck Berry, and The Beatles. Movie reviewers discuss Cary Grant, Katherine Hepburn, and Humphrey Bogart.

The comparisons between present and past, even the distant past, recognize the differences in the fields but still place modern and past giants on equal footing. Look at the "greatest ever" lists in any comparable area. Those connections bind generations and make the individual fields stronger within the consciousness of the public.

This thing is called tradition. Is WWE ashamed of its tradition, making everything a dollar-and-cents decision about pleasing an advertiser rather than building deep, continuing loyalties among devotees? Utilized properly, this is more than nostalgia.

Or perhaps VKM and his minions simply feel that wrestling is beneath them, comparing it to running a strip club and using the proceeds for higher purposes — like making B movies. Rebranding the operation is valid, but Vince's motives have a different edge. Apparently WWE would like to soften what they perceive as a tainted business.

If the media and the public have a negative impression about wrestling, whose fault might that perception be? Exactly who has commanded the public awareness of the product with their philosophy, angles, and product for almost three decades?

Ironically, like Sam Muchnick, Vince McMahon's father ran a highly respected, professional operation that elevated what was generally regarded as a shoddy business. Most wrestling impresarios left much to be desired in their business dealings and reputation. Yet Vince Jr. himself had an example right in front of him — his father — of someone who became a highly respected part of his community because of how he conducted his wrestling ventures.

The same formula was even more pronounced with Muchnick, who is a beloved legend in St. Louis thanks to his reputable, honorable presentation and conduct. Even now, years after the fact, wrestling itself is looked at more positively in St. Louis than almost anywhere else because of Muchnick's good business sense and restrained booking. It can be done. Nothing to be embarrassed about, Vince!

How lucky I was to grow up in a time when I could see, and at a very tender age actually work, in this fascinating field. I got to witness a vast collection of headliners because St. Louis picked and chose only the best for main events.

On top of that, I was spending afternoons from the time I was in high school in the wrestling office, sharing the amazing stories and deep knowledge of people like Muchnick and Longson. Unlike many modern promoters and followers, they did not say one era was better than another, that the product was so much better now or then. They just noted that the times were different. Keep in mind that Sam in particular actually saw Lewis, Thesz, and Flair — different times, different superstars, different styles. Equally successful. Muchnick and Longson would say the same thing today.

It was ingrained in me that just because things change does not necessarily mean the changes are better.

Let me deal with one issue directly. While most of my published work has been met with positive reaction, one criticism has popped up: "Matysik is a Muchnick mark."

Ignoring the misuse of the term mark, rest assured that I am perfectly capable of making my own decisions. On the other hand, how could I be foolish enough to disregard the feedback and opinions of a man who pretty much defined successful wrestling promotion in his time as McMahon does today? Yes, I understand that Sam had his weaknesses, many of which he acknowledged. We all have prejudices and defects, including Muchnick *and* McMahon.

But when it comes to professional wrestling, who in the history of the game ever had a more pragmatic, reasoned, and realistic grasp of the business and its practitioners, both in the ring and behind the scenes? Not taking Muchnick's insights and training into consideration would be pure folly, for me or anyone.

Nick Bockwinkel often maintained that Muchnick, or someone like him, was the best judge of talent. Wrestlers were influenced both by what worked for themselves and by what performance styles they'd had the best matches against. Fans, naturally, have the emotional connections of either liking or disliking a wrestler for whatever reason. As Bockwinkel pointed out and I learned firsthand, Muchnick made his calls based on what worked best in the ring, why and how the fans reacted, and how many of them paid to be present. No ego, no manipulation, no hidden agendas.

As I assembled this incredible list, I knew that some critics will claim that old school romantics only look at the past through rose-colored glasses. Yet isn't it true that some contemporary pundits look at the present and see only blue sky? Folks, there are strong and weak points in both.

My goal was to try to be balanced and fair, to struggle to be objective, especially in areas where I know too much. In fact, as I wrote this book, I constantly was fiddling with the positions of various wrestlers. Even when a decision seemed clear-cut, there was almost always a consideration that added another question: "But what if? Have I thought about this?" Until the very moment that Michael Holmes told me this was the last edit I could make because ink was going to paper, I was jockeying with who was number 26, who was number 41, did Triple H belong ahead of his trainer Kowalski or behind, was Bret Hart even close to the Funks, where did Michaels really belong compared to Valentine, is there more data on Jonathan to accurately place him, has Randy Orton caught up with the elite picks as quickly as Cena has, how does The Undertaker match up to Brody, Hansen, or Robinson . . . on and on and on. Those disputes and many more continue in my addled mind even now. Surprisingly, I am adding this sentence near the conclusion of the writing process after all the private contemplation and arguments with myself because I honestly feel that things have finally fallen into place.

How *do* you compare the different periods in wrestling's history? Are a couple moments in a national event like *WrestleMania* equal to the huge body of work from what were once dozens of *WrestleManias* at house shows in different major markets? The Rock or Buddy Rogers? Which mountain is bigger? How high on the pyramid did each star climb?

Pro wrestling does not lend itself terribly well to statistical analysis. Too many variables and way too much politics enter the picture. The sport is an emotional, gut-grabbing spectacle; that's how fans and participants both have to react for pro wrestling to be successful.

In the end, the choice comes down to trusting my instinct and my heart, what I've learned and seen. And I've seen, studied, learned, and understood a hell of a lot for a long time.

I wanted it to be fair. For those of us who care and take it seriously, this should be hallowed ground.

I want to quote John Sandford, an excellent mystery writer. While he may have been laying the groundwork for an investigation by his protagonist Lucas Davenport, Sandford could just as easily have been discussing what I often feel about professional wrestling. In *Mortal Prey,* Sandford said, "Much was speculative, but all of it . . . Lucas had lived with most of his working life. Not much could be proven, but much could be understood."

I understand the position of Sanford's hero, for I feel it resembles my years working in professional wrestling. Maybe it's like a theory in the philosophy of knowledge — you know because you know. I know. It's a gut feeling that this is correct, even if nearly impossible to prove.

For, in the end, with all the information and all the facts about these remarkable professional wrestlers, not much can be proven beyond a shadow of a doubt. But at least now the discussion can be informed, realistic, and respectful.

Let the arguments begin!

#50 RANDY ORTON
How good can this gifted star become?

He's here for two reasons. First, of the current talent on the WWE roster, Orton began building a strong body of work at the youngest age and has accomplished the most overall. Second, he is still young and he has an obvious gift for the game, with the potential to do even more. Randy is in a position to solidify his bid to stay among the 50 greatest of all time.

But it could fall apart just as easily. Late in 2011 and into 2012, Orton's bookings weren't doing him any favors as he took one — well, many more than one — "for the team" by doing jobs for lesser talents, in less than stellar fashion. Perhaps others climbing the ladder were supposed to get a rub by clashing with Orton, who was an established star and could afford a defeat or two. A *WrestleMania* loss to Kane, though, surely stung.

To keep Orton from burning out with one major PPV after another (against many of the same opponents), WWE gave him a less visible position for a chance to cool off away from the brightest spotlight. Allegedly Vince himself explained that philosophy to Orton, and Orton was comfortable with the move. Orton, however, could be undermined over the next few years by the creative team even if a strong push is inevitable sometime.

Furthermore, Orton has a long-term WWE contract, much as Mark Henry did. Depending on Orton's own drive and hunger, that security might coax him into sliding along, giving less than he has the potential to give, and failing to develop that potential further — and he is definitely capable . . . if he wants to do it. Plus, that old bugaboo injury (which has flirted with him often) could derail Orton's campaign to stay among the best ever.

Another possible problem is that in the summer of 2012, Orton served a second suspension for violating the WWE's wellness code. Randy is not alone in this position; for instance, Rey Mysterio has also been suspended twice. According to WWE public policy, a third suspension brings on dismissal. While Orton handled the penalty well and bounced back in action strongly, looking at his absence as "a six-week vacation," the danger of another violation does hang over Orton's head.

Bottom line: after securing a lofty spot among the top WWE hands at a tender age, Randy Orton has stalled. Part of Orton's challenge is how much early success he enjoyed: he ran through a galaxy of all-star opponents. Having new and meaningful rivals is vital to keep Randy strong.

Nonetheless, Orton has captured an esteemed status when simply being in the running for a spot among the 50 greatest would have been an honor. Randy is the youngest under serious consideration (John Cena is three years older, CM Punk, two).

Make no mistake, this is not a back-handed compliment. Consider all the outstanding pro wrestling talents Orton beat out for the position. Maybe including him is pandering of a sort to the new class of workers (and their fans), but it is not without evidence that he's earned the recognition. The obvious question is whether or not Orton has peaked yet; is there another step Randy can climb? It seems so.

Some early conditions could have worked against Orton's placement in the best 50. A finely tuned athlete, he has had problems with both injuries and maturity. Still, Orton was the youngest performer ever to

win the WWE World Championship at the age of 24, when in 2004 he dethroned Chris Benoit. (Lou Thesz was the youngest to win any major recognized world championship when in 1937, at the age of only 21, he topped Everett Marshall.)

While titles don't mean as much as they once did, the fact that McMahon and company gave Orton a turn with the crown spoke volumes about Randy's potential. The triumph showed him to be someone the company was going to rely on, a rare talent worth standing by as he developed.

The son of "Cowboy" Bob Orton and the grandson of Bob Orton Sr., Randy certainly had the correct lineage for wrestling stardom. He'd been in feature bouts almost since the moment he cracked through in WWE. What fans witnessed without realizing was that Orton was maturing as a performer right before their eyes. His natural gifts have always been so plentiful, though, that he never seemed overwhelmed, even in the early days.

Randy was prominent from the start because he was part of the Evolution group, along with Ric Flair, Triple H, and Dave Batista, another promising newcomer. Often partnered with Triple H, Orton also built the legend-killer reputation by beating up or disrespecting famous WWE names. Orton got a rub from it, with victories over Shawn Michaels and Mick Foley.

When Orton won the championship, his partners turned on him and put him in the babyface position. But Orton got back to the heel side, where some claim he is most effective, by rolling through many key bouts. It's almost a shock to look back and realize what superb duels Orton, as a comparative youngster, had with Michaels, Triple H, The Undertaker, Ric Flair, Rey Mysterio, Kurt Angle, Jeff Hardy, and even Hulk Hogan. This goes along with forming a sharp tag-team duo with Edge, and later feuding with him. For a few years, Orton occupied a major role on virtually every PPV, including *WrestleManias*.

All the while Orton was blooming as a performer, one who started with excellent natural instincts and athleticism. In retrospect, this was the way stars have been built for a century, and some thanks should probably go to his father and grandfather, who were well respected and liked within the business. In an ego-driven field, those who might have rebelled against the young stud's rise instead gave Randy room to grow, both because of his family and because of his respectful attitude in the dressing room.

Today, Vince and company don't seem to know exactly what to do with Orton. Randy has butted heads numerous times with Cena. While always thrilling, these battles risk becoming repetitive since they are played out on a national platform.

Likewise, Orton versus Triple H has received repeated play. This is because Randy was filling a gap for WWE as one of the very few new talents capable of performing on the main stage.

As noted earlier, all of those standout confrontations came so soon, so often, and with such attention that Orton seemed to have run through the entire roster. Nothing is left for him but to repeat these matches, yet in wrestling years, he is actually just hitting his prime.

Luckily a few new faces have climbed the ladder, helping Randy to meet worthwhile fresh foes as soon as creative and Vince pull the trigger and let Orton go full throttle against them. Randy might easily feel he has been handcuffed as to going all out in the ring. Additionally, in the history of pro wrestling, over time the best circle around and clash with the best again and again. With a little imagination and different issues, Orton versus Cena can happen once more and mean something major. Perhaps the time in a type of limbo (which included doing a movie late in 2012) can work to Orton's advantage.

Common sense says if something isn't broken, don't fix it. Randy Orton isn't broke. He just needs more opportunity, and maybe another good stint as the heel he wants to be. Much like David Von Erich or Ric Flair before him, Orton is blessed with a rare natural charisma, both inside and outside the arena. He is packed with talent; he has the size and the look to make him competitive with stars from any era. Orton would have excelled in any style, at any time. Stand him next to members of the WWE top 50 list. Orton is a main event piece of work, yet with more potential. Just a couple more steps, a little more versatility, that unique interview letting a spark of the real Randy emerge, a few more headline rivalries that break the mold . . . more. Something extra from Orton. The test of time, time on top of the mountain without growing stale.

Orton has been honored here among a unique group of performers. He has been selected as one of the leading representatives of his generation. Does he belong in this incredible company? All of us are greedy. Orton needs to prove it. He has hit the place in his career where it's up to him to carry the load, to be the top dog that the newcomers want to bump off, to lead the way.

The psychology and the physical ability need to blend together to make him even more than he already is.

Jerry Brisco, Jack's brother and a highly respected talent evaluator with WWE, told me something very wise in spring 2012: "The great ones aren't falling off trees anymore. They're few and far between. Anyone who really knows this business understands that it's hard to explain why and what makes them great. But you can see it. You know it. Even if you can't define or explain it."

Randy Orton can be one of those few greats. We want more, though, and Orton can give it to us — if he wants to and if the stars align. Can he rise higher on the ladder of the all-time greats? Ask again in about five years.

#49 STAN HANSEN
Beat up everybody who got in his way

Throwing this giant wildman into the mix when choosing the last few spots on the list of 50 became a difficult chore. Arguments could be made to place Stan Hansen much higher than number 49; in fact, one highly respected insider told me that he thought Hansen should be in the top 25 of the best, even if the group were to go worldwide.

Hansen was a much bigger star in Japan than he was in the United States or Canada. Hansen himself did an interview with Slam Wrestling where he admitted, "Stan Hansen was basically a Japanese wrestler, not an American wrestler." Maybe he didn't give himself enough credit. Those in North America who followed the sport knew exactly who Stan Hansen was.

Nonetheless, all of the normal comparisons can be made with other high-end stars and, like Dick Murdoch, Hansen might have missed the elite circle for the pickiest of reasons. Murdoch often did not get the big push in territories because he was so heavily booked in Japan; Hansen was booked even more there, to the point that Stan shunned many American offices. Thus, Hansen might not have gotten his due in certain

historical ratings because he didn't get as much name recognition in the English-speaking world as certain others.

What really is the difference between Hansen or Billy Robinson and studs like Wilbur Snyder or Big Bill Miller? Further, some might gripe that Dusty Rhodes was not the athletic talent that Hansen, Robinson, Snyder, or Miller was, so why is Dusty placed where he is? Now throw the multifaceted Murdoch into the mix. He could play with everyone named.

Can Edge or Chris Jericho really complain about being left out, considering Hansen's awesome talent? Think about Jericho or Edge against Hansen or Robinson, even in a work . . . could be a little nasty, couldn't it?

Really, I debated the merits of Hansen versus Billy Robinson. Hansen gets the advantage for four reasons, even if a large part of his career was in Japan:

1) The tale of Hansen breaking Bruno Sammartino's neck has stood the test of time and given Hansen's legend a boost. Hansen's challenge to Bob Backlund in 1981 during Backlund's run as the WWF champion is often forgotten, too. And, despite his rebellious reputation, Hansen seemed to have a good rapport with both Vince Sr. and Jr.

2) The story of Hansen and his abortive tenure as AWA champion, while making the "bad man from Borger, Texas," a bad guy in the eyes of staunch AWA enthusiasts, also demonstrates how a resolute independent could react when pressured by the wrestling establishment.

3) Hansen dominated main events in Japan like almost no other American, and that means a lot considering the fine talent in action there. Name one other American who holds victories over both Giant Baba and Antonio Inoki. Somebody higher up had to hold Hansen in the highest regard for that to happen. Also, because so many American superstars came to Japan, Hansen met a who's who of the era, including Andre the Giant in some classic bouts. Yes, Hansen body slammed Andre. Many felt that Andre had some of his best matches against Hansen, who was 6'4" and 325 concrete pounds, because the two styles clicked.

Stan Hansen (right) with tag partner Bruiser Brody in Japan

4) Like his longtime friend Bruiser Brody, Hansen represents the independent and combative nature that pro wrestling supposedly (though rarely actually) celebrates. Brody spent much of his energy in behind-the-scenes debates with American promoters. Hansen picked a different path, figuring it would be easier on his nerves. Too bad the timing and negotiations never worked out. While Vince McMahon certainly understood that big money was possible with matches like Hulk versus Hansen or Hulk versus Brody, whether it was finances or politics, the pieces of the puzzle never fell into place.

Hansen and Brody might have been the most physically dominant tag team ever. Fans of the Road Warriors will complain, but the Warriors never had the stamina that marked Hansen and Brody in their prime. Likewise, Brody and Hansen could do many different high-impact moves that the Warriors never bothered to learn. Always stiff and demanding, Japanese wrestling culture got even tougher after Hansen and Brody simply blew past some opponents. As Hansen has said, "We just beat the crap out of everybody." Everybody's game was stepped up a notch.

Hansen and Hogan did duel in Japan. Personalities got in the way of a proposed struggle on April 13, 1990, when Terry Gordy refused to do a job for Hulk at a supershow in Tokyo involving the WWF against All Japan stars. Baba went to Hansen, who readily agreed to put Hogan over. Hansen understood that the results were not nearly as important as the match itself because he was such a huge star in Japan and Hulk was such a huge star globally.

Hansen was a stiff, frightening worker. One reason for his bone-rattling lariats and tackles was that Hansen was nearly blind in the ring, where he couldn't wear his glasses. So Hansen tended to really lay in his offense, which caught the attention of fans and made him a giant in Japan.

The charisma was certainly there, for Hansen was just what he looked like — a rawboned athlete who chewed nails. He could draw money, and he certainly left a legacy. His interviews were like his style in the ring: blunt. They succeeded.

When it came to working, Hansen had the rough edge all aggressive heels needed. Sometimes it wasn't pretty. But it sure as hell *always* looked like it hurt.

Breaking Sammartino's neck also played into his reputation as painful to oppose. The story was that Hansen injured Bruno with the lariat during Stan's WWWF debut run. In truth, though, it seems that Hansen tried to slam Bruno but was soaked with sweat and lost Sammartino, thus sending Bruno crashing straight down on his head. A couple of vertebrae were broken as Bruno came within a millimeter of having his spinal cord cut. Despite the danger, Sammartino never expressed any heat for Hansen.

The rematch on June 26, 1976, which Sammartino naturally won, was part of the Ali versus Inoki extravaganza. Hansen had a ready-made selling point. But it wasn't long before he landed with Giant Baba and All Japan Pro Wrestling in 1981, after first working for Antonio Inoki's New Japan company. It was a marriage made in heaven, for Hansen captured Baba's major titles numerous times and pretty much put North America on the back burner. The politics and back-stabbing at home aggravated Hansen, particularly compared to the disciplined, upfront, and very lucrative business that Baba ran. Hansen earned guaranteed big bucks in Japan and enjoyed doing it. Brody, his buddy and tag partner in what most believe was one of the greatest teams ever, thrived on the U.S. conflict, but Hansen preferred to ignore it all.

When Stan finally was lured to the AWA in 1985, as Verne Gagne was fighting for his promotional life against Vince McMahon, the result was predictably controversial. Hansen won the AWA laurels from Rick Martel, another vastly underrated performer and a nice guy who deserves much more hoopla than he gets. Gagne wanted Hansen to drop the belt, but mishandled his explanation of the move. The independent Hansen was already irritated because he'd been booked in mostly lower-pay squash matches. Hansen walked out supposedly after talking to Baba. The AWA stripped Hansen of the championship, awarding it to Nick Bockwinkel. Though Stan respected Bockwinkel, he still had the physical belt.

Hansen went back to Japan, carrying the belt and defending the AWA crown of which he supposedly had been stripped. After the not-unexpected threats back and forth, Hansen mailed the belt back to Gagne — but, so the story goes, only after running over the belt with his truck and leaving mud tracks on the AWA symbol.

Hansen would have been a more major star in the USA if he had opened up more dates in more spots. The question is *how* big, since Hansen did answer only to himself. For him, it just wasn't worth the headache. A perfect example was his brief time with World Championship Wrestling in 1990 and 1991, when he knocked off Lex Luger for what was called the U.S. title. Hansen lost it back in a bullrope match and was never pinned. Then the bookers came up with some harebrained idea to make Hansen part of a goofy cowboy group, so Hansen quickly bid WCW adieu.

A few other meaningful candidates for the all-time top 50 had their finest moments in the wrestling hotbed of Japan, including Terry Gordy, "Dr. Death" Steve Williams, and The Masked Destroyer (Dick Beyer). In fact, The Destroyer was a roundly talented grappler who became a cultural icon in Japan, considered to be one of them and not a *gaijin* (foreigner).

Hansen was a step or two ahead of them all. In that Slam Wrestling interview, in his normal, laidback, away-from-the-ring fashion, he added, "I never really took myself too seriously. It's nice to hear that people remember me."

We remember Stan Hansen. He is one of the 50 greatest pro wrestlers of all time.

#48 BROCK LESNAR
This intimidating brute has unique credentials

Projecting real menace and danger has never been a problem for Brock Lesnar. The reason is simple. Brock Lesnar is real.

In professional wrestling circles, Brock Lesnar is a monster both visually and in attitude. He follows in the grand tradition of Killer Kowalski, Bruiser Brody, and Dick the Bruiser in their primes. Lesnar also has a varied history that both helps and, to some, hinders where, and even if, he should be rated among the 50 best of all time. Nothing like controversy to energize the discussion!

And this is indeed a controversial choice. Purists believe, with legitimate justification, that Lesnar has not done anywhere near what Harley Race, Gene Kiniski, or even Triple H did to earn a place among the greatest. As usual, though, there is another side of the coin.

Lesnar is a product of his time, to the most extreme end. Unlike the luminaries from the so-called old school — and even stars from the 1980s and 1990s — his pro wrestling career has been choppy and short. Look at The Rock, however: the general public considers both

The Rock and Lesnar to be representatives of professional wrestling. The Rock is a movie star.

Brock Lesnar is the only competitor to win a national collegiate crown, then the WWE title, and finally a UFC championship before returning to pro wrestling in 2012. That's why he is here, on the roll call of the finest ever. Despite, or perhaps because of, that varied background, to the general public Lesnar is a professional wrestler of special note.

For good or for bad, these stars get more attention from the mass audience that even wrestlers like John Cena cannot reach with the backing of major marketer WWE. It doesn't matter how much time and effort Cena puts in. What Lesnar has done on the pro mat, meanwhile, will never rival the depth of what Lou Thesz, Ric Flair, and "Strangler" Lewis did — but the world has changed and Lesnar represents a highly visible part of what this business is today.

Lesnar has not hurt pro wrestling. In the end, people have accepted Lesnar as a legitimate tough guy, and a skilled fighter and wrestler. What Lesnar did for UFC, when he was in the MMA cage, raised the image of professional wrestlers today. Even skeptics, upon seeing how rugged and successful Lesnar is, have to admit that pro wrestlers are reasonably tough and athletic. Lesnar's reputation contradicted the notion that modern pro wrestling has become nothing more than skits and gimmicks, a clown act with lots of flipping and flopping.

Still, of all those who were considered for the 50 best ever, Lesnar is questioned most about his passion for professional wrestling. Skepticism about Lesnar comes from his hard-nose business disputes with Vince McMahon and his movement from WWE to pro football to MMA/UFC and back to WWE.

It's easy to overlook how successful this prime athlete was in the amateur ranks. While competing for the University of Minnesota, Lesnar finished second in the 1999 NCAA tournament and won the national championship in 2000. His overall college record was 106–5, but it was his look — that always difficult-to-define "it" — that drew WWE scouts.

I'm told by certain key people, however, that they did recognize how difficult it was for Lesnar to concentrate on one objective. Amateur coaches had helped him to focus on the national title, but his mind was always running in 100 different directions. That tendency has been obvious throughout all of his professional careers. After winning the national collegiate title, he never made any effort to go after an Olympic medal, which seemed within his reach, apparently because his attention was diverted.

Lesnar rocketed through WWE's developmental and quickly became a major player there. The controversial Paul Heyman acted as his manager/adviser, and in actuality Lesnar trusted Heyman to give him good advice. Lesnar bounced through the Hardy brothers and Rob Van Dam, winning the 2002 King of the Ring. That led to a shot at The Rock, who was then WWE king. Lesnar, only age 25 at the time, dethroned him. Less than three years after turning pro Lesnar became the number one man in WWE. It was a crown he would hold three times in a relatively short period.

The following interval was tumultuous indeed. Lesnar got into hot feuds with The Undertaker, Big Show, and eventually Kurt Angle, whose amateur credentials including his Olympic gold medal win were even better than Lesnar's own. Few amateur tactics were spotlighted, but the battles were often stiff and dangerous. Following a showdown with Kurt Angle at *WrestleMania XIX*, for example, Lesnar misjudged a particular high-flying maneuver, which resulted in a concussion for Brock. Even so, the massive muscle package that is Lesnar catapulting through the air was mesmerizing.

Lesnar went on to engage in new, more memorable conflicts with John Cena and Chris Benoit and once again with The Undertaker, Big Show, and Angle. Many consider the Iron Man duel between Lesnar and Angle on *Smackdown* to be a classic. Bill Goldberg had also joined the WWE scene, but he was being booked poorly. In the collapsing WCW, Goldberg had been comparable to Lesnar — a monster who was unbeatable. WWE, though, seemed determined, perhaps by design, to take an edge off the dangerous aura that Goldberg projected.

By way of rivalries with Eddie Guerrero and Stone Cold Steve Austin, Lesnar was guided to what should have been a mind-boggling showdown with Goldberg — indestructible object and immoveable force colliding at *WrestleMania*. But, by then, Lesnar and McMahon were butting heads in the business world, and Lesnar wanted to try out for the National Football League. The bout in 2004 with Goldberg was a stinker, and many fans were turned off. McMahon had tired of Lesnar's financial demands and granted him a release from his WWE contract if Brock agreed to a non-compete clause.

Lesnar launched an all-out attempt to make the Minnesota Vikings. He came close but was a late cut from the team. The athleticism was reportedly there, but not the skill or experience. Lesnar hadn't played football since high school. Lesnar then accepted an offer to wrestle in Japan, which violated the agreement with WWE. Everybody ended up in court before a settlement was reached; the Japanese outings, even with another match against Angle, were a disappointment.

Perhaps it was inevitable that Lesnar would land with UFC at that point. His impact was overwhelming beginning in 2008, with MMA fans hoping that the pro wrestler would get his brains scrambled. Many pro wrestling fans followed Lesnar into UFC despite his often-bitter comments about how much he hated the lifestyle and difficulty of the pro wrestling world. He garnered enormous attention for UFC, and some seriously eye-popping buy rates for pay-per-views.

Lesnar bounced back from a bruising defeat at the hands of Frank Mir to rattle off thrilling victories over Heath Herring and MMA legend Randy Couture, thus earning the UFC heavyweight championship. He then blasted Mir in a rematch and won a savage struggle against Shane Carwin after surviving a battering early in the affair. The latter bout had been delayed when Lesnar was laid low by mononucleosis and then a serious case of diverticulitis.

In some form, Lesnar was a part of the pro wrestling business, taking it into a new realm just by his successful presence where nobody else had gone before. Even his loss in a wild, brutal brawl against Cain Velasquez in 2010 didn't lessen his appeal.

Many who'd once hoped for his failure now rooted for him, and the big-money PPVs continued. Lesnar was making serious cash, more than he could have with WWE. One estimate by *ESPN The Magazine* listed his annual earnings at over five million dollars. UFC was benefiting in even larger numbers. And every article or feature mentioned Lesnar's pro wrestling exploits.

Health once again became an issue when diverticulitis reappeared and a portion of Lesnar's colon had to be removed, knocking him out of a match against Junior dos Santos. Rumors floated that Lesnar might again enter professional wrestling. One of the hottest tales making the rounds was that Lesnar and Mark Calaway (The Undertaker in WWE wars) were lobbying for a match between them in a *WrestleMania* headliner. UFC president Dana White shot that one down.

Finally, Lesnar proclaimed himself healthy enough to go back into the octagon for a much-heralded test against Alistair Overeem. Many experts have since said that Lesnar looked less himself than usual, that either the health crises had taken something from him or that he had lost the desire for that type of competition. After the loss, Lesnar announced his retirement from MMA.

But that did not lessen his impact on UFC. Dave Meltzer of *Wrestling Observer* said, "Both businesses [UFC and WWE] are star-driven businesses and while wins and losses are part of the story, being a star supersedes wins and losses . . . a lot of people [don't] fully understand how important Lesnar was to UFC's growth, particularly in the U.S. and bringing in an audience they otherwise wouldn't have had."

A superstar like Lesnar had brought one audience to UFC and now might bring a portion of the UFC audience to WWE for his return. By spring 2012, Brock Lesnar was back on top in WWE. He reportedly signed a contract with unprecedented financial guarantees and minimal dates to work. Surely Vince wants to cash in on Lesnar's tough-guy reputation by showing WWE stars can run with him (e.g. John Cena bloodied and battered by Lesnar, but somehow scoring the victory). Much of what happens from here on out lands in the lap of booking and the relation between Brock and Vince.

Although McMahon and Lesnar have had testy negotiations, certainly Vince has never been afraid to bury the hatchet if he thought a business deal would make his company money. Lesnar was obviously motivated by a lot of money and a much easier schedule than he'd had previously with WWE. Of course, this means more attention and more pressure are focused on a few key matches and promotions — places where Lesnar's reputation can grow or diminish. The gross receipts must rise to justify Lesnar's fat contract. It's the curse of pro wrestling as it enters 2013.

Yet there's something else, and none of us who have spent our lives in this incredibly complex field ever doubted that somehow, some way, some day, for reasons even he probably cannot accurately articulate, Brock Lesnar would be back in professional wrestling.

His very modern tale gives him a shot to reside among the 50 greatest professional wrestlers of all time. Nobody has traveled these trails before, surely not with the type of success Lesnar has had despite all of the controversy. Can he stay in this select company? The deciding factors are being played out as this studied work goes to print.

#47 "SUPERSTAR" BILLY GRAHAM
Muscles his way in with incredible charisma

Sliding into the heralded crew of the 50 greatest pro wrestlers of all time, "Superstar" Billy Graham makes the case for eye-popping charisma, cool heel talk, and a bittersweet legacy that sometimes outweighs the fundamentals of the business. Not often would this be enough, but Graham was so overwhelming in his chosen role that he made it happen.

Graham, and to some extent Hulk Hogan, stretched the limits of what was expected for being a good worker and a real wrestler. While Superstar couldn't wrestle a lick, he was a tough guy and came across as such based on his size and the muscles he built hoisting iron (and that were inflated by other means).

But a first-class worker? Forget it. Apologies are due Don Leo Jonathan, Dick Murdoch, and Chris Jericho. Certainly those three could work rings around Graham and, based on that alone, would have far more claim to the position Graham has received on this list. It sure is nice when a guy whose work makes him look like a butt-kicker really can kick some butt if necessary.

Not that Superstar wouldn't have been more than a handful in a back-alley brawl, but much of his reputation was based on his extraordinary verbal talent and visual appeal. He had a knack for the catch phrase and sound bites that stuck with television viewers after one of his boastful promos. His brash, egotistical delivery made ears perk up.

What Superstar did, he did well, but he never elevated another performer. Other outstanding workers played off and sold Superstar's charisma and bully strongman tactics — that's what made Graham a serious star. Verne Gagne, Harley Race, Bruno Sammartino, and Bob Backlund all fit Graham's special qualities into their particular styles, thus making for some noteworthy scraps.

Graham was indeed a superstar, albeit a limited one who worked best against versatile stars who were willing to accentuate what he did. Fans got into his rap and his look. But don't overlook one key point. The fact that Superstar *was* Superstar made his bouts with all those other big names special too. He was skilled enough to carry his end. In other words, not just any pro wrestler could have stepped into Graham's boots. He was unique, warts and all.

Superstar's placement with the finest is proof that, on occasion, charisma and legacy can outweigh other considerations in this peculiar sport. Hulk is another extreme example, although he could also boast drawing power, mainstream recognition, and longevity that exceeded Graham's. Naturally, making money overcomes almost any other factor.

Hulk borrowed much of his repertoire from Graham. The history of pro wrestling is jam-packed with performers who picked up and built on the personalities, skills, and tactics of predecessors. A line, which branches off in many directions, can be traced from Hulk, Graham, and even Ric Flair to Buddy Rogers and Gorgeous George. Graham left a legacy by influencing many who followed him into the business. His character, confidence, and charisma are all fine. He could talk like few ever had before, and the camera loved his pumped-up physique. Ah, and there's the rub. From Hulk to Jesse Ventura to The Ultimate Warrior to the Road Warriors to Scott Steiner, muscles became the currency in the

1980s and early 1990s. McMahon, who was the television commentator for his father at the time, fell in love with Graham's entire picture, so the WWF pushed that type of cartoon body and extravagant personality.

Superstar had no more idea than did any steroid user in the early days of what the dangers were, of how many lives would be wrecked or even ended after steroid and drug abuse. Like all ambitious performers in many fields, these athletes did what they felt they had to do to compete. If it worked for Superstar, and that encouraged others in his realm to try the same method, this is a shame but it doesn't count for or against Graham as to where he belongs among the industry's elite.

Sadly, by 1990, he would be undergoing many major surgeries on his hips and ankles. He has battled drug dependence, constant pain, and liver problems that required a transplant. A couple of times wrestling journalists were waiting for word that the last bell had sounded. Graham's fight to live has made him somewhat heroic and mellowed him into something of an articulate philosopher. He has not hesitated to speak out on steroid abuse, nor to pin blame on Vince for his role in the catastrophe.

He really was a tough guy, this fellow born Wayne Coleman. He played football well enough to be lured to the Canadian Football League and was also a dedicated weightlifter and bodybuilder. He came under the influence of Stu Hart, the family patriarch and noted promoter of Stampede Wrestling based in Calgary. Hart trained Coleman, so the young athlete would have learned some hard basics about wrestling in Hart's noted "Dungeon."

The rookie teamed up with Abdullah the Butcher to start his career, which would have been quite an introduction considering Abdullah's take-no-prisoners approach. He changed his name to Billy Graham, borrowing from both the famous evangelist and wrestling's nasty blond bad guy Dr. Jerry Graham. He added the handle "Superstar" from the rock opera *Jesus Christ Superstar*. He was given surprisingly good opportunities for a newcomer with Roy Shire in San Francisco and Gagne in the AWA, but they both wisely recognized Graham's box-office potential.

Of course, one look explained why. You could hardly miss Graham. At 6'4", 275 pounds, he was shot full of steroids and had muscles bulging to the point of exploding. While there had been a few steroid users and bodybuilder types off and on in the business, none had ever been as blatant and attention-getting as Superstar, with his long blond hair and his in-your-face arrogance.

After a lucrative run with Gagne, Graham's name was made within the inner circles. This was not without some hesitance because the guy was an off-the-wall personality. He had big success in California, Hawaii, and Florida. Japanese fans got a kick out of seeing the flamboyant Graham as well. Graham was in and out of the WWWF and made a few stops in St. Louis, where he butted heads twice with NWA king Harley Race in 1977. While neither bout sold out, both came close and were intense physical brawls.

Ironically, in Graham's own book, he complained about having a lousy match with Pat O'Connor in St. Louis. Yet most of those who remember his two tussles against O'Connor felt that they were among his best locally, aside from his matches with Race. Graham felt O'Connor twisted him around and wouldn't let Superstar do his normal stuff. As former great referee Joe Schoenberger and I agreed while watching them work, it seemed that O'Connor was forcing Graham to do more athletically than he usually did, but this actually made Superstar look better because he was capable of it. Beauty must be in the eye of the beholder.

In the WWWF, though, Graham really hit the mother lode. He won the title from the legendary Sammartino on April 30, 1977, in Baltimore. Unlike earlier heel champions, Graham didn't turn the belt over to another good guy in a few days, but got a substantial stint as the ring monarch. Of course, he was a new concoction, a "cool" heel, and was a powerful drawing card. On February 20, 1978, the crown moved to the new all-American hero Bob Backlund in New York. Graham's sizeable vocal following has never forgiven Backlund for being the one picked to replace Superstar.

Graham became reclusive for a time before returning to the WWF in 1982. He had a new look, dressed in dark martial arts gear, the blond hair gone. Though still muscular, Graham used martial arts tactics and was something of a disappointment. In the mid 1980s, VKM tried to revitalize his former favorite into renewed stardom, but the health issues were already eating at Superstar.

Thus began Graham's long fight against the ravages of his demons. He's been in and out of McMahon's graces over the years. Outspoken and unpredictable, Graham still has the knack for getting attention. And, for whatever the reason, he has an influence — a legacy — that refuses to die and has helped bully him into a spot among the 50 greatest of all time. What could be more appropriate for Superstar Graham?

#46 BIG BILL MILLER
Masked or not, this doctor knew how to operate

Yes, the doctor is in. Dr. Bill Miller is "in" with the 50 greatest pro wrestlers of all time. Big Bill Miller was one of the most athletic and special big men in the history of the sport.

Miller really was a doctor, with a degree in veterinary medicine from Ohio State University. As Red Bastien always said, when other guys were drinking beer, Miller was reading a book. But Bill had respect from every segment of pro wrestling, from the performers to the promoters. He was smart, imaginative, very competitive, entertaining to watch, as tough as a rattlesnake, and able to draw money all over the place while having tremendous matches.

With his athletic background and the way he carried himself both in private and in public, Miller wasn't one to mess with. He certainly had all the necessary attributes to be a shooter. A legitimately big man, thick and hard with 290 pounds welded on a 6'5" frame, Miller was a two-time Big Ten heavyweight wrestling champion (in a hot rivalry with Verne Gagne and beating football Hall-of-Famer Leo Nomellini in the 1950 finals). Miller earned nine letters at Ohio State University in wrestling, in track and field as a nationally ranked shot putter and discus thrower, and in football. He was a star on the offensive line for the Buckeyes when they won the 1950 Rose Bowl, after which he was drafted by the Green Bay Packers.

Al Haft, the promoter in Columbus, Ohio, who clearly had a good eye for talent, lured Miller into professional wrestling instead. Only 13 months into his pro career, Miller won a version of the world title in Pittsburgh on May 1, 1952, by beating Don Eagle, who was very popular and had a short but impressive run on top. During his first professional year, Miller lost only twice, both times to Ruffy Silverstein, a former NCAA wrestling champion and leading contender for Lou Thesz's title at the time.

Haft, who was very influential behind closed doors, was able to book Miller around his Ohio home so Miller could continue his graduate work. His sons have told stories about the many nights their dad got back from a show as late as 5 or 6 a.m., attended classes most of that day, and then went back on the road to another show in the evening. Think of the discipline this required of Miller, and how hot pro wrestling was to have that many cards — all doing business — going on regularly.

All things considered, not too many stars or dissatisfied prelim guys wanted to test whether Miller was a shooter. Everyone knew the answer, so they let sleeping dogs lie. Stories about his workouts with Karl Gotch were well known. On top of everything else, he learned and excelled in submissions. Miller was a legitimately tough top-of-the-line athlete who felt no need to prove his mettle unless provoked. His ego was under control.

By the mid 1950s, he had his degree and was one of the strongest main event draws in the country. Miller topped shows from Portland to St. Louis to Boston. He had several tremendous battles with Buddy Rogers (who at the time was often a babyface), along with Bobo Brazil, Pat O'Connor, Hans Schmidt, and Dick Hutton. Miller also clashed often with Thesz, who loved to create great matches with competitors like Miller: a big, powerful athlete who could go for real. How in demand was Miller? In 1956 he often worked Philadelphia, Baltimore, Boston, and Montreal all in the same week in front of capacity, or close to it, crowds. Then Miller added New York, Minneapolis, Winnipeg, and San Francisco. No minor league territories were ever on his dance card. In San Francisco, he first met Japanese icon Rikidozan and also tackled Nomellini, the era's version of Bronko Nagurski, who was regarded as highly by fans and mainstream media as Nagurski was.

Miller also was an adept tag-team performer, forming a "brother" duo first with Ed Miller (real name Ed Albersand, a bear of an athlete) and later with his real-life younger brother, Dan. This opened doors for even more classic confrontations, in particular Bill and Ed Miller against Ben and Mike Sharpe. Each member of the quartet was truly a giant at the time, and their matches were absolute head-knocking masterpieces.

Bill and Ed Miller also headlined as a team from Ohio through Buffalo and into Canada, meeting combinations like "Whipper" Billy Watson and Yukon Eric, Joe Tangaro and Guy Brunetti as the Brunetti brothers, John and Chris Tolos, Gene Kiniski and Fritz Von Erich, and even the eye-catching pair of Killer Kowalski and Dick the Bruiser.

Somewhere in this grueling schedule, and make no mistake that Bill Miller was working close to 350 days a year, he headlined in Calgary during a rare boom time there against Kiniski, Thesz, Hutton, Watson, and the underground, generally forgotten hooker George Gordienko. Someone in power, likely promoter Stu Hart, wanted to see these two legitimate competitors in a match. He was not disappointed.

In 1959, Miller began one of his most famous runs as the masked Dr. X in Omaha, which was a smaller market that was a nationally recognized wrestling hotbed, consistently drawing sellout crowds of nearly 10,000. The mysterious hooded monster agreed to unmask if he were ever beaten by pin or submission. Dr. X won the AWA and world championships by downing Wilbur Snyder, who'd had a strong tenure as the kingpin.

Just consider some of the stars Dr. X knocked off: "Cowboy" Bob Ellis, Kinji Shibuya, local hero Ernie Dusek, The Crusher, Yukon Eric, Mitsu Arakawa, and Nick Bockwinkel. Finally, the masked terror had a one-hour draw against Verne Gagne that led to an absolutely incredible Texas death match on August 20, 1960. The conflict, which got national

publicity, went 14 — that's 14 — falls before Dr. X could not answer the bell and was unmasked as Bill Miller.

But Miller still had the title. He lost it to Don Leo Jonathan but later won it back in another mind-boggling battle of athletic giants. At the same time, Miller was also performing as Dr. X in the Ohio territory before he was finally defeated and unmasked there by Ellis.

Talk about being in demand!

Next, Miller made his Japanese debut as Dr. X on May 1, 1961, knocking off an emerging young talent named Shohei Baba who was destined to become one of the most prominent Japanese mat figures of all time. That set the stage for a series of matches against Rikidozan, who finally beat and unmasked Dr. X in a Japanese title versus the mask showdown.

Thus, Miller established himself as a superstar in Japan too. He formed a tremendous tag team with his training partner, Karl Gotch. Unknown to the public, though, was an incident that foreshadowed a well-known situation with Buddy Rogers. On the same tour was a huge strongman known as The Great Antonio, who was starting trouble with the public when away from the arenas. While Rikidozan shot on Antonio in a notable bout, it was Miller and Gotch who delivered the message to behave to Antonio — privately and in terms he understood.

When that tale spread globally, *nobody* wanted to argue with Miller about business — and he was a nice guy anyway!

By that point, Miller could choose where and when he wanted to work. He would debut as a monster heel, record win after win, and finally put over the local babyface star. It was a formula that made money for everyone, especially when the bad guy knew his business like Miller did. He took the old Dr. X gimmick to the AWA in Minneapolis, turned himself into the masked Mr. M, and eventually took the AWA prize from Gagne. Then Gagne regained the championship in the always-successful title versus mask showdown.

Right after that, Miller and Gotch had the famous dressing-room collision with Rogers. Buddy, the NWA champion, was creating havoc because of his relationship with Vince McMahon Sr. and Toots Mondt in what would become the WWWF. As noted, details are sketchy. The climax, though, was that Rogers was injured, missed numerous dates, and was eventually bumped off by Thesz for the NWA crown. Rogers then lost to Bruno Sammartino and that started the WWWF title lineage.

It went without saying that Bill Miller would square off with Sammartino in yet another highly regarded series. On July 12, 1965, in New York's Madison Square Garden, Miller went one hour against Bruno, and a three-judge panel made the decision ruling Sammartino as the winner. On August 2, 1965, the rematch went to Miller because Sammartino was counted out outside the ring, thus allowing Bruno to retain the title although Miller got the victory. The rubber match on August 23 was a shocking victory by Sammartino in a mere 48 seconds. Is there any question whatsoever that Bill Miller did what was right for business?

Bill and brother Dan also had a nice tour of duty as a tag team in the WWWF, at one point scoring a victory over Sammartino and Johnny Valentine. So respected was Miller that he was brought back several times in meaningful slots for the WWWF. He went back and forth to Japan, plus he did an excellent tour of Australia that included battling rising star Jack Brisco (another indication of how the best were seasoned to become even better down the road) and making a headline tag team with Killer Kowalski.

Then Miller began another historical feud, this one with Ray Stevens, who was on fire in San Francisco in 1968 and 1969. Stevens was cemented as a babyface after working *five* brutal and thrilling bouts against Miller. In the only Cow Palace title defense by NWA champion Dory Funk Jr. he took on — who else — Big Bill Miller.

But then, Dr. Miller cut back on his wrestling career, which had truly been one of the most impressive careers of any wrestling superstar. He got a job with the State of Ohio doing necropsies on animals. An intelligent, educated man, Miller knew he would never get a pension or insurance benefits in pro wrestling, so he decided it was time to reduce his mat schedule, which also meant having more family time.

One of the towns in which Miller continued was St. Louis, where I got to know him when I worked for promoter Sam Muchnick. Bill was one of my first interviews when I was a teenager, writing for *Ring Wrestling* magazine. He was a class act, someone with excellent insight into how the complex business of pro wrestling operated. Probably the most enthralling thing he told me in that first meeting was how much he loved teaching amateur wrestling to blind kids at the Columbus, Ohio, YMCA. This was a gentleman with many outstanding attributes.

One of his last major outings was in St. Louis as the masked Crimson Knight. Bouncing off a victory over the rapidly improving Jack Brisco (who Miller touted as a future champion from day one), the Knight got a crack at NWA champion Dory Funk Jr. by risking the mask against the gold belt. When Dory got the victory, Miller removed his mask for the final time. He continued to be an important part of many Midwest lineups right under the main events until he hung up his tights for good in 1976. Fans, promoters, and performers alike knew that Big Bill Miller added respect and quality to the business.

Indeed, it never hurts to have a doctor in the house. In particular, it adds honor and credibility to have Dr. Bill Miller join the 50 finest pro wrestlers of all time.

#45 RICKY STEAMBOAT
A brilliant babyface for the ages

At the top of the lineup, night after night, match after match, he often had the best bout on the card. Consistently excellent throughout his storied career, Ricky Steamboat was like that Hall of Fame baseball player who hit .300 every year and ended up with 3,000 hits. When he walked away, the fans gasped and said, "Oh my goodness, what a special talent we've had the honor of enjoying."

That was Ricky Steamboat, and it's why he has captured a hallowed position among the 50 greatest pro wrestlers. His feud with Ric Flair and his *WrestleMania* duel against Randy Savage were the stuff of history. Those may have been the most famous of Steamboat's battles, but it was that high quality he brought into action every single time against any foe.

Whenever someone speaks of traditional, classic babyfaces, one of the first names brought to the forefront is Ricky Steamboat. In grand fashion, Steamboat follows the tradition of beloved stars like Edouard Carpentier and "Cowboy" Bob Ellis. He was a good guy who never switched styles or personalities.

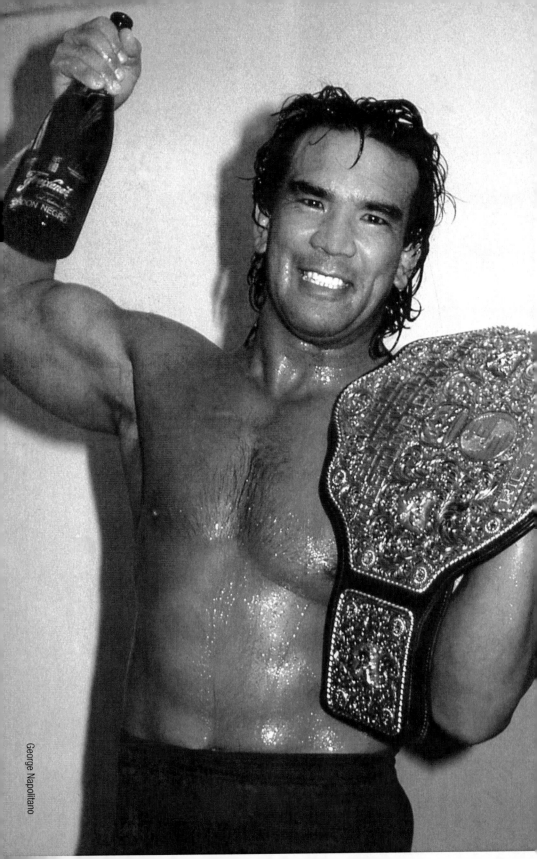

Steamboat was sleek and highly athletic, yet what set him apart from the others was his look. Handsome, with vaguely exotic features (Ricky's mother was Japanese), he was alluring and sexy too. His good looks didn't aggravate the guys, as happens with some babyfaces, for Steamboat earned their respect through his competitive nature and his remarkable athleticism. In other words, Steamboat wasn't just a pretty boy.

What really moves Steamboat into the top tier of talent is the ability he had in classic matches, particularly against Ric Flair and Randy Savage. Granted, those two brought a multitude of skills to the game, but Steamboat could match and complement them every step of the way. Ricky was a phenomenal worker and performer who had a firm grasp of the psychology that makes one match so much better than another.

The collisions with Flair and Savage were even more meaningful because they happened on national forums. The tussle with Savage occurred at *WrestleMania III* in 1987, giving it a special place in wrestling history thanks to the huge audience. As outstanding as the match was, it didn't even go 20 minutes! Actually, Savage and Steamboat had been blowing out buildings with longer matches on the road at various WWF house shows. But at *Mania*, the main event was Hulk Hogan and Andre the Giant, so there was pressure from the office to condense what Steamboat and Savage could do.

Nonetheless, the bout clicked so well that some observers considered it the top match of the 1980s. Steamboat and Savage probably had some better outings on the road without the big national audience. Add to his stellar record those duels when Ricky was in the WWF to his long, intense rivalry with Flair in the Jim Crockett Jr. promotion (a rivalry that was every bit as exciting as the one with Savage).

Flair had been one of Steamboat's earliest opponents in 1977 and 1978 while both were becoming stars for Crockett in the Carolinas. The chemistry was always great, aided by the fact that both Flair and Steamboat were trained by Verne Gagne. When Steamboat and Flair were reunited as rivals for the NWA title in 1989, they immediately sent sparks flying with state-of-the-art encounters, including one 55-minute dandy. The NWA crown was almost secondary to the explosive matches the two staged.

To rate Savage versus Steamboat ahead of Flair versus Steamboat, no matter how superb the former was, would be a slap in the face to the latter. Both were absolutely excellent. Ricky Steamboat was an indispensable ingredient for the best of what wrestling could be in the mid 1980s through the early 1990s. Yet what Steamboat could do against Lex Luger may have said even more about his innate feel for the business.

Steamboat actually defined the term *worker*, for he could make an exciting and interesting spectacle even when facing the stiffest or least skilled foe. Not that Luger was the worst, but he was an athlete who was very limited in the ring. Steamboat could take an event against much weaker foes and actually make it watchable. When he locked up against his peers in talent, the results speak for themselves.

Born Richard Blood, Ricky was a natural from day one and a state high school champion in his native Florida. He was dating a young lady whose friend turned out to be Verne Gagne's daughter. Blood sent his information to Gagne, and he was invited to enter Gagne's training camp. Verne was a stickler about getting in shape, being precise on the mat, and acting professional. The lessons all took for Ricky because he was that type of determined personality.

When Ricky turned pro, he borrowed the last name from well-known Hawaiian star Sam Steamboat. After a debut with Gagne's AWA, he bounced from Florida to Georgia to North Carolina, soaking up knowledge and experience every step of the way. Rugged Wahoo McDaniel was the one who recommended Steamboat to Carolina, where the Steamboat rocket was launched in 1977. The talent level in that territory was high, a fine mixture of clever old pros and hungry young tigers. Steamboat formed a scintillating tag team with Jay Youngblood in addition to starting that rivalry with Flair. Throughout the territory, folks still talk about the scraps Steamboat and Youngblood had against Sgt. Slaughter and Don Kernodle, in addition to a neat feud with the Brisco brothers. In singles, Steamboat had legendary struggles against Wahoo and also Tully

Blanchard. Ricky became outgoing in interviews as he became more comfortable and his natural personality began to shine.

But Crockett, whose booker was Dusty Rhodes, was going national, in response to Vince Jr.'s tactics and to the decline of once-strong territories. Steamboat and Rhodes reportedly had issues that led to Steamboat's defection to the WWF in 1985. McMahon gave Steamboat the "Dragon" identity, lizards to display as pets in the ring, and a couple of hot feuds with Don Muraco and Jake Roberts to begin his tour of duty.

Steamboat got over like the proverbial million bucks. He incited the audience's emotions even more after a powerful angle with Savage, who used the ring bell on Steamboat's throat. Despite Steamboat's success, though, hard feelings grew for both Steamboat and McMahon when Ricky wanted time off to be with his wife Bonnie for the birth of their first son. One thing led to another and Steamboat became a free agent.

About this time, Crockett's promotion was going under, and Crockett made a deal to sell his operation to Ted Turner's television and entertainment arm. Jim Herd and Jack Petrik, former St. Louis television executives, had made an unrelated move to Turner's broadcasting division and were put in charge of wrestling. Late in 1988, I was negotiating with Herd about leaving the WWF to go to the new entity. In a meeting with Herd and Petrik, one of the things I emphasized was how quickly they needed to move to get Steamboat on board. They looked numbly at me, for neither had a clue who this great, valuable talent was.

Regardless, in 1989 Steamboat went back to what would come to be called World Championship Wrestling. By this time, Steamboat had developed a sturdy business sense that led to another departure, a brief visit back to the WWF, and then still another return to WCW. Talent like Steamboat had is so rare that he was always in demand no matter how testy the business issues became. That's a trademark of those who belong among the top 50 ever. They are worth what they are paid and dealing with any headaches because they always brought something special to any promotion.

It was during this final stint with WCW that Steamboat tangled with one "Stunning" Steve Austin, who of course had a big future. He bumped with Brian Pillman, Paul Orndorff, and again with Flair. But Steamboat severely injured his back, then got into it with the latest WCW honcho, Eric Bischoff. The dispute culminated in Steamboat's dismissal in late 1994, and except for a brief run with TNA, he was out of the business until landing with the WWE as a road agent and trainer in 2005. After a few outings in the ring, where amazingly Steamboat still looked terrific, a serious health scare pretty much put him back to training newcomers. Whatever it was Steamboat had, if grapplers can learn from it then pro wrestling can only be improved. While others might have had a similar gift for brilliance, as the performance aspect changed, the high in-ring standard of excellence was set thanks in part to Steamboat's inspired work. Only the greatest deeply understood the art form.

Even WWE recognized what Steamboat did in his career, though I'd argue his place in their order is too high . . . which is not at all critical! Ricky was an awesome talent with great charisma. Simply being included is meant to be a tremendous distinction. And, most importantly, everyone from all sectors of the business seems to agree that Ricky Steamboat is one of the greatest ever. That's what happens when you hit .300 every year!

#44 DUSTY RHODES
The American Dream was an original

Hype, bluster, and flash get more than their share of attention in professional wrestling. This is proven true by the addition of Dusty Rhodes to pro wrestling's true hierarchy. That said, as someone who deeply respects both the working and the reality of the business, I enjoy the excitement an original, eccentric personality brings to the game.

Dusty Rhodes was that and more, someone who got himself over basically on the strength of his personality. Rhodes did what he had to do to be successful at the highest level. That worked out for Dusty, and he paid the necessary price along the way.

Virgil Runnels Jr. came from the wrestling and football factory area around West Texas State. The rough-and-tumble school produced football players who got hooked on wrestling thanks to Dory Funk Sr. and his Amarillo-based promotion. Stan Hansen, Ted DiBiase, Bruiser Brody, Bobby Duncum, the Funk boys, and Rhodes spent time at, if not graduated from, the school. Dory Sr. created a magical aura around the wrestling business that lured many an athlete.

Virgil became Dusty Rhodes when he broke into the pro wrestling ranks in 1969. According to one source, Dusty was actually a pretty good baseball prospect in college. Regardless, pro wrestling was where he made his home and, very quickly, got attention through that indefinable quality of charisma. Bad guy/good guy had nothing to do with it. Even though the tag-team combination he formed with Dick Murdoch was green, both members immediately got attention.

After a tour with the AWA, Rhodes and Murdoch parted company. Dusty ended up as a heel in 1974, teaming with Pak Son for wily manager Gary Hart in Florida. But Dusty violently split with Pak Son, and a hot new babyface was born. Dubbed "The American Dream" by Bill Watts, who was booking in Florida at the time, Rhodes caught fire. He was the plumber's son who was making it to the top with a jive-talkin' promo that stole timing and content from Muhammad Ali (only fair given that Ali had taken so much from wrestlers himself).

Before long, most of the Florida action built around Dusty, who was packing crowds in as he battled a long line of big-name heels. Thanks to smart and inventive promoter Eddie Graham, Florida always had influence in the business, particularly with the NWA because Eddie was close to president Sam Muchnick. That worked in Rhodes' favor, plus Dusty's interest in tangling with wrestling's politics was growing.

Though Dusty hardly had a physique like Jack Brisco or Superstar Graham, he was a 300 pounder who understood what he could and could not do. He built his style around that. Selling, bleeding, and coming back in fiery fashion . . . a simple formula, but one that usually works with the right person.

Rhodes went to New York for a series of events with WWWF champion "Superstar" Graham. These matches all drew huge business, although a blow-off on October 4, 1977, likely left a bad taste in some mouths. The Texas bull rope match only lasted about six minutes before 22,092 spectators plus a closed-circuit audience of 4,000 in the Felt Forum of Madison Square Garden. Still, both Rhodes and Graham understood the

strengths of their cartoon-like characters mixed with gory violence, so the feud succeeded.

Appearances in Georgia and on the growing WTBS cable show were added to Rhodes' calendar. Everywhere he went, he drew. Muchnick retired from the NWA, and Dusty got a few short runs as the champion. The hesitation, however, to give the belt to someone with Rhodes' build and limited pure wrestling knowledge was still there.

I was doing the ring announcing when we brought Rhodes as the NWA king to St. Louis on August 7, 1981. He faced Ric Flair, the man who would unseat him in a few weeks. Flair lit the fuse with his entry, but the blaring music and Rhodes' command of the ring when he bounced through the ropes sent the audience of 10,414 into a frenzy. I said to Dusty, "Man, it's great — like a rock concert!"

Rhodes laughed and responded, "Hey, I'm tryin', brother!"

By late 1983, Dusty had moved to Jim Crockett Jr.'s company, and Vince McMahon Jr. had launched his attack on the wavering wrestling establishment. In just a few years, VKM and Crockett were the only two organizations competing nationally. Crockett had the much-watched berth on WTBS national cable. Rhodes, who had become Crockett's booker by that time, built everything around himself as the top babyface, with his biggest rivalries against Flair and Tully Blanchard, yet another underrated heel of the time.

The difference between what Rhodes and Jerry Lawler were doing was the national platform. Bookers and owners who also wrestle usually look out for themselves first, some with success and some with failure. Dusty clicked in markets all over the country, while Lawler concentrated on Memphis. Granted, Lawler made a chunk of cash in his town, but only the rabid fans knew about his Memphis angles with Terry Funk and Nick Bockwinkel. Every wrestling devotee, and a good part of the casual crowd, was aware of Rhodes' collisions with Flair and the Four Horsemen thanks to the national scope of WTBS.

For a time, the Crockett-Rhodes combination held its own in parts of the country and drew big crowds in key towns. The productions were hot-shot top to bottom with plenty of blood and open-ended, no-finish decisions. But this approach is proven to burn out fans over a few months. Perhaps they believed they had to do it to survive in what became a nasty, expensive fight.

The so-called Dusty finish became famous because Rhodes did it way too often with Flair. In each battle it finished, champion (Flair) would have to be disqualified for some reason, but because the referee had been stunned or whatever, he couldn't call it. A second referee would come in as the challenger pinned the champion. Hooray! Everyone went nuts. That is, until they found out either at the time or on television a few days later that nothing had changed, the champ was still the champ because he had been disqualified. This ploy got heat but not necessarily good heat — especially after the second or third time in less than a year.

Executed correctly, done once every few years or so, it can work. We did it in St. Louis with Harley Race and Ted DiBiase on February 6, 1981. Because the story was told honestly and upfront, the angle led to a payoff on June 12 of 16,088 attendees, who generated record gate receipts at the Checkerdome. But did Dusty invent it? Well, the first time I saw the basic premise, Buddy Rogers and John Paul Henning pulled it off on April 7, 1961 (check *From the Golden Era: The St. Louis Wrestling Record Book* for details). Dusty would have been 15 years old, living in Texas. Muchnick and his crafty booker Bobby Bruns had probably seen the general idea used years before 1961. Nothing is new in wrestling, then or now!

Crockett's business began a steep decline, and the money started to run out in 1987. By the end of 1988, Ted Turner's video arm had bought out Crockett and started what would become the equally ill-fated World Championship Wrestling. Dusty Rhodes was a major star, but the new regime went in a different direction. Dusty was ousted as booker and performer even though he'd certainly been the key thinker and a strong drawing card in many glorious days before the fall — part of which was Rhodes' fault.

Dusty was, however, a national star. As such, VKM brought Rhodes to the WWF in 1989 for a campy role in a polka-dot bumblebee outfit, with

Sapphire (Juanita Wright) at his side. Most insiders felt McMahon was taking advantage of the situation to degrade Rhodes, something Vince had attempted to do with some other longtime notables. Nonetheless, Rhodes got over surprisingly well in the role before pulling the plug and returning to WCW as a booker. But turmoil was the byword, and soon Dusty was skulking around the fringes of the business.

By 2005, some wounds had healed and Dusty was back in as a legend in a creative and training capacity with VKM. He was still "The American Dream" and could still pop a crowd when he was brought out for an angle or appearance now and then.

Despite reservations on the technical side, Dusty Rhodes gets his place at the head table of the 50 greats. There is always room for that special breed of unique character upon which pro wrestling has always thrived.

#43 RAY STEELE
A policeman who could stretch any rival

A wrestler's wrestler: that's the epitaph that fits best for Ray Steele. Every insider knows he belongs with the best of the best.

Man's man. Kick-ass tough. Stood tall. Lived life to its fullest. Pick a cliché, because they're all true. He did it all.

Ironically, though, in terms of listing his achievements, Ray Steele may not look that impressive. This warrior's distinction comes in knowing the truth about him. In some ways, Steele might have been an early incarnation of underappreciated superstars like Dick Murdoch, Stan Hansen, or even Ray Stevens.

Steele won the world championship from Bronko Nagurski on March 7, 1940. On March 11, 1941, he lost the belt back to Nagurski, whose combined reputation as both football star and mighty wrestler was overwhelming. But the belt is merely the icing on the cake for Steele, who did so much for so long that the reign was almost like a reward from the industry.

Certainly Steele understood the game well. After a demanding training session, he is the one who told a young Lou Thesz that "you may have the aptitude to become a great wrestler, but if you don't learn to

make money at it . . . it's just a hobby." Thesz took the words to heart, for he knew Steele didn't sugarcoat the facts.

Born in a German colony in Russia, Pete Sauer was an immigrant who grew up in Lincoln, Nebraska, where he quickly demonstrated amazing wrestling skills. As a youngster he fell under the influence of Farmer Burns. Somewhere in that foggy, undocumented time between so-called amateur and pro, Steele also worked in the carnivals, making money by whipping locals who thought they could beat the wrestler. He also met Jim Londos, who was running the same gimmick.

Reputedly, the young Sauer-soon-to-be-Steele collided with Joe Stecher. While Stecher supposedly won the contest, it was only after Sauer broke free of Stecher's famed leg scissors and gave the famous champion fits.

Upon turning pro, Sauer moved to California and began using the name Ray Steele. He began training with mean-spirited hooker Ad Santel, who would later aid in the development of Lou Thesz. With the ring education imparted by Santel, Steele became a most dangerous adversary when he decided to shoot on a foe. Word got out quickly that Steele was nobody to challenge.

One source points out that Steele's transition to St. Louis coincided with his move to "repackage" himself. How often have modern fans heard Vince McMahon and WWE say they were repackaging a wrestler to improve his audience appeal? Steele did it in the early 1920s. History repeats itself in pro wrestling. For one gimmick, he would appear as the Masked Marvel, a disguise he lost in a match with Jim Londos. In Londos, though, Steele found a kindred soul, and the two had a long, friendly, profitable relationship.

St. Louis became a special place for Steele. The famous Business Man's Gym, run by noted referee Harry Cook (Cassimatis), was a hub for great wrestling talent. George Tragos, yet another shooter-hooker, was working with newcomers, including Thesz. "Strangler" Lewis was often there to challenge anyone who wanted to try him. Joe Stecher was in and out. Every major star made a stop at the place, which helped boost both Steele's knowledge and reputation.

Rugged Warren Bockwinkel, an unsung figure in wrestling lore, worked out at the gym and helped boost Thesz along the trail to stardom. Though never a main event regular, Bockwinkel was a legitimate tough guy and knew the ropes from A to Z. He also was the father of one of the 50 greatest of all time, Nick Bockwinkel (who wasn't yet born in the facility's heyday).

St. Louis promoter Tom Packs, who was rapidly becoming one of the major power brokers in the business, kept an eye on talent in the gym. And another young chap, one Sam Muchnick, was an avid handball player when he wasn't working as a sportswriter for the *St. Louis Times* newspaper. Steele was a regular opponent of Muchnick on the handball court, and Sam learned a lot about the inside of the business from him. Muchnick loved hanging out with the colorful grapplers.

Using St. Louis as a base, Steele was a key player from late in the 1920s well into the 1940s.

He loved the business and enjoyed the characters, of which he was one. In particular, Steele was loved — or feared, with a smile — for his ribs and jokes. Steele liked the carny types, the strippers and night club tribe who hung around wrestling in those days. He was popular with reporters so he stood out in the category that was the day's equivalent to mic work.

Appearing in main events all over the country, Steele made big money and lived comfortably below his means. In general, he was easy to do business with, putting an opponent over when it was the right thing to do. But he also could get testy if anyone needed to be put in his place.

Steele chalked up numerous bouts that today would be called five-star action. He tangled with Everett Marshall, George Zaharias, Gino Garibaldi, Danno O'Mahoney, and Orville Brown. He took on dangerous John Pesek in one particularly vicious scrap in 1933 that might well have turned into a shoot. Steele emerged victorious. Not all that many so-called stars were anxious to test, or trust, Pesek, but Steele did it willingly. Beating Pesek, whose losses were minimal when the chips were down, cemented Steele's stature as the real deal.

Steele had a couple of other claims to the championship, one of which was interrupted by injuries from a serious auto accident. But none were as meaningful as the time he topped Hall-of-Famer Bronko Nagurski, whom Steele respected for his outstanding athleticism and toughness. Steele had several hot affairs with Nagurski.

More headlines came to Steele in 1936, when he annihilated top-ranked heavyweight boxer Kingfish Levinsky in a boxer-versus-wrestler bout that most everyone seems to agree was a shoot. The bout discouraged many future boxers from accepting such a challenge.

Much of his fame stemmed from the period when he served as "the policeman" for Londos. Many wrestlers and insiders thought that Steele was a better wrestler than Londos, but Londos was the better showman; the only way to get a crack at Londos was to go through Steele. Terry Funk admirably filled the same role for his brother when Dory Funk Jr. was the champion 30 years later, and the idea has been used repeatedly by bookers over the decades.

Steele and Londos did often lock up, with Steele generally putting his buddy over. Does that answer the question of whether or not Steele could work? In many of Steele's other championship challenges against other wrestlers, he perfected the "come oh-so-close to winning only to lose by a hair" finish. Londos and Steele had numerous 60-minute time limit draws, plus a couple classic contests that went two hours. Needless to say, the champion going against his policeman was a great hook and drawing card for big crowds.

Another part of Steele's legacy was a duel against "Strangler" Lewis when political tensions were high, promotional factions were at odds, and too many tough guys were claiming the title. A deal had been struck for Londos to oppose Lewis, who had never liked him, on December 5, 1932. Londos was being pushed by Toots Mondt and Jack Curley at the time, while Lewis was allied with Paul Bowser. Somehow, Londos manipulated Steele into the corner across from Lewis.

This attempt to restore some order ended up in an uncomfortable, brief shoot between two legitimate hookers who liked and respected each other. Even though Lewis was older and near the end of his run, most still would have picked him in a straight-up shoot even against Steele. The battle ended with Steele disqualified for repeatedly fouling and punching Lewis. Nobody, least of all the two in the ring, was satisfied with that conclusion. But the commission and the referee apparently disregarded the agreed-upon finish. In fact, in Thesz's memoir, he claims that Lewis told Steele to begin punching for the DQ, so Steele went with the flow.

Steele had so many great moments in pro wrestling that this incident was nothing but a blip. He had the respect of all the boys, as did Lewis. Thesz in particular says Steele protected him when Lou was younger by giving him good advice and going to bat for him and other underneath talent to get paid better on a show.

Steele drifted away from pro wrestling around 1947 with no real retirement announcement. But like so many who've experienced the unique spotlight pro wrestling offers, he couldn't stay away. He was said to be training for a comeback when he died suddenly on September 11, 1949.

In the late 1970s, Sam Muchnick said that "Strangler" Lewis was the greatest he had ever seen. But he put Steele in a tiny group with Thesz, Stecher, Londos, and Pesek only a few steps behind Lewis. Anyone who knew anything about pro wrestling realized that Ray Steele was one of the special ones. Could he fit in today? Add what clearly were superior athletic talents to a great attitude about and love for the business, and you'd get a Ray Steele headlining pay-per-views now.

You see, there is always room for a wrestler's wrestler. Ray Steele belongs among the very best ever.

"CLASSY" FREDDIE BLASSIE #42

This character was no pencil-neck geek

"Pencil-neck geeks!" was a wrestling catch phrase before wrestling had catch phrases, thanks to the one and only "Classy" Freddie Blassie. He may not have zoomed around the ring in the manner of Ric Flair, but Blassie stirred every bit as much havoc as Flair did thanks to his expertise in the science of being a heel. Blassie wrote much of the book about how to be the bad guy.

It is said that comic Andy Kaufman, who came to cult wrestling fame for his feud with Jerry Lawler in Memphis, idolized Blassie and patterned some of his delivery on him. While Muhammad Ali is generally thought to have borrowed his talk from Gorgeous George, many believe that Ali was confused about which blond he admired, stealing a lot of his lines from Blassie interviews.

Born in St. Louis, Blassie had a tumultuous youth and ended up working in a meat-packing plant as a teenager. (Fred's cousin Nick would become the powerful president of the meat cutters union in St. Louis years later.) Pro wrestling was huge in St. Louis, and Blassie was an avid fan. He hung around referee Harry Cook's famous gym downtown where serious grapplers like Lou Thesz, Ray Steele, "Strangler" Lewis, and Everett Marshall trained. Promoter-to-be Sam Muchnick played handball there. Soon, some of the guys took a liking to the eager kid and taught Blassie some of the hookers' tricks.

Blassie got regular work at the carnivals, taking on all comers. He enjoyed the scene, and legend has it that he picked up the phrase "pencil-neck geek" during his days on the midway. He got more substantial wrestling work from the St. Louis and Kansas City promotions before World War II interrupted. After almost four years in the Navy, Blassie was back in the ring.

He had a horrific scare when he suffered a serious neck injury in a match with Rudy Dusek in 1947. Next, he had a brief run with notorious promoter Jack Pfeffer (who liked the carnival freaks most of all) before heading to Los Angeles in 1952 and then to Atlanta in 1953. Much of the time he was with another tough St. Louis native, Bill McDaniel, touted as either the Blassie brothers or the McDaniel brothers. Eventually, McDaniel got a job in the trucking industry to secure the insurance and pension plan that he could never have in pro wrestling.

Working as a single, Blassie bleached his hair blond, traded on his natural ability to get serious heat, and began his blood-and-guts approach to wrestling nastiness. It also made him a main event performer throughout the Southeast.

Promoter Jules Strongbow enticed Blassie to bring his act to Los Angeles in 1960. The World Wrestling Association was going so strong throughout southern California in those days that the company had its own world champion. Blassie, with his outrageous evil tactics, was a perfect fit for L.A. On June 12, 1961, he grabbed the WWA title from Edouard Carpentier and even went on to defend it against his hometown buddy Thesz, who was in between NWA title reigns.

Blassie made mat history with his classic interviews, where "pencil-neck geeks" became a catch phrase. In L.A., Blassie crossed paths with Japanese superhero Rikidozan and that opened the door to lucrative tours in Japan. In southern California, he traded the WWA title with Carpentier,

Rikidozan, and The Destroyer, a.k.a. Dick Beyer, who has always credited Blassie with teaching him how to get heat, often with the simplest of ideas. As paying customers packed the buildings, Blassie had bloodbaths with Dick the Bruiser, The Sheik, Mark Lewin, and Bobo Brazil, while also forming successful tag teams with Mr. Moto and Buddy Austin.

At one point, Blassie dropped the WWA crown to Bearcat Wright, who was one of the first African-American wrestlers to win such a trophy. Before regaining the WWA title, Blassie headed to New York for Vince McMahon Sr. and collided with WWWF king Bruno Sammartino in a wild, controversial series of brawls. He became close friends with Senior and Gorilla Monsoon, who was gaining power behind the scenes. Years later, as Fred neared retirement, he would return to challenge Pedro Morales for the WWWF crown.

L.A. was also a terrific location for making media contacts. Many celebrities were big fans of wrestling and in particular of Blassie. He cashed in and spread his fame, once doing a cameo on the Dick Van Dyke television show. Blassie appeared regularly on *The Regis Philbin Show* in San Diego. Philbin let Blassie run wild and, not surprisingly, loved the reaction Blassie got insulting host and guests alike while occasionally tossing furniture. Blassie also recorded a novelty record, loved by underground DJ Dr. Demento, which further extended his catch phrase.

In Japan, Blassie portrayed "The Vampire" on the highly rated television wrestling program over Nippon TV in the early 1960s. During matches, he would make his foes bleed by biting their foreheads. In between bouts, segments would show Blassie using a file to grind his teeth for an assault on some hapless foe. Wrestling lore has it that when Blassie battered Rikidozan, some viewers actually had heart attacks because the carnage was so graphic.

Blassie was a superstar in Japan. His feud with Rikidozan on live TV set viewing records and made Blassie a national celebrity. Thesz always loved to tell his story about going shopping with Freddie in Japan. Together on a tour in the early 1960s, Blassie and Thesz went to a specialty shop featuring china and other glass goods. Since wrestling was on national television at the time, they were soon followed by a huge bunch of people, primarily youngsters. Blassie grinned devilishly and told Lou, "Watch this." He pulled out a nail file and began to "sharpen" his teeth, as he did for his gimmick on TV. Thesz heard the kids gasp. Suddenly Blassie waved his arms in the air, roaring in anger. The kids panicked and ran, trampling other shoppers and crashing pieces of china. Almost every shelf in the store looked damaged as Thesz and Blassie scampered out too. "I guess they bought it," Blassie told Thesz. Later, according to Thesz, the store owner wanted to file charges against Blassie, but Rikidozan paid for all the damages, time, and trouble, writing it off as the cost of Blassie living his gimmick.

Perhaps surprisingly, Muchnick never used Blassie regularly in St. Louis. Once every year or two, Blassie would come to town to visit family, and Sam would give Blassie a win on *Wrestling at the Chase*. Blassie would then rant and rave during an interview about how Muchnick was afraid to let Fred meet the NWA champion. Afterward, the two buddies would shake hands and hug, and Blassie would head back to L.A. to create more controversy. Years later, Muchnick told me a character like Blassie couldn't use his kind of gimmick in his hometown because everybody knew better. Sam also thought that Blassie's gory tactics and bizarre promos didn't fit the St. Louis style of hard wrestling. In other words, keeping Blassie out of St. Louis was a business decision that both parties were comfortable with.

By the late 1960s, when Mike LeBell had replaced Strongbow as the promotional boss in L.A., Blassie had become the villain fans loved to hate so much that they now just loved him. The babyface turn would have come naturally, but a classic angle with John Tolos made the moment much more profitable.

Tolos supposedly blinded Blassie by throwing a substance called Monsel's Powder in Fred's face (the move was a forerunner of the Freebirds blinding Junkyard Dog years down the road in the Mid-South). The forced retirement of Blassie was announced. "Miraculously," Blassie made his comeback, and the subsequent blow-off with Tolos drew 25,847 at the L.A. Coliseum. This gave Blassie's career trajectory yet another jolt, but the end was near because his body was breaking down. His knees were shot, and California refused to issue a wrestler's license to anyone over 55 years old.

A perfect home awaited him, though: Blassie moved to the WWWF, reinvented himself as the Hollywood Fashion Plate, and became the manager of many leading stars in the company. Blassie's mouth helped get over many a challenger for the promotion title.

And, for what it's worth, Blassie was Hulk Hogan's manager when Hulk first invaded the WWF as a heel.

Just how many people have borrowed lines, tactics, or psychology from Blassie is impossible to know. What is easy to understand, however, is that Fred Blassie belongs among the 50 greatest pro wrestlers in history.

#41 RAY STEVENS
In recognition of all great workers

Naming Ray Stevens among the 50 greatest pro wrestlers in history is a salute to every outstanding worker in this fabled, complex sport and also a tip of the cap to Stevens himself.

Stevens was something of a pro wrestling child prodigy, competing in his first match at age 15 in 1950. He broke in around Columbus, Ohio, where wily promoter Al Haft had a stable of top hands. Buddy Rogers helped teach Stevens, praising him as one of the most talented and graceful performers Rogers had ever known. Stevens' in-ring philosophy was further crafted by several bouts he had as a teenager with none other than Gorgeous George.

Add to those influences a natural tendency to take risks (he was both a rodeo performer and a motorcycle racer), and it's easy to understand how Stevens became such a fluid, clever worker.

The mindset, along with the education, was there naturally. And that was key in Stevens' success, given that he was small, perhaps 5'8" and chunky at 235 pounds. To argue that size made some difference in where he was booked would be denying the obvious.

On the other hand, his working skills earned him huge respect from every promoter, even when Stevens didn't fit a particular office. Stevens was the absolute professional who had perfect timing and took frightening bumps. With a bottomless supply of nefarious tricks, he could get serious heat, then sell like few others could. And he was generous to a fault in doing so. Able to talk with fire, Stevens could project a personality that viewers loved to hate. Once he got over, size meant nothing.

The promoter who was most behind him was Roy Shire in San Francisco, where Stevens became a legend. Of course, Shire knew firsthand what talent Stevens had. Shire and Stevens had formed the Shire brothers tag team, working throughout the Midwest in the late 1950s. Roy was the "Professor" and Ray was the reckless younger brother. The combination obviously clicked — a major tag-team title came their way when they defeated Dick the Bruiser and Angelo Poffo in 1959.

Always ambitious even though he was getting older, Shire opened an opposition promotion in San Francisco in 1960, which started a war with longtime promoter Joe Malciewicz, who had no television promotion and Malciewicz eventually folded. Shire brought the fiery Stevens along and gave him a push to the moon, for which Stevens was more than ready. Shire's booking and Stevens' working set the Bay Area on fire and made it one of the top locations in the country. Stevens unleashed his bombs-away knee drop from the top rope to record win after win. The move was a masterpiece for the ages. His rip-roaring battles with Wilbur Snyder and Bobo Brazil filled the famous Cow Palace to capacity.

Possibly the hottest, most remembered angle involved Stevens against popular and powerful Pepper Gomez, a bodybuilder who reputedly had a "cast iron" stomach, or in today's parlance, "six-pack abs." Gomez had an open challenge for wrestlers to jump onto his stomach, but none were ever able to make him wince. Then Stevens dared Gomez to let him try the challenge — from a ladder.

Stevens jumped from halfway up the 12-foot ladder. Both feet landed on Gomez's stomach, and Pepper had no problem withstanding the blow. Once more, Stevens came off the ladder but Gomez shrugged it off. So Stevens climbed to the top of the ladder and abruptly switched to the bombs-away knee drop, coming down hard across Gomez's throat. Gomez was badly injured, spitting blood, and was out for several weeks. Needless to say, the resulting showdown between Stevens and Gomez packed the Cow Palace with 17,000 fans, a sellout that turned away more than 5,000 people!

For the rest of the 1960s, the territory was ablaze and Ray Stevens was the man. Stevens took on Snyder, Brazil, Bruno Sammartino (and was allowed to get a win by count-out so that Bruno kept the WWWF crown), "Cowboy" Bob Ellis, Karl Gotch, Dominic DeNucci, Big Bill Miller, Kinji Shibuya, Pedro Morales, Jose Lothario, and more — a veritable collection of mat stars of the day.

Adding to the fun, Stevens formed what became a classic tag team with Pat Patterson. The two could fly, taking dangerous bumps to sell the comebacks of heroic foes. They captured the area tag championship and generated another round of big gates by meeting various other teams. Naturally, like most wrestling partnerships, divorce came when the two turned on each other and drew sold-out houses for their battles. Stevens was the face, which was no surprise: a survey from the early 1960s showed that Stevens had been voted both the most hated wrestler *and* the most liked wrestler. Typical great heel.

By the turn of the decade, Stevens moved to the AWA, where Verne Gagne was a big fan. While Stevens captured the AWA tag prize once with Patterson as his sidekick, it was the unit he formed with Nick Bockwinkel that remains in history's headlines. Along with manager Bobby Heenan, they won the AWA title three times, first by downing The Crusher and Red Bastien, who was another superb worker and high flyer.

Think about Stevens, Bockwinkel, and Heenan. What a combination in the ring and on the microphone. How could it not work?

Stevens also picked up the nickname "The Crippler" when he used the bombs-away to "break" the leg of Dr. X (a masked Dick Beyer, before he headed off to become a legend in Japan as The Destroyer). The incident also gave the AWA a reason to ban the bombs-away move, leaving some room for angles and disqualifications. Stevens had a marvelous time in the AWA. He constantly gained new admirers through his savvy working touches.

But the accumulated bumps, bruises, and breaks took their toll, even on someone as gritty as Ray Stevens. After forming a fine team with Greg Valentine in the Carolinas, he had a shot with the WWF in 1982 when he did a hot angle with "Superfly" Jimmy Snuka. Unfortunately, though, the trend toward the blown-up steroid muscleheads was causing even a great worker like Stevens to be shuffled aside. He gravitated back to the AWA and a reduced schedule. Stevens officially put the wraps on his 42-year career in 1992.

Stevens' placement on this list calls attention to many terrific workers with somewhat similar claims. Dick Murdoch would be first to come to mind. But what about someone like Don Leo Jonathan, an agile giant who knew how to spark excitement? Or those two key members of the AWA crew when Stevens and Bockwinkel were dominant forces — Crusher Blackwell and Ken Patera?

A critic might snort, "Blackwell — a good worker?" But Jerry Blackwell was terrific, especially given the physical frame he had to work with. About 5'9" and tipping the scale anywhere from 450 to 480 pounds, Blackwell completely understood how to use his body to make lesser foes look good and better foes look great. Working the "fat man match" was his specialty. He could take head-shaking bumps for someone of his size, plus deliver a more-than-respectable drop kick.

He also did one of my wife Pat's all-time favorite interviews prior to a showdown with Andre the Giant, who was generously billed as seven feet tall at the time. Blackwell bellowed about people saying he's fat: "I'm not fat! I'm just short. If Andre the Giant were my size, they'd say Andre was fat!" It was the type of off-the-cuff riffing someone like Stevens, or Blackwell, could do to suck in a viewer. No soap opera writer needed.

Patera was a world-class weightlifter and athlete (track and field) who figured out how to be a star in the pro wrestling business. He knew how to crush someone, displaying his legitimate raw strength, just as he knew how to make his adversary look like a whirling dervish. The bouts between Patera and Bob Backlund were terrific examples of two stellar athletes putting together thrilling action and telling a story that brought the fans along. So were Patera's bouts with Ted DiBiase and Jack Brisco. Patera was right there, more than holding his own with members of the 50 best ever class.

Why mention Blackwell and Patera? Because of Ray Stevens, that's why. Patera and Blackwell both would have said that Stevens set the bar at record height as a worker. The way Stevens excelled in the ring should remind observers what a truly gifted worker means to the business. The master craftsman with charisma. He is the sparkling example of a worker's worker.

It's why Ray Stevens gets to dance with the greatest in history.

#40 "ROWDY" RODDY PIPER
Sound the bagpipes for a one-of-a-kind performer

At least Roddy Piper doesn't need to hire a band to celebrate his inclusion in the 50 greatest pro wrestlers of all time. He can just break out his bagpipes and play the appropriate upbeat music. Guaranteed, the fans will be clapping and dancing with him. That connection with the paying customers, even if most of the time they were jeering him, is a key reason why Piper has made the grade.

The reasons why Roddy Piper fits in with this elite group don't spring from the normal rationale. But, in the end, Piper's tale is totally pro wrestling. He came from nowhere and made something of himself on the strength of charisma, dedication, personality, and down-in-the-gut toughness. The whole mixture could probably only work in an unconventional field like pro wrestling.

Way back when he was a teenager on the streets of Winnipeg, Piper claimed he played the bagpipes for spare change to pay for a bed at local hostels or the YMCA for the night. He had bounced from Saskatoon to Toronto before ending up in Winnipeg. By every definition of the term, he was a rough and tough street kid. Ending up in boxing and wrestling seemed only natural.

Roderick Toombs lost his first pro wrestling bout in a mere ten seconds, although the story is that he was only 15 years old. He apparently fared better in boxing, winning a Golden Gloves championship. Additionally, he had a mouth and an attitude that wouldn't quit, so some wrestling promoters gave him a chance (and probably paid him ten bucks a night).

He got to the AWA, though, where he was beaten on a regular basis like any new guy. That led to the Kansas City office, which had a business relationship with Sam Muchnick in St. Louis. He would have been 20 years old when I was the play-by-play commentator for his loss to Lord Alfred Hayes on *Wrestling at the Chase* on November 9, 1974. Pat O'Connor, Sam's booker, stumbled with names so I was calling Piper "Ronnie" when he got waxed by the slick Lord Hayes.

But Piper had something nobody could teach. Call it personality, or fire, or charisma, or spunk. He was a good-looking, slender athlete who left it all inside the squared circle. Except for winning one tag-team bout, "Ronnie" lost often but always had the fans excited. Someone else who mattered even more got excited too — Sam Muchnick.

When Piper got the call to go to Texas for Fritz Von Erich, he might never have known that it was because Sam had called Fritz, saying he had a really promising youngster on television who needed experience. Could Fritz use him? Fritz did and found he liked him just as much as Sam did. And then Von Erich contacted promoter Don Owen in Oregon.

Before heading for Oregon, though, Piper stopped in Los Angeles and had a nice run for promoter Mike LeBell, who put Roddy in a mask. Roddy quickly shed the disguise and his naturally cocky, irreverent personality emerged. He put on the kilt, played the bagpipes, and irritated the daylight out of the fans, who hated him probably as much as they used to hate Fred Blassie — a compliment for a budding heel. Piper was a heat magnet and always added an unexpected touch to any proposed angle. His work was fresh and energetic. From 1976 into

1978, Piper bounced back and forth between L.A. for LeBell and San Francisco for Roy Shire while winning the requisite local titles.

In 1979, Piper invaded Oregon and finally met Owen. The two clicked, forming such a strong friendship that in the 1980s Piper refused to work for the WWF in Portland against Owen's withering promotion. Roddy made a home in Oregon and raised a family, despite the brutal travel schedule his fame would eventually require.

Rick Martel was another young star on the rise in Oregon. The two had some blazing battles. "Roddy was such a great worker, and could he ever talk," recalled Martel, who fits into that crew of deeply underrated talents. "Once we worked in a cage match, and at the very start I knocked him off the cage and he fell backward onto a table by the ring.

"All I could see were his legs sticking up out of his kilt, and he was wiggling and waving his legs. It was so hard for me not to laugh at him," Martel said. "But usually he was getting scary heat."

And that heat went past boiling once Piper moved to the Carolinas in 1980. The territory was red-hot then, and Piper added to the fire as he tangled with Jack Brisco, Ric Flair, and Sgt. Slaughter; he got into a feud with Greg Valentine that led to a famous and savage dog-collar match. Once, he was stabbed by an irate fan in a disturbance after a match. There were nights he literally fought his way back to the dressing room.

The temperature went even higher as Piper became the bad-guy color commentator with legendary Gordon Solie on the WTBS national cable show. Piper loved the mic, and the mic loved Piper. Promoter Jim Barnett gave Piper lots of room to operate, which probably added to the reasons Vince McMahon Jr. made Piper one of the original signings when the WWF began its march across the mat world in 1984.

Whoever came up with the idea for "Piper's Pit" deserves recognition as a genius. Various shows, including Vince's own, have tried to duplicate the fire created by "Piper's Pit." All of them failed. Piper, totally unscripted, was in his element. He would be interviewing a guest and end up going off like a volcano in all directions. Many a box-office feud started in the Pit, notably when Roddy smashed a coconut over Jimmy Snuka's head. Piper even shot an angle with Bruno Sammartino in the Pit. The recurring segments also moved the quieter "Cowboy" Bob Orton, a terrific talent, into the limelight as Piper's bodyguard.

From a historic perspective, it was the jumping-off point for the rivalry between Hulk Hogan and Piper, the spark for the first ever *WrestleMania* in 1985. On the Pit, Piper assaulted singer Cyndi Lauper, Hulk's good buddy, and attacked Captain Lou Albano, Cyndi's music video co-star. It all led to that giant night, and had *WrestleMania* failed, VKM's road to glory with WWF/WWE might well have been stymied.

When everything clicked, and the huge audience materialized, McMahon was off and running. Obviously, Piper's involvement was critical in the main event that set Roddy and Paul Orndorff against Hulk and television star Mr. T.

Mr. T's lack of athleticism had to be hidden but, used correctly, his image as a celebrity had plenty of legs at the box office. So Vince booked Mr. T against Piper in a boxing match for the second *Mania*. The crazy travel schedule for Piper made planning and literally rehearsing — which T needed — nearly impossible. I was working for Vince by then, and thanks to local connections I was able to secure a spot in St. Louis for a secret session involving Mr. T, Piper, and agent Black Jack Lanza, once a fine ring general himself.

Known to only a chosen few in town, I lined up a small black box theater on the Opera House side of Kiel Auditorium and had a Golden Glove boxing ring moved into the room. Nobody knew what it was for. Piper, Mr. T, and Lanza slipped into town and into Kiel, and the only person who knew about it was building manager Joe Failoni. Seems like a Secret Service operation when I look back on it now!

It was pretty obvious that Piper was going to have his hands full making a match out of the confrontation. T just didn't get it, nor were his reflexes quick enough to keep up, even when Piper slowed down. But Roddy was a patient coach, and T did try hard. Eventually, the two got through a mess of a match, but sitting on the ring apron after the grueling practice that day, Roddy told me, "Well, you saw what I saw. But don't worry. I'll get something out of it." Ah, the credo of a great worker.

And Piper proved that again and again, even after he ended up a fan favorite. It's the natural evolution of excellent heels. Through the 1980s, Piper might well have been the hottest heel in North America. More than two decades later the names best remembered from WWF in that hectic era are probably Hogan, Randy Savage, and Piper.

Even as Piper's body began to break down, he got mileage through the 1980s out of the Pit and his reputation. Whether Roddy dealt with Adrian Adonis or Andre the Giant, Bobby Heenan or Rick Rude, Bret Hart or Ric Flair, the fans were so into Piper that he always drew heat. And he produced even more heat during a four-year stint with WCW, including a win over Hulk in a steel cage.

The sporadic wrestling schedule he put together after the mid 1980s freed him up so he could pursue a movie and television career. While he hasn't become a screen superstar, he has been a fine supporting name who actually is quite good at what he does. His list of TV and film credits is over 50 and growing.

Moreover, after some less than pleasant times between Roddy and Vince — Piper has always been known to speak his mind — their relationship is good enough that Piper can always come back to the pro wrestling environment where it all began for that scrappy Canadian street kid.

Roddy Piper was one of a kind. Even today, Piper is recognized and positively associated with pro wrestling. He was made for this phenomenon.

#39 TED DIBIASE
One million dollars couldn't buy his versatility

One million dollars' worth of versatility earns Ted DiBiase a spot among the 50 greatest professional wrestlers of all time. DiBiase's WWF character The Million Dollar Man monopolizes most of the attention he earns. Unfortunately, some forget the remarkable wrestling work he did before VKM anointed him with Vince's personal gimmick.

As a wrestler and worker, DiBiase was at the head of his class from the late 1970s on. DiBiase was a handsome athlete who combined youth and fire with a humble and intelligent approach on the mic. The training he got from Dory and Terry Funk was obvious; Ted had to have been their best student ever. Those gifts served him well in hot spots like St. Louis, Atlanta, and the Mid-South circuit.

He was the classic babyface and never needed to beg or cheerlead for audience response. The go-get-'em roars came easily, and with intensity, whenever DiBiase made a fiery comeback against heels like Harley Race, Dick Murdoch, and Killer Karl Kox. The opponents are a huge part of the deal, but DiBiase had a natural feel for creating the depth and sense of competition that made every match, even a squash on television, a

Larry Matysik interviews a young Ted DiBiase

little more meaningful. He was much more than just a great technician, because he could emotionally connect with fans of all sorts and ages.

Obviously, adding this depth to the main event position meant DiBiase was a key part of drawing some pretty impressive crowds. His conflicts with Race and Ric Flair in St. Louis were box-office bonanzas, as were his efforts in Atlanta to gain revenge against the Fabulous Freebirds and especially Terry Gordy.

Giant Baba's All Japan promotion took note of DiBiase and made him a major part of their booking. He formed one of history's finest tag-team combinations a few years later when rugged Stan Hansen, an icon in Japan, personally chose Ted to fill the void left when Hansen's partner Bruiser Brody jumped to Antonio Inoki's New Japan.

The only real bump in the road came in 1979 during an aborted run with the WWF. Bob Backlund was having tremendous success as the young all-American hero who had become the WWF king by defeating "Superstar" Graham in 1978. Vince McMahon Sr., then the undisputed boss of the company, wanted to duplicate the success of Backlund by adding another young, explosive stud.

Muchnick was a close friend of Vince Sr., even during business disputes in the early 1960s. Sam had recommended Backlund to Vince Sr., and that was a rousing success. When McMahon asked for Sam's opinion again, he spoke up strongly for DiBiase.

But this time the idea fizzled. DiBiase came in billed as owner of the North American championship. He quickly lost it to Pat Patterson, who supposedly united that title with the South American crown he reputedly owned, calling himself the first Intercontinental champion. Then DiBiase did the job for newcomer heel Hulk Hogan at Madison Square Garden, and it was goodbye New York for Ted. Whether it was a fuzzy booking plan or DiBiase too much resembling Backlund as a young wrestler type, the entire episode left a sour taste for all involved.

The incident also hinted at a perceived weakness, according to the always blunt Bruiser Brody. "Ted's a nice guy, too nice. He's got a soft ear," claimed Brody, alluding to his belief that DiBiase let others talk him into things that were not always good for him. Nonetheless, way more often than not, things were going quite well for DiBiase.

Around this time, Bill Watts suggested that DiBiase try working as a heel in Mid-South. Ted was hesitant after all the success he had enjoyed as a face. Maybe the New York experience had made him a little gun-shy too. He brought up Watts's idea in a St. Louis dressing room. Sam Muchnick, who'd seen and done it all, was there, along with Race and me.

Muchnick understood Ted's concern, but explained, "You could be a great wrestling heel. Someone the people know is good enough to win without cheating, but you cut corners and that gets them angry."

Race agreed, saying, "Ted, you've got the skills to do it. Not everybody can. A guy who can wrestle and then does heel stuff, he can get real heat. It's in how you carry yourself and when you do what you do — just like always."

So Watts got his new heel, and DiBiase discovered another card in his winning hand. He was excellent in the role.

By the mid 1980s, DiBiase was among a small handful of performers considered the best workers in the world. Most observers have noted that DiBiase seemed to be a logical world heavyweight champion for the National Wrestling Alliance. But by this time, the NWA had deteriorated. It comprised only the Jim Crockett Promotion out of North Carolina, which meant DiBiase wasn't in the discussion — the politics were decided by Ric Flair and Dusty Rhodes. DiBiase was Watts's guy, and Watts and Crockett were only united at this point by their desire to upend the surge of WWF and Vince Jr.

If someone like Muchnick, who loved DiBiase's breadth of ability, had been in charge of the NWA around 1980, DiBiase could easily have been in the mix to move the title between the likes of Flair, Race, Rhodes, and David Von Erich, depending on the ole devil politics. But that's just conjecture, and times were changing.

So along came VKM, turning the industry topsy-turvy after taking over the WWF from his dad.

Vince brought DiBiase to his Connecticut office and explained his great idea for DiBiase. He had a role Ted would be perfect for, but he would not explain what the gimmick was until DiBiase committed to the WWF. McMahon said that he loved how DiBiase carried himself as a heel; Vince loved Ted's demeanor and his arrogance. He also told Ted that he wouldn't explain further because he didn't want DiBiase to reject the offer and then take the idea back to Watts, Crockett, and whatever was left of the NWA.

McMahon had to leave the room to take another call, so Ted was left with Vince's trusted soldier Pat Patterson. It was Patterson who told Ted that since this idea was Vince's, all Vince's, it was going to get a huge push, and that DiBiase really was — in Patterson's opinion — the perfect player for the part.

When DiBiase got home, he called Terry Funk for Terry's opinion. Funk laughed and told DiBiase, "Pack your bags, get on a plane, go to New York and don't look back." Which was exactly what Ted DiBiase did, and The Million Dollar Man — in many ways the personification of Vince McMahon and his business philosophy about pro wrestling — was born.

In all likelihood, Vince still believes every person in the business has a price. He should, because events in the real world have proven the point almost 100 percent correct. DiBiase, in Oscar-winning fashion, played the part of the tumultuous and fictional pro wrestling world on the big screen. McMahon wanted DiBiase to be in character as a filthy rich performer at all times so that fans who spotted him would believe in the character. So Ted got to travel first-class and stay in the finest hotels.

"Tough job, but somebody had to do it," DiBiase laughs today.

When the program got running late in 1987 into 1988, the cynical Brody declared to me that this was McMahon's way of getting a fabulous worker out of the ring. Most of the early booking had Ted as a person who set others into action while he himself did not wrestle. Brody, among others, thought that McMahon was devaluing workers to make it easier to replace them with weightlifters and lesser athletes who would work cheaper.

Of course, it was inevitable that DiBiase more and more became an in-ring performer. Over time he squared off with everyone from Hulk to Randy Savage to Jake Roberts to Dusty Rhodes.

Even with those and other outings, a critical observer could argue that WWF never got all of the best ring work Ted DiBiase could have given them.

DiBiase missed the much more physically demanding action in Japan, where he returned briefly in 1993 before serious back and neck injuries led to surgery and the finish of DiBiase in the ring.

He continued as a manager/entrepreneur in WWF, made a disappointing jump to what was then World Championship Wrestling in a similar position, and finally backed away from the pro wrestling scene. When he couldn't really compete anymore, an important part of his fire was extinguished.

DiBiase was a born-again Christian with deep beliefs and a man who had been helped through personal problems by sincere, good friends like Pastor Hal Santos now in Fairview Heights, Illinois. In 1999 DiBiase became a Christian minister and founded the Heart of David Ministry.

As Brody had said, he was "a nice guy" who was not burdened with the enemies many make in wrestling. He became involved again with McMahon and WWE, even working as an agent for the promotion for a while. But the situation just wasn't for him. Today, he has found a balance with wrestling that leaves him content, and his religious beliefs and work keep him fulfilled.

Look at all that variety, notably going from the torrid young favorite to the greedy, nasty manipulator. Clearly, Ted Dibiase is a unique pro wrestling personality who utilized his versatility to become one of the most elite performers ever in the mat game.

#38 PAT O'CONNOR
Never got the credit he deserved for all that talent

Pat O'Connor never got the credit he deserved for restoring faith in the ability of the National Wrestling Alliance champion as a drawing card, or for what a fantastic performer he was.

When Lou Thesz ended his hugely successful reign as NWA champion in 1957, Dick Hutton was chosen to be the new titleholder. While Hutton was a brilliant grappler, he was considered to be too bland and quiet for such a visible position. But he had the politically powerful support of NWA president Sam Muchnick, Thesz himself, and a few other promoters who insisted that Hutton's overwhelming amateur credentials would be sufficient to carry the load.

Unfortunately for Hutton, a decent fellow who was highly competitive if uncomfortable in the wild wrestling world, business was falling off and promoters got antsy, leading to some bogus title claims. Hutton shouldn't have been blamed for all the box-office disappointment. The entire industry suffered after overexposure on television into the mid 1950s and then hardly any television coverage at the end of the decade.

The board of directors decided to make a change. While strong names like Verne Gagne, Edouard Carpentier, Buddy Rogers, and Wilbur Snyder were bandied about, it was Pat O'Connor who emerged as Hutton's replacement. Not only was he a personal favorite of Muchnick and politically acceptable to a contentious membership, O'Connor was another excellent pure wrestler. He was aggressive, had mastered mixing fundamental strengths with spectacular pro moves, and could project a strong personality. Gagne split from the NWA in anger and created the AWA so he could be the world champion too. It was a development that the wrestling community seemed able to accept.

Somewhere in the back of Muchnick's mind had been the thought that another major claimant, an idea the NWA had toyed with in 1957 for Carpentier, might be good for the business, particularly in the area of booking. (The 2011 angle with John Cena, CM Punk, and WWE is hardly a new idea.) The key for the NWA was that O'Connor was recognized as the real deal, a legitimate champion.

Growing up on a New Zealand ranch and working as a blacksmith, O'Connor's wrestling talent earned him a spot training with famous coach Anton Koolman. When O'Connor won the New Zealand championship, thus earning entry into the British Empire Games, he was spotted by touring pro Joe Pazandak. Before long, Pazandak had arranged for O'Connor to come to the United States, where he trained with both the University of Minnesota team and with promoter Tony Stecher (Joe's brother) and Verne Gagne for his professional debut.

On national television in 1952, O'Connor was an immediate hit with his wide-open style that relied on flying tackles, drop kicks, and flashy variations of basic maneuvers. He was so hot as a fan favorite that he got a match with Lou Thesz at Chicago's Wrigley Field that year.

Sam Muchnick loved him from the beginning, starting him with a victory over The Mighty Atlas in St. Louis in 1952. By 1954, O'Connor was headlining shows in Madison Square Garden, Toronto, Montreal, Denver, and throughout Ohio. He competed on even footing with the biggest superstars, winning against (and seldom losing to) the likes of Rogers, Gagne, Carpentier, Killer Kowalski, Yvon Robert, Bobby Managoff, and Gene Kiniski.

When the time came to strap on the gold belt, O'Connor was firmly established among the best performers in North America, and also as a solid drawing card. He took the NWA honor from Hutton on January 9, 1959 in St. Louis, and for the most part the NWA calmed down with O'Connor as their leading man. O'Connor had the goods and nobody who thought of an in-ring swerve was anxious to test him.

O'Connor was a popular and respected representative of the business who always drew well and never made waves. But the politics, as always, were swirling and pressure built to switch the crown to the colorful Buddy Rogers, with some promoters pointing out how successful heel champion "Wild Bill" Longson had been in the 1940s. And here was the arrogant, strutting Rogers primed to set new gate records, or so the argument went.

On June 30, 1961, Rogers took an unforgettable battle from O'Connor to become the new NWA ruler before 38,622 fans in Comiskey Park. The attendance record stood for years before it was broken by *WrestleMania III* in 1987. A rematch that summer had drawn another 20,000 spectators. On July 29, 1960, at the same venue, O'Connor against Yukon Eric and Rogers against Bearcat Wright had drawn 30,275. Since it always takes two to tango, make no mistake that O'Connor was every bit as important as Rogers to the successful equation.

It hurt O'Connor's visibility and reputation that he settled in Kansas City, where he became part-owner of the promotion. Kansas City was a mid-level territory, relying on smaller markets, and it slipped down the ladder later in the 1970s. But O'Connor was a trooper, doing the right thing for business, and the business often put him in smaller venues and doing jobs for what would be considered lesser talents. Looking back, it's obvious that making weaker foes look stronger is the hallmark of a great worker.

KC was also a good training ground for newcomers. Dick Murdoch, who started there in 1969, told me, "It was a pain. Thanks to guys like O'Connor and Bob Geigel, I had no skin left on my back after a week. All I did was look at the lights while they beat me up." Then Murdoch added, "But I really learned how to work and take care of myself too."

Fortunately, O'Connor had St. Louis, where he eventually became the booker for Muchnick and also someone who taught me important parts of the game. Until he slowed down and willingly moved himself to a mid-card role, O'Connor had historic matches and drew sellout crowds when he met Kiniski, Dory Funk Jr., Dick the Bruiser, Fritz Von Erich, and others. As far as skill and excitement, his series of duels with Thesz were right there with those to come between Dory Jr. and Jack Brisco. Every budding star, from Ric Flair to Roddy Piper, always got a taste of and a lesson from O'Connor.

O'Connor never got the credit he deserved for being such a creative performer. He had a unique way of doing things so he never had the same match twice. Quite often O'Connor would add or change something in how he executed some of his favorite moves.

The so-called O'Connor roll-up, which Pat actually named the "reverse rolling cradle," is a good example. While many grapplers pull off the maneuver, none could do it as smoothly as O'Connor could. A few, like Bob Backlund, were athletic enough to add a bridge at the end, and that was impressive. But O'Connor moved behind and took down a foe in a sleek, graceful fashion that nobody could match.

His arm drags were things of beauty, yet sometimes O'Connor could cinch in deep and hurl an opponent up and over. Other times, O'Connor would be farther away and would use more of a whipping motion.

Pat told me that it all depended on the opponent he was working with. "Some guys it's just a matter of guiding into the right position. Others, well, you have to yank them into the right spot," O'Connor said. "With some, they're either too bulky or just not flexible enough to offer much help. So you move them around yourself." And O'Connor was talented enough to do exactly that.

He could move even the capable ones. Once Nick Bockwinkel, as fine a worker as there ever was, marveled about how O'Connor could put him into positions that made Nick appear in command, with either a hold or winning a spot, and Bockwinkel wasn't even sure how Pat got him there. It just happened by the magic of how O'Connor controlled the ring.

Dory Funk Jr. talked about catching O'Connor in an airplane spin. "Usually you have to lift your opponent, get him spinning around. With Pat, it's like he wasn't even there. He was flying! I had to look to make sure he was up there, because I could hardly feel him," recalled Funk.

How often has anyone used the spinning arm lock? O'Connor did the move in such beautiful fashion that crowds would yell in delight as he punished a heel by spinning around and around, cinching in on the shoulder. Dory Funk, a marvelous scientific grappler himself, claims that he has studied tapes of O'Connor applying the hold but can't figure out how O'Connor made the move look so exciting and painful.

Modern fans who don't know the background might scoff, not realizing how important it was that O'Connor could combat ruffians with his scientific wrestling. By working the psychology and selling properly, O'Connor could elicit the same screams from crowds for a spinning arm lock or a hard takedown that less skilled performers could only get with halfway decent punches. Everything *looked better* because of the way O'Connor did it. His command of movement, his and his opponent's, was second to none.

Speaking of punches, Pat O'Connor knew how to fire them too. In a particularly effective moment, he clamped on a side headlock and popped his rival on the forehead. If the atmosphere was right, O'Connor would unleash a rapid-fire sequence of four or five shots to the face of a heel. Every blast looked like a potato!

The best, though, was the hard right cross O'Connor would deliver, a sizzling shot that seemed to bounce off the chin of O'Connor's foe. When O'Connor used punches like those, it indicated he was either enraged or realized he was in a fight for survival, so the punches never failed to bring fans to their feet.

When a performer can make a crowd erupt with either a spinning arm lock, a reverse rolling cradle, or a right cross, it proves how special a worker that star is. Pat O'Connor was special — special enough to be worthy of entrance into the company of the 50 greatest pro wrestlers ever. He finally gets the credit he deserves.

#37 GORGEOUS GEORGE
My goodness, what did he start?

The legacy of Gorgeous George might well outlast whatever professional wrestling becomes down the road, for the legend of the bland workman turned flamboyant showman and cultural icon will resonate through the generations.

Pretty flighty writing to describe a wrestler who bleached his hair blond and acted prissy to draw money, right? What he did, though, has influenced a huge number of pro wrestling performers and promoters for years and likely will continue to do so for the foreseeable future. Sometimes, the simplest ideas have the most potential for growth. That certainly was true for George Wagner, whose simple idea was born as much from frustration as inspiration.

In the late 1930s, solid wrestlers were a dime a dozen. Wagner was one of them. Perhaps he possessed a bit more instinct for stirring up the crowd than the others, but he was missing that extra something to put him in the spotlight and earn him the big bucks. He could wrestle. He was good, but not quite good enough. Competing with the likes of Londos and Thesz left George a few steps short.

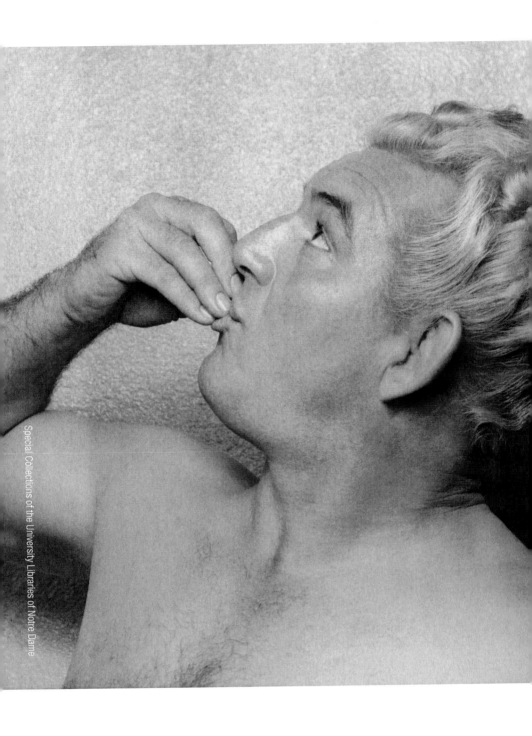

First, Wagner concentrated on being the ruffian as he moved around among territories. Then, he added the nickname "Gorgeous" to his billing. Next came the bleached hair. Borrowing from a rather effeminate personality that one of his buddies, an eccentric performer named Dizzy Davis, was using in Mexico, George added certain mannerisms to his own solid ring repertoire. He wore a long, gaudy robe for the introduction.

Johnny Doyle, a California promoter always open to ideas, loved what Wagner was doing. He made the ring name just *Gorgeous George*. Soon the robe was festooned with sequins, the tune "Pomp and Circumstance" blared when George came to the ring, and, like the worker Lord Lansdowne who came before him, George added a valet to the entourage. Often dubbed "The Human Orchid," he had golden bobby pins that he'd toss to the eager crowd. His valet would spray perfumed disinfectant in the ring and on the referee's hands. Then the valet would hold a mirror before George so the star could make sure his hair was just so before the bell rang. By any standard, it was a scene to remember!

Having perfected what he did as a wrestler, George was the first bad guy who played the coward, cheating and running. Not a big man, George looked and acted like a snotty male diva who really deserved a butt-kicking. Fans hooted and hollered in dismay, but they all struggled to grab one of those bobby pins. Oh, and the most important point — Gorgeous George drew money. Lots of it. Even the more traditional hard-nose competitors like Lou Thesz understood what George Wagner was doing, and they all enjoyed working with him.

The entire gimmick came together in the 1940s, ready for the spotlight when that invention television changed the world. Since George was still excellent to work with, everyone was happy to jump on the gravy train and help keep this most intriguing character a star. It wasn't just his appearance and conduct in the ring — George could also talk. Whether it was on radio or television, George talked the talk like it had never been done before. He made bragging an art form, and entertaining to boot.

All in all, it was everything Vince McMahon does today with more bells and whistles at his disposal. Dame Fortune deserves a nod, for Wagner was the right guy in the right place at the right time. He absolutely thrived on being Gorgeous George. Whether it is entry, appearance, or work philosophy, many different threads today lead back to what Gorgeous George did.

Wagner's roots were in amateur wrestling and working the carnival promotions, taking on all comers. Morris Sigel, a highly respected promoter in Houston, began using Wagner around 1937. George was respected and got bookings, but the lucrative main events were not on his agenda until, with the help of his wife-to-be Betty, the personality of Gorgeous George began to emerge. Betty's mother actually sewed some of his colorful early capes.

When it all came together on the magic box, George became one of television's biggest stars. Talk about being larger-than-life and part of pop culture. George was all that and more, delivered right into America's living rooms. Along with Bob Hope, Lucille Ball, and Milton Berle, he was one of the biggest stars in the country. Hope, in particular, was a huge fan of George. So was the famed stripper Gypsy Rose Lee.

In the end, though, it all came back to that little squared circle under the lights. Night after night, he headlined bills and brought in houses. Often overlooked in the glare of his fame, George won several regional honors and even briefly one version, Boston-style, of the world championship when he downed Don Eagle in 1950. He could also claim a triumph over talented Enrique Torres to grab the Los Angeles crown in 1947.

More often than not, though, George lost the big main events. Not that it mattered in the long run, because his persona allowed him to keep his heat, something bookers have always strived to do for lesser heels. Beating someone up after a loss has nothing to do with keeping heat. It's all about the context around big matches and, perhaps most important, about the personality of the villain getting whipped. After the initial years of notoriety, George was often in a prime position on the card to add a different taste to a more serious feature.

Somehow when George lost, it was never quite enough and the folks always wanted more.

As his career wound down, Gorgeous George had one of his most noted duels squaring off with "Whipper" Billy Watson in Toronto's historic Maple Leaf Gardens on March 12, 1959. They had been involved in a long-running feud, with Watson always getting the upper hand but never quite satisfied.

But this showdown was the "more." Hair versus hair, the dignified Canadian hero Watson against the resplendent and arrogant George. When it was over, George was defeated. Photos of Watson shaving off George's golden locks hit the wire services and were published everywhere by the mainstream media.

By then, years of punishing wrestling and serious alcohol abuse, plus financial setbacks, were taking a toll. His final bout again risked his hair against the mask of The Destroyer (Dick Beyer) in Los Angeles on November 7, 1962, and he left the ring bald. Gorgeous George was dead only 13 months later in 1963.

But what a ride.

Muhammad Ali always gave credit to George for both content and advice on how to get and keep attention. Although Ali also had contact with another great heat magnet in Fred Blassie and may have borrowed some of Blassie's chatter, it was George who seemed to have the most effect on the boxing great's self-promotion.

Soul singer James Brown openly admitted that he copied many of George's histrionics in developing his own stage performance. Think of George with his cape, and then consider what James Brown did. Even Bob Dylan, a totally different type of singer than Brown, talked about the influence of Gorgeous George.

Is it any surprise how deep the current runs for Gorgeous George in pro wrestling? Youngsters today often try out what they think is a new idea without even realizing that George already did it. It's in their heads that bleaching hair or acting the chicken heel is effective.

Yes, Buddy Rogers had influence. So did Thesz. So did other stars. But when it's all added together, nobody ever delivered quite the earthquake to professional wrestling that Gorgeous George did.

#36 THE UNDERTAKER

Mark Calaway injected soul into a gimmick

Injecting a soul into a gimmick character might be the most difficult thing to do in modern pro wrestling. Mark Calaway has done it with The Undertaker, incorporating portions of old and new school. Calaway's personality and talents have made The Undertaker a historic figure who gets a home with the top 50 greatest pro wrestlers of all time.

The wrong person portraying The Undertaker would have turned what is now an intimidating, powerful character into just another cartoon caricature. WWE has been plagued by many of them. Calaway, though, had a passion that overwhelmed and took control of what otherwise might have been a comic book fiasco rejected by the general audience for being too over the top.

Actually, The Undertaker has survived a number of over-the-top gimmicks plenty of times, but Calaway's portrayal is always wrapped around his solid physical work. He's been sealed in a casket, betrayed by manager Paul Bearer, and buried alive; he's from a dysfunctional "family" with "brother" Kane in a storyline far too bizarre to go into; he's disappeared from a locked casket that was set on fire, "embalmed" foes and played with druids; he became a motorcycle ruffian nicknamed "The American Bad Ass"; he was once more buried and proclaimed "dead forever," only to make a triumphant return as an almost-supernatural monster; he got carted out by druids when knocked unconscious, found hell in a cell regularly, and amazingly enough even got badly burned for real when pyrotechnics malfunctioned. And that's just a brief overview of the drama.

Got all that? "Strangler" Lewis he isn't! Of course, some of the swerves and double-crosses in the 1920s and 1930s read pretty screwy too, without the science-fiction twists. Lewis worked with the hand he was dealt, exactly as Calaway did more than 60 years later. And Calaway claimed a special niche just the way Lewis had.

Consider what follows as the main reasons for Calaway's success: Shawn Michaels, Triple H, Stone Cold, Ric Flair, John Cena, Randy Orton, Hulk Hogan, Randy Savage, Kurt Angle, Superfly Snuka, Ultimate Warrior, Jake the Snake, Diesel (Kevin Nash), Mick Foley as Mankind, Edge, Mark Henry, Batista, Big Show, Brock Lesnar, and dozens more. Every WWF/WWE stalwart locked horns with The Undertaker for some reason.

The Undertaker clashed with them all. Heel or babyface, he's been both numerous times. For some 22 years, The Undertaker has been bread and butter, the glue for WWF/WWE booking geniuses. Regardless of how ridiculous some of the plots were, Mark Calaway redeemed it all by generating good to great matches against a massive variety of opponents. What made The Undertaker more than campy, more than surreal, was the truth that Calaway could engineer a tough, exciting, smart match when the chips were down.

Isn't that the mark of someone who deserves to be part of the greatest 50 pro wrestlers in history? Not number two, as WWE would trumpet, but certainly somewhere fitting for a rare talent who has risked life and limb to excite a hungry audience. Just like "Strangler" Lewis in his own way and time did.

Calaway's size alone would have made promoters of any era rub their hands in anticipation. At least 6'8", coming in around 300 pounds at his peak, Calaway had been a high school basketball star, which

perhaps informed his agility in a wrestling ring. His athleticism and competitiveness would have always made him more than just a novelty attraction with a short shelf life.

Born in Houston, Calaway grew up on the quality wrestling product of promoter Paul Boesch. He broke into the business in 1984, stepping into the ring for Fritz Von Erich's World Class Championship Wrestling. Legend has it that in his first bout he received a thumping from Bruiser Brody. Certainly something stuck about Brody — look at the way The Undertaker did no-sells during squashes against lesser foes, not to mention starting comebacks against anyone by abruptly sitting up from the mat. At one point in the WWF, he zipped up battered rivals in body bags. Calaway would surely have seen television bouts in San Antonio, in which Brody had an ambulance on hand to take out those he had vanquished.

I remember Brody telling me, after using the rookie in a mask as Red River Jack for a role Brody was actually playing, that Calaway was "a big kid. Aggressive. He's starting to get it. I think he'll be okay." Good scouting, huh?

After a couple of years getting his feet wet in Texas, Calaway bounced through Jerry Lawler's struggling Memphis operation before landing in WCW, the Turner-owned company that had its own learning curve to face, in 1989. Even though he got a decent push at times, somebody missed the boat and decided not to renew Calaway's contract. And Calaway clearly had the requirements for wrestling in that day.

Calaway made his debut as "Cain the Undertaker" for Vince McMahon on November 19, 1990. The name Cain was gone fast, but The Undertaker would be on top for years to come. In a way, fate was kind to Calaway because he was still learning the business, figuring out what did and didn't work for him. Actually, he and The Undertaker grew together. Calaway never had to try on three or four different public personalities until something clicked.

He became The Undertaker, and The Undertaker became him. Calaway excelled at using the tools he had, whether they were spooky promo scripts or special effects and fireworks. It might be a shame the audience couldn't discover more of Calaway's true personality, but why fool with a winning equation?

In the ring, parts of his game matured. Naturally, Calaway had to work within the parameters of The Undertaker persona. With a growing interest in mixed martial arts and the Ultimate Fighting Championship, Calaway modeled the way he punched and some of his moves on the MMA style in order to toughen up even more of his work. Some of the cartoon action and the crowd manipulation stuck, but there was plenty of hard-nosed action too. The Undertaker became much more than just the gimmick over the years. He was one tough, mean dude.

It helped that Calaway gained a large measure of influence with VKM. It seems Vince felt that Calaway understood this Frankenstein role as well as Vince himself did. Calaway became one of the honored few whose suggestions about matches and angles were listened to. Apparently he hasn't been shy about flexing his muscle when he believed in a direction. By all accounts, The Undertaker is also a strong presence, highly respected by other wrestlers, in the dressing room.

To obtain this esteemed position, Calaway paid a hefty physical price. He made bundles of money along the way but left pieces of his body scattered behind him. Injuries and surgeries have been plentiful, especially in these later years. The damage has taken a toll, just as age and combat have always done on even the finest performers, for this is a torturous profession in any era. Those who've been through it salute those before or after. For instance, when Nick Bockwinkel heard criticism of some WWE bouts, he responded by saying, "Vince must be doing something right for the guys to take the chances of getting hurt that they do. Look at Undertaker! What an athlete . . . a 300-pound man running across the ring and leaping head first over the top rope to crash into something or someone."

It was The Undertaker who stood out as an example. Dory Funk Jr. praised Calaway: "He has really become a master of 'less is more.' He has established what works, so when he takes those big, dangerous bumps at the right time, they mean something. His psychology is great."

Nonetheless, all that punishment adds up, and The Undertaker has cut back on his schedule in the past few years to concentrate on his appearances as a magnetic television personality who works only the biggest match. The Undertaker has kept his *WrestleMania* winning streak alive with what have possibly been the three most memorable matches of his career.

In 2010, The Undertaker whipped Shawn Michaels. In 2011, he downed Triple H and then was carried out of the ring on a stretcher, likely a symbolic touch. What irony that as their bodies wear out, every great star understands better than ever how to produce a fabulous match.

The point was reemphasized emphatically in 2012 at *WrestleMania*, as once again Undertaker and Triple H squared off. A grueling, vicious donnybrook, the match was won in dramatic fashion by The Undertaker, the culmination of a war built on violence and well-known finishing moves. The work actually was old school. It is fresh in the minds of fans and more critical observers, so naturally they rate it as maybe the most brutal brawl ever.

Whatever — it was a dandy, especially considering it was the ONLY outing for The Undertaker in an entire year. That, however, is the way professional wrestling operates today. Because The Undertaker has become such an icon, he can pump up a buy rate in the right situation at the right time. And he, along with Triple H and Shawn Michaels as a special referee, were smart enough to use the attributes they still had to make it work.

Does that mean he should land higher in this superstar-spangled list of the best ever? Sit back, relax, let time calm everyone's emotions, and then judge all of the talent and all of the fabulous matches. It's a tribute to what Calaway did, with what could have turned into a cartoon gimmick, to score as well as he has.

Somewhere in this character was a competitor that diehard followers and casual fans alike have come to recognize as a performer who provides unique thrills. Yes, The Undertaker was a tremendous gimmick, a brilliant idea. But without Mark Calaway, The Undertaker might have been a gaudy but empty shell.

With Mark Calaway at the controls, The Undertaker takes hold of his rightful placement among the 50 greatest pro wrestlers ever.

#35 BOB BACKLUND
Did exactly what was needed with style

Here is the truth. Bob Backlund belongs on the roster of the 50 greatest professional wrestlers of all time. He was an amazing athlete, stayed in incredible condition and was a superb fundamental wrestler. He had a most impressive tenure holding *the* major championship of the biggest territory of the day. He was an excellent drawing card. He met and was equal to every major name of his time. He was a good worker who could elevate lesser talents than his. He was in public much as he was in private, a down-to-earth good guy.

For all that, Backlund is probably plagued by more acid-tongued critics than any other superstar, with the possible exception of Bruiser Brody. Unfortunately, what is likely a small percentage of haters have loud voices and, particularly with the Internet, a forum on which they can yell. Check the facts, not the complaints to assess Bob Backlund.

And remember — the large majority of fans loved him.

Backlund was the last of the classic babyfaces. Well, so what? Ever hear of Ricky Steamboat? Some scoffed at Backlund's comebacks, yet 90 percent or more of the audience stood and screamed when Backlund exacted revenge on a heel. He had a different style, more wrestling and less brawling. Variety is the spice of life, and of pro wrestling. The style he used was simple. Have these critics watched any of Hulk's matches?

Backlund's interviews were vanilla. Why, because he talked like a professional athlete with a college background? When he got angry, his talking sounded forced and uncomfortable, or he made unnatural facial expressions when making a heated comeback in the ring. His was likely a style forced upon him by someone else in power. His personality was not put together that way, which may have rubbed those who felt "he didn't fit in" the wrong way. Reminds me of high school cliques.

The guy he followed as champion, "Superstar" Graham, was more flamboyant and bizarre. Perhaps it was just that Backlund was far more technically sound and didn't need to disguise what he did in the ring with glitz. When he came back to the WWF years later, Backlund played a goofy professor, a political type. Is it really necessary to bring up all the solid professionals (including Dusty Rhodes dressed in a silly bumblebee outfit and Dory Funk Jr. with a goofy cowboy hat and billed as "Hoss" Funk) who were thrust into ridiculous cartoon roles by a company whose philosophy favored sizzle over steak?

Backlund didn't really draw the money; someone else did. After studying all the available information about pro wrestling and entertainment, isn't it clear that the main event, the featured performer(s), draws the money? Let's follow up on that last complaint about Backlund, since it is certainly a prominent gripe and easy to disprove.

Business was good for the WWWF when Backlund upended Graham on February 20, 1978, in New York. Backlund headlined show after show before capacity (or close) audiences all over the Northeast. From my days in Sam Muchnick's office, hearing the telephone chats between Sam and Vince McMahon Sr., I can personally guarantee Senior was very pleased about the revenue flow.

Those who snipe at Backlund conveniently forget that, almost unanimously, fans liked how his quick style energized a product that had moved slower with titleholders like Graham, Pedro Morales, and Bruno

Bob Backlund sends Ric Flair flying

Sammartino. Those champions were often pitted against other powerful, more ponderous opponents. Backlund opened the door occasionally to a different kind of challenger and a different sort of combat that involved less strength, punching, and kicking but more maneuvers, motion, and bumping.

Nothing is wrong with either method; both have been proven effective time and again under the correct promotion. These different styles can even fit together well for the right practitioner. Backlund also brought a different personality on board. Vince McMahon Sr. wanted an all-American boy to follow the counter-culture, over-the-top outlaw that Graham portrayed so well (maybe because to some degree that persona reflected reality). Remember too that Sammartino in his long service at the top had evolved from the young powerhouse sensation to the respected statesman who had paid more than his dues while honorably defending the title.

Consider this progression to what had happened with the NWA. The comparisons aren't direct, but the situations are similar. Buddy Rogers was in some ways a Graham type in how he appeared and performed. Lou Thesz and Gene Kiniski had been through the wars and earned their positions, as had Bruno.

In the NWA, along came Dory Funk Jr., the skilled new star who had some vulnerability due to his youth. And Dory was a red-hot commodity as champion. In the WWWF, the talented, fresh fireball who was at some risk because of his youth was Bob Backlund. And Backlund was a success as champion.

Some of the haters whined that at one point the big crowds that came to see Backlund were really drawn by undercards featuring Pat Patterson versus Sgt. Slaughter. Of course, Backlund had been packing them in quite nicely for a long time without Patterson and Slaughter. Research should probably be done on how cards not topped by the champion drew.

The most laughable complaint is that cards led by Backlund were loaded top to bottom. The same thing happened for Graham and Bruno, Funk and Thesz. Perhaps a check of *WrestleMania* lineups would be in order here. To turn a profit, the promoter always wants the best card possible. In St. Louis, title cards at Kiel Auditorium were generally packed. If we moved to the Checkerdome, which held 8,000 more seats than Kiel did, the lineups always added a couple more big names and extra angles. That happened everywhere in pro wrestling! It was and is common practice to deliver the largest payday, especially in the biggest buildings or for major pay-per-views.

Big-name talent liked to be added to title cards in every alliance and promotion. They all knew this type of show was most likely to get the strongest gate receipts, which meant *everyone made more money*. This is a business, and the goal is to put money in the bank. Backlund was hardly the only titleholder who had strong support beneath him.

All this for a kid from Minnesota who had a gift and love for wrestling. He wrestled and played football at Waldorf Junior College in Iowa and earned all-American honors on the mat. Moving to North Dakota State, he captured the Division II NCAA title at 190 pounds in 1971, and he finished fifth in the heavyweight class in 1972. By then the bug had bitten. Backlund was training with Eddie Sharkey in Minnesota, a well-known trainer and something of a rival to Verne Gagne. In fact, Backlund made his debut for Gagne and the AWA, immediately clicking thanks to his fresh looks and sharp technique.

From there, Backlund got important work with the Funks out of Amarillo, Texas. He did a quick stint in Georgia and then went on to Florida, where he caught the eyes of Harley Race and promoter Eddie Graham, both of whom told Sam Muchnick that this was a kid who could go places. Sam looked at tapes of Backlund in action and heartily agreed.

The St. Louis debut came for Backlund in 1976, and he was quickly in feature bouts with the likes of Race, Gene Kiniski, Jack Brisco, and eventually Terry Funk, the NWA titleholder at the time. Bob also crossed paths with none other than "Superstar" Graham in a tag elimination bout.

And fate was getting ready to change Backlund's career. For years, Vince Sr. and Sam had been in regular contact. I had just met both Vince Jr. and his right-hand man Howard Finkel at the time Senior was moving the WWWF title to Graham. He understood that Superstar's style might have a short shelf line in comparison to someone like Sammartino. After the success Sam had had in St. Louis with young all-Americans, Senior was thinking that type might be the logical successor to someone like Superstar. When Vince asked Sam about prospects for the role, Muchnick suggested Backlund, someone relatively new on the national level and therefore unscathed for those into looking at records. Backlund's earnest, serious approach to his work and interviews appealed to Senior just as it had to Muchnick. So Backlund won the WWWF crown from Superstar.

During his lengthy stint as champ, Backlund, more than any other kingpin, had several title versus title confrontations as he faced Race and also AWA king Nick Bockwinkel. Bob even had a showdown with Ric Flair after Flair got the NWA hardware. While history treats those collisions as big deals, the truth is most every fan, rabid or casual, understood that no championships were going to change hands. Nonetheless, all were excellent displays of talent at the top of their games. Backlund more than held his own, which is also a credit toward being in the finest 50 ever.

The list of those Backlund dispatched is, not surprisingly, overflowing with the big names of the time. Particularly thrilling were matches with Superfly Snuka, Greg Valentine, Bob Orton Jr., Sgt. Slaughter, Ray Stevens, Hulk himself when Hogan was a heel, Ken Patera, and even Antonio Inoki.

All champions lose some appeal after a long time on top, but from what I saw of Backlund in the fall of 1982, he still had some distance to go. I was on hand for a 30-minute struggle between Backlund and Bob Orton at Madison Square Garden, and the near-capacity crowd hung on every move, bump, and false finish. Maybe some fans were calling Backlund "Howdy Doody," based on an interview by the Grand Wizard, but I certainly heard nowhere near the jeers and boos that John Cena gets today. Clearly, the Backlund-Orton bout was the one the audience wanted to see most on that show.

Afterward, both Backlund and Orton were celebrating how well it went. Both were pleased that in almost a half hour of work, only *two* punches had been thrown. They brought the fans to a psychological climax with fast-moving action, established Orton as a strong heel, and made Backlund's victory meaningful. It was a great example of a certain kind of work that apparently VKM wasn't excited about when the business changed hands. VKM, a big fan of Superstar, wanted a new look and a new direction.

Granted, Hulk was the right personality to headline an all-out assault for national dominance, especially with a wrestling promotion that had a different concept of how to please the people. Backlund was pushed aside, and though he made a couple of rather bizarre returns to the WWF, he now never gets the respect he deserves for doing exactly what was asked of him at a certain place and time.

Was he perfect? Is any pro wrestler perfect? Backlund emphatically had all the talent and credentials to guarantee himself a spot in the industry's highest echelon. While he didn't do the 20 or 25 years as a main event guy like a Gene Kiniski, a Race, a Sammartino, or a Thesz, some of that is accounted for by the change in tastes that was actually inspired by the company for which Backlund excelled. Make a comparison between Backlund and Cena.

But Backlund was a huge contributor at a time when pro wrestling was on the cusp of a monumental upheaval. He performed excellently and has legitimately earned a place among the all-time greats.

#34 DANNY HODGE

A hidden gem who could whip anyone

Danny Hodge sits in a place of prominence among the 50 greatest pro wrestlers in history. He deserves the recognition because, in truth, he probably could have beaten most if not all of those at the table with him. He represents a certain group of performers who fail to get the respect that their unique talents demand.

Those who never saw Hodge in action need to understand that he did not offer a boring takedown, escape-and-roll-around amateur-style event. He tailored the crisp amateur moves he had learned to the pro game. Everything was jazzed up a little. Yes, he gave and received flying tackles, something that once prompted Johnny Valentine disdainfully to ask, "Did you ever see someone bounce off the ropes in a real fight?" Hodge, the master wrestler, could do it so forcefully that no fan had that thought in mind.

What Hodge did was make the basic maneuver look more exciting while still retaining the realistic edge. Let's face it. Certain pro wrestling moves clearly cannot be done without the cooperation and assistance of the opponent. This is more true now than ever before with pro action as it is in WWE and TNA, especially with the heavy reliance on stunt bumping. Hodge could fit the puzzle together smoothly and make the crowd perk up for what at its base was a wrestling move. He was as quick as lightning and understood how to sell and drive a match to climax.

The goods were always there, starting with an undefeated high school career in Perry, Oklahoma. At the University of Oklahoma, Hodge was also undefeated, going 46–0 with 36 pins. He became one of only two three-time NCAA Division I champions, along with Earl McCready, who had become a pro star in the 1930s. Never once in three years of competition (freshmen were ineligible at the time) was Hodge taken down from a standing position. Hodge competed twice in the Olympics, grabbing fifth in 1952 and winning a silver medal in 1956. He was so dominant that the Dan Hodge Trophy was later initiated, honoring the best collegiate grappler every season.

On April 1, 1957, Hodge became the first wrestler ever to be featured on the cover of *Sports Illustrated*. But he apparently had a little extra time on his hands, so Hodge went into boxing and won both the national Golden Gloves and AAU boxing championships. Nobody had ever won a national title in both boxing and wrestling until Hodge came along.

After a brief flirtation with pro boxing (he was hyped as a better prospect than Rocky Marciano but was paid pennies), Hodge was immediately swept into pro wrestling, trained by Tulsa promoter Leroy McGuirk, himself a great amateur star, and "Strangler" Lewis. After a debut late in 1959, Hodge became the NWA Junior Heavyweight Champion by whipping Angelo Savoldi on July 22, 1960, in Oklahoma City.

The title, which the NWA left up to McGuirk to handle, became Hodge's personal property for most of the next 16 years. The territory was primarily composed of small towns, but Hodge was a terrific drawing card and became one of the sport's top earners. He also became an idol for Oklahoma youngsters Jack Brisco and Jim Ross, an announcer who became world famous calling television matches for WWE among others. On March 15, 1976, Hodge was in a terrible car accident and suffered a broken neck, which led to his retirement from wrestling. Medical

accounts said the wreck would have killed him had Hodge not been such an amazing physical specimen. His legacy, however, was firmly established.

Here was this slender, wiry little guy who apparently had steel cables running through his body. His grip, which could squash an apple, was legendary. More than one big guy, especially as newcomers to wrestling, made the mistake of trying to push Hodge around, ending up with their elbows shoved into their own mouths. A young Frank Goodish, who would become Bruiser Brody, broke in around the Mid-South. He was in a match against Hodge and couldn't understand why he was the one doing the job. Goodish, raised in Detroit and mainly a baseball and football fan, didn't know who Hodge was and roughed him up.

Jim Ross, who saw the incident, maintained that the way Hodge physically tied Goodish into a knot was almost gentle and made Frank understand what a real wrestler — a shooter — could do. Years later, Brody told me, "Hell, I barely knew what a headlock was then. As soon as Hodge grabbed me, I knew I was in deep trouble!"

Lou Thesz once called Hodge a freak, meaning it as a compliment of the highest order, because Dan was so talented on the mat. Dick Murdoch, another tough guy, recalled being made to beg for his mother when Hodge got hold of him. John Molinaro wrote that Hodge "instilled the fear of God in everyone around him."

While Hodge usually clashed with other junior heavyweights, he also took on his share of the heavyweights and more than held his own. At his so-called weight limit (the barrier seemed to vary a lot), he had some incredible battles with Hiru Matsuda. His match against Bobo Brazil inspired a chuckle, as the two hardly seem complementary. Hodge loved facing Mad Dog Vachon, a tough nut and terrific villain who had a fine amateur background.

When Hodge made a few bookings in St. Louis late in 1973, I found him an affable and fascinating personality. Kidding around in the office with Hodge and "Wild Bill" Longson was a learning experience, as was watching him break a pair of pliers in his bare hand. His bouts had a different look, but the crowd responded eagerly. Hodge was used in the middle of the lineup, getting victories over solid journeymen.

I asked Sam Muchnick about the possibility of building Hodge to a duel with Jack Brisco, who was a serious admirer of Hodge's and who then held the NWA heavyweight title. This was nearing the end of the famous series between Brisco and Dory Funk Jr., so I figured fans would buy into another serious, intense scientific test. I also recognized that Brisco versus Hodge might not be so hot in other markets. St. Louis was educated and appreciative of the more serious side of pro wrestling, even while loving the wide-open, spectacular stuff.

Muchnick, though, said no and, as usual, had a pragmatic reason why. He asked who, if anyone, would benefit from a showdown between the heavyweight and the junior heavyweight kings.

If Brisco won, the perception would be that lighter guys could not go with bigger men.

If Hodge won, aside from all the political in-fighting among NWA members to move the title, it would hurt Brisco personally since he would look as though he could not handle the smaller foe. Also, it would do some damage to the entire heavyweight side, especially if Hodge earned a crack at Brisco by beating one or two other leading big men.

Going to a draw, while undoubtedly exciting to watch, would lead nowhere because there could not be an eventual resolution in a rematch. It would be what most folks expected and therefore probably wouldn't draw well. In the end, of course, drawing money had to be the primary purpose.

For all concerned, it was best that Hodge stay within the junior heavyweight ranks, with only an occasional foray elsewhere to display how good he was. Take advantage of Hodge's credentials to get a few newspaper or television features. Let the media and the general public see that pro wrestling had a star athlete with legitimate credentials. In 1973, lighter weights didn't draw in major markets, even if Hodge was so good that in the correct position he might have been the exception.

Sam thought it would be good for the business if the junior heavyweight ranks could add more talent capable of drawing crowds, but he pointed out that finding new blood was always a problem at all levels. If Muchnick only knew what it would be like in 2012, with mixed martial arts siphoning off so many potentially good performers!

Therefore, Dan Hodge maintained a hidden-gem quality, like a cult rock star that all the insiders know is fabulous. And everyone in pro wrestling knew that Hodge was the real deal.

For pure wrestling ability, only a select few in the annals of the sport can compare to Hodge. Unfortunately for him, Hodge's time at his peak was when the primary attention in large markets was on the bigger competitors. Nonetheless, his presence and exulted cult status in the industry is historically meaningful. Danny Hodge has earned his due as one of the greatest ever to lace up the boots.

#33 KURT ANGLE

Had all the tools in every form of the game

Had this exercise been more strictly formatted to the 50 greatest *wrestlers* of all time, the final lineup might have looked somewhat different. If the concentration had been on who could best execute the takedowns, the escapes, the pins, and the submissions, some names would have risen to the top while others would have tumbled downward.

Professional wrestling, however, asks more of its participants, and especially from its most famous stars. It's a mixture of different ingredients, although the ability to just plain wrestle can be a big help. What Kurt Angle did as a collegiate and Olympic competitor most assuredly added a special element for someone who had a surprising aptitude for the business.

Kurt Angle has done some great things for pro wrestling, some awesome accomplishments in both daredevil moves and mind-blowing matches. Yet that little suspicion won't go away: with all his attributes, for all he achieved, there could have been more.

Of course, the likes of Lou Thesz, "Strangler" Lewis, Joe Stecher, and a couple other earlier gladiators did not have the opportunities to go to

George Napolitano

college to train and compete at the level Angle did. They still became fantastic wrestlers, perhaps more skilled than Angle in the area of hurting someone due to their hard-scrabble backgrounds.

Make no mistake, though, that Angle could really go when going was required. Once again, the different demands of different eras make it interesting to wonder what Thesz or Lewis would have done with the opportunity for extensive training and competition at the amateur level. Likewise, how would Angle, Dan Hodge, and Jack Brisco have developed if they'd come up in the less structured but brutally competitive gym scene like Thesz did? No matter the answer, Angle is and was the real deal. Somehow, though, looking at the potential, we wanted a little more.

As outstanding as Angle has been in the pro game, he could have been better. That is mainly the fault of injuries and, most recently, an inept promotion. But at the start, those basics Angle had mastered paved the way for one of the smoothest transitions into the play-for-pay ranks ever. He does have some competition from the likes of Verne Gagne, Jack Brisco, and, of course, Dan Hodge.

Angle twice captured the national collegiate title while at Clarion University, which added to his triumphs in the junior nationals and the amateur world championship. He put a giant cherry on the sundae of his amateur career when he won the gold medal in freestyle heavyweight wrestling in the 1996 Olympics. That achievement was even more eye-catching because Angle had a broken neck — literally — with two cervical vertebrae fractured and two discs herniated.

Apparently, Angle was hesitant about pro wrestling before joining what was then the World Wrestling Federation in 1998. After a brief apprenticeship in the WWF Memphis training facility, Angle stepped onto the big stage.

It was obvious from day one. Even though he'd never been a fan of pro wrestling, Kurt Angle was completely natural. The moves, the instincts, the expressions, the intensity — everything was there in the perfect package for pro wrestling at the beginning of the twenty-first century.

He quickly and surprisingly was scripted into being a heel, using the character of a great American hero to be arrogant. Perhaps some perverse booking psychology of Vince McMahon's was at play there. Some of the angles he was dumped in were ridiculous (the three-way love affair with Triple H and Stephanie McMahon), but the superb in-ring battles Angle had with the likes of Triple H saved the day. Angle was so doggone good in action and comfortable in front of a camera that he could have portrayed any character effectively.

Almost overnight, Angle became a key player for the WWF's major pay-per-views. In the ring, he always delivered. At one point I was talking with Jack Brisco, who told me of all the talent pushed to the top in that period, the person he would have wanted to work with most was Kurt Angle. "Two amateur champions, combining the mat stuff at the level we'd be along with the babyface-heel fireworks — we'd have brought down the house anywhere," Brisco guaranteed.

Sam Muchnick dearly loved a spectacular athlete with legitimate credentials, and I knew without question that in another time Kurt Angle would have gotten a *huge* push in both St. Louis and the entire National Wrestling Alliance. A potential NWA kingpin? Believe it.

But life wasn't simple in the pro ranks, as nerve and spinal injuries took their toll on Angle. So did the attendant addictions, which led to some scary and erratic behavior. Still, Angle was there for standout battles with The Undertaker, Steve Austin, Brock Lesnar, Edge, and most every pushed name the WWE had. Even when the booking (not just involving Angle) brought some criticism from the real world, Angle's matches were so outstanding that many casual fans forgave the promotion just for the opportunity to watch Angle perform.

The marriage of Angle and WWE ended in 2006 with not-unexpected controversy. From Angle's point of view, he'd worked hurt most of the time and the schedule made the situation unbearable. From the WWE position, the company feared for his well-being so they released him from his contract. That's a short explanation of a much deeper dispute, but eventually Angle was a free agent, though a damaged one.

After a couple of much-heralded trips to Japan (including another highly anticipated battle with Lesnar, which Angle won), Angle signed a deal with Total Nonstop Action, which had a home on Spike TV. It looked like, and in many ways it has been, a good home for Angle, providing him with an easier schedule and more say in the direction of his career.

It should have been a game changer for TNA, but instead that promotion blew it. With Angle as the hot, lead personality, TNA had a chance to boost ratings, increase pay-per-view rates, and lure in that elusive casual audience. The booking of Angle should have been so simple, so easy, so direct, but none of the geniuses in charge could see that, much less build the outline to execute it.

TNA completely missed the boat on what should have been a long-running and profitable rivalry between Angle and Samoa Joe, who was new and getting over at the time. Instead, the booking rushed in, did what should have been the blow-off too early, and never got full value.

After a couple brief jumps in both ratings and buys, some further muddled and incomprehensible booking pulled Angle down into the crew rather than using Angle as the instrument to bring up the action and the storytelling. He sank to their level (ask any viewer about TNA booking at that time), rather than being allowed to raise the bar for the plotting.

Angle, after more domestic turmoil, legal problems, injury, and the simple drain of getting older, is still a key player, the one who might pull ratings or add a few buys in the right circumstances. When his marriage broke down, the controversy and resulting divorce was turned into an angle — no pun intended — that put Kurt into repeated confrontations with Jeff Jarrett. Good opponent, good matches, but not at the lofty level at which Angle once performed.

Unfortunately, between slipping a notch or two himself and being in a stumbling promotion, Angle may no longer be able to hit that grand slam home run when it comes to competing in a five-star match or drawing the big crowd. He picks his spots better, and he can still take a giant risk that makes everyone gasp. But at what cost? And for what gain?

Nonetheless, he has proven that he deserves a spot among the pro wrestling gods. It just leaves that little hint of disappointment; if fate had worked more in his favor, maybe his professional efforts would have generated the excellent results his amateur career did. And wouldn't that have been something?

Regardless, no matter the form, whether in structured wrestling or its much more liberal professional cousin, Kurt Angle is deserving of his status as one of the greatest ever.

#32 BRUISER BRODY
Wrestling's true rebel

Any wrestling follower has heard the name Brody. Whether it is Bruiser Brody or "King Kong" Brody, the name *Brody* has a connection to a legendary, perhaps epic, character with a unique spot in the history of the business. Students of the game may grasp parts of Brody's saga, some surprisingly accurate, some muddled with mystery, some flat-out wrong.

But it is that enigma, combined with what Bruiser Brody did to earn recognition, that places him among the 50 greatest pro wrestlers ever.

The ironic part for me is that when Dave Meltzer originally contacted me to complain about the WWE version of the best of all time, and I began to think about who should or should not be included, I told Dave, "There are so many terrific pieces of talent, I don't know if my ole friend Brody will make it." I was serious, not trying to look unprejudiced by eliminating a friend I'd worked with. There really were so many stars to consider in over a century of wrestling. Was he that good or was it me rewarding our friendship?

My wife, Pat, heard the chatter and jumped on me. "He was great," she admonished. "How can you doubt that he belongs in the 50 best?"

To Dave's credit, he chuckled and said, "Well, see how it works out before you decide." Of course, then came conversations with Michael Holmes at ECW Press, the book concept was born, and I really *did* have to start evaluating a lot of tremendous names and finally make a decision.

Yeah, Brody makes it. Safely. Objectively. What was I thinking?

When Vince McMahon and Hulk Hogan upended the wrestling business from 1984 onward, Brody was the rebel, the independent who picked up every remaining television wrestling show that he could in order to keep his controversial name alive. He drew big money across the board, operating on a different plane from Vince. Brody was the grass-roots politician going door-to-door, and anyone who followed the business at that time knew the one dream match that would pack any joint was Hulk versus Brody. But it never happened.

In Texas for the World Class promotion, Brody could lure the bucks in for brutal, bloody donnybrooks with Abdullah the Butcher. He and Abby bounced through many smaller towns and always sold out or came close. In the AWA, Brody was responsible for the company's last big house at the Metrodome in Minneapolis, where he elevated John Nord for a tag-team collision against Jimmy Snuka and Greg Gagne. The cliquish AWA dressing room was leery of Brody, but they accepted the payoff that day. He kept Kansas City on life support for an extra year or so, able to steal a house for them when even the mediocre crowds had pretty much said goodbye.

The man was making money without selling his soul to a corporation, as many viewed the WWF in those days. He'd grab independent dates for fat guarantees on sold shows in small towns (he and I worked together often, along with local promoter Herb Simmons, all over Missouri and Illinois), and the crowds turned out in droves to see national superstar Brody. Some of his trusted friends, like Crusher Blackwell or Killer Brooks, came along for the ride to fill their wallets. Youngsters who had dreams, most of which never came true, met and learned from him along the road. Mark Calaway was one such lucky kid. At Brody's idea, he imitated Brody by donning a mask as Red River Jack for an angle in Texas. Calaway became The Undertaker a few years later.

Bruiser Brody had carved out a singular identity in towns all over North America during earlier boom days in the mid 1970s to the early 1980s. And *carved* is the correct word, for Brody never hesitated to carve his own head when that was the right thing to do for business. Brody was hardcore before that became a promotional buzzword. He busted furniture and opponents with equal glee.

And he was very picky about when and for whom he did jobs. Brody knew winning and losing mattered, so to his mind it had to be done correctly. He'd do it for Sam Muchnick in St. Louis, for Vince Sr., for Baba, and probably for Fritz Von Erich in Texas when it made sense. That stubborn trait is also why the possibility of Hulk against Brody always floated around — Brody was unblemished and that was what Hogan would have needed in a monster heel at the time.

Of course, the real key to it all for Brody from a business standpoint was his lucrative business in Japan, usually for Giant Baba with All Japan but also briefly for Antonio Inoki with New Japan. Dory Jr. and Terry Funk were booking for Baba and lined up Brody to tour. One trip was it — Bruiser Brody was over like dynamite in Japan and quickly making big bucks from Baba.

Fans could see the danger in his eyes. His interviews were riveting. At 6'5" and tipping the scales around 300 pounds at his peak, Brody could launch a perfect drop kick and execute some eye-popping athletic moves. As he honed his skills, Brody could brawl, move, even wrestle a bit and — my, oh my, could he take over a television screen by talking when the camera was focused on him.

He first burst onto the national scene in 1976 as a challenger for WWWF kingpin Bruno Sammartino during Bruno's second title reign. Both Bruno and his promoter, Vince McMahon Sr., knew that this monster was going to be box-office gold. It was actually Vince Sr. who gave Frank Goodish the name Bruiser Brody. For a publicity picture, Senior also posed Brody next to a large poster showing the famous scene from the *King Kong* film where the monster climbs the Empire State Building. Brody's huge body and growling face next to the classic poster was the

Bruiser Brody about to dispatch one of Japan's greatest — the legendary Antonio Inoki.

inspiration for us in St. Louis to name him "King Kong" Brody. After all, St. Louis already had one Bruiser in Dick the Bruiser.

It didn't much matter which nickname got attached over time. Brody. Fans knew what it meant. And if he was new to a territory, Brody had the magical ability to get himself over as a character and drawing card in one or two television outings.

Of course, he was an independent. He was a rebel who marched to the beat of his own drummer.

Brody learned early that most promoters and bookers were not to be trusted, and he often bumped heads with those he had learned not to count on. Brody had some battles, though these were usually exaggerated in both number and intensity, with other wrestlers who made the mistake of not dealing honestly with him.

Most of the big guns knew, though, that Brody was great to work with and had a strict personal integrity. Some who complained about him actually wished they had the guts to be like him when it was time to stand up for themselves.

At certain moments, promoters hesitated to book him because of his stubborn reputation, especially if they'd already had a run-in with him. Please keep in mind that so much has been blown out of proportion over the years. Either way, though, reality set in. No matter who was trying to screw whom about either booking or money, Brody was someone who drew that money. Those who were a little shady bit their tongues and got dates on him. Some whose business was floundering because they actually weren't very good bookers or promoters needed help and got dates on him. Quite often Brody was the only big name who would risk a business relation with some of those promoters. Guaranteed pay was occasionally involved, sometimes after a bit of arm-twisting, which showed good sense on Brody's behalf.

What complicated the issue for those who wanted to tarnish Brody's reputation was how wonderfully he worked for Sam Muchnick in St. Louis, Fritz Von Erich in Texas, and Giant Baba in Japan. There was never a problem, although he did leave Baba to go with Inoki's rival operation before returning to Baba. Brody decided that Baba was the honest promoter, and he should not have been lured away by the promise of more money. And Baba was paying great money anyway.

Von Erich, who helped start Brody after his professional football dreams floundered, always considered Brody part of his family. Brody quickly became a mainstay along with David, Kerry, and Kevin Von Erich as the promotion caught fire around 1980.

Muchnick believed in finding out about talent for himself, not basing decisions on rumors and gossip. Brody and Sam quickly came to respect each other, much as Muchnick had with another crazy character named Dick the Bruiser more than a decade earlier. Brody packed in the fans for his duels with Ric Flair, Harley Race, and Andre the Giant in St. Louis.

Brody's philosophy was simple. If someone tried to fiddle around with his payoff or finish one time, not only would he never trust them again, he would go out of his way to double-cross them. No gray area. No second chance. I trust you, or I do not trust you.

He did have plenty of supporters who had learned they could rely on this explosive and eccentric personality when the chips were down. The Funks, Stan Hansen, Gary Hart, Buck Robley, Jimmy Snuka, and Big John Studd all knew that Brody fought the hardest fights of all behind closed doors and in the offices. They also knew the big man could deliver the goods in the ring. Flair has always raved about working with Brody, pointing to a spectacular one-hour draw with Brody in St. Louis on February 11, 1983, as one of the highlights of Flair's career.

In all of this discussion, often marred by inaccuracies or lies by his detractors, the fact that he had a wife and son to whom he was dedicated gets shunted aside. And so many forget how bright Brody was about the game, in particular because his viewpoint was not obscured by illusion.

Tragically, the final entry into Brody's legend is his death. He was murdered by wrestler/booker Jose Gonzales in a Puerto Rican dressing room in 1988. Like many of the other stories about Brody, this tale too has been twisted and tainted. Those who say he "had it coming" because of disputes about pay or finishes need a serious morality check. With that kind of thinking, how many employers would kill employees who disagreed with ownership? Is there any rationalization for murder? I think not.

Bruiser Brody stood up for himself, was the true rebel so many others falsely claimed to be, and provided some of the most wild, crazy, absolutely entertaining action of any figure who ever answered the bell.

So here is how it works out. Brody is firmly entrenched as one of the 50 greatest pro wrestlers of all time.

#31 JOHN CENA
Meets the challenge of twenty-first century wrestling

How about second guessing myself, because I certainly did when it came to placing John Cena in his rightful position. And the question originally was whether or not the rightful position is among the top 50 pro wrestlers of all time.

At first, my answer was "no." This is what I initially wrote for the chapter about why some of the high-ranked WWE representatives did not even deserve to be included on the roster of the greatest 50.

John Cena is the face of McMahon's WWE today, for Cena is a handsome, attractive, charismatic performer. He was a Division III all-American football lineman who went into bodybuilding before he started wrestling. When Cena was getting his feet wet on "indy" cards in California, he was billed as The Prototype.

Now he is indeed the prototype of the modern professional wrestler at the top of WWE's pyramid. Just the fact that he fought his way up from the bottom, that lightning did strike for him and he got the opportunity to perform for McMahon, makes Cena someone special. John Cena seized the moment. He does everything humanly possible for his employers, and he often goes the extra mile for charity endeavors. Without question, Cena is a public-relations dynamo.

Cena has headlined countless pay-per-view events, and while this promotion is mostly based on brand name, Cena on top has never hurt a buy rate. Has it helped? Hard to tell, as it depends on opponent and circumstances. He recites his scripted lines with vigor and a wink, even when the copy is truly inane. Cena's feeble yet cocky attempts at humor have done him no favors. The movies he's done for the company generally drew poorly outside the confines of the core wrestling audience — though his performances were fine. His television series work on the USA Network has been better received.

In the ring, Cena is also the prototype for what is called working today: signature moves, better timed by him than most of the newcomers. Plenty of so-so punching. Wrestling only when necessary. Bumps similar to everyone else. A patterned match that fits into the WWE concept. Once again, in the right spot against the right foes, able to build for a suitable climax. Improving psychology within the context of what WWE calls sports entertainment instead of wrestling. Excellent facial and body language. Intensity that is good, sometimes great.

Hardcore Internet fans hate him. The casual audience generally likes him but doesn't tend to connect emotionally. Teenage girls love him and cheer frantically, while teenage boys, for the most part, despise him and chant minor vulgarities. At least all this makes for a noisy arena during a Cena bout. There is actually some genuine heat.

Of course, he's not the first babyface who appealed to the younger set and garnered that response. It happened for Dory Funk Jr. in the mid 1960s and for David Von Erich in the 1980s. Good company for Cena.

With the mammoth exposure of WWE today, if he stays healthy long enough, it's likely nobody will question if John Cena belongs among the best of all time. The propaganda will drown out any doubts. And he will belong in a real Hall of Fame, for he did exactly what his owners wanted him to do and he did it well, with a magnetism that caught the audience's eyes. He's got that indefinable "it."

But take away the impact that WWE adds to John Cena. Does anybody really think that only 15 wrestlers in history were better than he is? Versatility in the ring or on the mic, toughness, individuality, personal drawing power. Is Cena better than Bruno Sammartino? The Funks? Bruiser Brody? "Wild Bill" Longson? Jim Londos?

Maybe he's more like Antonio "Argentina" Rocca and benefits from a large promotion that is fully behind him, pushing as hard as Vince's father did for Rocca in the late 1950s and early 1960s. Rocca had "it," particularly for a certain audience, but he's not joining this elite group. Yet I have heard arguments for including Rocca (and won't do it!).

So, does Cena qualify as one of perhaps a couple dozen solid main event babyfaces who were products of their time, all-around popular performers who consistently drew good houses in different locations? Cena became bigger than he was because of the national marketing might of WWE; he is the key player in the only game in town. "Cowboy" Bob Ellis had "it" too, but he isn't on this list. Why should Cena be on if he's not better than Ellis, a respected "good hand" who was a consistent and excellent drawing card around the country but didn't benefit from a WWE boosting him?

John Cena is very good, likely better than many give him credit for. But is he among the greatest ever? Perhaps more to the point, considering how long he has been the flag-carrier for WWE nationally, is it possible he could move into that elite 50 with a another good year or two or three? Or should he be there NOW, and in a prominent position? How much does the needle move up for a guy who has repeatedly been in main events for one pay-per-view after the other?

To quote Dave Meltzer in the Wrestling Observer, *"In actuality . . . Cena does not have the universal appeal that the top tier legendary figures had. He is still that level just below The Rock, Austin, Hogan, Sammartino type of babyface and from a business standpoint has been a successful top guy, just not top tier successful." I agree, and suggest more of Cena's story could still be told in the future.*

But after writing that, I had second thoughts and took time to reconsider Cena's entire body of work as I had for many others. I reassessed the realities

George Napolitano

and looked again at the hard numbers of TV ratings and gross receipts. I also discovered that I had a greater appreciation for his passionate effort in the ring. What he brings to the table is indeed substantial.

After then talking to various learned folks in the business, after wondering whether Cena was suffering from the fallout of any disenchantment I might personally have with Vince or his product, after going through all the frustrating comparisons with other big names throughout history . . .

John Cena is on the final version at number 31. Right or wrong, good or bad, flaws and all, just like every other entrant, John Cena is in and he belongs. He is among the 50 finest pro wrestlers ever, a group that includes the subcategory of sports entertainers, to satisfy all viewpoints.

Just as I was comfortable arguing that Cena did not belong, I am equally comfortable explaining why he *does* belong. Dissatisfaction with WWE or Vince is not a reason to disqualify a wrestler who has done everything asked of him and done it well.

The more I looked at the whole picture and the more often I shuffled people around into different positions, the more likely it became that Cena had a right to be at the party.

Consider the irrefutable fact that a huge percentage of pay-per-views for more than eight years have been built around Cena at the top. Others who are alleged to be superstars by WWE might have enjoyed this position once or twice, if at all, but Cena has again and again been the man around whom everything is built. My original argument is flawed. Cena does make a difference — with the right opponent in the right context. In other words, he's just like all but the few most explosive greats ever.

Furthermore, considering how much pressure there is to draw ratings for *Raw*, Cena's resume is made all the more impressive because he is almost always booked into an important position to lure the audience. Between *Raw* and the PPVs, that's a truckload of exposure and Cena has not burned out yet.

While the argument that he is not a mythical figure in WWF/WWE annals like Bruno or Hulk is true, it is equally true that Cena's tenure on top in terms of hard results and financial return is right there with Sammartino and Hogan. That speaks volumes on Cena's behalf.

So does the fact that he is such a polarizing figure for fans, love him or hate him. They *care* . . . and that's what makes it work.

With regard to his ring work, logical reasoning would hold that he accomplishes what WWE wants today and, by virtue of its position as a near monopoly in the field, this is what pro wrestling is today to most people. In other words, Cena is at the top of his field in his era, just as "Strangler" Lewis was in his time, Lou Thesz was in his, and Ric Flair was in his.

When other factors such as the diversity or lack thereof in his ring performance are added in, perhaps Cena does slide down the ladder from the true giants in the field. But what happened at *WrestleMania XXVIII* in 2012 demonstrated how well Cena and his esteemed foe The Rock understand today's pro wrestling. Maybe this execution or that maneuver wasn't done with the skill of Thesz or Brisco, but all were spectacular, timed perfectly, and tailored to the expectations of the modern audience. One time-tested truism of professional wrestling states that sometimes you get over better losing if you lose in the right way, than you do winning. Cena was just as strong, maybe stronger, after the 2012 struggle with The Rock.

Politics and destiny are surely part of this. Cena fought for his breaks, earned every one, and took advantage of them. It's not his fault that he had a greater opportunity on the national scale than other equally talented stars did years earlier. Cena is one of the few, if not the only, character Vince generated who got over to anywhere near this level in the past decade.

And if Cena had come along in the territorial time, would he have been smart and athletic enough to benefit from the greater variety of training and experiences? Would he have become a more well-rounded performer in the ring, as was required in that era? Honestly, that answer is "yes." Cena would have headlined everywhere (although he would have struggled in the Lewis-Londos-early-Thesz time period).

Jim Ross calls Cena "a lifelong fan with a great work ethic who is living his dream." And the perceptive JR is right on target. It's time to recognize that this attitude and energy has paid off. Cena is a successful product of his time.

Finally, irony of ironies, if John Cena adds a few more years atop the WWE managerie, he might become this era's version of Bruno Sammartino. Rough edges are being smoothed off while Cena is *the* key player again and again. Think of that! Cena as Bruno.

John Cena fits into the 50 greatest pro wrestlers ever. This is the correct verdict. Plus, over time, he could climb up a few more rungs of the ladder.

#30 JOE STECHER

Thesz called Stecher "a wrestling god"

Probably the most difficult opponent Joe Stecher faced was himself. The inner demons seem to have spelled an end to a most impressive career, while his reserved nature kept Stecher from being accepted in a bigger-than-life category with outgoing, colorful personalities like "Strangler" Lewis and Frank Gotch.

Yet denying Stecher's wrestling ability is impossible. That ability alone, along with some famous bouts, puts Stecher among the 50 greatest pro wrestlers in history. Some who have researched the time period felt that Stecher struggled to keep the sport as legitimate as possible, while accepting that the industry was changing to more of a performance style.

To whom would he compare in later times? Maybe someone like Karl Gotch in the 1960s, or Billy Robinson in the 1970s. Robinson and Gotch were both workers, and each had a cantankerous streak about being shooters (they were both seriously skilled) but lacked some visible personality elements that would have made them stronger characters. Thus, neither made the cut to be included in the fabulous 50. Perhaps

232

Stecher was a more skilled Wilbur Snyder, who also lacked that bombastic personality that draws attention.

Understanding that Stecher was dealing with wrestling culture in the 1910s and 1920s, and also noting that he was involved in some truly historic confrontations, Joe Stecher logically belongs with the greatest of all time. With or without title recognition, Stecher also was a consistent box-office draw in many different geographical areas.

So what if he lacked a little in what today are called "mic skills"?

After Frank Gotch retired while still in control of the championship, the wrestling business fell into a recession of sorts as promoters eagerly sought "the next Gotch." A sensation even as a teenager, when he reputedly took the measure of a hooker sent by Farmer Burns to "put the kid in his place," Stecher had all the athletic tools necessary to fill the bill. At the tender age of 22, he jumped into national fame by winning the world championship from Charlie Cutler on July 5, 1915, in Omaha, which was a leading wrestling metropolis. Gotch was actually in attendance at the crowning and gave his blessing to the new titleholder.

Stecher introduced the leg scissors to professional wrestling, as the naturally strong farm boy had powerful legs. Stecher often won by squeezing either the head or midsection of an opponent. He had mastered many of the basics of shooting too. Stecher often trained by using the leg scissors to squeeze 100-pound sacks of grain until they burst open.

About 60 years later Kevin Von Erich started doing the same trick to demonstrate the power in his legs as he became a major star, along with his brother David. Of course, Kevin mainly used the Iron Claw his father Fritz had invented, but the sack-crushing gimmick got Kevin some good attention early in his run — decades after Joe Stecher debuted the idea.

What's more, Sam Muchnick was the person who gave the idea to Fritz to pass on to Kevin. Growing up in St. Louis, the young Sam had been a big fan of Joe Stecher and recalled all the details of Joe squashing those bulky bags with the leg scissors. What an intertwined world pro wrestling was and is!

At any rate, though, much of Stecher's publicity (would that word be *marketing* today?) was generated by his brother, Tony, who had a gift for the politics and ballyhoo, which Joe generally disdained. Tony Stecher eventually became part of a few nasty promotional wars. The owner of the Minneapolis promotion that was the forerunner of Verne Gagne's AWA, and one of the originators of the National Wrestling Alliance, Tony was smart, sharp, and guided his brother's career in the best fashion he could.

During this period, none other than Ed "Strangler" Lewis also charged into prominence a few steps after Stecher. Lewis and Stecher first locked up on October 20, 1915, when Lewis was counted out of the ring after reportedly falling through the ropes and hitting his head on a chair. The duel lasted two hours. At the time, pro wrestling was in a zone of switching from work to shoot to work, and that finish definitely tells a tale. Didn't that finish happen a lot in some configuration over the next 97 years?

The first battle led to a rematch on July 4, 1916, when Stecher and Lewis tangled for more than *five* hours before the match was ruled a draw. While the event is part of pro wrestling lore, the truth is the outdoor duel in a huge field was a stinker, even with approximately 20,000 fans on hand. According to accounts by many, including Billy Sandow, Lewis's manager, the bell rang at 1:30 and by 7:00 p.m. fans were pulling their automobiles onto the grounds so the headlights would shine on the ring. All this was in the stifling heat too. Allegedly, neither man was ever taken off his feet.

If ever a match in those times shouted "shoot," this was probably it. Both competitors recognized how dangerous the other was, and neither was willing to take a chance and risk losing. Who knows what manipulations the promoters and managers did or did not do behind the scenes? Think how similar that must have been to the first mixed martial arts match, billed as boxer versus wrestler, when Antonio Inoki took on Muhammad Ali in what was also a stalemate.

A third struggle between Stecher and Lewis in New York's Madison Square Garden ended in a fast-paced, exciting draw that sent everyone home happy. Obviously, an understanding had been reached. The seeds were sewn for a rivalry that lasted years. Let's concede the two had a testy, challenging feud that boosted the stature of both. Take a look at the section on Lewis for more.

According to research by historian Steve Yohe, Lewis and Stecher met 19 times with Stecher winning six, Lewis nine, and four ending as draws. Before 1928, when Stecher had begun his downhill slide, he was ahead of Lewis five wins to three. Now try to factor in whatever part shoots, double-crosses, works, and politics played in those statistics. Good luck.

But recognize this: in the ring, Joe Stecher could hang with Ed "Strangler" Lewis, whose stature is well-established. That alone makes Stecher, who may have been Lewis's equal or more in some areas, deserving of his ranking among the greatest in history.

In addition, Stecher has a lot more going for him. He dropped the belt to Earl Caddock, another talented performer, in 1917 and enlisted in the Navy during World War I. Upon his return, Stecher went on a long winning streak, which included victories over title claimants Lewis and Wladek Zbyszko, Stanislaus's brother. The drive culminated in Caddock's defeat on January 30, 1920, in Madison Square Garden, Stecher regaining the crown after eliminating some other claims to the championship.

Yet along came Lewis, and he knocked Stecher off the perch in December 1921. Some point to that battle, and Stecher's resulting injuries, as the moment Joe began to slip from his dominant position. He kept on winning and drawing money; however, a promotional war erupted that pitted his brother Tony on one side against the so-called Gold Dust Trio of Lewis, Billy Sandow, and Toots Mondt on the other. Several sources maintain that Joe was upset that Lewis and company changed the emphasis of ring action to a worked show, with reliance on shooting slipping away. At least, that's the story.

Eventually, a deal of sorts was struck after Stanislaus Zbyszko, on behalf of Tony Stecher, had double-crossed and shot on Mondt's champion, Wayne Munn. But Zbyszko, older by then, wanted nothing to do with "Strangler" Lewis, who was out for revenge. So, in 1925 before 15,000 fans at the Federal League Field in St. Louis, Zbyszko dropped the championship to — guess who? — Joe Stecher.

It took the business entities until February 20, 1928, to put it all together for yet another showdown between Stecher and Lewis in St. Louis. But there was no final shoot, as Stecher was exhausted from the demands of being champion. Lewis assumed the throne. Stecher began to take fewer dates, although he had high-profile bouts with Lewis yet again and Jim Londos, which established more credibility for both of the victors thanks to Stecher's remarkable reputation.

Unfortunately, the demons caught up with Joe Stecher as he battled severe depression and finally had a nervous breakdown. He was institutionalized for the last 30 years of his life. Today, he probably could have been helped. In his book, *Hooker*, Lou Thesz talks about how sad it was to see Joe in those days, as brother Tony often arranged for wrestlers to work out with Joe. Thesz notes that while Stecher clearly wasn't the same person when instinct took over on the mat, he still had the ability to more than hold his own.

But what did Thesz remember best? That when he was eight years old, he looked up to Joe Stecher as a wrestling god. To Thesz, Stecher was Babe Ruth. That's good enough for me. Joe Stecher is on the list.

#29 "WHIPPER" BILLY WATSON

Brought dignity and class to a rowdy business

"Whipper" Billy Watson might be the most dignified figure on the inventory of the 50 greatest pro wrestlers in history, if *dignified* is a word that can be applied to the absurd mat world. Watson did actually bring a hint of repute to a business that always needs it.

Above and beyond charisma and skill, Watson became a legend throughout Canada for the way he used his fame to contribute to the community and help charitable efforts.

He was a link from pro wrestling to the real world, something that has seldom happened but is badly needed by the grappling clan. Consider how hard today WWE trumpets its efforts in visiting the troops, or with the Make-A-Wish Foundation and other altruistic organizations.

For WWE, it's about public relations. For "Whipper" Billy Watson, it was what he honestly wanted to do. He wasn't seeking public recognition, though it came regardless.

Of course, Watson loved the recognition he earned by excelling in the wrestling ring. Around 1931, his brother talked young Bill Potts into skipping a piano lesson to attend a wrestling camp at a local church. The

kid loved it and began training at both a local athletic club and the YMCA when he wasn't selling newspapers on a Toronto street corner.

Soon he was appearing on cards advertised as amateur wrestling shows. He had ability and was lured for a tour of England, where the action often evolved into hardcore shooting. Potts got a fractured shoulder, broken ribs, and the ability to take care of himself when the need arose. He also began using the ring name of Billy Watson.

Returning to Toronto after four years of rigorously paying his dues, Watson connected with emerging promoter Frank Tunney, who was slow to embrace the local youngster. But when Watson got his chance, he exploded into prominence. In the end, Watson and Tunney became business partners in the promotion. Tunney once estimated that between Watson's debut at Maple Leaf Gardens in 1940 and his final match in 1971, Watson drew more than five million fans for his main events in Toronto alone.

But that was nothing compared to his renown across Canada. He laid the groundwork for there to be a national hero, which Bret Hart tapped into decades later. Everyone in the country knew "Whipper" Watson. Plus, as he became a main player in struggles for the world championship, Watson gained prestige throughout the United States as well.

"Whipper" picked up his catchy nickname when he began using the Irish whip to flatten foes right and left. The move was originated by Danno O'Mahoney, a noted mat figure in the 1930s, and Watson took the move to new levels. He understood the psychology of selling, always portrayed himself as the good guy even when the breaks of the game went against him, and used the Irish whip to level adversaries of any size. Fritz Von Erich and Gene Kiniski, who were Watson's main heel rivals in the late 1950s, had a running wager about who could fly the farthest when getting the whip from Watson. That money probably went back and forth a lot, because one night one flew furthest, the next night the other. Watson loved to send the two aggressive villains sailing.

Watson was debonair, with matinee idol looks that fit the times. His trademark thin mustache was part of a carefully crafted image that made "Whipper" as big a national celebrity in Canada as any hockey star. He was careful not to make himself a superman; he wanted fans to buy into him as a hard-working, talented athlete — who was beatable. This made Watson even more popular. Sometimes he lost flat-out clean in the ring, but because he always bounced back and got even, "Whipper" earned an emotional connection that no performer today has with his audience.

The bruising collisions with Kiniski, "Wild Bill" Longson, Lou Thesz, both Fritz and Waldo Von Erich, Hans Schmidt, Bulldog Brower, Don Leo Jonathan, Nanjo Singh, Yvon Robert, Pat O'Connor, Bobby Managoff, Gorgeous George, and The Sheik were blockbusters that drew big money all over the country, and plenty of battles topped bills in the United States as well. Against scientific foes, Watson stayed clean, and the fans appreciated it. Against brawlers and rule-breakers, "Whipper" did exactly what he had to do to stand up to them. Fans ate it up.

Watson won the world championship by knocking off the highly respected Longson in St. Louis on February 21, 1947, ending the rowdy Longson's four-year reign. It meant something, actually causing reverberations throughout the global fan community. Thesz then upended Watson on April 25, 1947. Longson and Thesz traded the crown back and forth before the National Wrestling Alliance came into being, and Thesz had a seven-year tenure until toppled by none other than Watson on March 15, 1956, in Toronto. Boxing great Jack Dempsey officiated that match.

As was his nature, Thesz was hesitant to praise Watson's pure wrestling skills but was high on "Whipper" for the business. "He was a great performer," Lou told me. "'Whipper' was a quality guy in a business that is often short on that kind."

But Watson was indeed tough when necessary. Dewey Robertson, who spent time as the notorious Missing Link in the Dallas promotion World Class, was a Watson protégé. "If anybody pushed their luck, Billy would stretch them just like that. Nobody was in a rush to cross him," said Robertson.

Hans Schmidt, an underrated heel from the 1950s, felt that Watson was much tougher than advertised. "He could take it and dish it out," recalled Schmidt. "'Whipper' had a great feel for the crowd, how to whip up the heat. I loved working with him."

Kiniski had tremendous admiration for Watson. "I was still young when I went to Toronto, and I learned so much from Watson," Gene said. "He'd call the match, coaching me, making me even meaner than I was, and I was pretty damn mean back then."

Jonathan, who had no doubt about the crowd favorite when he met Watson, said, "If you won, you'd have to literally fight your way to the dressing room, the people loved Billy so much."

By the late 1960s, as his wresting career slowed, Watson found a new calling as he raised funds for Easter Seals and started a safety club for children comparable to the baseball star Ted Williams' efforts in Boston. He made countless public appearances for charities big and small. The community was shocked and saddened when a car rammed into Watson as he was loading a fireplace screen into his trunk on November 30, 1971.

He nearly lost a leg and battled the pain of disability for the rest of his life. It did not, however, stop his tireless work for others. He generated millions of dollars for Easter Seals and was director for the Ontario Society for Crippled Children. After Watson's death, many regular folks related stories of surprise visits during hard times, or special attention given by Watson when he was approached for an autograph or handshake and a conversation.

This is different from most wrestling stories, and that is good. Watson's legacy for pro wrestling is beyond reproach. He was never embarrassed about what he'd done, and he presented the sport in the best possible light. "Whipper" had no messy divorces, public scenes, or ugly bankruptcies. He didn't fight private duels in public just to further his own reputation.

That alone is worth something when considering his place among the 50 greatest wrestlers ever. What he did in the ring was superb, without question, but what "Whipper" Billy Watson added to the business guarantees him a special spot in the mat hierarchy. He may have been better for pro wrestling than pro wrestling was for him.

#28 FRITZ VON ERICH
Inventor and master of the Iron Claw

From the moment Fritz Von Erich became one of the sport's most compelling heels, he wrapped an Iron Claw around a position in the top 50 greatest pro wrestlers ever. The Iron Claw was just the icing on the cake for Jack Adkisson, whose portrayal of the sneering, strutting, and brutal Von Erich earned him all sorts of attention and gobs of money, which he invested wisely.

Sadly, though, none of that could protect him from the reality of a devastated family that lost five sons through tragic circumstances. Once again, reality was stranger than fiction. The tragedies have overshadowed what a giant he was as a wrestler. He was one of the greatest heels ever, and as a promoter he was both influential and ambitious.

But it is Fritz Von Erich the performer who should be considered here.

Three factors combined to get Von Erich over as a sinister bad guy — appearance, athleticism, and that scary Iron Claw.

Adkisson looked the part of a snarling, arrogant Nazi bully. I don't think anyone in the business has ever had a better sneer than Von Erich. Thickly built at 6'5" and 265 pounds in his prime, he had that smooth movement all the good athletes have. Crowds reacted to him as he strutted confidently to the ring, glaring at anyone close to him. They were hooting and hollering by the time he got through the ropes. Fritz would smile coldly, gaze first at the balcony, then ringside, and point at the assembled spectators, making each one think he or she was the target of his scorn. It was a hell of an entry without fireworks or music.

Von Erich's voice boomed out in interviews as he commanded the television screen. When the floor director would swing his finger around in the signal to wrap it up, Von Erich would roar, "Don't you wind me up! Don't you dare tell me what to do!" The first time it happened on *Wrestling at the Chase*, the floor man was so startled that he actually jumped back from the ring. The audience was stunned because it was such a sudden, explosive verbal attack on somebody who wasn't part of the action.

George Abel, the announcer in the mid 1960s, once stood up to Fritz. Remember, at this time the planning for interviews was minimal, absolutely zero scripting with little contact before the show. As fans hooted and Fritz ranted about a future foe, Abel bravely asked, "What makes you so arrogant?"

Surprised, Von Erich hesitated only a moment before blustering, "What makes you so arrogant to ask a stupid question like that? What makes these fans so arrogant to think they can boo me?" And off he went, neatly tying together the unexpected query with his upcoming main event and further projecting his dominating character.

When the bell sounded, Von Erich was stiff and mean. He loved colliding with the likes of Johnny Valentine and later helped to train Bruiser Brody. Every punch and chop was laid in snugly, and Fritz expected the same in return. Despite his size, Von Erich had a terrific dropkick, which he could follow with the Shawn Michaels–style kip-up. One of his favorite spots was to hit his first drop kick, then miss the second drop kick, which opened the door for a comeback by the babyface rival. Or, if he was up against someone like Lou Thesz or Wilbur Snyder, both men would throw simultaneous drop kicks, causing a tremendous crash. If the mood hit, he could even leapfrog a charging opponent.

Mostly, though, he was a vicious heel. Punching, choking, kicking — staying on top of his prey until the heat hit fever pitch. This was serious "hate you" heat, not unlike that drawn by Buddy Rogers at his peak. The smart opponents knew that Fritz would likely cut off their first couple of attempts at a comeback, simply to guarantee an emotional fireball when the good guy finally got the upper hand. His ring psychology was unmatched.

The Iron Claw was the masterstroke. Fritz had huge hands. He would clamp the right hand over his foe's face, digging his fingers into the temple until the victim collapsed, either in horrible pain or total unconsciousness. Naturally, a lot depended on his opponent selling the Claw but that never seemed to be a problem. Von Erich *was* a strong alpha male personality.

One of the most effective photos I have ever seen is a close-up of Von Erich putting the Claw on "Cowboy" Bob Ellis, a willing bleeder. In this particular shot, the blood is all over Ellis's forehead and, most important, running over the hand and fingers of the snarling Fritz, whose face is contorted as he punishes Ellis. Wherever Fritz went, that picture found its way into the printed program for the card.

The Claw was versatile. Fritz could be applying the Claw, trip and fall backward, and have his shoulders down to be pinned while still holding the Claw on the surprised winner. Or a desperate, enraged good guy could be near the corner and somehow break the Claw by slamming Fritz's wrist into the turnbuckle, thus setting up an inventive finish. Those kinds of conclusions only happened once a year, against an iconic opponent.

But the key was that the Iron Claw was over so strongly that as soon as Fritz applied it, the building would implode.

Baron Von Raschke learned that when he worked for Fritz in Texas in 1969. During a bout against Pat O'Connor in St. Louis on October 4, 1968, O'Connor whispered to Raschke to "put on the Claw." The problem was that the relatively inexperienced Raschke didn't know what the Claw was. Somehow, with O'Connor's wiggling about, Raschke applied something that looked like the Claw, and the crowd reacted.

Later Raschke moved to Texas and saw how Fritz utilized the Claw. Von Erich graciously gave Raschke some advice on how to make the grip effective; thus, another master of the Claw had his start.

The Claw, of course, was a huge weapon for Fritz's sons when they got rolling. Few who saw it would ever forget when Harley Race tried to nail David Von Erich with a diving headbutt, only for David to catch him in the Iron Claw on May 27, 1979. Race donated gallons of blood to help get David and the Claw over. The tape of the match played everywhere David was headed, including Japan.

And it was all because of Fritz. Jack Adkisson grew up in Dallas. He was a legendary athlete in high school, where he set a record for the high jump (foreshadowing those surprising drop kicks). He played football as a powerful offensive lineman at Southern Methodist University, and he also threw the discus for the track squad. As usual, old tales conflict, but it seems that Adkisson got nowhere trying to make pro football a career. Either, or perhaps both, Dallas promoter Ed McLemore and Canadian icon Stu Hart were involved in getting Adkisson started in pro wrestling. His ring debut appears to have been in January 1953 in Dallas.

Adkisson quickly started using the Nazi gimmick to gain attention, not an unusual ploy in the years after World War II. Fritz supposedly was a family nickname and Erich was his mother's maiden name. As often happens for those who truly have the gift, Fritz quickly jumped into main events.

He became a titanic box office magnet in the Toronto-Buffalo area as well as the budding AWA territory. That opened the door for matches with "Whipper" Billy Watson, Verne Gagne, Lord Athol Layton, Pat O'Connor, and Ilio DiPaolo, a huge local star in Buffalo. Fritz and Gene Kiniski often combined for tag bouts. Fritz headed into the Carolinas, joining his "brother" Waldo (Walter Sieber), a fine piece of talent who is now usually overlooked. Unfortunately, tragedy struck early for Fritz when his first son, Jack Jr., was electrocuted by a downed wire after a thunderstorm in Buffalo in 1959.

Visits back to Texas were easily paid for by sellouts between Fritz and the likes of Bull Curry or Dory Funk Sr. Von Erich started headlining in St. Louis, Indianapolis, and Detroit. Dick the Bruiser joined Ellis and Snyder as favorite opponents, drawing serious money at the gate. Fritz even had a very short run as AWA champion after beating Gagne on July 27, 1963.

The travel never let up, for Von Erich was an amazing performer in heavy demand. He went to Japan in 1966, when that country's wrestling community was rebuilding after the stabbing death of superstar Rikidozan. Fans there knew Von Erich had twice beaten Antonio Inoki in Texas. That, combined with the Iron Claw, its attendant blood, and Fritz's excellent facial expressions, finished getting him over big time. Von Erich and Giant Baba's match on December 3, 1966, drew the first sellout ever in the famous Budokan Hall. The meeting was also telecast live nationally and drew a huge audience, securing Fritz's position in Japan.

A promotional war erupted in Dallas in 1965, but Fritz had become close to NWA president Sam Muchnick during his bookings in St. Louis. He even lived in the area for a while, and his son Kevin was born in 1957 in Belleville, Illinois (where I was a ten-year-old wrestling fan). Muchnick helped tip the balance in the promotional fight so that Fritz came out on top. Fritz later told me that Muchnick made him promise to involve those he had battled, including McLemore, in the formation of the rearranged promotion. "I promised, kept my word, and Sam was right," Fritz told me at his ranch in 1983. "He said it was best for our business, which it was, to give everybody a piece once I was in control."

By then, Von Erich had sons, plus he'd made big money and invested it well in real estate around Dallas and Fort Worth. By the late 1960s, Fritz cut back on his frantic travel schedule to concentrate on his own promotion and his family.

Over time, Fritz slid into the good-guy role as the enforcer of last resort, the legitimately tough superstar who could batter the latest heel terror into submission. Fritz confronted Ernie Ladd, The Spoiler, Professor Toru Tanaka, Black Jack Mulligan, and eventually Brody, among others. Gary

Hart, one of the best managers ever, became Fritz's booker and created plots where Gary was the manager of one brute after another attempting to shoot down Fritz (and eventually his all-American sons Kevin, David, and Kerry). It was a strong, profitable territory.

Politically, Fritz had excellent rapport with Vince McMahon Sr. and often funneled big-man talent to and from Senior. This included monsters like Brody and Big John Studd. When Muchnick stepped down as NWA president in 1975, Fritz accepted the job, but for one year only to find out how stressful the position really was. Over the following years, Von Erich's business in Texas faced numerous problems, with Joe Blanchard eventually going on his own in San Antonio and Paul Boesch setting up independent shop in Houston.

Yet Fritz was the guiding light of what became World Class Championship Wrestling, a red-hot show based in Dallas that was syndicated around the United States in the early 1980s. It set new standards for lighting, music, and production. His sons were on fire. Fritz seldom got in the ring; there was no need, plus all those drop kicks and bumps for a 265-pounder were coming back to haunt him.

And then it all fell apart. David died in 1984, Mike in 1987, Chris in 1991, and Kerry in 1993. Suicide was the reason, certainly on the last three. The company itself fell into turmoil as drugs haunted World Class. Another young star, Gino Hernandez, died suddenly. The NWA collapsed. Vince McMahon Jr. took over the wrestling business. Fritz fought violently, often with shady promotional ventures. It was a disaster. The promotion collapsed before Jack Adkisson himself died of cancer in 1997.

Nobody will ever know the why of the Von Erich tragedies. Forget bloggers' theories. They weren't there. I was a close friend of David Von Erich. To this day, I refuse to accept that David may have committed suicide. I believe he suffered an accidental overdose from mixing alcohol with pain pills, following the crib death of his child, a shattering divorce, and the strain of being a wrestling star in the 1980s. But nobody knows — nobody.

Jack Adkisson — that proud, strong, aggressive, intelligent man — had to be torn apart by what life did to him and his family. What toll did it take on him? Did he blame himself? Who *really* knows? Does it matter? Is it anybody's business? Accept the tragedy and pray it never happens to you or anyone else.

Perhaps that is why it is best to remember Adkisson when he was Fritz Von Erich in that mesmerizing illusion called pro wrestling. The excitement he could generate, the emotion he could ignite. Any record of the 50 greatest pro wrestlers must include Fritz Von Erich. He was at his best as the nastiest villain of them all. The Iron Claw still has its hold.

#27 KILLER KOWALSKI
Possibly the most relentless performer ever

Relentless and ruthless, Killer Kowalski is an enduring name in the pro wrestling annals. He generated a fury that few could match in the ring, but away from the lights he was a solitary, eclectic individual who went his own way whether anybody liked it or not.

He was a frightening figure who actually had two different physiques in the course of a nearly 30-year career. When he began in 1948, Kowalski was a mountain of muscle. Standing 6'7" and tipping the scales around 285 pounds, he had a narrow waist, a thick chest, and wide shoulders. Nobody questioned whether Kowalski was able to rip apart opponents. The Polish-descended native of Windsor, Ontario, first had plans to become an electrical engineer. He paid his way through college by working at an automobile plant in Detroit.

Athletes who saw his physique and the way he attacked the weight room at a local YMCA told him he should try professional wrestling. When he finally took their advice, he was an immediate hit. His size, his build, and his aggressive nature had promoters clamoring for his services almost from day one. Few athletes at the time were as big as Kowalski, and those who were couldn't move as athletically and smoothly as he did.

He legally changed his name from Walter Spulnik to Wladek Kowalski, but he usually was billed as Tarzan or Hercules Kowalski. He used the nickname Killer early, but at first it didn't stick. Most everyone on the inside called him Walter.

He was a natural for national television in the early 1950s. He became a celebrity because he was a contrast to Lou Thesz, Verne Gagne, Gorgeous George, and Buddy Rogers. Kowalski was a monster. Kick, kick, kick. Pound, pound, pound. He just never stopped moving and attacking.

Certainly one story about Kowalski will survive the ages. This situation was as extraordinary as the man himself. In a 1954 match against powerful Yukon Eric in Montreal, Kowalski leaped off the top rope in an attempt to obliterate his foe. Eric rolled just a little bit, enough for Kowalski's knee literally to slice off Eric's ear. The ear was badly cauliflowered from years of wrestling, so it was a big target. Kowalski later said he thought he had missed entirely until he saw something on the mat: Yukon Eric's ear. Some versions claim that the referee picked up the ear, just in case a doctor could reattach it.

The incident was made even more bizarre when Kowalski visited Eric in the hospital. Naturally, Yukon's head was wrapped in bandages. When the two rivals saw each other, they both smiled and broke out laughing. Kowalski recalled the two simply couldn't stop.

Apparently, a reporter either was at the hospital or heard about what happened from employees there. The newspaper got the story right but misrepresented the context. The headline the next day read that Kowalski had visited Yukon Eric at the hospital and had begun to laugh. That definitely played up his image as a heartless heel more than anything else could have. During a match that followed, someone threw a pig ear at Kowalski in the ring. A female fan managed to stab him, leaving a superficial wound in his back. He always got heat, but this was more serious than ever. People called him "a killer," and this time the name stuck.

Killer Kowalski was a huge gate attraction in every major territory. Like all the greats, he clashed with everyone, everywhere. Lou Thesz loved the challenge of working with Kowalski, whom Lou called "tireless, and a true money-making machine." Montreal was a particularly successful stomping ground for him: he made various title claims after wins over Verne Gagne, Edouard Carpentier, Don Leo Jonathan, and Pat O'Connor there. He headlined in Texas, Hawaii, St. Louis, and New York. When Kowalski went to Australia for wily promoter Jim Barnett, he proved that his method of violence could draw sellout throngs everywhere. Japanese mat followers were in awe of this giant and his ring tactics.

Over time, though, his physique changed. Kowalski always was intrigued by various health kicks, although he was hesitant to contact doctors. In 1955 he decided to become a vegetarian but first went on a fast. Hans Hermann, a good friend and another solid performer in the 1950s, was shocked when he visited Kowalski, who had lost a huge amount of weight and looked like a skinny basketball player. According to both Hermann and Jonathan, Kowalski explained that it was healthier to refrain from eating meat and instead live on various juices and "the air." Kowalski apparently declared that he wanted to lose weight "scientifically."

Sam Muchnick, who highly respected Kowalski on a personal level, said some promoters didn't want to use Kowalski during that period, until they discovered he had just as much energy and could still draw the bucks — fans clamored to see Killer walloped, which seldom occurred. He now looked different; instead of mass, Kowalski was all sharp angles and hard bones attached to lean muscle. Either way, he was a frightening sight when on the attack. His interviews were intelligent; he spoke with power and confidence. People believed in him, knowing he was dangerous.

During the 1960s, Kowalski was one of the finest challengers for Bruno Sammartino and the WWWF title. Bruno getting the upper hand in a fight with Kowalski had true meaning for fans, who had learned to respect and fear Kowalski. In 1972, Kowalski pinned and body-slammed Andre the Giant in Quebec City. But Kowalski also did all the right things to make Andre, billed as Jean Ferre at the time, a budding international superstar. Likewise, Kowalski generously went out of his way during bouts against Giant Baba to help make Baba's reputation in both Japan and North America.

Promoters trusted Kowalski, not a small item. During the confusion over Buddy Rogers and the NWA crown during 1962 and 1963, Kowalski had many matches with various claimants to the honor. Both sides trusted Kowalski to stick by his word and do the right thing. And he did.

Could Kowalski work? It's a good question about a big, aggressive athlete. Kowalski, though, understood how to get something out of every type of opponent, as long as they gave 100 percent. Foes had to match Kowalski in expenditure of energy or they would be trampled. What he demanded of himself raised the bar for anyone in the ring with him.

Kowalski did not smoke or drink, and seldom hung out "with the boys." He wasn't, however, a loner. Kowalski was a fascinating individual with a good sense of humor. Away from the arena he got along well with everyone from wrestlers to fans. But he didn't force his own views on anyone. Kowalski was a student of theology and different religions. He was a thinker and a reader, studying new ideas. He only ever jumped another performer if that performer had done something Kowalski felt hurt the pro wrestling business. He was dedicated to keeping the image of pro wrestling strong, for he knew that was always a difficult chore.

As his career wound down, Kowalski got into training newcomers. He was well liked in his Boston community. His best-known student is, of course, Hunter Hearst Helmsley — or Triple H, as Paul Levesque came to be known. Kowalski also got Big John Studd started and worked with Chris Nowinski, who after a short burst with WWE is now active in the study of concussions in sport. Killer would be proud of that.

Once more, finding that perfect fit for Kowalski among the 50 greatest pro wrestlers ever is tricky. But he does belong. Killer Kowalski is a concrete part of pro wrestling's heritage, wherever he goes.

#26 TRIPLE H
Puts it all together as one of the best

Paul Levesque paid his dues as he became Hunter Hearst Helmsley. He has displayed the heart and the talent to batter his way into the select society of the 50 greatest pro wrestlers of all time. A big, agile, competitive athlete who would have surely found success in any era of the sport, Triple H also has demonstrated his cunning in navigating the labyrinth of wrestling politics.

In all likelihood, even if he'd had only a modicum of political smarts, Triple H would have been a major star because he had the goods in the ring. His size at 6'4" with bulging muscles caught eyes. He could deliver a strong match against capable foes, and he could draw money. The fact that he was trained by someone as highly respected as Killer Kowalski would also have opened doors for Levesque.

And Levesque is bright. He was a student of pro wrestling, growing up studying tapes of various performers such as Ric Flair and Harley Race. Levesque had a knack for talking to those in power, never putting forth his thoughts in a way that seemed pushy. (Maybe "respectfully persuasive" is a better description.) He seems to understand how to deal with decision-makers. Naturally, it was easier to be heard when he had proven to be a good worker and a solid attraction at the gate.

Marrying the boss's daughter, especially when the boss is the most powerful man in pro wrestling and you happen to be a pro wrestler, is a doggone good political move as well. That statement obviously is unfair to Paul Levesque and Stephanie McMahon. No claims are being made that their relationship was motivated by anything more than what happens between any young couple. Plus, they are both reportedly pro wrestling fanatics. People often marry partners who share their interests. This marriage just happened to involve a man and a woman in unique positions.

But this business being as cynical as it is, rest assured that more than one dressing-room lawyer has brought the marriage up when Levesque is not around. If the couple can ignore any back-stabbing and gossip, more power to them.

As a youngster, Levesque was into not only wrestling, but also bodybuilding. He won a teenage bodybuilding contest in 1988 and found his way to Killer Kowalski's wrestling school. Good body, good size, good look, good background — it was inevitable he'd go somewhere. Levesque landed with WCW in 1994, but primarily shuffled around their lineups. He left for the WWF in 1995 after realizing the future looked bleak where he was.

He was given the "Hunter Hearst Helmsley" moniker along with a supposed "blue blood" background. Even though he got a moderate push, it was mainly mid-level stuff for a cocky young guy trying to find his way. But he kept getting decent spots, which most felt were because of his backstage maneuvering along with Shawn Michaels, Kevin Nash, Scott Hall, and Sean Waltman. Known inside as The Kliq, the group seemed to have VKM's ear. Apparently, though, Vince cooled on Levesque after the infamous incident at Madison Square Garden where Levesque, Michaels, and Waltman all broke out of character in public, in the ring, to wish Nash and Hall good luck when they jumped ship to join WCW in 1996.

Nonetheless, Triple H later clicked with Vince. The character gained a lot of steam in the next year when the original D-Generation X (or DX)

George Napolitano

Triple H batters Stone Cold as Jim Ross watches from the announcer's table

was formed by Triple H, Michaels, Rick Rude, and Chyna, who was also H's girlfriend. The high-society personality was long gone, with Michaels and Triple H crotch-chopping and chanting "suck it" on most if not all WWF television shows. When Michaels was laid up by injury, Triple H got the spotlight to himself, and it boosted his stock. Audiences liked the rebellious attitude, and DX became favorites rather than heels.

DX also opened the door for Triple H to take on The Rock, who was a bad guy at the time. The pair had strong chemistry against each other; therefore, an exciting series of bouts raised both men sky high. When Triple H broke away from the remains of DX, he reverted back to the bad guy chasing the championship and also supporting the McMahon family. Triple H did win the WWF crown for the first time by beating Mankind (Mick Foley).

That led to a fateful chain of events, as real life imitated the worked world of the WWF. Triple H lost the WWF crown to none other than Vince McMahon Jr. (that's right, the promoter with no wrestling experience became the champion) on September 16, 1999. Hunter did regain the championship and then lost it and then . . . well, you get the bouncing-ball title picture.

The key point was that Triple H tried to "get revenge" on Vince by marrying his daughter, Stephanie, in a convoluted set of scripts that tested patience and the ability to suspend disbelief. Triple H also did get the even-up victory over Vince. That marriage was a work of fiction, but it kept the two together in action that lasted well over a year. Not surprisingly, Stephanie became a meaningful player, but much of the booking clicked in the long run. In real life, their relationship also bloomed. On October 25, 2003, the two really did get married.

After 2000, Triple H hit his stride in the ring, but not without setbacks due to injury. All that muscle perhaps couldn't fit comfortably onto a human frame. During a live *Raw* on May 21, 2001, Triple H tore his left quadriceps muscle while he and Steve Austin battled Chris Jericho and Chris Benoit in a true thriller. Continuing to perform and even doing the dangerous finish after he was hurt rightly earned Triple H a lot of respect.

Kowalski would have been proud of his student. Afterward, surgery laid him up for eight months.

Neck problems in 2005 sidelined Triple H for four months. In January 2007, he tore the quadriceps in the right leg, again during a match in which he gutted it out to the finish. Once more, though, Levesque was on the disabled list for several months. In 2010, various aches, pains, and torn muscles took Triple H out of action. Still, Triple H was in major main events and important PPV slots. He had excellent struggles with Jericho, Austin, The Undertaker, Michaels, and Bill Goldberg. Additionally, the formation of what was called Evolution with Flair, Dave Batista, and Randy Orton launched numerous angles, with members as both partners and enemies.

Naturally, as John Cena moved to the forefront, Triple H got to square off with him repeatedly. Michaels and Triple H kissed and made up so that DX could reform. H went through duels with Edge, Orton, Big Show, and Jeff Hardy. Sheamus, Levesque's workout buddy, got booted up in the pecking order when he and Triple H had a few dances, the last of which supposedly injured Triple H so badly that he didn't work for almost a year. This mirrored the reality that Levesque needed time off to heal.

Through all this, Triple H was the glue when healthy. He could be counted on for a high quality of performance, and he fit in well against all sorts of opponents. Without being too flashy, Triple H struck the correct chord to connect with his audience and to be as credible as possible in a wrestling universe that is often anything but.

Rumors circulated that he might be finished, but the need for proven superstars at the top of the lineup brought Triple H back to meet The Undertaker on *WrestleMania XXVII* in 2011. While H put Taker over, the effort was so destructive that The Undertaker had to be carried from the ring. It also marked the end of anything remotely resembling a full-time schedule for either combatant.

The rematch, billed as "The End of an Era," came in *Mania* 2012 and was a slugfest sure to be remembered and also to be exaggerated through the marketing blitz of WWE. It was a legitimate classic on par with

Von Erich versus The Bruiser, Kiniski versus Kowalski, and Valentine versus Race, with the added impact of a zillion sizzling chairshots and an irresistible story to tell.

When Triple H returned to WWE television in 2011, he was the acting chief operating officer or some such position that made him a boss. This further allowed Hunter to get into a feud with Brock Lesnar. In the real world, Levesque did truthfully have a major position in the front office of WWE and was focused on training and developing new talent. As he had for years, Levesque continued to wield huge influence on booking and, obviously, his own angles. As this book goes to press, Levesque is one of those who make the final call along with Stephanie and VKM.

Politics and performance had somehow become wedded. In this business, that's not unusual, but perhaps it has never been as visible as it is with Paul and Stephanie. Keeping a marriage together has never been easy with the demands of pro wrestling. The Levesques deserve every credit in the world for making their relationship work.

As a performer in the ring, we must give credit where it is due. Nobody expects a shooter in this day. Triple H gives them what they need and might well have had the gifts to cut it in another era. Whatever part politics played, the truth is that Triple H could get it done at the highest level. He joins his teacher in the congress of the 50 greatest pro wrestlers in history.

#25 RANDY SAVAGE

Oh yeah, he could hold his own with anybody

"Oh, yeah!" There was a time when it looked like only a precious few would ever know how good "Macho Man" Randy Savage really was.

Randy Poffo already had dealt with one dream that fizzled, as his hopes of playing major league baseball ended following a shoulder separation and the realization that he wasn't quite a good enough hitter to reach the highest level. The son of solid pro wrestler Angelo Poffo, Randy was a skinny, athletic kid obsessed with becoming a baseball player. His parents were supportive, as Angelo settled down in Chicago to work with his kids (Randy and his brother Lanny) and calm the usual nomadic life of a grappler by living in a central location. The Poffo clan regularly attended both Cub and White Sox games.

After a standout high school career at Downers Grove North, Randy was invited to a free-agent tryout with the St. Louis Cardinals in 1971. His dad had been a reliable performer for St. Louis promoter Sam Muchnick, who had close ties to the baseball team and especially to legendary scout Joe Mathes. I had just begun working full-time in Muchnick's office when I was invited to join Sam in the press box to watch the tryout.

George Napolitano

What sticks out in my mind is how many line drives the Poffo kid laced into the outfield and off the walls. He could hit! The Cardinals signed Randy as a catcher-outfielder and sent him to the rookie league in Florida. Teammates remember him as a great guy, one who worked out constantly, regularly doing 1,500 sit-ups every morning. But after moving up one class, disaster struck in a home-plate collision that left Randy with a serious shoulder injury.

The mishap ended his catching career, taking the edge off what some scouts felt was a major league arm, and he was eventually released by the Cardinals. He played a season with the Cincinnati Reds' farm club before teaching himself to throw left-handed so he could play first base. While he did get a short trial with the White Sox, in 1975 baseball was put on the back burner and he went into the wrestling business.

Randy quickly gained a reputation for his ring instincts and excellent athleticism. Always intense, Randy also was careful with money, following in Angelo's tradition. Randy's dad was famous for being tight and bright on investments. By 1978, the Poffos had started the outlaw promotion known as International Championship Wrestling.

The promotion was in direct competition to established NWA groups owned by the Fuller (Welch) family and Nick Gulas in Kentucky and Tennessee. The Poffo operation eventually led to conflict with Jerry Jarrett and Jerry Lawler. The fight was nasty. Talent was stolen from the rival operations, physical threats and occasional altercations broke out with hot-tempered Randy right in the middle, and lawsuits flew back and forth.

ICW had some outstanding wrestlers. By then, Randy had become "Macho Man" Randy Savage, given the name by booker Ole Anderson when Randy worked in Atlanta. He topped lineups featuring brother Lanny, Bob Orton Jr. (a superb worker who could also stretch a foe), Bob Roop (a legitimate shooter, collegiate champion, and underrated professional), Ron Garvin (one tough dude), and the big guy who would eventually become the One Man Gang. Also on hand as a television personality was Liz Hulette, who was only a few years from becoming the lovely Miss Elizabeth of WWF fame.

The position of ICW, though, hurt Savage in the industry. In effect, he was blacklisted. When I got deeply involved with Pat O'Connor in the St. Louis booking in 1981, O'Connor sadly told me we could not use Randy because of the politics, even though he was the best young talent in the business.

My initial connection to Randy came in 1983, after Muchnick had retired and his successors had different ideas about how to operate what had been wrestling's model franchise for 30-plus years.

With Muchnick's support and tacit encouragement, I started an opposition promotion to the St. Louis Wrestling Club and began looking for independent talent. Fritz Von Erich was a major power in the NWA who quietly helped me in the hope that a deal could be brokered to restore peace in St. Louis. Fritz highly praised Randy Savage and said I should open the door for him and his dad, which I did eagerly after I saw him work in Springfield, Illinois.

For a highly emotional and exciting six-month run, before I struck a deal with Vince McMahon Jr. involving St. Louis and the longtime television slot of *Wrestling at the Chase*, I came to see how badly Randy wanted to succeed. On our first card on June 18, 1983, he was so psyched up that he walked and walked and walked, pacing relentlessly in the halls of The Checkerdome. Bruiser Brody took me aside and said, "For crying out loud, try to calm him down. Everybody's nervous anyway, and he's gonna have a meltdown." But that was Randy.

His talent was apparent to everybody. He could fly, he was totally fearless, and he had a perfectionist streak in the ring. His timing was consummate, the intensity almost frightening. Further, Randy was blessed with the gift of true charisma, which nobody can ever teach. When my operation closed late in 1983, ICW was also struggling and eventually a truce put Savage together with Lawler. Cautiously, they had in-ring showdowns that did business in the territory's core towns, including Memphis and Lexington, Kentucky.

By now, though, the WWF was on the march, sucking in talent, towns, and television times. Vince became aware of Savage, especially since it seemed that Randy had settled down psychologically due to his work with Lawler. After assuring McMahon that Savage had been no problem in the dressing room, I told Vince my honest opinion: Randy Savage had the potential to be a superstar. That was no profound prediction by me. Golly, couldn't everyone see the obvious?

The decision was made and the scenario worked out to bring Liz along as Miss Elizabeth, and the stage was set for everyone to discover why Randy Savage was destined to be among the 50 greatest pro wrestlers ever. Aside from Hulk Hogan, Savage was as hot as any property from the mid 1980s through the mid 1990s. McMahon and his bookers took their time, did it right, and got maximum mileage from Macho Man and Elizabeth.

During this period when the promotional war was going full blast and pro wrestling was so hot that Vince often ran three shows every evening, talent was on the road constantly, lucky if they had one day off per month. Savage was consistently providing some of the finest in-ring action. Consider only the biggest of multiple big moments Randy was responsible for during that time.

At *WrestleMania III* before some 78,000 at the Pontiac (Michigan) Silverdome in 1987, Savage had one of the greatest matches in WWF/WWE history, against Ricky Steamboat. Always wanting things done just so, Savage planned the match move-by-move in advance and many claim the duel stole the show from the main event of Hulk against Andre the Giant.

In 1988 at *WrestleMania IV*, Savage captured the WWF crown by defeating Ted DiBiase in the finale of a tournament for what was then a vacant championship. Since Savage got assistance from Hogan, the battle also laid the groundwork for a year-long story revolving around Savage, Elizabeth, Hulk, and the title.

On February 3, 1989, headlining a prime-time NBC special, Savage and Hogan teamed against Big Bossman and Akeem (who was One Man Gang and Randy's former running mate in ICW). This was the first and most successful modern soap-opera booking done at this level. Liz was accidentally injured by Akeem. Hogan went to help Liz and took her to the dressing room.

Not realizing why he was alone, Savage fought two-against-one while Hulk did some hokey acting, imploring medical personnel to "save" Elizabeth. Finally, Hulk ran back to the ring, only to be slapped by an irate Savage and deserted. Hogan made his usual Superman comeback, got the pin on Akeem, and then charged to Liz's side as she was being treated.

At that point, it was Savage with his lunatic intensity who made the angle, accusing Hulk of making a move on Elizabeth, clobbering Hogan with the title belt, and threatening to smack Liz when she tried to intervene. In an instant, Savage was the hottest heel going. It was the second-most-watched pro wrestling program in U.S. history, with 21 million viewers tuning in.

Needless to say, Savage and Hogan headlined *WrestleMania V* in 1989, and Hulk regained the WWF prize. Supposedly Elizabeth was neutral for the showdown but was involved throughout, trying to protect one or the other. After that show, Savage was on fire as a heel and Liz more or less slipped out of view.

By *WrestleMania VII* in 1991, the wheels were turning for Randy and Liz to be reunited, leading to a PPV wedding later that year and another strong angle for Savage with Jake Roberts. Of course, in real life, they had married in 1984. By late 1992, they had divorced. And by late 1994, Randy Savage had jumped from the WWF to Ted Turner's WCW.

Legend has it that WCW made its big charge to challenge Vince when Kevin Nash and Scott Hall switched sides from the WWF to WCW. While there is truth to that version of the tale, the business turnaround for WCW had already started when Savage came on board and began a series of arena-rattling battles with Ric Flair. Once again, Savage's work was flawless.

In roughly 12 years, Randy Savage had gone from being a supremely talented performer who couldn't get work with the big promotions because of politics to being a major superstar and historical figure who helped change the ebb-and-flow of the entire pro wrestling business.

As usual, though, WCW managed to botch a good thing. Vince juggled his talent and booking to regain the advantage, finally buying out the remnants of a collapsing WCW in 2001. By then, Savage was paying the price for his hard physical style and Mother Nature was suggesting a finish to his career. He was, however, established as a mainstream personality, doing commercials for Slim Jim using his patented "Oh, yeah" line and popping up in movies here and there.

Randy flitted around the edges of the wrestling scene but something was missing. The fire was gone. He probably didn't want — or need — it anymore. Whatever had happened with McMahon, the two never made up. On the personal side, Savage had found a former lady friend from his baseball days, gotten married, and seemed happy with life when a sudden heart attack struck down the Macho Man on May 20, 2011.

When it was over, though, had the entire wrestling world discovered just how good Randy Savage was? Had Randy Savage established his place among the best ever? Anyone who knows pro wrestling would answer those questions with a hearty "Oh, yeah!"

#24 ANDRE THE GIANT
There is only one REAL giant

It's pro wrestling. There's always a giant. Even if the big, gangly guy is really 6'7" and weighs 290 pounds, eager promoters will bill the poor fellow at 6'10" and 330 pounds and call him a "Giant." Once in a while, someone like Sky Hi Lee comes along, fitting most of the height dimensions of a "giant," but without the bulk or athleticism. "Big Show" is *a* giant. But were any of them *the* giant?

In the end, everyone knows there has only been one *GIANT*. He is *the* giant. He is none other than Andre the Giant. It didn't matter if psyched-up publicists couldn't resist adding a couple of inches or a few pounds on his introduction. One look told the story every time. He was Andre the *Giant*, and finding another like him is probably a futile effort.

When Andre locked up with Hulk Hogan in front of a record throng at *WrestleMania III*, he'd established his reputation through years of touring everywhere. If anyone had a tougher travel schedule than the NWA champion, it was Andre, and he didn't get to drop the belt after a couple of years. He was still the Giant, and he was in demand for bookings.

His size, the result of a glandular disease called acromegaly, was evident early when he was growing up in the French Alps. Andre Roussimoff was said to be a good athlete, playing soccer and rugby, who struggled to find a future before he moved to Paris. After fiddling with boxing, Andre made contact with the wrestling promotion in Paris and a marriage was made. Soon, under the moniker Giant Jean Ferre, he was hailed as a star in Europe. He also made his Japanese debut as Monster Roussimoff in 1970.

Myth has it that Edouard Carpentier connected Andre with the Montreal promotion. In fact, journeyman Frank Valois may have played a big part in the move. Nonetheless, Jean Ferre was a huge star in Quebec until a basic booking fact reared its head. A giant only has so many competitive foes that he can tackle in one area before there is nobody left for him to face. And then gate receipts dwindle. Thus, it was time to move on, and there was no lack of suitors. Andre wanted the smartest deal.

With the trusted Valois helping negotiate, Andre settled on Vince McMahon Sr. and the WWWF. Senior encouraged Andre to actually BE a giant: no more drop kicks, which Andre actually did at the time. The deal was simple. Andre got a major percentage of the gate equal to or slightly better than what the NWA and WWWF champions received, while McMahon got a smaller percentage for doing the booking. Senior used the WWWF as Andre's home base, pumped up the publicity barrage, and made Andre available to promoters everywhere.

It worked. Andre immediately hit the road and lured big crowds consistently. Along with Hulk Hogan and Stan Hansen, Andre followed in the footsteps of Lou Thesz, the most famous foreign star in wrestling-mad Japan. All of that would continue until Senior, his health failing, sold what was then the WWF to his son in 1982, and the face of the industry began to change.

The advertising on The Giant said 7'4" and 450 pounds. The truth was probably about 6'11" and, as time rolled on, he definitely weighed over 400 pounds. But nobody argued. Andre's head was huge, framed by massively curly hair. His hands were truly like hams, each palm as big as most people's faces. His frame and bones were thick and powerful. He was *THE* giant.

On February 15, 1974, Andre made his first St. Louis outing. Like the fans, I had seen tapes of him, but the fact was that his physical being in person was more eye catching than expected. He weighed maybe 380 pounds back then. That evening, he stunned the crowd when he executed a perfect sit out and switch on "Baron" Scicluna to a collective "ooohhhh" by 9,500 people. Maybe that athleticism dwindled over time, but Andre was always special in how he handled his immensity.

As the wrestling war raged, Hulk Hogan was just becoming nationally known, but Andre was already famous. He had all sorts of fans because he'd been going town to town for more than nine years. Hitting each spot once or twice a year, he avoided overexposure and never burned out his appeal. But the ravages of his size and his disease were getting to him by the early 1980s, and he had a difficult time coming back from a broken ankle. His bone structure was beginning to collapse. His weight ballooned, making travel a harder chore than ever before.

Yet Andre was a terrific attraction for the WWF. A feud with Big John Studd was a big deal, and Andre had no lack of good rivals as the WWF added or stole talent from dying territories. Andre was still huge in Japan, but in 1986 he got involved in a dirty little war with Akira Maeda, who had a reputation as a shooter. Andre was unimpressed and didn't sell for Maeda, and the situation culminated when Andre attacked Maeda in the ring. But he lost his balance and fell after taking some wicked kicks to his already battered knees. Maeda was scared to death to get close to Andre, knowing that if the Giant grabbed him, he was dead meat. So he'd kick and run, while Andre lay there and laughed. Finally, Antonio Inoki rushed to the ring and stopped the fiasco.

VKM pitted Andre against Hogan for one mammoth run, but it did mean turning Andre heel with the aid of Ted DiBiase. Everything worked perfectly, with the main plot points playing out on a live television special in 1988 on NBC. The special drew a record number of viewers

for a wrestling show. It all led to *WrestleMania III*, where Hulk slammed Andre and handed him his "first" defeat ever.

Of course, the idea that Hogan was the first to body slam or defeat Andre is baloney. This may not be a complete list, but Andre was slammed by Inoki, El Canek (a Mexican star), Killer Kowalski, Stan Hansen, Harley Race, Ken Patera, Kamala, Otto Wanz, and Hulk himself a couple of years earlier. No matter, though. Those were little blips in a fragmented wrestling world. To the mainstream, Andre had been untouchable for years.

The huge casual audience, hooked by the WWF through the NBC programs, had no idea. They knew Andre as *the* Giant. With all the glitter surrounding the angle, that group of occasional fans was happy to buy into the storyline even with Andre as the heel. The avid fans who knew better were vastly smaller in number and happy anyway to see pro wrestling getting so much attention. In retrospect, the entire scenario was using the supposed climax of one icon's career — that of Andre the Giant — to bolster the standing of yet another icon — Hulk Hogan. The goal was to make a lot of money and draw a gigantic crowd.

That's fine, because it's the way of wrestling, and sports in general. What bothered many observers was the aftermath, which saw Andre in the same position, hopefully to elevate the Ultimate Warrior. Simply put, the booking laid an egg; crowds were lousy. Because of Andre's failing physical stature, the matches that were called main events lasted less than five minutes, and they stank. Worse yet, Andre had to put Warrior over. The public, avid or casual, didn't buy that Warrior deserved the position, nor did they want the mess against Warrior to be their last memory of a true legend like Andre.

Life for The Giant was not easy. Perhaps I first sensed this back in 1974 when I picked Andre up from the airport for his St. Louis debut. The poor fellow had to cram himself into my Grand Am and bend forward to rest his chin on the dashboard. One can only imagine what other drivers thought when they saw that big face almost against the windshield! But, how did it feel for Andre?

Andre the Giant dwarfs Mil Mascaras and Dusty Rhodes

A giant doesn't fit like other folks. Airplane seats, even in first class, weren't comfortable. Even the best hotels seldom had beds that were made for someone of Andre's dimensions. Despite being the good guy, he knew some unthinking people looked at him as a freak; he might have to dodge the icy snowballs kids hurled at him when he left a building where he'd been cheered by thousands only an hour before. He'd always been a heavy drinker, and that got more out of control near the end.

He was friendly with everyone, but only close to a chosen few. He called most everybody "boss" because he had met so many people that remembering names accurately was impossible. Only later, as nasty pain consumed his body, did he become crabby, aloof, and difficult to work with. And did anyone consider the private moments when Andre cursed his size and wished he could be normal? Even for the Giant, the spotlights turned off, and he had to go home and be himself — all alone.

I kept Andre company on a few trips in 1982 when I did some television commentary for Verne Gagne, promoter Wally Karbo, and the AWA. It was difficult to imagine that anyone could drink so much wine, beginning with breakfast at 7 a.m., and never seem drunk, but Andre did it before the flight from Minneapolis. Enjoying his company once in Winnipeg when he actually seemed comfortable is a fond memory.

Andre arranged a mid-afternoon lunch at the Polo Park Inn when the café was empty. He invited John Ferguson, one of the toughest hockey players of all time, who was then an executive with the Jets, and Serge Savard, a Hall-of-Fame defenseman who had played for the Montreal Canadiens with Ferguson. They'd become friends with Andre because he owned a popular restaurant in Montreal where they hung out. Andre knew I was a hockey nut so he invited me to join them, along with his foe that evening, Jerry "Crusher" Blackwell.

As always with athletes at the highest level, the talk turned to injuries and how to deal with them. Savard and Ferguson brought up a couple of bad mishaps they'd had. Then Blackwell rolled up his sweatpants above one knee. "Look at this," said the 450-pounder. He looked to be about half the height of Andre but was a great opponent for him. Jerry began pushing his kneecap up and down, side to side, around and around.

Ferguson and Savard were aghast, groaning and telling Blackwell to stop it. While they moaned, Andre just sat back and laughed. He was delighted that the two hockey ruffians were impressed by what a wrestler goes through. "Everything's torn in there, so the cap just floats around. No pain at all! Hurt like hell when it all got torn, of course," Blackwell explained. One of the hockey studs asked him how long he'd been out of action. "A couple days, maybe. No insurance and don't get paid if you don't work," he said. Savard and Ferguson were appalled.

Leaving the room after lunch, Andre bumped into me and said, "See? Now they know. That was good," and he laughed some more.

Blackwell certainly would have been one of the many who vouched for Andre's generosity in the ring. Naturally, The Giant couldn't sell like a normal performer for an opponent, not even a superstar, because of his size and reputation. But when he could, Andre would try to repay those who worked with him. Kowalski always praised Andre, maintaining that Andre's attitude made what could have been difficult much more enjoyable.

Stan Hansen has always made a point to thank Andre for helping make his reputation in Japan. "I couldn't believe all the offense he'd give me," Hansen said. Bruiser Brody also had enormous respect for Andre. "Think what all he goes through to make money for all of us. He was always great for me. I loved working with him." Big John Studd lauded Andre repeatedly during a feud he had with The Giant. "Andre always knew how much to give me, and he never hesitated to do it. He made me a lot of money," noted Studd.

Sam Muchnick claimed that only three wrestlers in history ever drew money on their own, simply by putting their name on top of a card: "Jimmy Londos, Buddy Rogers, and Andre the Giant." Everyone else needed context, booking, and publicity.

Andre was, without doubt, *THE GIANT*. How could anyone disagree that Andre is right there with the 50 greatest pro wrestlers ever?

#23 EDOUARD CARPENTIER
The Fabulous Flying Frenchman

The Fabulous Flying Frenchman. Doesn't that say it all about Edouard Carpentier, whose combination of ring smarts and high-flying acrobatics earns him a place among the best pro wrestlers in history? Carpentier turned out to be much more than just a singular performer and robust gate attraction. Because his work turned up the intensity well past a novelty, Carpentier was smack in the middle of some historic turning points in the game.

Compact and handsome, Carpentier was already 30 when he made the move to North America in 1956. Born in France, his real name generally is accepted as Edouard Weicz, a shortened version of a Polish surname. Along with his family, the young man lived through the horrors of World War II. Legend says that Weicz joined the French underground resistance, which may indeed be true. Some claim the tale came from the office of Montreal promoter Eddie Quinn, who was pretty good at hyping a new star.

Another part of the tale is that Weicz competed in the 1948 and 1952 Olympics as a gymnast, though records have been difficult to find. Supposedly he was already wrestling professionally in 1950. Perhaps more

accurate are the stories that he was a dynamic circus performer after the war, thrilling spectators both as a gymnast and as a trapeze artist.

He caught the eye of one Lino Ventura, the European Greco-Roman wrestling champion, and Ventura, who also ran a stunt team, led him to pro wrestling. He also did some movie work, becoming even more of a physical fitness fanatic. It is certain that from 1953 on he became well known for his sensational style in wrestling rings. Frank Valois and Larry Moquin spotted him while touring Europe and brought the new guy to the attention of Montreal superstar Yvon Robert. The trio then sold promoter Eddie Quinn on bringing him to Canada. Quinn renamed the rookie Edouard Carpentier, hinting at a supposed relation to Georges Carpentier, the French boxing star who fought Jack Dempsey.

What better controversial background could there be for a pro wrestler? Whatever the shadings of truth were, Carpentier was an immediate sensation. His Montreal debut was on April 18, 1956. By July 18, 1956, Carpentier tackled Argentina Rocca at Montreal's Delorimier Stadium before 23,227. Later that summer, Carpentier faced Killer Kowalski and broke the 20,000 attendance mark again. A star was born, and every promoter in wrestling wanted a piece of the action.

One early comparison was made to Rocca, for there was a similarity in approach because they both had acrobatic backgrounds. Carpentier, though, had a meaner edge and fans sensed that he was more competitive. Once he figured out that Quinn was cheating him out of money, Carpentier learned to stand up for himself. Rocca had a simpler nature and was used as a cash cow for years. Lou Thesz said Rocca had no wrestling ability and less performing aptitude — slapping an opponent with his bare feet, while it made fans laugh, was "flimsy," as Thesz called it.

Carpentier's toolbox included acrobatics that ended up in pretty solid physical contact. He could execute solid wrestling skills, which made the aerial explosions more effective. He was not indiscriminate in flying, only going airborne when it was most valuable. His drop kicks were high and on the money. A patented back flip off the top rope was followed by a back body drop or a drop kick. His steamroller, also called a cannonball, ended with a massive "splat" right on the gut of a foe.

Only listed — generously — as 5'10", Carpentier could sell and get sympathy. He was so thickly muscled, the audience believed it took a lot to hurt him. When Carpentier made a comeback, it was electrifying; the Flying Frenchman understood what worked for him and why.

Thesz called Carpentier "a helluva performer who understood how to use the acrobatics. He had a lot of pride in what he did." The battles involving Carpentier against such massive monsters as Kowalski, Don Leo Jonathan, and Gene Kiniski were classic little man versus big man tests.

When his comet took off, Carpentier quickly won the respect of the promoters. Look at the political position he was placed in within three years of coming to North America: picked to be the key performer in a historically significant championship commotion during 1957 and 1958.

Carpentier was involved in matches that, by hook and by crook, led to title claims by Verne Gagne for the AWA and Fred Blassie for what was the WWA in Los Angeles. The fabulous Flying Frenchman had become such a strong figure that fans accepted what he did as having tremendous meaning. He had connected with his audience so tightly that they *believed* he was in tough competition at the highest level.

On the surface it all started June 14, 1957, in Chicago as Carpentier went after NWA king Lou Thesz. After splitting falls, Thesz could not answer the bell for the decisive fall. Other reports said that the referee stopped the match during the final stanza because Thesz clearly had a back injury. Most agree that the decision was called a victory for Carpentier by disqualification. By NWA rules, that verdict would not allow the belt to change hands, except this time the match had been stopped because of injury. That left all sorts of room for spinning the result regarding who the champion was. The NWA, with the approval and assistance of both president Sam Muchnick and Thesz himself, would have two titleholders during a period when Thesz had accepted some very lucrative bookings in Asia and would not be available for booking by the NWA membership.

After a period of controversy with two claimants, the apparent plan was that Thesz would defeat Carpentier and unite the two claims.

See what WWE could have accomplished in their two-title scenario with CM Punk and John Cena if they had had some patience and imagination? Of course, the scheme that Muchnick and the NWA set up didn't work as planned.

Before the plot climaxed, Thesz lost the NWA crown to Dick Hutton. Quinn, the Montreal promoter who booked Carpentier got into a bitter disagreement with Muchnick and the NWA about how the deal was going down. In addition, Carpentier rebelled after he and Quinn, who had a contract to book Carpentier and who handled payments from other promoters, got into a dispute about whether Carpentier was getting the right amount of money from Quinn. Fred Kohler, the ever-aggressive Chicago promoter, managed to steal Carpentier from Quinn. In the chaos, it's often overlooked that Carpentier had been involved in yet another world championship claim thanks to battles he had with Kowalski in Montreal for what Quinn called the IWA.

While still claiming some version of the world championship, Carpentier put over Kowalski in Boston on May 3, 1958, then lost to Gagne in Omaha on August 9, 1958, and completed the triple play by losing to Blassie in L.A. on June 12,1961. Yet in Montreal on July 21, 1960, Carpentier downed Buddy Rogers and one year later, before 20,618 at a Montreal stadium show, flattened Hans Schmidt. And he again tackled Rogers, by then the NWA ruler, before a huge crowd at Comiskey Park in Chicago on July 27, 1962.

Obviously Carpentier, who was accepted as a legitimate title claimant, was a major superstar from one coast to the other. Plus, he was doing big business both before and after that booking melee.

In some ways, Carpentier became a less-noted version of Andre the Giant (with whom he often teamed and whom he had supposedly discovered). He was a good drawing card whether or not he was a regular in a territory. Throughout the 1960s and into the 1970s, using Montreal as a base, Carpentier was in main events from the WWWF to the AWA to Los Angeles. He was a big favorite in St. Louis.

In the AWA, his matches against Maurice "Mad Dog" Vachon were all-time favorites of those who saw them. His feud with Kiniski jumped all over the map. Dick the Bruiser was a perfect foe for many wild evenings of fun and frolic. Actually, Carpentier formed an aerially dynamic tag team with Rocca (their differences made the partnership work well) on a few occasions. Johnny Valentine and John Tolos had bruising combat with Carpentier. The Destroyer, who respected Carpentier's basic skills, would produce a heel versus face event that was more wrestling-oriented. Always the good guy, Carpentier protected his reputation and made sure that bookers understood if he lost, it had to mean something.

He was a private person, described by many of his peers as something of a loner. Harley Race once called him "crusty," explaining that Carpentier knew what he wanted and how he wanted it.

Ivan Koloff said that Carpentier was not someone who could be kicked around, even comparing him to Billy Robinson. Plus, according to every observer, he was always in great condition and could go forever at a fast pace.

But he slowed down in the 1970s, all that high-flying coming home to roost with a litany of aches, pains, and injuries. Edouard made a few carefully selected outings and then quietly disappeared from the scene. He did, however, do French-language commentary on television for the WWF/WWE.

Anyone who saw him can remember the burst of fire that ran through the crowd when Carpentier did that letter-perfect back flip high off the top rope. And the superstar knew what to do both before and after. R. Kelly could have been thinking of Carpentier when he sang "I Believe I Can Fly." No wonder the Fabulous Flying Frenchman has stuck a landing right in the heart of the 50 greatest pro wrestlers ever.

#22 DICK THE BRUISER
The one and only

It's like a nuclear explosion. A madman, his eyes on fire and mighty muscles bulging, begins to stomp on the heavy wooden steps leading to the ring. All of the massive muscles in his chest and shoulders flex as his foot slams down heavily into the two-by-fours. Then, suddenly, crrrraaaaack! The entire building can hear it, all 8,000 people gasping.

The wood, once broken, can now be kicked and yanked apart by this monster. Wood chips fly into the air and land by startled ringside spectators. The steps are destroyed as he rips the structure to bits. And then the jagged piece of wood appears in his hand. Triumphant, the bad guy carries the wood like a knife and charges the stunned favorite.

Ah, that sounds like fiction, doesn't it? Instead, it's an accurate description of Dick the Bruiser going on a rampage during a main event with "Cowboy" Bob Ellis. That was 1963, and The Bruiser was doing serious hardcore long before anyone ever gimmicked a plywood table. You see, there's a little bit more to the incident.

The Bruiser began pounding the wood against Ellis's forehead, poking the jagged edges into his skin as ringside fans shrieked. And did

Ellis's blood ever flow! Gordon Solie, the famous Florida announcer who coined the phrase, would have been proud, for soon The Bruiser had turned Ellis's face into "a crimson mask."

But then from somewhere, maybe the desperate roar of the fans, Ellis found strength after The Bruiser crawled up on the turnbuckles. "Cowboy" snatched the 250-pound bulldozer and slammed him. The wood lay on the mat. Ellis spied it, grabbed it, and gouged The Bruiser's forehead in return.

Soon both wrestlers sported crimson masks. From that point on, referees got dropped, help was called, the bell sounded, and the match was supposedly stopped. Yet The Bruiser had one last act of defiance in store.

Enraged, Dick went to the concrete floor and honed in on the biggest missile he could find — the old-school press table, eight feet long and made of sturdy two-by-fours. With the building in turmoil, The Bruiser somehow got the awkward piece of furniture overhead, pressed it upward, and hurled it — actually hurled it! — into the center of the ring where it nearly decapitated Ellis and a hapless referee.

For good measure, The Bruiser then pitched three metal folding chairs high over the ropes and into the bloody ring before he stomped head-first through the hostile crowd — the hostile crowd that parted because everyone believed this guy could snap at any time.

As much as they all hated The Bruiser that night, and he repeated that performance with Ellis among others all over the Midwest before big gates, it would only be a few years before Dick the Bruiser became one of the first and best character babyfaces in pro wrestling history. The fans had already seen his act in New York's Madison Square Garden, where Dick's outburst ignited a riot during a tag duel that featured him and Dr. Jerry Graham against Argentina Rocca and Edouard Carpentier in 1957. The ensuing suspension discouraged The Bruiser from ever coming back to the Northeast (Vince McMahon Sr. may have been startled as well by the intensity of Dick's shenanigans), so folks were deprived of the chance to cheer the guy they had hated because he was so damn exciting to watch.

Dick the Bruiser (left) squares up against Dick Murdoch

He was always unpredictable. In 1982 Dick the Bruiser stole Ric Flair's gaudy robe and paraded around in the garment. The Bruiser's wrestling tactics comprised a punch, a kick, a slam and then ramming a foe into a ringside table or whacking the poor chump with a chair. This was The Bruiser's version of scientific wrestling.

Since he now generally did that to bad guys like Black Jack Lanza, Baron Von Raschke, and Harley Race, the fans now stood and cheered. And they wanted him to hurt his rival even more. So Dick did. Oh, and did he ever love to chase and batter one of wrestling's absolute best managers, Bobby Heenan.

William Richard Afflis did not invent Dick the Bruiser: he *was* Dick the Bruiser through and through. What happened when action started was spontaneous, seldom planned past certain moments.

Talk of hardcore. The Bruiser was hardcore before the original Extreme Championship Wrestling was ever thought of. Talk of attitude. The Bruiser was a bully whose attitude of bluster and intimidation made him stand out from the pack. Once the adrenalin started flowing, it was blood, guts, and violence, especially when he was the villain.

What a surprise Dick's antics must have been to those who knew the Afflis family, which was stable, affluent, and politically connected in their native Indiana. Dick was the stereotypical high school jock, a superb athlete with more than a hint of arrogance because he knew how good he was. He played football at Purdue before switching to the University of Nevada. He also worked as a bouncer at various rowdy but well-known clubs, such as Harold's in Reno.

From 1951 through 1954 he was a starter for the Green Bay Packers in the National Football League. He had a reputation for being athletic, mean, tough, and undisciplined. No surprise in that. Too bad Afflis left the Packers before Vince Lombardi took over as coach, because the media was deprived of what would likely have been some juicy stories of two stubborn guys butting heads.

In the summer of 1954, Afflis made his debut as a wrestler in Reno. While he's always had a reputation for being wild, look a little deeper after considering who trained him: football all-star and talented wrestler Leo Nomellini, an excellent amateur and scientific pro grappler by the name of Joe Pazandak, and none other than Verne Gagne. The Bruiser knew about hammerlocks, even if he seldom used them.

Dick the Bruiser quickly became a mainstay at the top of lineups for the simple and usual reason — he was box office. He made a deal with promoter Jim Barnett, who promoted in Detroit and then Indianapolis, and clashed with the likes of Gagne, Ellis, Wilbur Snyder, Hans Schmidt, Don Leo Jonathan, Yukon Eric, and Bobo Brazil. Eventually he went to Los Angeles and battled Fred Blassie. He formed a famous tag team with The Crusher (Reggie Lisowski) and had knock-down, drag-out brawls with teams like Larry Hennig and Harley Race. He invaded St. Louis, surprised many by settling into a longstanding friendship with Sam Muchnick, and established an even stronger reputation for packed houses and red-hot battles. He made several successful tours of Japan. He got national publicity for a feud with football all-pro Alex Karras, who had been suspended from the NFL.

Even then, there was something in his personality that made him the heel fans loved to hate. He was one step away from being a babyface even from his debut performances, which was amazing because his tactics weren't vaguely scientific . . . unless kicking, punching, and plain old bashing are scientific. Of course, some who recall The Bruiser from the end of his career forget or don't even know how athletic and powerful he was into the early 1970s.

The guy was a stud who scared fans by his very looks. He was a bully, the worst of anyone's imagination. And he had that personality, a magnetic presence, that nobody can teach or invent. A volcano primed to explode at any second, he was real.

Not surprisingly, considering his background, it wasn't long before The Bruiser was fiddling around in the politics of wrestling. He formed a business alliance with Snyder, who was much more laid back than the aggressive Afflis, and forced Barnett out of Indianapolis, taking over the town and territory. Along with Gagne, Afflis and Snyder bought Chicago from Fred Kohler. Afterward, Gagne and The Bruiser were always fussing and feuding about control of that lucrative town.

For years the operation in Indianapolis was strong and profitable. But things cooled. The Bruiser hurt a few feelings by supposedly being tight on payoffs, and the continued emphasis on putting over both himself and Snyder after their primes took a toll on gates, as it usually did anytime a wrestler got control of a promotion and failed to inject enough new faces into the mix.

But Dick the Bruiser had long since secured a spot among the greats of all time as an explosive heel and a character babyface, perhaps one of the first.

When he finally made the so-called switch to babyface, the audiences were absolutely passionate in pulling for this "man's man." Dick positioned himself as the world's most dangerous wrestler.

Many of his interviews were classics. He shot right from the hip and connected with the gut. He could face the most clean-cut and talented good guy, such as Jack Brisco, and somehow turn Brisco into the villain just by how The Bruiser presented his own position. In that unforgettable interview before a title match with Brisco, Dick described Brisco as a great champion, a close friend, someone he loved, and promised, "When they wheel out Jack Brisco's bloody, beaten carcass on that stretcher, I still love him and he's still my best friend . . . [I'll] help load my friend's body into the ambulance."

Or he could go into a rant, for example about Ric Flair dressing in women's robes and prancing about, that left audiences torn between laughing and cheering. Once, before a duel with Gene Kiniski, Dick somehow got started about how his bookie "Louie" had money on this match, making it crucial that The Bruiser whip Kiniski so he wouldn't have to defend himself by dropping "Louie" into the Mississippi River. A writing team couldn't make up material that witty and sharp. It was all Bruiser, off the cuff.

Was he a great worker? Well, not by most standards. Maybe it wasn't smooth, maybe it wasn't high-flying, but crowds absolutely bought and believed what Dick the Bruiser was doing. Isn't that what matters? And especially until late in his career, if The Bruiser was in with a quick and clever opponent, he was a good enough athlete to stay stride for stride — before he popped the cork and began brawling. Dick certainly didn't sell much, but when he dropped to one knee, fans would react, knowing he was in trouble.

Once, in Kansas City, The Bruiser was in a bout against Bobby Jaggers, a solid hand trained by the Funks and then relatively new to opposing The Bruiser. Bobby threw a couple of punches and — oops! — realized he had potatoed The Bruiser, causing blood to trickle from above Dick's eye. Jaggers hesitated. Dick touched his forehead and saw the blood. "Oh, damn," thought Jaggers.

But The Bruiser rasped, "Hit me harder!" Jaggers threw another punch, this time being more careful.

"No!" growled The Bruiser. "Damn it! Hit me hard! Hit me, hit me!"

So Jaggers let loose, pounding on Dick's head. The blood really started to flow. Dick dropped to one knee and the crowd yelled. Dick got back up, taking still another shot from Jaggers.

And then Jaggers heard a guttural snarl as The Bruiser rumbled, "Way to go, kid. That's it!" At that point, Dick the Bruiser made his comeback and beat the holy hell out of Bobby Jaggers as the fans stood and cheered.

Those folks would probably be cheering now: Dick the Bruiser has a prominent spot among the 50 greatest pro wrestlers ever.

#21 BRET HART
All the qualities of the best in one package

Bret Hart is fond of proclaiming that he is "the best there is, the best there was, and the best there ever will be." A proud competitor, Hart can be forgiven for this burst of ego-fulfillment because wrestling promos today are all about hyperbole. Humility is dead. Everyone brags. Good guys, bad guys — can't tell them apart when they talk — they all brag. They also strain mightily to work in an assigned catch phrase at the expense of telling a story that might require some thought from the audience.

The truth about the Hitman is that he isn't, he wasn't, and he won't be the best ever. Nonetheless, Hart did have enough of all the qualities necessary to earn recognition among the 50 greatest pro wrestlers ever. This gladiator was quite good in every aspect.

While he wasn't the biggest drawing card, he was solid at a time the promotion needed stability. And, aside from the rare personalities like an Andre the Giant, a good part of drawing a crowd is context and booking. Although Hart wasn't a particularly outstanding promo guy, he got the important points across.

In the ring, Hart could flat-out go. The genes were there, and so was the opportunity. Finally. As everyone likely knows by now, Bret's father was Stu Hart, the famed promoter, shooter, and trainer located in Calgary. What a mixed background Bret had, watching his dad train newcomers in the noted Dungeon, seeing the worked matches and absorbing things like instinct, plus having a fine amateur career through high school and into college.

Not surprisingly, Hart got into play-for-pay wrestling pretty quickly. According to some stories, he at first hadn't decided to commit to pro wrestling, considering filmmaking instead. But he had a rare aptitude for the mat game, and soon he was a key performer for his dad's promotion, picking up even more experience in matches against the Dynamite Kid and unselfishly doing whatever jobs were required to make the shows successful.

This also opened the door to Antonio Inoki's New Japan, where Hart got to clash with the legendary Tiger Mask.

Now here's a hard reality that might make a reader or two squawk in dismay. In the late 1960s and most certainly in the 1970s, the Stampede promotion was near the bottom of territories where top wrestlers wanted to go. It was down there with Memphis. Romantic history has served both territories well, but neither was the place for a guy capable of making big money. Young men with some potential went to Calgary because of Stu's knowledge, but many high-level athletes chose training with Verne Gagne instead. Stampede had lousy pay, small towns, long trips, and miserable weather for a high percentage of the year unless a guy was used to the climate.

No established star went there. The territory did, however, have some strong workers, often smaller guys or new talent from foreign locales using Calgary as a stepping stone. Who knows whether Bret Hart would have gone to the major markets if territorial wrestling had survived in some form. Because other promoters liked his dad, he might have gotten an opportunity. His size was okay, and obviously he could work. The question would likely have come down to charisma and booking. But he

might have been happy mixing home with well-paying trips to Japan. It's a question to think about.

Of course, the tumult of VKM running roughshod over the wrestling world changed the landscape for everyone, particularly Bret Hart. When McMahon made the deal to buy out Stu, which wasn't completed as agreed upon financially, Vince also promised to use some talent that was dear to the elder Hart. Thus, Bret joined Dynamite Kid, Davey Boy Smith, and Jim Neidhart in the WWF in 1984.

Bret became part of the Hart Foundation, teaming with Neidhart in a duo managed by irrepressible Jimmy Hart. Bret added a dimension of wrestling to the heel duo, which was positioned in the middle of most lineups. Of course, having swept up many big names at the time, VKM had an abundance of known and talented stars at his disposal. Bret, though, made a lot of folks take notice through impressive singles duels with Ricky Steamboat and fiery tag combat against the British Bulldogs. Hart started to climb the ladder, which was no easy task.

The Foundation, mainly due to Bret, was turned babyface as Hart got more opportunities on his own. A feud with the Honky Tonk Man was well received, and after a bout against Andre the Giant, Andre emphasized to Vince how well Hart could do as a single. In the early 1990s, Hart was rising rapidly thanks to rivalries with Curt Hennig, Roddy Piper, and eventually Shawn Michaels.

In addition, the WWF faced a new climate when business fell off drastically by 1992. Scandals about sex and especially steroids, along with a federal trial involving McMahon, sent the company reeling. Strict testing was introduced, and the days of giving pumped-up muscle monsters all the main events ended. Suddenly smaller, more athletic, clean-cut types became the choice for the WWF, which was under pressure from both the government and the media; thus, the torch was handed to Bret Hart.

Hart became the WWF champion for the first of five times between 1992 and 1997 by defeating Ric Flair. While it was a marketing phrase, Hart's "excellence of execution" was obvious and kept the promotion afloat. Business leveled out domestically but surged overseas where Hart was a hot number, a trend that was already rolling in 1991 when Hart and Davey Boy headlined before 78,927 fans at London's Wembley Stadium.

Certainly on display was Hart's inborn professionalism. He shrugged off injuries, appeared on time for every date, moved heaven and earth to elevate opponents, and generally made so-called old school look pretty good in a crisis. As well as facing other big names of the time, Bret even made a feud with his own brother, Owen, come across as serious and passionate.

In 1996, Hart dabbled with acting. He dropped the WWF crown to Michaels in a famous 60-minute Iron Man match at *WrestleMania XII* on March 31. In what was yet another chapter of the promotional wars, World Championship Wrestling came calling with a huge monetary offer for Hart to switch sides. But Hart stayed with the WWF, signing a jaw-dropping 20-year deal that McMahon almost immediately began to regret offering.

Quickly, the WWF title went back to Hart. At *WrestleMania XIII*, Hart and Stone Cold Steve Austin pulled off one of wrestling's most difficult feats to do correctly and effectively, making a double turn in the same match. After a bloody brawl, Austin ended up being the red-hot lead babyface and Hart was the heel. That, however, did nothing to change the situation between Hart and McMahon, who decided he would breach the 20-year contract and told Hart to cut whatever deal he could with WCW. The company had been losing money, and McMahon felt he could get better terms on loans without the $28,000 guaranteed weekly for Hart. Vince asked Hart to take less. Bret refused. Feelings were still raw as business began to improve, but by then McMahon apparently had decided Michaels and Hart could not coexist. The money likely helped him to decide to keep Michaels and cut Hart.

On November 3, 1997, Hart signed with Eric Bischoff and WCW. He gave notice to McMahon, although he was already booked and announced for the *Survivor Series* pay-per-view in Montreal on November 9, risking the WWF laurels against Michaels. Backstage politics flew thick and hard regarding how and when Hart would drop the title. Bret had creative control in the last days of the contract, and McMahon feared Hart would end up appearing on WCW television with the WWF title belt. Hart, always proud about his Canadian heritage, did not want to lose the title in his native country. Apparently, a compromise was worked out to satisfy everyone and eventually get the WWF title to Michaels — but not that night. Egos and politics were running amok!

In the match itself, Michaels clamped a sharpshooter on Hart. The plan was that Hart would reverse the hold. Before he could, however, referee Earl Hebner called for the bell and said that Hart had submitted. McMahon came to ringside, where a fuming Hart spat on him. Later in a dressing room, he allegedly punched McMahon. Austin was now the top babyface in the company, McMahon was the top heel for his actions, and Hart was on his way to WCW.

The entire scenario ended up the subject of a well-regarded 1998 documentary called *Wrestling With Shadows*. Skeptics might ask, "It just happened to be filmed as part of a movie?" Well, it's unfair and likely incorrect to suggest that. The Montreal screwjob, as it came to be known, has been an integral part of various booking plans ever since — to the point of "Give me a break!"

Granted, to a new audience this is something unexpected. Those who have taken the time to understand the business, though, know that double-crosses happened surprisingly often before World War II. All readers need to do is check the stories of Frank Gotch, Joe Stecher, "Strangler" Lewis, Jim Londos, and Ray Steele. Once in a great while it even happened when one wrestler shot on another. Regardless, the incident between Hart and Michaels will stand in history because the background and details have become so public.

On the other hand, the WCW excursion is probably one Bret would just as soon erase from the record books. Not that all of his bouts were bad — to the contrary, all were at least adequate and some were good. But, as was usual in a company that would blunder into extinction, the booking was a mess, the internal politics a disaster. WCW was handed the hottest babyface in the world after the McMahon double-cross and botched it up. By 1998, they tried to turn Hart heel, which was nothing the audience wanted to see. It took the edge off.

Things got even worse for Hart in 1999. Owen, his brother, was killed when a stunt entry backfired and he plunged from the ceiling of Kemper Arena in Kansas City on May 23. Needless to say, the ill feelings between the Harts and McMahon were made 100 times worse by the tragedy.

Then, only a few weeks after Hart won the WCW title on November 16, powerful Bill Goldberg kicked him in the head during a match at Starrcade, causing a severe concussion. Reliable as always, Hart worked a few more matches after the blow and likely suffered additional concussions. Hart never blamed Goldberg for what happened, but the injury led to his release from the WCW contract and his retirement in 2000.

As he flitted around the fringes of the business, another disaster struck. Hart had to fight even harder after suffering a stroke, which left many friends fearing for his recovery. But he bravely rehabilitated himself, and the fact that bridges in wrestling can seldom be burned proved true once again.

Bret Hart made peace with Vince McMahon Jr. and WWE. Bret shook hands with Michaels on live television, thus burying the hatchet. His return also led to a match of sorts at *WrestleMania XXVI*, when Hart got his public revenge by pounding a mostly defenseless McMahon into defeat. Since then, Hart has occasionally appeared in televised skits, and his reputation has been protected and polished.

He has a right to brag. Bret Hart has been a major figure in pro wrestling for many years. He has earned his fame with his well-being, both physical and emotional. That he belongs with the finest 50 in pro wrestling annals is unquestioned. He is *one* of the best there is, there was, and there ever will be — *one* of the very best.

In this assembly, that's the highest praise anyone can get.

#20 THE ROCK

Movies and wrestling — a magic celebrity

Dwayne Johnson is what every person today who dreams about becoming a professional wrestler wants to be. The Rock needed only eight years to become a movie star, of all things, in addition to being one of the hottest properties ever in pro wrestling history. Even more than Brock Leshar, The Rock is a product of the times, blending entertainer and athlete to become a mainstream celebrity bigger than any wrestler ever was.

Of course, The Rock has the right tools to work with. While he stumbled a bit at first to find what worked for him in his wrestling career, certain elements of personality and athleticism almost guaranteed that sooner or later he would break through as a gigantic star. Nobody expected just how colossal that notoriety would be.

His position at the pinnacle of global recognition does not, however, make him *the* greatest wrestler of all time. It does put him among them. The Rock is too big to fail as he navigates today's path of celebrity. He can step back into pro wrestling, as he has done in the past two years, and still energize the product to such a degree that he draws a record audience.

Not being around on a regular basis helps, of course, because it keeps The Rock, as a wrestling persona, fresh and unblemished.

A valid question is how well The Rock would have drawn had he stayed in wrestling full time after the hot spell. He would have still meant a lot at the gate, but would the big highs have dropped if he did PPV after PPV after PPV? Would his act, which is pretty intense, have gone stale with week after week of television exposure?

World Wrestling Entertainment and The Rock were made for each other at a particular moment in the history of the business. Keep in mind that Dwayne Johnson left WWE before he really hit the jackpot as a movie star. He believed he had something special and was willing to roll the dice on his own.

Yet The Rock is still hooked to some degree on the pro wrestling community, a community both his father Rocky Johnson and his maternal grandfather Chief Peter Maivia were part of. It never gets out of the blood.

On February 18, 1978, little Dwayne was there when his dad fought to a one-hour stalemate with NWA champion Harley Race at Kiel Auditorium in St. Louis. Shy yet smiling, the little fellow mostly hung onto Dad's leg amid the usual chatter of the dressing room. That kiddo grew into an impressive young athlete as he and his mother traveled around North America, following Rocky's career as a main event performer in various territories.

Dwayne got a full ride to play football at the University of Miami, where he was part of the Hurricanes' national championship team in 1991 even though he was injured. After a brief time with the Calgary Stampeders in the Canadian Football League, Dwayne decided to try pro wrestling. His dad did his best to discourage him but eventually agreed to train his son — with the warning that nothing would be made easy for him.

Of course, it didn't hurt that Rocky had been a popular figure in the WWF for years. After a few tryout matches, Dwayne was signed and sent to Memphis to make his debut as "Flex Kavana." Not surprisingly, Dwayne took to wrestling easily and was headed for the big time by the

George Napolitano

end of 1996. He was billed as Rocky Maivia, the "Blue Chipper" and future of the company.

WWF pushed, but fans pushed back. They obviously resented being force-fed this rookie, no matter how promising and handsome he was. Working against him to a degree was the growing popularity of Stone Cold Steve Austin, an anti-establishment, outlaw good guy. Early on, the chemistry worked against Dwayne despite outstanding battles with Triple H and Bret Hart.

The logical response was to slide Johnson into heel mode, which really allowed Dwayne's personality to cut loose during entertaining promos. More and more he was billed as The Rock and he got into a feud with his erstwhile partner Faarooq (Ron Simmons). A high-impact ladder match against Triple H in 1998 is often considered the turning point, when fans began to accept and respect The Rock.

Once firmly entrenched in the feature mix, The Rock was given a juicy role as the enforcer for Vince McMahon and his family in their dispute with Austin. In not unusual fashion with WWF booking, The Rock bounced back and forth on the good guy–bad guy scale, but by now the reactions were always explosive. He was over, in no small part because of his wild-and-wooly duels against Mankind (Mick Foley in one of his several identities).

This also led to scuffles with Austin and with Ken Shamrock. The Rock quickly landed major roles in several *WrestleManias*. When The Rock reluctantly buried the hatchet and became Mankind's partner, they did a parody of *This Is Your Life*, which lured a record viewing audience for *Raw*.

He threw in more catch phrases in one promo than most performers do in a career. His delivery was dynamic. If pro wrestling was indeed only entertainment as VKM maintained, The Rock was able to cash in and still do enough athletically to satisfy the portion of the potential audience that preferred action.

More importantly, as 2000 dawned, the WWF was taking control in its promotional war against the failing WCW. While Austin has probably received the most praise for leading this charge, The Rock was a critical part of the picture. In retrospect, VKM was the beneficiary of a crew of charismatic and talented performers who all ended up in the same place at the same time, and Vince wisely gave them room to roam creatively.

Again, in not surprising style, The Rock won and lost various titles, including the WWF crown. That, along with his oft-broken relationship with McMahon, gave The Rock the opportunity to meet the best talent that the WWF had to offer in spotlight matches against Chris Benoit, Triple H, Kane, The Undertaker, and even Vince's son Shane. This meant The Rock could shine both in the promos leading up to the battles and then in the conflicts themselves. Naturally, Austin was always available for that much-awaited monumental showdown whenever circumstances warranted.

By the time Stone Cold and The Rock squared off at *WrestleMania XVII* on April 1, 2001, they were able to ring up 40 million dollars in income from PPV buys, merchandising sales, and live gate. It set records in all areas. On the heels of that triumph, Dwayne caught fresh eyes in the movie industry with his role in *The Mummy Returns*. He then inked a deal for *The Scorpion King* that was reportedly the highest salary ever made by an actor in his debut starring role. Maybe there was more out there than wrestling and the WWF.

Thus began a level of mainstream celebrity that probably no one anticipated. After becoming only the second wrestler (Hulk Hogan was the first) to host *Saturday Night Live*, The Rock made the cover of *Newsweek* and *TV Guide*. He was the subject of numerous major magazine stories and a guest on David Letterman's show. Another part of Dwayne's life was getting into high gear with his focus on the movies and acting.

The Rock found room, however, for a couple of major angles. In *WrestleMania XVIII* on March 17, 2002, The Rock took on Hulk in a battle of the icons that brought in boatloads of money to the WWF coffers. One year later, Austin and The Rock clashed again in another highly profitable *Mania*. New directions, however, were pulling The Rock away from wrestling. He was a sporadic participant in the WWF hijinks and made what was then his final *Mania* outing in 2004. It would be seven years until The Rock was back at *WrestleMania*.

In that long gap, The Rock built a strong resume as he expanded the types of movie roles he could play. The Disney people cast him in several lead roles and were reportedly very pleased with his work. For a while he distanced himself from wrestling by using the name Dwayne Johnson on the marquee. He eventually went back to using The Rock. He has moved gracefully and effectively between family, comedy, and action roles.

But the pro wrestling bug kept biting. Though he'd stopped wrestling, he apparently never stopped thinking about where his fame began. Tease, talk, an unexpected drop-in . . . The Rock kept himself alive on the perimeters of what has become WWE — until 2011. That's when Dwayne Johnson got the ball rolling for a feud with John Cena for at least two *WrestleManias*.

The collision between Cena and Rock in 2012 was a crowd-pleaser that delivered the best of each performer for more than 30 exciting minutes. Most importantly, the two utilized their skills to tell a compelling story that helped cement both of their positions among the greatest ever. Some critics might have griped about technical points in the match, or the audience manipulation by WWE during the buildup, but the fact is that the intensity and emotion were right at the top of the scale.

The Rock should have had an even greater match than he did, since he'd barely worked in recent years. The point is, though, Dwayne did it and did it with style and fire. For that matter, was "Strangler" Lewis anywhere near his peak when he had the classic showdown with Jim Londos in 1934?

The other side of the coin, of course, is that the 2012 Cena versus Rock demonstrated why Dory Funk Jr. and Jack Brisco landed so high among the greatest 50 ever. Brisco and Funk were in their primes physically, mentally, and emotionally when they battled for hours and hours all over North America. Those two staged their time period's *WrestleMania* main events probably hundreds of times. Nonetheless, The Rock had everything to be proud of when he crawled back through the ropes again.

What brought The Rock back to pro wrestling? He clearly didn't need the money, although a one-time gig in *Mania* can pay big bucks. Maybe he felt the visibility would revitalize an old fan base while winning some new followers, thus helping boost his movie career. Yet those factors seem a little too crass, a little too business, to be the entire truth.

Make this bet and expect to cash a winner. Down deep, The Rock came back, if only for an occasional taste, because he missed what pro wrestling did for him. A movie can be a big rush and last seemingly forever. But pro wrestling, with all that energy and excitement concentrated completely on *the moment* before a live crowd, carries a charge unlike any other.

The Rock missed it. He needed it again. And those who watch and enjoy the spectacle are happier for that. Why is he headed back for both the *Royal Rumble* and *WrestleMania* — at least — in 2013?

Pros and cons about The Rock? One thing is certain. He deserves to be in with the 50 greatest ever. The question is where.

In his favor, whenever he does make that rare appearance, it's going to be a big deal and get much more mainstream play than anything or almost anyone else. Whether Vince likes it or not, the media will hype it even more because it is *pro wrestling*. The Rock's going to draw a much larger buy rate than WWE would normally get for a particular event without him. Although he can't be as sharp in performing as he once was, with current pro wrestling based mostly around spots, The Rock is smart enough to put together an extremely memorable bout with any competent opponent. He understands crowds and how he appeals to them, so he can blow the doors off the building. This is especially true because he's only in action once in a great while, so overexposure and boredom are unlikely to harm him.

Against him, that last statement also plays as a negative. The Rock isn't challenged to change what he does, but rather to stick with what has worked before. Contrasting him to the others in the upper echelon of the 50 finest, The Rock falls short when it comes to having a long career with a variety of accomplishments. It's all about WWE for him, but that isn't his fault. Maybe if he'd had the chance to clash with a greater variety of opponents from different backgrounds, The Rock would have become an even better performer in the ring. Still, how can anyone blame a magnetic personality like Dwayne Johnson for cashing in on the movie opportunity when that door was opened?

In the end, the results seem pretty clear. Accept that The Rock has a unique spot in pro wrestling history that must be celebrated and honored. Enjoy any time that this unparalleled talent can spend where it all began — in professional wrestling. And welcome him to his place at the table with the greatest ever.

#19 JACK BRISCO
A world-class athlete with expert wrestling skills

Crisp and precise. Dedicated and disciplined. In a nutshell, that describes Jack Brisco. His idols, the superstars on whom he patterned himself, were Lou Thesz and Dan Hodge. That he successfully managed to emulate Thesz and Hodge demonstrates why Brisco joins his heroes among the 50 greatest pro wrestlers ever.

If ever anyone carried himself like a world-class athlete, it was Jack Brisco, and he probably was one of the two or three best all-around athletes in the history of major pro wrestling stars. With the look ladies love and guys envy, only a glance confirmed that Brisco was indeed the stud athlete, the best player on the high school football team, or the college athlete most likely to be drafted first by the pros.

In high school, the only match Brisco lost was as a sophomore. Three times Jack was an Oklahoma state champion. He was also an All-State fullback in football and took second in the state in high jump, an event for which he never had time to train. He was just that naturally talented. At Oklahoma State University, after turning down a football scholarship from legendary coach Bud Wilkinson at the University of

Oklahoma, Brisco finished second in the nation in 1964 (his only loss in college) and won the NCAA wrestling championship in 1965 during his final year of competition, when he was nationally dominant. He lost one year of eligibility (not counting his first year because freshmen then weren't eligible) because he had to work as a janitor to earn money for his new family.

Partially because he needed the money, and partially because it had been a lifetime dream, Brisco jumped into pro wrestling immediately after taking the collegiate title. He also politely declined an offer from Tom Landry, then the coach of the Dallas Cowboys, who knew all about Brisco's exploits and wanted him to take a shot at the National Football League. Brisco, however, had grown up in little Blackwell, Oklahoma, reading *Wrestling Revue* and watching the televised exploits of Thesz and Hodge.

Plain and simple, Jack Brisco wanted to be a professional wrestler. That was his dream. And damned if he didn't make it, becoming one of the very best in history. The only question is how high to rank him. I was fortunate enough to be working for Sam Muchnick in St. Louis during most of Brisco's career and can attest that, move for move, I cannot remember anyone who was better than Jack.

With all due respect to Bret Hart, Brisco was better in execution. When Kurt Angle was serious, what a wonderful competition against Brisco that would have been in a pro wrestling ring. Jack told me several times that he would have loved to work with Angle. Brisco also liked shooting, so that might also have entered into the picture with someone of Angle's caliber.

Whether it was sharp suplexes, lightning takedowns, stunning fireman carries (perhaps the predecessor of John Cena's attitude adjustment), or blistering, fiery comebacks that immediately brought supportive fans to their feet, everything was just so "on the money." Oh, and those drop kicks! In his prime, Brisco's vertical leap would allow him to plant his boots right into the jaws of Big Bill Miller or Black Jack Lanza, both of whom stood around 6'5".

The charisma was as natural as the talent, for Brisco connected with his audience immediately. By any definition, Brisco was a babyface. His natural humility came across in interviews that didn't have catch phrases but rather established Brisco as serious a professional athlete as any football or baseball player. Brisco was not a huge man, at perhaps 6'1" and 230 pounds, but he looked like he could easily be an NFL running back or a .300 hitter in baseball. The casual sports audience took Jack to heart. Even when he became the National Wrestling Alliance champion, and sometimes cut a corner or two to save the crown, the crowd might boo then but still applaud when Jack retained the title. He had their respect.

In competition Brisco was so confident and efficient, proving that he was a stubborn competitor who resided at a higher altitude than almost any other. Everything flowed smoothly, with an edge that advertised he would do what it took to emerge triumphant. Rip Hawk, a talented worker himself, said that wrestling Brisco "was like wrestling glass, he was that smooth." Don Leo Jonathan described Brisco as "probably the greatest champion of the twentieth century," and Jonathan had met Thesz plenty of times.

Brisco's path to the top had a few bumps, not the least of which was as a rookie working for the Memphis territory and getting 10 to 15 dollars a night. But word spread quickly about this exquisite talent as he moved to Texas and then Australia, where he met Joe Scarpa (who would eventually become Chief Jay Strongbow). Scarpa got Brisco into Florida with promoter Eddie Graham, a superb operator and trainer who smoothed Brisco's rough edges and gave him many of his biggest breaks.

The other opportunity, of course, was in St. Louis where Muchnick absolutely loved to give potential stars a shot. Between Muchnick and Graham, Brisco got to collide with the finest talent in the business, every match making him that much sharper and surer of himself. It was inevitable that fans everywhere would want to see the match that occurred as 1971 dawned — Dory Funk Jr. defending the NWA honor against Jack Brisco. More tasty intrigue was added when a tape circulated of Pat O'Connor showing Brisco how to counter the Funk brothers' favorite spinning toehold.

Brisco's dogged chase of Dory Funk Jr. and the NWA's gold belt was like a movie with multiple plot twists. In St. Louis alone, they had five of the most exhausting and exciting one-hour matches ever.

And that was the tip of the iceberg, for Brisco and Funk had the unique chemistry only a few capture. Red Sox versus Yankees, that was Brisco against Dory Jr., and the rivalry played itself out all over North America. Sixty-minute draws, even a couple 90-minute battles. Controversial disqualifications. Absolutely screaming fans, rabid in their loyalty to one or the other. Somehow the two told a different story every time out. One thing, though, was consistent — sellout crowds. One *WrestleMania* after another, in major market after major market.

On March 2, 1973, in Houston, the stage was set for Brisco to win the title at last. Dory Jr. was ready to step down after a lengthy reign, but his father Dory Funk Sr., an influential player in the NWA, balked. According to the chatter going around, he didn't want his son to lose the gold belt to another scientific wrestler in straightforward fashion. Think if there had been the Internet then! There was some heated dispute before Muchnick, as Alliance president, got the decision nailed down. But just before the switch, Dory was allegedly involved in a truck accident on his father's ranch.

The Funks never changed their description of what happened and why Dory was sidelined. Brisco always believed that Dory ducked the match. Muchnick himself always was discreet in what he told me, though his suspicion was obvious. Harley Race took advantage of the situation, winning the title from Funk on May 24 after the situation calmed and then losing the crown to Brisco 57 days later. Race politically, and rightfully, set himself up for a lengthy turn as champion down the road, while Brisco got what he had earned at that moment — the NWA title.

There are those who feel that Brisco was not as successful a champion as he was a challenger, that his box-office appeal was less than anticipated. My personal opinion, though, is that the gap from March and an expected title win until July 20 when Brisco finally dethroned Race took the steam away from what would have been a hot new champion. Booking momentum was disrupted, taking something away from Jack that a new champion normally has his first time out.

For instance, the booking before March 2 in St. Louis was perfectly laid out for Brisco to defend against Dory's brother Terry in April. This would be followed by a test from Race later in the spring and then a collision with Gene Kiniski, whom Brisco had never beaten in the market. All three matches would have drawn big, and none could happen under the circumstances. Instead, Brisco was thrown into limbo while the controversy worked itself out, losing another match to Kiniski and going to a draw with Terry Funk.

Other territories were in similar circumstances, with plans having been neatly constructed as they had been in the past for other fresh titleholders. The new champion was to have a hot contender or two right on his doorstep. But it didn't happen since the gold belt hadn't changed hands as planned, and Brisco was thrown into a waiting pattern that slowed his momentum. The triumphant parade didn't get to develop the way it should have.

Nonetheless, Brisco did have a noteworthy campaign as the titleholder until he dropped the championship to Terry Funk on December 10, 1975. Name a major star of the period, and Brisco met him . . . Johnny Valentine, Harley Race, Wahoo McDaniel, Edouard Carpentier, Gene Kiniski, Bobo Brazil, Terry Funk, Dick the Bruiser, the top hand in every territory. He hit Japan, and those sophisticated fans loved him and his work against their stars. Brisco had memorable struggles with them all. The feud with Dory Jr. was revived, but this time it was Funk who could not get the best of Brisco. Generally, Brisco drew very well.

Most promoters were thrilled to have him as their sport's representative. Don Owen, a salty veteran of many a double-cross while promoting in Oregon, wrote Muchnick to say how good it was to "have a champion who can protect the belt." Jack was, of course, a shooter, which everyone from Roddy Piper to Pat O'Connor found out when they tried to get serious with him. Brisco's legitimate credentials made him an easy sell for promoters dealing with a skeptical media. Brisco was also charming and professional in all social situations, just as Dory Jr. was, thus elevating the impression of the business.

But the grind gets them all, sooner or later. The NWA hierarchy was willing to stay with Jack as the champion, but he made it clear that he wanted to step out. He'd been careful with his substantial earnings and he'd seen enough of wrestling's closet skullduggery, so he wanted an easier schedule out of his adopted Florida home base. After stepping down, Brisco was a main-eventer everywhere he went and the key guy in Florida rings. He enjoyed teaming with his brother for action-packed tag matches in the Southeast and was still a fabulous performer, but he had proven what he wanted to prove to the most important person — himself.

He and younger brother Gerald, also a fine performer, had bought into the Georgia operation that ran on WTBS nationally. When Vince McMahon was in the process of starting that war we always talk about, the Briscos ended up in the middle, engineering a sale of the promotion and its contract with WTBS to Vince. A lot of those fighting McMahon were incensed but it was the right business deal for the Briscos, who saw the future clearly. If they didn't sell, Vince was going to take it anyway. It was the way of the professional wrestling business.

At one point, Ole Anderson, the booker and part-owner of the Georgia group that had been aced out, called Brisco and warned that he was sending the Road Warriors to Tampa to get even with Jack and his brother. When Brisco told me this, I asked seriously, "Does he really think you've slipped that much?" Jack gave a relaxed and gentle smile, perhaps recalling all of the jacked-up muscleheads he had twisted into knots during his career.

The Brisco brothers had a run against Dick Murdoch and Adrian Adonis in the WWF, but the travel wasn't any more fun than it had been before for Jack. In the middle of a blizzard at the Newark airport, Brisco decided his career was over. He later told me, "Larry, I lost a step, couldn't do some of the things I'd always done as well as I wanted to. I don't want fans seeing me at less than what I was. That and the travel, it was time to go."

Brisco did not have the ego-inspired drive of some others who hung on. He wasn't consumed by money either. There was no unquenchable need to fill anymore. So Brisco quit and never looked back, quietly enjoying life and knowing what he had accomplished.

Why mess with success? Jack Brisco knew that there was nothing like a dream come true.

#18 NICK BOCKWINKEL

Set the bar for an intelligent, maddening heel

Maddening: what a perfect word to describe Nick Bockwinkel, the consummate professional and the first cerebral assassin. He's who Michael Holmes, my editor at ECW Press, called his favorite performer from his childhood.

Why maddening? For the simple reason that he was an obviously talented bad guy who could wrestle and was completely full of himself. If anyone ever needed to be both defeated and beat up, it was Bockwinkel. Guess what, though — it seldom happened because he was so crafty and clever. Just plain maddening.

But looking back, Michael added, "It was also wonderful, the great excitement Bockwinkel created."

What a blend of techniques were at play when this distinctive performer was in the spotlight. He was an athlete, he could wrestle, and his psychology was second to none. "I wanted to keep the level of wrestling at a high plain, while I pulled every dishonest and despicable trick I could at the right moment when it meant the most," Bockwinkel explained.

It took a few years, however, for Bockwinkel to find the role that suited him best. After tearing up his knee playing college football for Oklahoma, Bockwinkel started wrestling around 1958 with the help of Sandor Szabo in Southern California. This was no surprise, for Nick's father was one of the forgotten grand masters of the business.

Warren Bockwinkel helped train and develop the likes of Lou Thesz, Ray Steele, and "Wild Bill" Longson. He was a solid professional with a knack for the intricacies of the game, most of which he quietly imparted to his son Nick. Nick says he often felt he could hear his dad whispering in his ear, saying, "Do this. No, not that. Slow down. Be patient. Feel the crowd. Now."

Early on, Nick had the opportunity to form a tag team with his father, but it was stressful. No matter how gifted a rookie is, the command of the ring takes time to learn. "My dad would snap at me, 'Get over here, you dumb SOB!' and I'd be like a whipped pup going to make the tag. What did I do wrong?" recalled Bockwinkel.

Ah, but the kid "got it." He learned and improved rapidly. Before long, he was billed at the top of lineups from Oregon through California. He beat The Destroyer, Tony Borne, and Johnny Barend. Bockwinkel also joined forces with Wilbur Snyder and Edouard Carpentier. He headed to Atlanta, then moved on to Indianapolis and Omaha — Bockwinkel was part of the reason all of those towns were booming in the 1960s. He tackled Dick the Bruiser, Big Bill Miller, and Joe Scarpa, and was part of yet another superb tag duo with Joe Blanchard.

The instincts were just so outstanding. Nothing wrestling offered could shatter Bockwinkel's concentration, thanks to his quick wit and the experience of growing up in the business. How many bouts, the moves and the timing, had he absorbed via osmosis before Nick ever answered a bell? He had seen and understood both the absurd and the serious sides. For instance, Nick had a rather unusual job as a kid one summer thanks to his dad.

Yukon Eric was in some ways the Andre the Giant of the time, a colorful 300-pound strongman who went from territory to territory for a

week or so at a time. That year, basing his travels out of Buffalo, Eric had bought a Cadillac convertible from Ed Don George and had the expensive vehicle painted bright lime green. He had a trip planned and matches booked from Boston to Baltimore, through several Pennsylvania markets, and back to Buffalo.

In each new destination, Eric planned to ride around with the top down during the day so everyone would see this giant muscleman and realize wrestling was in town and he was in the main event. Eric needed a driver for the tour. Warren offered his son. Nick still remembers it: "I was sunburned and looked like a tomato, but it was so smart. People would come up to the car at stop signs. Kids would run along the street next to us. Word-of-mouth spread that Yukon Eric was in town and wrestling tonight. And I was his driver. Lots of ways to learn about this business."

Wally Karbo, Verne Gagne's partner in the AWA, was mightily impressed with Bockwinkel's efforts in Omaha and made the offer for Nick to work out of Minneapolis in 1970. Karbo and Gagne had talked and Wally suggested that Bockwinkel work as a heel for the first time in his career. Nick loved the idea and quickly found the role suited him perfectly. He had always had a touch of arrogance even as the good guy.

Karbo, by the way, is another character who rarely gets the credit he deserves. Sam Muchnick maintained that other people (I assumed he meant Gagne) often took credit for Wally's ideas and plans. Behind the scenes, Karbo was an important operative in making the AWA the big, successful territory that it was.

Once more, it was Karbo who suggested Bockwinkel hire Bobby Heenan as his manager. Wally thought the dynamics would trigger big-time heat. When Ray Stevens came on the AWA scene, Karbo figured that Stevens and Bockwinkel managed by Heenan would guarantee terrific matches and draw big gates. Bingo! Wally hit the nail right on the head.

In short order, Bockwinkel and Stevens won the AWA tag honor to start their first of three reigns by disposing of The Crusher and Red Bastien. In between AWA dates, the duo went with Heenan to Florida and got that promotion's tag title from Tim Woods and Hiru Matsuda.

The chemistry between Heenan, Stevens, and Bockwinkel was perfect, not to mention that Nick, with his deep catalog of skills, fit in exactly with what worked in the AWA towns. Eventually, Karbo called Nick in and told him that Verne wanted Wally to give his blessing for moving the title to Verne's son, Greg. "I can't go along with that," Wally told Bockwinkel. "Would you want the title? I think Verne might accept that, and you'd be a great champion."

Thus it was that Nick Bockwinkel defeated Verne Gagne for the AWA championship on November 8, 1975, in St. Paul, Minnesota. Bockwinkel would hold that title for 2,990 days over the next decade, a most impressive accomplishment to say the least. He began another reign in 1981 following Verne's retirement, which angered many fans, but think about it, folks — Nick was the heel.

And what a terrific heel he was, but with a slightly different perspective on the role than the usual. Articulate. Intelligent. Talented. Not a brawler, more like a shark. Heenan added one aspect to the promos, Bockwinkel quite another. "I picked up the idea from watching Lord James Blears with his manager, Captain Leslie Holmes," said Bockwinkel. "Blears hardly spoke because he was above the lower classes. Holmes was eloquent in getting the points across. I thought that's the track I should take."

If any fans weren't upset with Bockwinkel's sneaky tactics, they *were* upset with how he talked down to them, throwing out 50-dollar words right and left. Then Heenan would clinch the deal, mocking "the 9-to-5 ham-and-eggers" who were beneath Bockwinkel.

Once, Bockwinkel blasted a future opponent for being "an obsequious sycophant." (I had to look it up too. In basic English, Nick called the guy a fawning, flattering, self-serving suck-up).

An English professor from Wisconsin University was so upset that he wrote an angry letter to the AWA office, accusing Bockwinkel of using the words incorrectly and in the wrong context. Delighted, Nick responded in his next television promo. "The professor is a blithering idiot to attempt to correct me, of all people!" fumed Bockwinkel. Off-camera, he told the chuckling Gagne and Karbo, "I hope he bought tickets to see me get my ass kicked."

Years later, as he told me the story, Nick added, "I learned very early that if you can irritate those at the top of the ladder, you can definitely irritate those at the bottom of the ladder. When Sam Muchnick explained to me his concept of always trying to hook the smartest fans, I understood exactly what he meant. It works."

At different points as AWA champion, Bockwinkel had to fend off Gagne, Hulk Hogan, Dick the Bruiser, The Crusher, Mad Dog Vachon, Jerry Lawler, Germany's Otto Wanz, Stevens after their team broke up, and many more leading lights of the sport. Additionally, the excellent battles between Billy Robinson, the unique scientific master, and Bockwinkel, the epitome of a tricky, talented villain, provided yet a different flavor. Plus, Bockwinkel had a one-hour draw with Andre the Giant.

In a title versus title bout, Bockwinkel and WWWF king Bob Backlund were involved in a top-quality draw on March 25, 1979. His one-hour stalemate with Curt Hennig on December 31, 1986, on ESPN was an all-time classic. It was Hennig who finally broke for good Bockwinkel's grip on the AWA belt in 1987.

During his time on top, Bockwinkel had more than his share of disqualifications to save the title, especially when he met Gagne or Hulk. This was particularly true in 1982. But Bockwinkel, with Heenan's aid, was a genius at never losing his heat. While Nick has always praised Stevens as the best worker in the universe at the time, insiders were well aware that Bockwinkel was right on Stevens' heels.

Outside the ring, Bockwinkel's ego was under control (which would naturally surprise fans who only knew what they saw in the ring) as Nick handled the potential personality minefields of Verne and son Greg. Karbo was always an essential ally in the drama, keeping the waters calm.

Some kudos went Bockwinkel's way in the NWA controversy with promoter Paul Boesch in Houston. Houston had been a solid NWA supporter from the days of noted promoter Morris Sigel, but it was put in play when Harley Race, the NWA champion at the time, messed up his schedule and no-showed an important date in the city. Boesch was infuriated and opened the door for both Backlund and Bockwinkel to defend their respective titles in what was a highly profitable freestanding market for wrestling, similar to Toronto and St. Louis.

Boesch was well respected by all and had been a good friend of Nick's father, Warren. Nick and Paul hit it off so well that Bockwinkel began to risk the AWA crown in Houston regularly. What's more, as Boesch considered what the business would look like down the road, he wanted a stable and honest partner to look out for his wife and nephew when Paul phased out. He offered Nick the opportunity to buy points in the promotion. Bockwinkel jumped at the chance, and it was a good marriage, for it also opened the door to a whole new cast of quality opponents in Texas.

After Muchnick had resigned as NWA president and Fritz Von Erich (Jack Adkisson) had assumed much of the power in the organization, Fritz approached Nick and offered him the NWA crown. Bockwinkel asked Fritz and secretary Jim Barnett, who booked the champion and knew Nick from their days together in Indianapolis and Atlanta, how many days per week he would work. Barnett grinned and said, "Six and a half days out of seven, if not more."

So Bockwinkel graciously turned down the deal. As AWA champion, he always had a couple of days a week off, much the same as wrestlers do today in WWE. In addition, Bockwinkel was making a healthy income, not all that much less than what the NWA titleholder earned. He was content, understood the pitfalls of the company he was with, and liked the lifestyle he had.

Rejecting that offer probably best explains Nick Bockwinkel's success as one of the 50 greatest pro wrestlers in history. While completely confident in what he did, Bockwinkel was intelligent and didn't allow himself to become ego-driven. Nick knew what worked for him. And what worked for him he did in such a suberb fashion that Bockwinkel is clearly among the best ever to step between the ropes.

#17 "WILD BILL" LONGSON
A tremendous attraction — the first bad guy champion

Some bad guys are just bad guys. And that is high praise for the swashbucklers who drive many of the emotions that energize pro wrestling.

"Wild Bill" Longson is widely recognized as the first heel owner of the world heavyweight championship. That wasn't by choice or plan, but rather was an extension of the rough-and-ready personality of an aggressive tough guy.

Why did Longson get over so well as both a magnificent drawing card and a tremendous heat magnet? It was because that was him when the bell rang. He was a tough guy, and it showed. That was the style of "Wild Bill" Longson, the athlete and competitor and performer. He was tough and mean even when he was supposed to be the good guy.

In some of his earliest bouts with slick and smooth Dean Detton in 1931, Longson got the crowd riled up because he was so aggressive, pushing the envelope. From then on, "Wild Bill" just followed his instincts, which led to him becoming one of pro wrestling's all-time great performers. Once he had more experience and had figured out why it worked, Longson was a great villain for whom no underhanded trick was too nasty to pull. He thrived breaking the stricter rules of the day, as his antics infuriated — and drew — massive crowds.

As the serious heat built and the good guy started a comeback, Longson would run around the ring and then catapult himself high over the top rope, at one point being virtually parallel to the concrete floor, before executing a perfect landing on his feet outside on the floor. The babyface and his fans would howl in frustration, all building the intensity for the ultimate comeback, which Longson would milk until exactly the right moment.

At his peak in the 1940s and the early 1950s, Longson packed buildings from Montreal to Dallas. Capacity crowds came to enjoy, and enjoy booing, the thumping attack Longson would unleash on his foes. Many researchers credit Longson with keeping wrestling alive during World War II, a time the business sagged except when Longson headlined the bill.

Why didn't Longson end up in the service? Blame wrestling for that as well, because on January 5, 1937, in a match with huge Man Mountain Dean, Longson suffered a broken back. Longson actually wrestled three more nights before his opponent, Billy Hanson, took Longson home to Bill's wife, Althea, and begged him to go for medical aid because he clearly was suffering badly. Doctors wanted to fuse bone from his shin into his spine, where a large piece of bone had broken away. Longson refused, fearing it would definitely end his career even though doctors were already telling him he would never wrestle again. He ended up in traction and a full body brace for months, then rushed through intense rehabilitation so he could return to action at the end of 1937.

He never again worked a match without pain, but he never complained and few even knew what he had gone through. All it would have taken was one bad bump and Longson would have been paralyzed or worse. But he was a *real* tough guy. Times were different, so what medical advice he got was probably different as well. No complaints, no missed dates. And he went on to become a celebrated titleholder and to produce some of the most bruising physical contests in pro wrestling history with Lou Thesz,

Buddy Rogers, "Whipper" Billy Watson, Yvon Robert, Bobby Managoff, Gorgeous George, the Duseks, Earl McCready, Bronko Nagurski, Argentina Rocca, Killer Kowalski, and so, so many more. Clearly, he could engineer an exciting bout against any type of foe, making someone mediocre look better or having sensational struggles against his equals.

Who could have imagined that the youngster who, as a teenager, did hard labor on road crews putting in highways through his native Utah would become a world-class ring psychologist? Who could have guessed that the kid who rode and broke the most spirited mustangs at ranches throughout the state would turn out to be one of the meanest, roughest wrestling warriors ever?

The fresh-faced Longson also trained at the famed Deseret Gymnasium in Salt Lake City, built by the Mormon Church to spread a gospel of physical fitness and competitive athletics. While all levels of athletes in sports from racquetball to swimming to boxing worked out there, it also became the spawning ground for more than a dozen pro grapplers. This was mainly due to the dedicated work of John Anderson, a noted wrestling coach and competitor, and Verne McCullough, a worker and more notably a promoter, both of whom knew their stuff in boxing and wrestling. When local wrestling ace Ira Dern spotted Longson's obvious gifts, Bill gained yet another superb tutor.

Longson and Detton, who later ended up headlining for Paul Bowser in the Northeast, were the prize pupils. Not only did Longson repeatedly win the AAU Intermountain Championship, but he also went to the semi-finals in the national tournament in wrestling. Often forgotten due to his brawling reputation is his solid, fundamental background in the sport.

That wasn't all. Longson also was a superior AAU boxer, again capturing the AAU Intermountain title. His record was 63–7–10 with 50 knock outs. While Longson always preferred wrestling, he was so impressive that he got a lot of pressure to go into boxing. Thus, in a bout for charity, Longson had his first pro boxing match against none other than Jack Dempsey on September 14, 1931.

Only a couple of years removed from being boxing's most dangerous performer, Dempsey had heard about Longson's reputation. At the very start of the bout, Dempsey nailed Longson with a short, vicious punch to the heart that buckled the youth's knees. Dempsey clinched Longson and told him, "You ain't going down yet, kid." Bill fought back, but Dempsey kayoed him in the first round, thus reinforcing Longson's decision to go pro in wrestling. Some years later, in a boxer versus wrestler match, he did knock out George "KO" Koverly, and also became friends with Dempsey.

News of Longson's mat prowess spread quickly, and he went to work for noted promoter Joe Malciewicz in San Francisco. Of course, that's where the giant splash of Man Mountain Dean nearly ended Longson's budding career. When Longson made his amazing comeback, Malciewicz brought him back under a mask as the Purple Shadow starting in San Francisco on April 18, 1938. The character took off like a rocket. Longson unmasked for the first time after a loss to Bronko Nagurski in San Francisco on August 23, 1938, and then unmasked in Sacramento after a defeat at the hands of Jim Londos on September 26, 1938. (In those days, communication was not as sophisticated as today and most fans did not know what happened from one spot to the next.) These bouts, though, demonstrated that Longson was already at that lofty superstar level — battling the likes of Nagurski and Londos — in the minds of pro wrestling power brokers to face main event opponents of that caliber.

Eventually, with the blessing of Malciewicz, Longson pondered major offers from Tom Packs, the promoter in St. Louis, and Morris Sigel, the promoter in Houston. Longson chose Packs and St. Louis, but as it turned out Houston and the entire Texas territory were among his strongholds when he caught fire almost instantly. Shades of a future Bruiser Brody, in that "Wild Bill" Longson got over right away and drew money immediately everywhere he went.

On February 19, 1942, Longson won what was the most widely recognized world championship of the time by beating Sandor Szabo in St. Louis. During this reign, Longson worked as the masked Superman II in Louisville and parts of Missouri to set up a championship unification with Orville Brown, who had in some form laid claim to the title. Longson beat Brown, in part by taking off his mask and using it to choke out Brown to set up the pin. Yes, Bill was the bad guy!

He dropped the prize to Yvon Robert in Montreal on October 7, 1942. Robert was then dethroned by Bobby Managoff in Houston. Longson then began his greatest title run by knocking off Managoff in St. Louis on February 19, 1943. He would be on top until losing to "Whipper" Billy Watson in St. Louis on February 21, 1947 — a four-year reign packed with sellouts everywhere. Air travel was minimal, so Longson often drove from Montreal to Toronto to St. Louis to Houston to Atlanta, working various towns around each city.

While Longson may not have been the first to use the maneuver, he most assuredly was the first to really demonstrate how dangerous the piledriver was. As he knocked out one opponent after another, some commissions banned the piledriver and called for disqualification if anyone, in particular Longson, used it. Even now, the public looks at the piledriver as a dangerous move, and not every wrestler is able to use it correctly. Thus, Longson's deadly piledriver that struck fear into fans and foes alike in the 1940s is seldom seen today.

His fabulous rivalry with Lou Thesz got rolling during this period. In fact, according to most research, Longson had more victories over Thesz than anyone else, a significant fact indicating the respect Thesz had for Longson. "Wild Bill" beat Thesz 15 times, while Thesz had only two wins over a couple years. There were many grueling draws, including a two-hour — that's *two-hour* — stalemate in Houston on May 21, 1943. While Thesz eventually caught up in the win column during his seven-year tenure as kingpin, nothing changed how exciting their battles were.

The chemistry was there. Longson was sharp enough as a fundamental wrestler to hold his own with Thesz, who noted that while "Wild Bill" may not have been the greatest hold-for-hold competitor he met, Longson was as mean and strong as a bear. "Bill was a fighter first," Thesz said. "He was not a sophisticated wrestler and didn't pretend to be. He was, however, a legitimate tough guy who would put knots on your noggin in a heartbeat." Not surprisingly, Thesz versus Longson was box-office magic everywhere.

In St. Louis, where the most detailed records are available, Longson headlined 58 events that drew 573,671 customers for an average of nearly 10,000 per show between 1941 and 1945. And, at his best, he did similar business everywhere else. Realistically, for nearly an entire decade, he was wrestling's biggest draw.

His last turn as champion began November 21, 1947, when he knocked off Thesz. But Thesz regained the laurels from Longson in Indianapolis on July 20, 1948, under controversial circumstances.

After taking a beating from Longson, Thesz went on the attack and chased Longson, who escaped by leaping high over the top rope. But when he landed, his foot slammed down into a bucket of ice a beer salesman had left on the floor by the first-row seats. Longson's ankle was badly injured, and he was counted out outside the ring. Titles changed hands back then on a count-out. A work? Well, yes. But a pretty unique one all things considered.

The wrestling world went on to change drastically over the next few years, but Longson was a solid main event guy in all towns and never failed to bring in the dollars. When Sam Muchnick and the National Wrestling Alliance came into power, Tom Packs sold his promotion to a group including Thesz and Longson, with those details naturally not told to the public. Muchnick became part of the company, even though he had his own opposition promotion running at the same time.

"Wild Bill" technically retired from the ring to concentrate on the St. Louis promotion in 1956 but still had a plateful of bouts because he could draw and he loved performing. He battled Dick the Bruiser and Wilbur Snyder in Indianapolis, beat Gory Guerrero in New Mexico, and even had a couple of dandy scraps with Dick Hutton and Pat O'Connor after both became the NWA champion. Longson was so rowdy on November 24, 1959, during a tussle with Argentina Rocca in Kansas City that a riot nearly broke out. The bad guy hadn't mellowed at all! He finally stopped crawling between the ropes after he broke his pelvis while riding an unbroken stallion at Leo Newman's ranch (Newman was a worker and manager) in the summer of 1960.

When *Wrestling at the Chase* was born on St. Louis television in 1959, the two promotions got together with Muchnick as the promoter and Longson as a beloved associate. Maybe once or twice a year even into the early 1970s, whenever a wild angle threatened to get totally out of control in St. Louis, Longson would come to the ring to help restore order. And the fans would say, "Oh, this is real. It's out of hand. Muchnick sent 'Wild Bill' to break it up."

Ironically, for those who knew him outside the squared circle, Bill Longson was a big teddy bear. He was a loyal friend with a neat sense of humor. He was married to the same woman for 55 years, perhaps a record in the business. In my case, he was also a quiet, subtle teacher of all facets of pro wrestling. Am I prejudiced on his behalf? Maybe. But the facts and the aura are all there in ample amount. Longson's credentials speak for themselves.

When everything is added up, "Wild Bill" Longson is high on any group of the 50 finest in pro wrestling history. Would he adjust to modern training methods and a different style? Obviously. The brain, the athleticism, the competitiveness, and the instinct were there. He would excel, likely much better than many of today's stars would going back to butt heads with him in the 1940s.

After all, when it comes to pro wrestling, some bad guys are just the real deal like Bill Longson.

#16 JOHNNY VALENTINE
The toughest of the tough

How tough was Johnny Valentine, whose name is etched in stone among pro wrestling's legends? Joe Garagiola knew.

Before Garagiola came to national fame as the host of *The Today Show* on NBC, he was the original play-by-play commentator on *Wrestling at the Chase* in St. Louis in addition to working with broadcast giants like Jack Buck and Harry Caray on Cardinals baseball games. One of Joe's favorites in wrestling was the magnetic and rugged Valentine.

In one *Chase* appearance in 1962, Valentine battered a foe and finished the beating by delivering a pair of wicked elbows to the top of his victim's skull before getting the three-count. Garagiola wasn't sure what to call the move and was seriously impressed when ring announcer Eddie Gromacki, after asking Valentine, intoned, "With a series of *brainbusters*, the winner of the match is Johnny Valentine."

On air as Valentine raised his hand, Garagiola mused, "Boy, that Valentine must be tough. Did you ever try to bust a brain?" Though that is a cute and funny story about Valentine, the truth is that Valentine was anything but cute and funny inside the ring. Johnny Valentine was one of the toughest, meanest, most intense, most colorful, and most successful pro wrestlers in history. The question is not whether Valentine belongs among the 50 finest ever, but rather exactly where he should be listed. Any study of the greatest 50 that does not include Valentine is a fraud, plain and simple.

An all-around athlete who excelled in football and boxing in his native Washington, Valentine was spotted by a local wrestling promoter, who hooked him up with the Zbyszko brothers. He trained and worked at the noted shooters' farm in Missouri before heading to Argentina, where he made his professional debut in 1947. By 1950, Valentine was a top hand for Vince McMahon Sr. in the high-profile Northeast and never lacked for bookings all over the country.

Early on his style was evolving, but it wasn't long until his natural roughneck tendencies took over. Lou Thesz once told me that right behind the hookers and shooters, who were dwindling in number, the toughest guys of all were Valentine and Gene Kiniski. A big man at 6'4" and 250 pounds, lean and hard, Valentine was a handful for anyone and he quickly got title matches for one simple reason — he drew crowds. Everyone made money.

Apparently, every now and then in battles between the two, Valentine liked to test Thesz by shooting on him. Thesz had the edge in skill and experience but never made the mistake of thinking Valentine couldn't hurt him. The brief scuffles within the context of a worked event were not in anger; they were two tough guys wanting to push each other, and themselves, to the limits. Fans would tell promoters or announcers, "Oh, I know this stuff isn't real. Except for Thesz, or Valentine, or . . ." Those are the special characters who stand out over time.

One moment that made other performers wary of Valentine happened early in his career. Apparently a dispute about money (what else?) between the promotion and wrestler Joe Pazandak led to a match between Pazandak and Valentine, with the quiet acknowledgment that this would be a shoot. Pazandak had a terrific amateur background, and he could go for real on the mat. Valentine didn't try to test grappling skills with Pazandak, who knew that Valentine was also a legitimate ruffian. But Valentine lured Pazandak in and landed some vicious punches, opening up a gash by Pazandak's eye. From that point on, Valentine dished out a brutal pounding for a couple of minutes before the referee stopped the lopsided contest.

Afterward, Valentine told Thesz that he knew the fight could have gone the other way, for Pazandak had the goods too. Shooter versus street-fighter can always become nasty and is unpredictable. But the story of what happened, obviously, got around and made Valentine an even more dangerous figure to some performers. The real tough guys loved working with him because his style immediately hooked the fans into believing. Many Carolina fans still remember duels between Valentine and Wahoo McDaniel, where the pair literally beat each other black and blue.

Rip Hawk, a colorful ruffian who had a superb career, told the newspaper columnist Mike Mooneyham about working with Valentine: "When he hit you, he would hit you. And if you hit him, he wouldn't cry. None of that 'loosen up, loosen up.' The tougher the better."

Another moment that added to Valentine's legacy happened nowhere near a wrestling arena. A Texas promoter got publicity by entering Valentine in a rodeo, where Johnny was to ride a bull. While game, Valentine had no bull-riding skills and was tossed after a couple of jumps. For some reason, perhaps because Valentine was green in a bullring and turned the wrong way, the bull started snorting and took a charge at Valentine. In self-defense, Valentine hauled off and, in his own words, unleashed the hardest punch he ever threw, connecting directly with the nose of the bull.

Pow! The bull stopped cold. Urban myth says Valentine kayoed the bull, which was an exaggeration. But the punch gave Valentine time to do a "Wild Bill" Longson imitation and launch himself high over the fence, away from the irate animal.

Those tales, added to how hard Valentine hit and twisted and slammed foes, meant he was as much feared as respected in dressing rooms. Dory Funk Jr. remembered being on a card with Valentine when Dory was

breaking in. Valentine opposed a youngster with a good body but not much sense who tried some moves and blows that were inappropriate for what was needed. The kid, bleeding from the chest and mouth before it was over, took a ferocious beating from Valentine.

Funk talked to Valentine as he cooled off after. "Too bad," Valentine said simply. "That kid doesn't belong in the business, and I have an obligation to get over. I'm going to be in the main event. I have to draw. I owe that not only to myself but everyone in the dressing room. If I get over and draw a house, everybody makes more money. I do my job. If he can't do his, that's too bad."

Valentine loved to pull pranks on other guys, but some had a mean edge to them, cutting up personal clothing or making a mess of someone's private property. When he sat alone in many dressing rooms, some performers were simply in awe. They didn't know what to expect. With "the Valentine stare," he could be tremendously intimidating. He was a presence in the ring and out. According to Mike Mooneyham, Hawk recalled, "A lot of guys didn't like [Valentine] because he liked to rib a lot. Some of his ribs were pretty bad, but he was great to work with."

In a magazine interview, Mark Nulty asked Ric Flair if he patterned himself after Buddy Rogers. Flair got irritated. He told Mark that if he modeled himself after anyone it was "that man right there" and pointed to Johnny Valentine, then retired but a visitor to the dressing room.

Both Dory Jr. and Terry Funk talked about Valentine's intimidating image too. If someone was sincere and took the time to get to know and understand Valentine, they would discover he had a deep knowledge and many clear theories of how to work. Of course, those at his level had no trouble communicating. One doctrine Valentine had is still valid now and will be valid in the future: work for the front row, not the balcony. If the front row believes, if the front row gets into the action, the balcony and the whole house will come along. So basic, so true.

Probably no performer captured more regional titles than Valentine did. Valentine had repeated cracks at the world championship. He was in constant demand in every principal wrestling center, including Japan.

Johnny Valentine inspects the battered fist of "Cowboy" Bob Ellis

It's a safe wager that there is no major, or even minor, star in wrestling from 1950 until 1975 that Valentine didn't face. Part of his genius in the ring was that Valentine could lose and somehow become stronger for it. One of his finest rivals was Buddy Rogers, and the two had many a bloody skirmish as they carried out their rivalry all over North America.

I can recall, as a kid in St. Louis, on June 15, 1962, when a hot angle had been shot on television — Rogers defending the NWA laurels against Valentine at Kiel Auditorium. The building, sold out in advance, housed over 12,000 rabid spectators. Somehow Rogers got his hand up after being on the edge of defeat again and again. Valentine had applied the hanging backbreaker, but Rogers kicked off the ropes, got under Valentine, and delivered a back body drop for the pin.

Slowly the crowd started to applaud for their fallen hero. He stood, looked, and slowly turned, the noise building every second. Then Valentine asked for the ring microphone and said simply, "I did my best. I'm sorry I lost." And that audience just exploded.

I was the ring announcer on January 19, 1973, when Valentine emerged from a savage war with Harley Race and captured the Missouri state championship, winning a title in St. Louis for the first time. Valentine didn't have to say anything; he just held the title belt, did that slow rotation so every person could see him with the prize, and brought the emotion out of every single person in Kiel Auditorium. To this day, I've never heard a louder crowd (and this was without blaring music or fireworks).

Of course, Valentine was not always the good guy. What a terrifying heel he was. Like all the greats, he knew how to get heat. In his case, though, as with Rogers, the heat was more intense, turned up a few degrees higher than anyone else could do it. His matches methodical, even slow to some critics.

But everything meant something. From a front facelock to a blistering forearm smash, Valentine used his body language, sheer toughness, and psychology to hook the fans in, one by one, until they were all hanging on the climax. Terry Funk said that when Valentine came to the Carolinas, during the first week or ten days, some of the talent criticized him behind his back because his pace was slower than everyone else.

By the second week, nobody was saying anything. By the end of the first month, with houses up and fans completely fascinated and screaming during Valentine's matches, all of those who had griped were now trying to copy Valentine's style and, if they had the courage, asking for advice.

Would that philosophy work today? Well, consider just one modern superstar — The Undertaker. Instead of rattling off spot after spot rapid-fire, do one or two things that mean a lot. Something that makes the crowd gasp, that grabs them and shocks them. Less is more, especially if it is done correctly. That is the lesson from Johnny Valentine, one that I'd bet The Undertaker picked up somewhere along the line.

On October 4, 1975, destiny stopped Valentine when it seemed nothing else would. He had already made a comeback from heart problems in 1973 and was in the midst of a hugely successful run in the Carolinas, which were becoming a red-hot territory partially because of Valentine.

A twin-engine Cessna aircraft carrying Valentine; promoter David Crockett; Tim Woods, who appeared as the masked Mr. Wrestling; Bob Bruggers; and a budding young star named Ric Flair crashed while approaching the Wilmington, North Carolina, airport. The pilot was killed. Bruggers' back was broken, and he retired from wrestling. Flair's back was also broken, but he made a comeback and continued on for a storied career.

Johnny Valentine was paralyzed, his back also broken and a bone wedged into his spinal column. The same fate might have befallen Flair had he been in the front seat where Valentine was. But Valentine never got angry and never cursed the gods, at least that anyone knew. As tough as he was in the ring, this proved he was even tougher outside the ring. His love for wrestling was still there, even when he lost his final match for real in 2001.

In every category that defines the 50 greatest, Valentine earns an "A." But even that grade is too low when the subject comes to legacy. How tough *do* you have to be to bust a brain? Johnny Valentine was that tough.

#15 SHAWN MICHAELS

A fabulous performer at his peak

No matter what WWE maintains, Shawn Michaels is NOT the finest performer in the history of the business. Even though it fit neatly into the company marketing plan, Shawn Michaels is NOT the best there ever was.

This has nothing to do with old school, new school, politics, or personalities. No attempt is being made to belittle Michaels himself here. Nor is this blunt statement an attempt to stir up controversy or curry favor with any particular segment of those who work in or follow professional wrestling.

This is a fact. It's truth.

Probably down deep, unless the delusions of grandeur run terribly strong, Shawn himself realizes it.

Even though the might of the WWE marketing machinery claims otherwise, Shawn Michaels is NOT the epitome of all those who answered the bell for more than 100 years.

That said, Shawn Michaels *is* pretty damn good. When he finally hit his peak, Michaels was indeed *great*. But not the greatest ever. Does he

George Napolitano

deserve a place in a legitimate top 50, such as we are putting together? Of course he does. Just not at the top, and, honestly, not even threatening those at the pinnacle.

But look where he finished! Look who he is ahead of, though I still struggle to accept some of that. And it's what he accomplished in the last eight or so years of his career, when he wasn't working a full-time schedule, that bounced Shawn Michaels this high.

Ironically, but not unusually when the best of the best are considered, Michaels' physical peak probably came before his career was at its apex as a worker in the early 2000s. A brash comment made recently by Buck Robley, who worked in San Antonio in 1984 when Michaels got his start, ties it all together.

Never one to pull his punches verbally, Robley described Michaels as "an ass-kisser. A whiny crybaby. But I guess he got better at it [playing the politics], and he finally learned how to work too. Everybody should if they last 20 years like he did. He got pretty good finally." That is praise, considering the rather cynical source.

By the same token, Michaels inspires admiration from the greats in the business. Dory Funk Jr. praised Shawn to the skies when he said, "Michaels is one of the very best ever. Great psychology. He's excellent. I wish our times had coincided so I could have worked with him."

Nick Bockwinkel was finishing up in the AWA when Michaels and Marty Jannetty came in as the Midnight Rockers. "You could see all the talent, all the potential Shawn had," noted Bockwinkel. "I've told Shawn often how much I enjoy and respect his work. He's tremendous."

After the usual rugged introduction to the business way back when, the breaks did finally fall Michaels' way, and he was sharp enough to take advantage when opportunity knocked. He first gained some attention in that high-energy tag team with Jannetty. They caught on with AWA in 1986 when that company was dying and needed new blood. A brief trip to the WWF ended when the duo's immaturity caught up with them and got them tossed. But the look was there, and Vince McMahon brought Michaels and Jannetty back as just The Rockers.

As usual, the individual details pale in comparison with the overall trajectory of Michaels' career. Into the 1990s he was a middle-of-the-card act — as was his rival Bret Hart — but he zoomed upward when he became a nasty villain nicknamed the "Boy Toy" and later fell in with a politically savvy and pushy group that included Hunter Heart Helmsley (the future Triple H and future husband of Vince's daughter Stephanie).

Shawn earned an insider reputation as unreliable, often injured, and ducking doing important jobs for other wrestlers. He was reputed to be nosing around — or is that sucking up? — to McMahon and playing politics in the dressing room. Business, however, was down for the WWF and with public pressure on the promotion about steroid issues, the door was open for fiery smaller competitors to catch the brass ring. Michaels was one who did. So was Hart. But at the start of the run, neither actually was drawing that well — although their matches, against others as well as each other, were often top of the line.

And some of Shawn's behavior continued to stir controversy. For instance, in 1997 Michaels vacated the WWF championship, saying he had to retire due to a knee injury. This let him avoid losing the crown in the ring, doing the job for Hart. But because he had previously "retired due to injury" in 1995, and there had been a few other controversial absences, not everyone took Michaels' reason as gospel (although he eventually did undergo knee surgery). How much was angle, how much politics, how much pure baloney — who knows?

By the end of the year, Shawn was part of the original D-Generation X (DX) along with Triple H, Trips's girlfriend Chyna, and Rick Rude. Michaels was also back feuding with Hart over the WWF throne. Supposedly some of the angle spilled over into the real world, festering dislike between Michaels and Hart. The personal acrimony culminated in the infamous "Montreal screwjob" at the Survivor Series PPV.

Essentially, McMahon was afraid Hart would not lose the belt before leaving for a new deal with World Championship Wrestling. So he concocted a secret finish (a secret to Hart most assuredly!) in the bout between Michaels and Hart where Michaels and referee Earl Hebner grabbed a quick decision by supposed submission, which Hart never expected. Hart's outburst after what happened underscored the alleged trickery, although Michaels claimed innocence in the plot. Of course, few fans even knew that stolen decisions or surprise shoots had a lengthy history in pro wrestling, especially from 1900 into the 1930s.

The entire scenario and booking has been repeated ad infinitum to the point that fans who remember are sick of it, while those who didn't see it no longer care.

Michaels was seriously hurt when he herniated and crushed discs in his back after taking a bump during a casket match with The Undertaker in 1998. This led to another retirement. He was definitely ahead of Lou Thesz in number of retirements but far short of the many failed retirements of Terry Funk. For certain, this meant more time away from the ring for Michaels.

No matter how good his featured bouts were, and they were often awesome, in retrospect if Michaels were to be number one, the best ever, he needed to be in the ring more and playing politics less.

Thesz, who of course had many awesome duels with major stars, also had some time off. In his case, however, his time off occurred first while serving in the military during World War II and then after finishing a seven-year — that's *seven-year*, at approximately 300 bouts annually — reign as the NWA champion. Not quite the same thing, especially when considering who was the better wrestler in the eyes of history.

In any case, it was after that particular legitimate absence that Michaels did catch fire as a drawing card through hot rivalries with Triple H, Chris Jericho, Kurt Angle, and even Hulk Hogan. The reunion of D-Generation X and a well-booked feud with the McMahon family got Shawn right back on top. Again, though, Shawn had to take time off for knee surgery.

As usual, Michaels came back with a roar, feuding with everyone from Randy Orton to John Cena, while often reforming DX with his buddy Triple H. On television at least, Michaels buried the hatchet with Hart. Shawn was not full time, but to the general crowd it had to seem that way. He was involved in many television angles and major PPVs. And he didn't disappoint in either talking or wrestling, although some viewers were getting tired of his trembling lower lip in the more preposterous angles.

In a 2011 website interview, Michaels explained that in the final eight years of his wrestling career he almost never thought about wanting a long reign as WWE champion. It was his belief that the guy with the belt "needs to be the workhorse and I in no way wanted to be that." He recognized how to present himself within the concept of WWE and could take advantage of the bigger opportunities, which meant he was always taking time off and never worked a regular house-show schedule. This was a wise choice, for the house shows of today are at the bottom of the pecking order, behind television and PPV events, for both money and exposure.

Michaels knew he could pick and choose, landing the biggest matches against the biggest opponents before the biggest potential audiences. Think about it. Compare Shawn to those rated ahead of him, like Flair, Londos, Race, Kiniski, the Funks. That crew had a match that qualified under those conditions — big matches, big money in a house-show format as there was no PPV — a few times every month, maybe once a week. To make the money, they had to work *and produce* soul-stirring action more often than Michaels did.

Ah, but this is not a criticism of Shawn Michaels. To the contrary, tip your cap to Shawn Michaels. He learned and then perfectly played the system as it had become — no easy task since he was dealing with the wily Vince McMahon. He could gear to a giant outing in two weeks, and again in two months, and yet again maybe four or five months later. And he did deliver.

Just remember, the Brunos and Gagnes and Valentines all had awesome bouts too, all of them surely more often than Michaels did because that was how pro wrestling was presented at the time. Thanks to national PPV and a national promotion, a huge audience only needed to see Shawn do it once.

But Michaels did it correctly. He was right. Back in the late 1980s, Bruiser Brody told me, "The idea of this is to make as much money as possible while working as little as possible." He obviously didn't know it at the time, but Brody nailed Michaels' philosophy. It wasn't that simple to do back in Brody's time, which is not Michaels' fault. But when the chance was there in the 2000s, Michaels grabbed it with both hands.

Salute Shawn Michaels, and I mean that. Now, while trying to figure out who goes in at which number among these fantastic names, it is also fair to ask if Michaels was big enough and sturdy enough to endure the type of schedule he would have faced in a different era.

Another question that has been raised is, considering Michaels' many mind games and swerves, would he have gotten the type of push he eventually did with WWE? It's been strongly pointed out to me that most promoters have overlooked the double-crosses that angered them once the stars involved could draw money. Thus, the theory goes, Michaels would have been on top as well in the '60s and '70s. Bruiser Brody is usually pointed out as the first example of this. As much as some promoters hated to deal with Brody, they kept booking him because he brought in the bucks.

But here is the other side of that equation: would Michaels have been able to establish himself as that type of attraction at that time? He was much smaller, plus the number of comparable talents was much larger back in the day. More wrestlers, more good ones. Would a major-market booker (i.e. Tampa, Minneapolis, Dallas, or — oh — New York) have taken a chance on Shawn when that booker had several other tempting choices who had drawn in different locations no matter how testy they were doing business?

Michaels might never have had the opportunity, or he might have been shunted into that popular realm of really exciting tag teams such as the Rock 'n' Roll Express or The Assassins. Remember, his earliest chances in what was still "sort of" the big time came as a partner with Jannetty. And most guys who were in tag-team combinations that drew in mid-level circuits were not main event performers as individuals.

Personally, I think Michaels would have climbed above the tag-team label, much as Ricky Steamboat did. But Steamboat was easy to work with and had an early reputation as a true professional. Michaels' early reputation was as a pain in the butt. His trip upward would have been more difficult and required more patience, if Shawn indeed could summon that type of perseverance.

The difference in the size and quality of the talent pool definitely worked to Michaels' favor in the early 2000s. Actually, Chris Jericho inadvertently alluded to the situation when he said that in the future a lack of diversity in training, plus fewer guys in the sport, would mean a three-star match today would be considered a four-star match in the future. Actually, that trend has been going on for some time.

By that calculation, Michaels, and actually Jericho too, stood out even more in 2007 or 2008 because there were fewer outstanding performers in a smaller talent pool than there had been 20 or 30 years before.

Certainly Michaels benefits from the memorable conflict he had with Flair in Ric's sort-of retirement bout at *WrestleMania XXIV*, and even more from the classic struggle in Michaels' goodbye duel against The Undertaker at *WrestleMania XXVI*. Although Michaels did this often as the years went on and his game became smarter, those battles were on the money for pace, context, and content. The fans cared about who was wrestling; they got a dizzying up-and-down ride while seeing all of the action they craved so badly. Those outings in particular solidified a prestigious position for Michaels in wrestling's annals.

When all the smoke clears, Shawn Michaels is not number one of all time. But fortune smiled on him, and he was indeed the right talent and the right player at the right time. He belongs with the very best, and there he shall reside. Case closed.

#13 THE FUNKS

Different sides of the same coin, the Funk brothers have a revered position not only in a gathering of the 50 greatest pro wrestlers of all time, but also as a part of the history of the industry. Individually or together, Dory Funk Jr. and Terry Funk are nothing short of treasures to be safeguarded for the ages.

Dory, the elder brother, was one of the most respected scientific performers ever. Moving smoothly and quickly, he could slide from a headlock to a hammerlock to a toehold. Because of his intensity and seriousness, Dory could draw any audience into the competition he was having. Yet, when provoked, Dory would erupt. Not so much with punches, but rather with hard body slams and thudding forearm upper cuts that could make fans believe in his comeback. And, every so often, if that angry response got a little nastier, a little meaner, then spectators were really emotionally connected to the spectacle.

Terry, the younger brother, was equally respected, but he was a tornado ripping around an arena. Off-the-wall and unpredictable, Terry tricked fan and foe alike, often because everyone forgot that he was well schooled in wrestling and could evoke a reaction with a fundamental move. But it's the wildman they remember, crashing through tables and bashing opponents. At times, Terry could switch personalities and styles in the middle of a match. Yet everyone was with him because whichever tactics he used, whether scientific or hardcore, they were so solid and sound that they put Terry in a class by himself.

Or with his brother.

Therefore, why agonize over incremental differences about which one might have a bit of an edge over the other? That would tell more about the tastes of the judge than it would about the talents of the Funks. Yes, Dory got more praise and recognition, especially with the NWA title reign in the early part of his career, but Terry capitalized on the hardcore style to get more of the spotlight later.

When it was time go home, however, they both had extraordinary careers, Dory as the scientific master and Terry as the hardcore king. Call it a tie and give them both their rightful due among the greatest.

#13 TIE, TERRY FUNK

The hardcore legend could wrestle too

On April 2, 1978, Terry Funk told me he was thinking about retiring from professional wrestling.

I remember it to this day.

The movie *Paradise Alley* starring Sylvester Stallone had just made its debut. Funk not only played nasty Frankie the Thumper in the movie, but he also choreographed all the action segments and lined up a number of leading wrestling stars for appearances. Stallone and Terry got along great and worked together on a few other films, plus the flick opened the door for Funk to do *Road House* with Patrick Swayze.

Furthermore, Funk's knees were a wreck. His reign as NWA champion had ended on February 6, 1977, with a loss to Harley Race in Toronto, and was followed by knee surgery.

We were driving from the wrestling office in St. Louis to the KPLR-TV studio for a taping session of *Wrestling at the Chase*. Terry was in an introspective mood as he mulled over his plans. Having been in town for a few Kiel Auditorium cards plus the television shows as they fit in, he was reminded that St. Louis could provide a safe haven if he still wanted to keep his hand in wrestling.

I explained to Terry how he could work four Sundays a year, which would equal ten to twelve television appearances, and that was more than adequate to hype headlining perhaps eight or nine well-paying house shows on Fridays. Depending how the cards drew, and if a championship shot were worked into the mix, picking up 12 to 15 grand or so from St. Louis seemed a reasonable expectation.

Interesting plan. No need for it, though, as it turned out. I'm telling this story 34 years later, and Terry Funk probably planned on retiring 34 different times in the interim. Instead, he became much more famous for his wrestling exploits since 1978 than he probably was after serving as the NWA champion. Most assuredly, Funk scored big in the murky area of cult hero when he was the face and spirit of hardcore wrestling, catching on with the Extreme Championship Wrestling promotion in the mid 1990s. Terry put his body, blood, and reputation on the line, and it paid off for all concerned.

When Vince McMahon and the WWF began running roughshod over the territories in the 1980s, Terry was one of the few established stars without the WWF pedigree to get himself over. Live television on NBC was right down Terry's alley. With his imaginative and unpredictable conduct, Funk got much more attention than anyone expected, even when he was working with Junkyard Dog. Every time Terry worked for the WWF, he found a way to distinguish himself from the pack.

Never less than a clever politician, Funk also got himself into prime positions for Ted Turner's WCW, the opposition for the WWF from 1989 through the 1990s. Funk and Ric Flair staged some of the most brutal and memorable conflicts ever on behalf of WCW. On November 15, 1989, Terry dropped an absolutely amazing "I Quit" decision to Flair. Of course, it kept Terry Funk in the limelight for all the talk the epic struggle stirred both within the business and among its fans.

Years of experience had taught Terry a critical lesson — know when to get in, and more important, know when to get out. Understanding

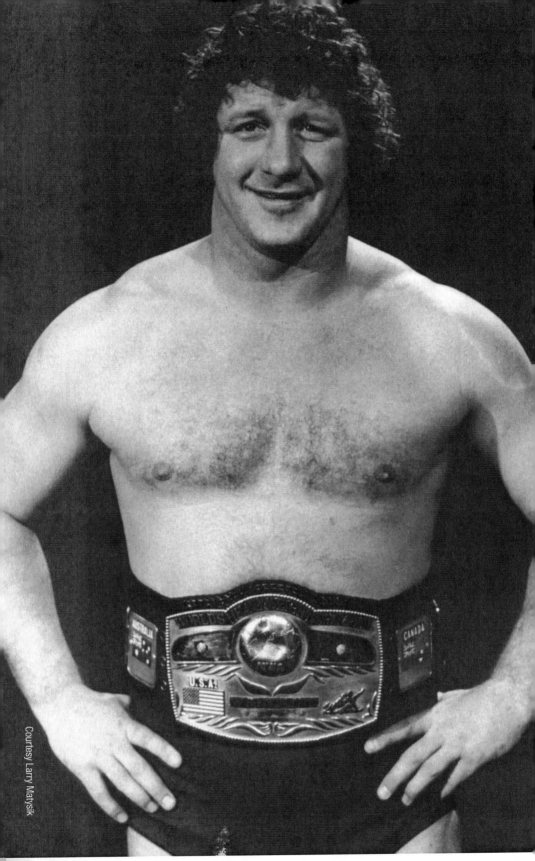

that concept, Funk was always fresh and never wore out his welcome. Naturally, he could also pick and choose among the many lucrative offers he had for independent shows (think of a series of battles with Jerry Lawler around 1990 in Memphis) along with staying on good enough terms with both WCW and the WWF to bounce back and forth.

Of course, he was always retiring, on the verge of retiring, or thinking about retiring. But that ole devil wrestling was just too strong to get away from. And Terry Funk was extremely good at it.

Added to all of that was Japan. This was yet another perfect spot for Terry to indulge all parts of his wrestling personality. He and brother Dory captured various tag-team titles and tournaments, clashing with duos such as The Sheik and Abdullah the Butcher or Stan Hansen and Bruiser Brody. Each sparkled individually as well. Blood and guts were surely part of it for Terry. The difference in approaches between the Funk brothers actually worked to their individual advantages.

For years the brothers together booked American talent for Giant Baba's All Japan. The two helped train such Japanese superstars as Jumbo Tsuruta and Genichiro Tenryu. That was once more the other side of the fascinating Terry Funk personality popping up.

All business, smart, and imaginative. In dressing rooms around the globe, when he was appointed to the task or asked for an opinion, Terry was a great "finish man," always tweaking and adjusting how a bout would end to both satisfy the customers and leave something in their memories for the next time.

When the business in Japan changed and All Japan could no longer entice foreign talent with big bucks, Terry traded on his reputation in that country and added to his hardcore credentials by taking part in gory, savage Texas death matches with Atsushi Onita and also Mick Foley as Cactus Jack. In 1995, when he was hardly a spring chicken, Terry did three consecutive death matches in a tournament in Kawasaki, Japan. Thumbtacks, ladders, barbed wire, and exploding rings all took bites out of Terry's hide. Much of the same scenario was imported to the original ECW through Terry.

Terry always navigated the changes in the professional wrestling landscape quite well. He grasped how to take advantage of opportunities as they presented themselves. Ironically, that was true even from 1969 into 1973 when his brother was one of the biggest superstars in the world as the NWA champion.

It's almost too easy to forget that Terry came out of the so-called wrestling factory of West Texas State University, where Terry played football and was considered a good prospect for the National Football League. Many of the athletes of the time at West Texas were also exposed to the wrestling promotion run by the brothers' father, Dory Funk Sr. The list would include among others Ted DiBiase, Tito Santana, Stan Hansen, Bruiser Brody, Tully Blanchard, Barry Windham, Scott Casey, and naturally Terry and Dory Jr. That bunch would form a nucleus for a potent territorial operation. It was a credit to the Funks' father that he opened the door to the wrestling business for such fine talent.

Needless to say, Terry and Dory both had the benefits of growing up in the business. As youngsters, they had the opportunities to see, meet, visit, and learn from Lou Thesz, Gene Kiniski, Johnny Valentine, Pat O'Connor, Jose Lothario, and many more. The lessons that make great pro wrestlers were ingrained into the brothers.

It might also be suggested that Terry and Dory saw more of the good side of a business that can also have its dark, dangerous parts. They picked up on the camaraderie of extremely talented men in a rare and unusual endeavor. Beer and barbecue were the choice of most appetites at the time, as opposed to steroids, cocaine, and painkillers.

Dory got started first in January 1963, and his obvious talent and potential to headline in the leading role opened a lot of NWA promoters' eyes. Terry had his first match against Sputnik Monroe on December 9, 1965, and then began the journey that somehow — for Terry — seems destined to never end.

Early on, Terry had a wild streak, a more unpredictable side than his serious brother. This wasn't something planned or thought out but rather a natural extension of each Funk's true personality. I've done radio interviews with both Dory and Terry, and that question came up. In both cases, they seemed surprised at the suggestion that anything was planned and said that Terry was just Terry, Dory was just Dory.

Even the great ones take time to mature into their promise, and Dory was always a few steps ahead of his kid brother. That made it logical to portray Terry as more short-tempered and immature, when he really just had a different style. Then Dory captured the NWA crown from Gene Kiniski on February 11, 1969, and began one of the longest and most respected title reigns in mat annals.

But the Funks knew pro wrestling and how to take advantage of any situation. Dory Sr. and Terry both eagerly laid the groundwork for Junior's upcoming title defenses in a territory or specific market like Houston or St. Louis. Senior would do some interviews, or maybe an occasional angle. Terry would be the policeman, daring a potential challenger to knock him off before the challenger could get to the champion.

Of course, that also meant Terry got beaten a lot but he learned, learned, learned every time out. Much of his schedule mirrored his brother's except he was always one or two shows ahead of Dory, so Terry was also facing cream-of-the-crop performers. Naturally not every challenge worked that way, though, so the youngest Funk had many other outings in which to create his own ring persona without having to put over yet another contender. The business knew that Terry, like his brother, was a unique talent.

Sometimes he was a babyface, straight up and scientific with a short temper. Other times he was a heel, mean and ornery with a touch of Dick Murdoch because Terry could clown with the best when he had the urge. When it came to getting full-bore heat, however, Terry was right there with the tops in the field ever. Whatever role he assumed, Terry had the natural ability to hold the fans on a string, like a puppet-master manipulating the marionettes.

His brother's lengthy championship reign gave Terry a chance to try out a lot of different ideas. The moment Dory was dethroned May 24, 1973, by Harley Race in Kansas City, with a quick turnover to Jack Brisco in Houston on July 20, Terry Funk was thrust into the position of being a leading contender and a natural foe for the new champion.

After many thrilling bouts with Brisco all over North America, on December 10, 1975, in Miami, Terry caught Brisco with an inside cradle when Brisco went for the figure-four leglock and the Funks became the only brothers to win the world championship. Terry became the NWA ruler but he had a difficult act to follow, for his brother had been a robust standard-bearer as champion for the NWA when that organization was at its strongest. Dory had been one of the very best box-office draws in the history of the title.

Terry Funk did doggone good as the champion. His matches were wilder, more helter-skelter than Dory's had been, but every bit as demanding and exciting. Maybe the long time serving as the steppingstone to his brother hurt Terry's gate appeal somewhat, although intuitively that seems wrong. Seeing a title change hands is usually motivation for ticket buyers. Whatever the reason, while he drew well as the champ, Terry fell short of what Dory brought in at the box office.

Additionally, Terry's knees became severely painful and the brutal day-after-day schedule of 30- to 60-minute grinding matches did nothing to help him recover. No fan ever knew that, for Terry had some fabulous duels against a wide variety of foes. Like all champions, Terry's chore was to make the challenger look like he was right on the verge of knocking off the king.

Sometimes that was easy because it was true; sometimes it was difficult because there was a wide gap for Terry to conquer on behalf of his challenger. He proved his mettle by handling both tasks. A master worker and psychologist, Terry Funk was simply a different sort than his brother was.

Terry handed over the gold belt to Race in 1977, his reign considerably shorter than Dory's had been, and started thinking about acting in movies and retiring from the ring. History notes, though, that those plans went in a different direction. Terry still had many of his famous moments yet to perform in the squared circle.

Terry Funk is at the head of the class in the 50 greatest. So is Dory Funk Jr. They are both here, without question. Terry got the biggest headlines late, while Dory grabbed the top of the page early in their respective careers.

It's a draw. Let the Funks figure out who should go first if it ever comes to that.

#13 TIE, DORY FUNK JR.
Smooth and sleek, a wrestler's wrestler

Command. That's a word experts use a lot in sports. To be "in command." This is what separates the good ones from the pretenders.

A pitcher has command of his "stuff." Justin Verlander has command now; Greg Maddux was in command in his heyday. A quarterback is in command of the field and his offense. Tom Brady has command now, just like Joe Montana used to.

In pro wrestling, Dory Funk Jr. had command of the ring. Command of the psychology. Command of his own actions. Command of the pace. Like an orchestra conductor, Dory subtly and effectively commanded the action, building to a climax.

In a pro wrestling discussion, that command leads to another critical word: credibility. If the fans do not believe, if they don't find what they see to be credible, they won't buy tickets or PPVs. Dory completely understood this concept. What he did had to be credible. Perhaps almost as important, his opponent had to be credible.

Thanks to his vast command of what went on between the ropes, Dory knew how to make any foe credible, giving him the rub and putting

Dory Funk Jr. attempts to submit fellow World Champion Harley Race

him in the correct position to look competitive. Like all the great ones, when Dory squared off with someone whose talent was close to his, the music they made was hypnotizing. And that is what makes Dory Funk Jr. one of the greatest pro wrestlers ever. He fully understood how to mix the ingredients together to construct a thrilling product.

While his main reputation will forever be as a scientific wrestler, someone who excelled at holds and takedowns and escapes, it would be wise to remember that he could turn into a brawler whenever the occasion demanded. Find a video of Dory against Bruiser Brody or perhaps Harley Race for proof.

Like his younger brother Terry, Dory had a phenomenal teacher in their dad. Dory Sr. was a political operator and in-ring shooter with excellent psychology about the business. Terry took what he did best and used the knowledge one way. Dory Jr. took what he did best and used the knowledge another way.

Dory was in the ring only days after concluding an outstanding football career as an offensive tackle on the West Texas State team that won the Sun Bowl in 1963. Within the first year of his pro wrestling career, Dory had tangled with Lou Thesz, Gene Kiniski, Verne Gagne, Pat O'Connor, Sonny Myers, and Moose Cholak. Talk about being groomed for success, but it was a tribute to both Senior's influence within the sport and to Junior's potential for greatness that established names at that level *wanted* to get into the ring with the kid.

And that kid was a sponge, soaking up every trick and nuance he could from the absolute masters. Dory recalled that his dad told him it would take four years before he really had learned enough to be comfortable in the ring. Was Papa Funk correct? Dory laughed and answered, "Not even close. I was still learning from my challengers when I was the champion."

His path to the title might have taken some different turns had it not been for Gene Kiniski, the titan Dory would eventually dethrone. Arrangements late in his rookie campaign were made for Dory to spend some time in Vancouver, which was a hot territory in the 1960s. Kiniski was a major player and part-owner of the promotion there. In an early bout, Dory apparently tore up his knee. He made plans to go home and find a surgeon because he'd obviously torn some ligaments.

Kiniski, however, ordered Dory to the building for his scheduled bout that evening. After a brief look at the knee, Kiniski proceeded to tape Dory's leg as tightly and securely as possible. Dory worked that night, and all the rest of the tour, without a hitch. He learned how to tape the knee, never needed surgery, and never was sidelined for the problem. Again, the youngster had learned something.

St. Louis was a key domino that had to fall for Dory to become a superstar. Promoter Sam Muchnick was always eager to give young talent a shot, plus Sam was a buddy of Senior's. Thus, Dory Jr. began the building process in St. Louis in May 1964, working with everyone from Corsica Joe to Dan Plechas, from Bob Geigel to Hercules Graham. Meanwhile, he was in the ring somewhere every night of his life, just as brother Terry would soon be. It was a college education in pro wrestling with the finest professors available.

By the summer of 1965, Dory was partnered with Johnny Valentine against Dutch Savage and Dick the Bruiser on television's famous *Wrestling at the Chase,* where Muchnick was shooting an angle for the kid's first St. Louis main event with Bruiser. Along came another lesson in the politics of wrestling.

Dory wanted to ask Sam for a couple of complimentary tickets so Dory's in-laws could attend the big show at Kiel Auditorium. When he mentioned the request to his dad, Senior told him, "No, no. They can buy their own tickets." The business in those days was built around gross receipts, and word of a big house spread quickly and boosted the stock of whoever got credit for drawing the money. Every buck counted. When word got around that Dory Jr. had drawn that well, more promoters wanted to book him. A little lesson, perhaps, but valuable nonetheless.

Florida promoter Eddie Graham also taught Dory something that is valid as much today as it will be tomorrow. "When the bell rings, be sure to give [the fans] a little extra. Give them *more* than they paid for and they'll probably be back," Graham explained. "If you only give them what they paid for, *maybe* they'll buy a ticket again. If you do *not* give them what they paid for, they're not coming back."

He went on to tell Dory, "Make it easy, kid. Give 'em more than they expected."

In retrospect, it all came together very quickly. On February 11, 1969, in Tampa, after delivering seven consecutive body slams followed by the spinning toehold on Kiniski, Dory Funk, Jr. became the new NWA champion and the second youngest ever to hold the world title. Dory was an impressive athlete as he strapped on the famous gold belt.

And he caught fire as the champion. Kiniski had been a big draw for the first couple of years he was kingpin, then cooled off toward the end of his reign. Funk presented a completely different dynamic as the champion. For one thing, Kiniski was a vicious heel. The natural instinct when a fan makes his purchase is to want a new champion crowned, and that instinct was reinforced by the fact that Kiniski could make enemies in a church. Folks wanted Kiniski, like "Wild Bill" Longson or Buddy Rogers before him, to get his comeuppance.

Suddenly, though, here was this clean-cut, handsome, confident yet humble, supremely talented young athlete in control of wrestling's biggest prize. People really *liked* him, liked him a lot.

After Rogers, Thesz, and Kiniski, Dory looked so young and vulnerable. They wanted Dory Funk Jr. to keep the championship and worried that he was so young that his time on top might be short. Dory wasn't a good guy like Thesz or O'Connor had been, for they had more salt on them. No matter how good Funk was, and the audience recognized he was very good, was he tough enough to survive?

The paying customers across North America in every NWA stop (and even in Japan, where Dory made a couple of trips) turned out in capacity numbers to find out. Generally, they wanted to cheer Dory against Kiniski, Black Jack Lanza, Fritz and Waldo Von Erich, Johnny Valentine, Baron Von Raschke, Wahoo McDaniel, Billy Robinson, Dick the Bruiser, and Big Bill Miller. The matches were terrific, the houses were wonderful, and God was in his kingdom for the NWA.

It got even better when the casual audience kept turning out to see Dory tangle with the different styles of favorites like Pat O'Connor. While there were, not unexpectedly, a few subtle heel moments on behalf of the champion, the result was primarily a great action wrestling match, not slow and on the mat but with movement and bumps and surprises.

Then the fun began with Jack Brisco. This rivalry is one of the greatest feuds of any era of pro wrestling. The value of the championship, the way Dory conducted himself as the titleholder, and the way Brisco conducted himself as the challenger made winning and losing box-office magic everywhere. It didn't hurt that every battle between the two told a new story and set a new standard for action.

All champions run their course, naturally, and by late 1972 the time was ripe for a change. For one thing, Dory had been a busy, busy ruler and had gone through most of the likely candidates to unseat him. While still drawing solid houses, the regular sellouts weren't regular anymore. Most importantly, Dory was simply worn out after four grueling years of non-stop work and travel. Brisco was rightfully chosen to replace Dory. But just before the switch was scheduled to happen in Houston on March 2, 1973, Dory was involved in a truck accident on his father's ranch. A shoulder injury put the champ on the disabled list.

Controversy still lingers today over the what and the why of this time. Everyone involved has his own take on it. Suffice it to say, the original Houston bout did not happen, and Dory got back into action several weeks later. He dropped the NWA prize to Harley Race on May 24 in Kansas City, then Brisco dethroned Race on July 20 in Houston, and finally it was Dory chasing Brisco for the gold belt. The change in hunter and hunted kept that conflict humming along with another set of healthy box-office returns around the horn.

And Funk and Brisco kept the action at a peak. They gave the folks more than they paid for every time, which would make Eddie Graham happy.

Dory became a consistent draw and lead performer throughout the NWA into the 1980s, notably in the Carolinas, Atlanta, Florida, and St. Louis.

Of course, Japan became a big priority. Dory Sr. had been booking Americans for Japan when Senior died unexpectedly on June 3, 1973. By this time, Dory and Terry were well versed in how the Japanese did their business. In fact, Dory was in Japan in 1972 only a few hours before a title bout against Antonio Inoki when Inoki walked out on the company, busting up a partnership with Giant Baba. Inoki landed his own television deal and started New Japan in opposition to Baba's All Japan. The Funks stayed with Baba. When Senior passed away, Baba offered the booking job to the brothers.

To keep the legal people happy, Dory was listed as booker but, in fact, the two worked together evenly and closely to open the doors for lucrative Japanese tours for the biggest American stars. Since Inoki was also mining the same field, competition was fierce. Whichever brother had the best relationship with the performer they wanted to book would make the approach to him, after which Dory and Terry coordinated the dates.

As noted, of course, the Funks were key talent for Baba, both as a tag team and individually. When Stan Hansen jumped from Inoki to Baba, a huge move at the time, the Funks were right in the middle of it all, both behind the scenes and in the ring. Until the Japanese business deteriorated and Baba passed away, Dory was loyal to his longtime associate.

Dory was a bright and innovative booker throughout, lending his insight and help in both Florida and the Carolinas. In the ring, he still had every on-target instinct. He made the poor look good, the good look better, and the great shine. He eventually found time to make a few ventures into the hardcore world with Terry as a tag partner.

When the NWA crumbled and Vince McMahon began the drive to take over everything, Terry fit in easier than Dory did. The smooth, methodical, intelligent wrestling that Dory utilized so well was not a favorite method for Vince, who went for big muscles and garish characters. Comfortably, Dory slid into an independent training role.

Just as Dory got national prominence early in their respective careers, Terry often gained the spotlight later with his explosive excursions.

Each brother has won one fall. Now, the time limit has expired. It's a draw, and that's the bottom line.

#12 HARLEY RACE

Paid every price it took to be the best

Whatever it took, whatever had to be done, whatever physical punishment was required, whatever price had to be paid as a performer . . . Harley Race willingly and expertly did it all, and that's why he has earned such a conspicuous position among the greatest who have ever laced up the boots.

Race didn't move up the ranks from amateur wrestling or college competition. For Harley, it was the school of hard knocks from the start, and it was a dream he had to chase, particularly after overcoming polio as a child.

He was expelled from high school after striking the principal, who was trying to break up a fight between Harley and a classmate. Determined to become a wrestler, he connected with the famous Zbyszko brothers. Unfortunately, wrestling instruction played second fiddle to the farm work that the Zbyszkos tied in with their supposed training. Luckily, though, after that, Race connected with promoter Gust Karras of St. Joseph, Missouri, and Kansas City, who got Harley started on the long, winding road to wrestling immortality.

Like any kid in pro wrestling, though, Harley had to pay his dues. While he learned, and got even tougher than he already was naturally, he was Karras's gofer. Because Race drove a large Cadillac, he was often the chauffeur of choice when Karras brought in outside talent. The most memorable customer had to be Happy Humphrey, a bigger version of the Haystack Calhoun "fat man" gimmick and one who hit the smaller territories, including Kansas City.

Race had to drive Happy around to all the towns, but his chores were a little more difficult than just that. At probably 750 pounds, Humphrey had a terrible time cleaning up after a match. Therefore, Race usually got a garden hose, hooked it up in the dressing room, and helped poor Happy lift up his massive belly so Race could squirt the water from the hose all over Humphrey's body. All part of paying dues, and Harley can laugh about it, remembering that Humphrey was a nice guy.

Those days didn't last long, because the kid clearly had a natural feel for the ring and absolutely no fear of taking any bump. At the time, Kansas City was the hub of a good learning territory and had salty, knowledgeable characters like Pat O'Connor and Bob Geigel to work with the kids. In addition, there was a business relation with Sam Muchnick and the major league town of St. Louis, so the youngsters were often recruited to do jobs on television's *Wrestling at the Chase*, thus gaining even more experience. Race's first St. Louis match was a loss to Joe Tangaro on June 20, 1964.

Using the name Jack Long, Race began working out of Nashville at the age of 18 in 1961. Everyone loved his potential, but a horrible car accident nearly put a halt to everything. Race's first wife was killed in the wreck, and doctors wanted to amputate his leg. Karras rushed to the hospital, refused to allow the leg to be amputated, and through sheer will and hard work Harley eventually made a full recovery.

When he went back to the ring in 1964 for the Funk family in Amarillo, Race was using his own name. His father had asked why his son would want to make a different name famous. And the name Harley Race was absolutely perfect for wrestling, as so often happens when reality is better than fiction.

George Napolitano

From that point, Race hooked up with Larry Hennig. The duo invaded the AWA and became one of the most famous tag teams in history, notably for their money-drawing feud with Dick the Bruiser and The Crusher. As always, the AWA crew was among the best, but the young Race fit right in and learned with every step up the ladder. Working regularly with O'Connor, Verne Gagne, Wilbur Snyder, and "Cowboy" Bill Watts did nothing but help.

By the early 1970s, Race was back in K.C., with side visits to St. Louis and the Funk portion of Texas. He was in many a bloody scrap with both Terry Funk and Dory Jr., who was then the NWA titleholder. Fate then smiled on Race at the end of Dory's reign. While Race actually had some support within the NWA board of directors, who made the decision, the majority clearly wanted the belt to go to Jack Brisco after Funk's four-year reign. But Junior's dad, Dory Funk Sr., balked because Brisco had been involved in a lengthy and profitable rivalry with his son. He didn't want Brisco to beat Junior clean for the crown.

Nonetheless, the switch to Brisco was set for March 2, 1973, in Houston. Several days before the match Dory Jr. was allegedly injured in a truck accident on his father's ranch. This incident caused consternation throughout the NWA and set into motion much backdoor politicking. Muchnick, the longtime NWA president, made noises about going his own way if the alliance could not hold together over the original decision.

When the dust settled, Dory Jr. went back into action and that very week (what a surprise) dropped the championship to Race on May 24 in Kansas City. Yes, it was a work. But, to many seasoned and cynical eyes, a lot of care went into taping up the package that evening.

Race had developed a reputation as a mean street fighter, someone who wasn't afraid to get dirty if the situation required it. The days of shoots and swerves in the ring had almost disappeared, but everyone with any experience in the business remained concerned that such a double-cross could happen. They had all heard the tales. Harley and Bob Geigel, by then the promotional power in K.C., had a long, friendly relationship with the Funks. And, naturally, there was always the referee. As I've said,

Harley Race bloodies Ric Flair

the Montreal screwjob in the WWF doesn't seem so unusual once pro wrestling's real history is acknowledged.

The ref was only involved to the extent that Richard Moody executed the agreed-upon finish. After a bump, he missed what would have been a pin on behalf of Dory Jr., thus satisfying the Funk clan. Race then jammed Dory's shoulders to the mat, putting a new champion in charge. Only 57 days later, on July 20, Brisco flattened Race in Houston to become the titleholder, calming the NWA waters.

Race had a lot of favors due him after all those histrionics. During the ensuing four years, he managed to buy percentages of the promotions in both Kansas City and St. Louis, which helped his political-insider status. He was a busy former champion, bouncing all over the NWA map to top cards and draw good crowds. He became a steady headliner in wrestling-crazy Japan. The brief spin as king gave him extra credibility to bring his sturdy, sterling work into previously off-limits areas. In some ways, Race was like a presidential primary candidate working conventions and fundraisers around the country to garner support for a run at the big prize from his party.

Muchnick often spoke with me about how Race got over as a drawing card with fans. "He takes a little time, because his style is methodical. But he's tough and knows how to get heat. Everything looks good, so he'll click, but it won't happen overnight," Sam explained to me. He also showed me a thank-you letter that Race had written to Sam after Harley's first St. Louis main event in a loss to Edouard Carpentier in 1969. Harley promised to get over if he got another chance, which Sam never doubted.

The analysis was true. Once Race was over, the heat would build like boiling water on a stove. He shed gallons of blood and took countless spine-rattling bumps as his reputation spread globally. Some moves were unorthodox (which was actually good), for he lacked the extensive formalized scientific training that someone like Brisco had, but everything was solid, sure, and effective. His diving headbutt was spectacular and new. His high vertical suplex has been copied in so many forms that Harley's original maneuver, so stiff-looking it made even the audience hurt, is underappreciated.

Of course, I came to know Harley well because I had been Muchnick's gofer in my high school days in the mid 1960s. By the 1970s, I was in the office, handling the publicity and public relations, doing play-by-play for *Wrestling at the Chase*, and learning from Sam, the sport's rendition of Obi-Wan Kenobi. Race was one of the first performers way-back-when to let me inside about finishes.

In 1977, after the title had passed from Brisco to Terry Funk, Race was ready, waiting, and able to be the champion. Harley dethroned Terry on February 6, 1977, in Toronto and began what was, in essence, a four-year command. One indication of the weakening of the NWA, though, was the one-week wonders, title changes from and back to the same person (in these cases, Dusty Rhodes, Tommy Rich, and Giant Baba), that chipped away some of the title's credibility.

Race handled a back-breaking schedule, particularly as Muchnick phased out of power, because no authority in the NWA was trying to get the champion a few days or even a week off each month. The only bump in scheduling came in Houston, a great wrestling market, when Race missed a date. Promoter Paul Boesch was so infuriated that thereafter he stopped booking the NWA champion and made a deal with Nick Bockwinkel and Verne Gagne to risk the AWA prize instead.

Although usually in the heel position, by this time Race had so much respect from the fans in most markets that he could take on heel challengers and gain cheers as the champion. Therefore, the list of possible opponents was enlarged. While no records exist, it's likely that Race had more one-hour draws than any other titleholder. His endurance was amazing, especially considering some of the scary bumps he took, but Race was a master at pacing both himself and the match.

On June 21, 1981, Rhodes finally ended Race's rule in Atlanta, but Race continued to be a top challenger who drew the big gates in many major markets. When Muchnick retired and the promotional battle in St. Louis erupted, Race got another short run as titleholder by beating Flair in St.

Louis on June 10, 1983. That led to the first *Starrcade* of Jim Crockett's promotion, as Ric Flair began *his* second reign (Flair had knocked off Rhodes in the interim) as NWA boss by defeating Race in a classic duel on November 24, 1983.

Of course, the wrestling world was flipped topsy-turvy when McMahon and the WWF began their drive to conquer the entire business, Muchnick retired on January 1, 1982, and his old promotion fell into turmoil. The new owners, including Harley, had such a different philosophy from Sam about how wrestling operated that I left to start my own promotion. Before long, I was with Vince and the WWF, the remnants of the St. Louis operation died, the K.C. office went broke, the NWA became just a public name of Jim Crockett's company, and Race suffered serious financial setbacks.

Harley, managed by Bobby Heenan, ended up on the WWF roster in 1986. Therefore, when all was said and done, by the mid 1980s Race and I were again on the same side and both getting checks from the same boss. Through all of the upheaval, and there were definitely hard feelings during that period, I never lost the respect, appreciation and affection I had for Harley.

Generally, at that time whether they would admit this or not today, the WWF tried to either downgrade or embarrass any wrestler who had been a major star outside the McMahons' promotion. In the end, that didn't happen with Race, who somehow brought prestige to a gimmick of being "The King" because he'd won a *King of the Ring* tournament.

I was working for Vince in those heated days when the war was breaking many established promotions, and talent was jumping sides. When he told me that Race was coming on board and asked for any ideas, I suggested that since Harley was known as such a serious competitor, he should be cloaked in a black robe with a black hood. He could be the incarnation of hard, tough, and mean wrestling, a dark, deadly, and intimidating figure in the menagerie.

Oh, well, Vince didn't agree. While dressing the hard-nosed Race in a gaudy crown and cape might have caused a chuckle or two in the office,

Harley understood how to get heat better than most anyone. He used his abilities to generate exciting matches that got him into the spotlight despite his cartoonish entry. To make the comparison to today, how much good did a crown and robe do Sheamus when WWE cast him in that gimmick? Most think it hurt. That's what Race had to overcome in the WWF.

But the injuries were mounting by this point, particularly when Race missed his patented diving headbutt while trying to flatten Hulk Hogan on a ringside table in 1988. The table broke and ripped into Race's midsection, causing such serious damage that the WWF ran an angle to find a new King. After a brief return to the WWF, Race took on a role as a manager with Ted Turner's World Championship Wrestling before a serious car accident ended Race's days on the road.

Yet the business was in his blood, and Race formed what is now called World League Wrestling. He trains young talent. His respect in dressing rooms around the world is through the roof, as it should be. Race had that unique ability to make new stars, elevate weaker talent, stage mind-bending wars with superstars of comparable talent, and still make it clear that when push came to shove, he was a performer who nobody would want to test.

Indeed, Harley Race paid the price in full. His reward is a home among the finest pro wrestlers who ever stepped into a ring.

#11 VERNE GAGNE
Was there a hold he didn't know?

Exactly where does Verne Gagne fit into the firmament of wrestling's brightest superstars ever?

He belongs, no doubt about that. In fact, Gagne surely has a home in the upper echelon. The puzzle is, where? Where does Verne Gagne go?

Obviously his credentials built from the birth of his career. By itself, his early history would indicate Gagne was much rougher and tougher than some later observers would have expected. After a tour of duty with the Marines, Gagne went to college and finished third behind Dick Hutton and Ray Gunkel in the NCAA wrestling tourney. His senior year in 1948 saw him avenge the loss to Hutton as he won the NCAA title. All told, Gagne won two NCAA championships, one AAU title, and four Big Ten championships while also being picked as an alternate for the Olympic team. A strong football prospect, Gagne was courted by the NFL and was drafted by the Chicago Bears before promoter Tony Stecher and Joe Pazandak brought him into pro wrestling.

Some of his first bouts in Minnesota were officiated by Wally Karbo, who would become Verne's partner and "front man" promoter in Minneapolis.

After an early run through Texas, where he learned from Paul Boesch and then worked with inventive bad guy Danny McShain, Gagne became an overnight sensation on the Dumont Network's nationally televised wrestling program. Gagne was butting heads with Lou Thesz, going to exhilarating one-hour draws, and proving himself a drawing card every bit the equal of Buddy Rogers. Battles with Wilbur Snyder, Dick the Bruiser, and Killer Kowalski earned even more credibility for Gagne. At one point, Gagne topped five consecutive shows at New York's Madison Square Garden. In Boston, box-office records in existence since Jim Londos were shattered when Gagne and Argentina Rocca met Hans Schmidt and Karl Von Hess. Like the business itself at the time, Gagne was a big deal to the public. In action, he was a complete performer.

Gagne was closely aligned with aggressive and controversial Chicago promoter Fred Kohler in this period, which led to some political headaches with the NWA. When Thesz stepped down as NWA king in 1957 and was replaced by Hutton, seeds were sewn that would lead to Gagne forming his own company, the American Wrestling Association, and claiming the world championship for himself. Eventually, Gagne would base the AWA laurels on a win he scored over Edouard Carpentier, who had been previously involved in a controversy with Thesz, Carpentier's own promoting angel Eddie Quinn in Montreal, and the NWA itself.

Who says wrestling politics were dull in the late 1950s? It's a funny world, for Tony Stecher had been one of the early originators of the NWA and now his protégé Gagne, along with Karbo, was up and running the opposition to that organization when they bought out Stecher in Minneapolis. Yet relations always were friendly between the two groups, partially based on the mutual respect and friendship between Gagne and NWA power Sam Muchnick. Gagne almost always attended the NWA conventions.

Technically, the AWA gave Pat O'Connor, who had become the NWA champ after Hutton, 90 days to defend the title against Gagne. Naturally, that didn't happen, so Gagne was proclaimed the AWA world heavyweight champion on August 16, 1960. At no point thereafter was the AWA without top-line talent, many of whom were serious candidates for the 50 greatest in history.

And they all tangled with Gagne at one time or another.

The sleeper was a feared weapon for Gagne, but he was such a smooth wrestler that he could incorporate many different fundamental moves into a believable, exciting finish. The likes of Big Bill Miller and Mad Dog Vachon were great foes for Gagne, because both had terrific heel tactics to mesh with their excellent wrestling skills. Of course, when The Crusher as a heel dueled Gagne, their encounters made for an engrossing evil versus good test. Nick Bockwinkel was perfect in the 1970s, for as Gagne's athleticism ebbed, Nick played to Verne's strengths perfectly. And Verne was smart enough to do what he did best.

Gagne was well known everywhere, likely earning recognition as a celebrity. With his excellent work and serious background, Verne was one of those who brought credit to a business that often needed good will. The AWA became established throughout the upper Midwest and parts of Canada.

In the early 1980s, after Gagne had bought a minority position in the St. Louis promotion and I'd had several years as the play-by-play voice of *Wrestling at the Chase*, I made a couple of trips to the Twin Cities to do TV when Gagne's regular announcers were unavailable. Verne was a class act. We ate dinner at his country club and enjoyed the National Hockey League from his prime season seats. It was like being with Muchnick in St. Louis; Gagne was just as well liked in the Twin Cities. When Verne wasn't available, the fascinating Mr. Karbo made sure I had company to dine with at the best steak house and entertained me with one hilarious wrestling story after another. And running around town with Ken Patera, who was one of the top AWA stars at the time, made me realize what a strong position the promotion had built in the community. As in St. Louis, wrestling people were respected stars.

Gagne dominated the crown off and on, including his historically long run from August 31, 1968, until November 8, 1975, when he was unseated by Nick Bockwinkel. Verne finally regained the AWA crown from Bockwinkel on July 18, 1980, before an announced crowd of over 20,000 at Chicago's Comiskey Park. After almost another year with the belt, Gagne retired as champion.

While he bounced back in now and again (and it was obvious he had slipped some), generally those bouts still helped at the box office.

During that entire time from the mid 1950s into the 1980s, Gagne had actively been training promising prospects for the wrestling business. As Muchnick always complained to me, the business needed young blood and new faces but never had enough of them. Gagne would scout the college ranks and even go to international competitions. Romantically, historians like to fawn over Stu Hart's Dungeon in Calgary, and indeed some excellent talent came out of there. But consider this list of athletes and what they became in pro wrestling after working with Gagne: Ric Flair, Curt Hennig, Ken Patera, Ricky Steamboat, Buddy Rose, Baron Von Raschke, his own son Greg Gagne, Jim Brunzell, Jesse Ventura, Chris Taylor, Brad Rheingans, Sgt. Slaughter, Iron Sheik, and plenty more supporting types. While churning out quality hands like that may not speak so much to Gagne as a wrestler per se, it certainly does vouch for a strong legacy unparalleled by anyone else.

Of course, the AWA was the spot from which Hulk Hogan jumped to land in the WWF when Vince McMahon Jr. began his drive to conquer the globe. While Hogan was well on the road to superstardom at the time, working in the AWA with the likes of Bockwinkel certainly helped hone Hulk's character, which exploded for Vince. The loss of Hogan wounded the AWA badly, as did the other talent McMahon raided from Gagne. Vince also grabbed some key television production people, and that hurt too.

One of McMahon's favorite rationalizations was that if he didn't go national, Gagne would. Everyone politely ignored the potential of the WTBS national cable show and whatever intentions Jim Barnett had in Atlanta. In truth, Gagne was ambitious and had made attempts to promote in San Francisco and Los Angeles. A major upheaval was beginning, and

Gagne fought the WWF to his last penny and cost himself most of the fortune he had made as both wrestler and promoter.

Within the business, Gagne was not without enemies and, particularly, detractors. The ambitious streak rubbed some people the wrong way, and his ego was immense. Verne aggravated more than a few who worked for him. While he never was ripped for bad payoffs, the feeling existed that he favored certain performers (including son Greg) with more money. Of course, Gagne must have paid well enough, for his roster was always solidly packed with established stars who could have found regular work elsewhere.

Others were also irritated with how little credit Gagne gave to Karbo, who added a lot in terms of imagination and experience to the AWA. Did Gagne push himself too strongly after his peak had passed? Yes, but then, which star in history didn't do that? Gagne was also sniped at for being rigid and stubborn, and for not changing with the times.

In later 1982, after Muchnick had retired and the St. Louis promotion was crumbling, Verne and I had a long talk about the town's future and our philosophies on booking. His idea about finishes was more open than that in St. Louis, for he had gone through a series of bouts between champion Bockwinkel and challenger Hogan relying on disqualifications and phantom pins. I told Verne that I still believed in clean wins and losses when it came time to blow-off a feud, which I guess made me the old-line conservative thinker. But I also brought up the use of new technology available in television production to make the shows look better, and at least he didn't seem negative.

This is not intended to duck the original question of where Gagne fits into the overall aggregation of the greatest pro wrestlers, but rather to demonstrate what a significant figure Gagne was as both wrestler and operator. His wrestling made the rest possible. As much as his ownership of the AWA leads to criticism that he was its champion, the reality of the promotion's huge profitability for more than two decades demonstrates that the audience bought him as that champion. And AWA shows drew well even when Gagne was not working.

The fans, including the elusive and valuable casual portion, bought him because Verne Gagne was indeed a major superstar with all the requisite talent and personality. While nobody ever called Gagne a shooter, he clearly had the wrestling skills to take a roughneck or a pumped-up bodybuilder to school and did whenever the situation demanded. The fact that he competed on even ground with an unknown great like Hutton and a famous great like Thesz says it all. He must have done something right, because his student Ric Flair turned out pretty good.

I asked some very serious people with real knowledge of and experience in pro wrestling where they thought Gagne fit. One didn't think Gagne would have been able to handle the torturous schedule of the NWA champion. Interesting, but think about this. While the AWA calendar was easier than the NWA's, it was certainly busier than today's WWE, with the possible exception of the toll foreign tours take. Maybe 200 matches annually against 150 or fewer?

Further, that evaluation of Gagne comes from Verne's work in the early 1970s — when he was almost 50 years old! Even Thesz slowed down at that age. Mother Nature always makes sure that time wins the fight, and Gagne wasn't going as hard as often, quite naturally, as he had been 20 years earlier. In fact, by the time Gagne was 49 years old and lost to Bockwinkel in 1975, he had been a major star nationally for almost 25 years. Talk to anyone who saw or faced Gagne in the 1950s or 1960s; there is complete agreement that he was a superior worker who busted his tail every time out. He went over as a serious athlete that fans liked and respected.

Now to make those devilish comparisons. While a few observers will squawk, Gagne falls just short of the Thesz-Flair-Lewis triumvirate. Hogan, Sammartino, Austin, Londos, and Rogers are all part of certain important historical chords. That leads to a select company of perhaps 20 incredible performers who each offer something different to the discussion. How perplexing to uncover the miniscule advantages or disadvantages that make Gagne higher or lower than Kiniski, Race, the

Funks, Longson, Michaels, Valentine, Brisco, and so on. And, oh man, how to weigh Frank Gotch in that collection?

Like it or not, the AWA title gives Gagne a boost, not so much because of the crown itself but because of the quality of the opposition and the matches it provided. All of them were drawing cards, some great and some just good. A point added for someone here, a point subtracted from someone else there.

Impact on the country or the home community? Well, that edge might go to Gotch, Gagne, or Michaels, with Shawn and Verne each getting a boost from a national television show. In his own town, though, Gagne would be hard to beat. Yes, Michaels could do a terrific promo, and some of it was probably from his input. Find a video of Terry Funk or Kiniski doing an eye-opening rant. But Gagne delivered what the audience of his time wanted, as did Dory Jr. and Brisco. Gotch and Longson could charm any newspaper editor or radio announcer. All were great in what was required of them.

The best true wrestler of the bunch likely comes down to Gagne or Brisco, or perhaps a look at Angle, Hodge, or Lesnar. Everyone could work, each in different style. The toughest of them all — I wouldn't even begin to guess.

Once more, the decision comes down to instinct, feeling, and common sense. And anyone who doesn't see that Verne Gagne is a vital part of that upper echelon of the top 50 needs to work on the common sense thing.

#10 FRANK GOTCH

It may have all started with him

Consider this: A century ago — 100 years! — Frank Gotch set the standard that any professional wrestler has to meet if he wants to be considered the greatest ever.

Of course, the business was different. Night and day. So was baseball, then and now. So what? Certain basics still apply and the DNA was established. Once again, the ability to dominate the time frame in which a superstar competed and performed demonstrates in some way that he would be able to do the same thing had he come along in a different period, even 100 years later!

The same gifts that made him a star in 1912 would have made him a star in 2012, because so much of that stardom revolves around his personality and his motivation to be the best no matter the cost. On top of that, when appraising Frank Gotch within the categories that have been used to judge all the stars, he stands out.

Projecting reality, working ability, mic skills or getting over with the era's media, drawing power, charisma, legacy. Those are the same regardless of what years are covered. Isn't this all common sense when looking at the big picture?

By golly, Frank Gotch had all of that. He established the starting point of a line of champions that connects Gotch, Joe Stecher, "Strangler" Lewis, Jim Londos, and Lou Thesz. Succession is skewed a bit after that, with many claimants following Thesz. Clamoring for acknowldgement are Bruno Sammartino, the Funks, perhaps Verne Gagne, possibly Buddy Rogers, and one or two more, before the progression narrows down to most definitely Ric Flair and Hulk Hogan prior to the monopoly of WWE names.

It began, though, with Gotch. His professional effort started in 1899, after rigorous training with a master grappler and shooter by the name of Farmer Burns. At 5'11" and some 200 pounds, Gotch was famed for his quickness, his superior mechanics, and his unbeatable endurance. Sportswriters of the day praised his courage and his skills, and described him as "a remarkable physical specimen." The genetics obviously were present. Gotch concentrated on handball for explosive movements and 5- to 10-mile runs up and down hills to further develop his endurance.

Translate that into the training methods Gotch would have added in the 2000s, and he would still be at the very head of the pack. Rest assured a competitor of his nature would have jumped on the advantages of specialized diet and weight-training, to say nothing of what steroids might have added for someone who was in reality a phenomenal athlete.

Bluntly, many of the modern performers who used chemical enhancement were not in the upper reaches of athleticism. Take that away from them and how would they compare to Gotch, or for that matter "Strangler" Lewis or Lou Thesz?

While some of the early results are fuzzy when it comes to dates and places, most researchers agree that Gotch in some form established a meaningful championship claim by whipping one Tom Jenkins, reputed to be a talented and nasty competitor, in 1904 in Cleveland.

Gotch and Jenkins had several battles before Gotch peaked and proved to be superior. So highly thought of was Jenkins that when he retired he

became the boxing and wrestling coach at West Point. Gotch's reputation got a huge boost because he had finally topped Jenkins.

This led to Gotch's most famous rivalry against George Hackenschmidt, the fabled Russian Lion who trained with weights and was the monster of the day. He too had managed to beat Jenkins so a showdown was logical, not unlike how modern-day booking would set up two leading contenders. On April 3, 1908, in Chicago, Gotch took two straight falls from Hackenschmidt in roughly two hours. Reportedly Hackenschmidt was bloodied from Gotch's headbutting and thumbing Hackenschmidt's eyes before Gotch clamped on his dreaded toehold. Others said that Gotch simply outmaneuvered Hackenschmidt, using different methods to wear down the giant who usually won in speedy fashion. Whatever the case, Hackenschmidt submitted and did not answer the bell for the second fall. As reports of the triumph, which established Gotch as the true world heavyweight champion, spread, a wild and happy celebration broke out in his hometown of little Humboldt, Iowa.

The titleholder went on a tremendous run, solidifying his reign over the next few years, including a win over Stanislaus Zbyszko, another serious star whose name would pop up well into the 1920s, and who might be a performer who fails to get the rating he deserves in this list of the greatest 50 ever. Hackenschmidt, however, kept up the pressure for a return go with Gotch, similar to today's storyline or booking.

Finally, Gotch and Hackenschmidt locked up on September 4, 1911, in the new Comiskey Park in Chicago. Again, reports vary but almost all seem to agree some 30,000 fans were on hand for the eagerly anticipated duel. The battle, however, was shrouded more in infamy and controversy than anything. Gotch again captured two straight falls from Hackenschmidt, who allegedly suffered a knee injury during training. Claims were made that Gotch had someone (one story says Ad Santel, a notorious hooker, but Santel's dates don't seem to match up) shoot on Hackenschmidt during a workout to cripple him before the bout. According to Hackenschmidt, he was accidentally hurt by sparring partner Dr. Benjamin Roller, another reputed tough guy of the era.

And to digress for a moment, how often have worked finishes been built around one combatant being attacked and injured before an important match to make an excuse for his defeat? How many wily bookers in the 1930s, or the 1980s, stumbled onto this very scenario when putting together a finish? Did this story just keep repeating itself in some fashion over the century? That booking continues today, for WWE has done it often. One hundred years apart and we see the same finish, whether work or shoot. Think about that while mulling Gotch's position in the top 50 ever.

Supposedly, Gotch knew about the injury regardless of how it happened and agreed to carry Hackenschmidt to a decent, interesting bout. Why? Logic would say that neither wanted to cancel and miss the gigantic payday. But then Gotch allegedly double-crossed Hackenschmidt and pretty much wiped him out.

Still another twist to the story came from an allegation that Hackenschmidt made up the injury to cover for the fact that Gotch smashed him. Whatever the truth, from that point on, Gotch was considered unbeatable, something he proved repeatedly until his retirement in 1913. Depending upon which date is used to start his reign as champion (1904, 1905, or 1908, as different versions have it) Gotch had one of the longest reigns — if not *the* longest — as champion. Either way, he was the man for a long time.

But, wait! Isn't something missing? Was it all a shoot? Was it real? How much was a work?

When did it all change? It would seem Gotch often did worked matches. More and more, promoters and wrestlers were finding that a work made the best economic sense. Sometimes the best drawing card is not necessarily the most skilled competitor, so accommodations have to be made. Yet many still believe the first Hackenschmidt confrontation was for real, while the second is clouded in controversy.

This much can be verified: Frank Gotch was, and in most circles still is, seen as the real deal. If *working* means making a foe look better than he is, Gotch may have been somewhat deficient, for most of his outings are described as one-sided. On the other hand, he would have been *the* target for a double-cross, so perhaps it was easier for him to just blast his opponents.

When it comes to the so-called mic skills, clearly Gotch was more than efficient as he was a superstar on the level of boxing great John L. Sullivan at the time. Certainly the evidence indicates that Gotch had plenty of charisma. All of his matches drew big crowds. He was a darling with the press and in demand for public appearances. When he went to Chicago Cubs baseball games, the players flocked to get his autograph.

Furthermore, he was twice invited to the White House by President Teddy Roosevelt. By presidential request, Gotch wrestled a Japanese judo ace and forced him to submit in the East Hall. How many WWE stalwarts have been invited to the White House? Gotch was even considered as a potential candidate for governor in Iowa before his early death.

But, you say, WWE talent gets to be in movies, even if those movies jump to home video pretty quickly. Well, Frank Gotch starred in a play. There wasn't television, or much in the way of movies back then. Getting the starring role on stage was a big deal, and the production also went to Europe. The critics loved Gotch's performance.

Frank Gotch made professional wrestling a big deal and brought it to the mainstream with his stardom. Has this not been the ultimate goal of Vince McMahon and WWE from the start?

One hundred years later and the question is not whether Frank Gotch should be included in the finest 50 pro wrestlers of all time, but where his rightful place should be. Even common sense probably is not enough to help on that.

But now, in cozy Humboldt, Iowa, they still remember Frank Gotch as the town's most famous citizen. At Bicknell Park on a small bluff overlooking the Des Moines River, Humboldt is planning to build an eight-foot-tall bronze statue of Gotch in his wrestling attire. On that site, Gotch trained for the rematch with Hackenschmidt. Fans and sports reporters from all over converged to watch him train.

Humboldt, Iowa, remembers. As wrestling fans and students, we should remember Frank Gotch too.

#9 GENE KINISKI

This dynamo was a superstar everywhere

His finely tuned motor never stopped running and that, perhaps more than any of the multitude of talents that he contributed to this celebration, made Gene Kiniski one of the very best of the 50 greatest pro wrestlers of all time.

Almost from day one in 1953 and well into the 1970s, Kiniski worked in main events in wrestling's principal markets. Historian J. Michael Kenyon, who has compiled a detailed record of Kiniski's outings, wrote for Dave Meltzer's *Wrestling Observer* that he wouldn't doubt that "Kiniski made more money [during that period] . . . than any of his contemporaries. I mean he worked almost without time off, and spent years going between big paydays in St. Louis, Toronto, Montreal, Indianapolis, Minneapolis, and Winnipeg." And Kenyon didn't even bring up the trips to the Northeast, Texas, Florida, California, and especially Japan.

Add to that how well Kiniski drew as the NWA champion from January 7, 1966, when he dethroned Lou Thesz in St. Louis, until February 11, 1969, in Tampa, where he was bumped out by Dory Funk Jr. Especially during the first two years with the gold belt, "Big Thunder" drew sellout after sellout in every NWA town. In the NWA headquarters of St. Louis, Kiniski was on top of bills that drew ten consecutive shows at capacity over 18 months at the start of his reign. The rugged, garrulous, colorful champion was drawing that much *everywhere* before tailing off at the end of his run. Overall, the wrestling business in general was cooling after the long boom that had started late in 1959.

But Kiniski was always a superstar and a drawing card, one of a handful of the era's dominant personalities. In the ring, Kiniski was the bad guy. For all the brawling, mixed in with some surprising mat skills, Kiniski was a cardio dynamo. Any opponent, even in a work, had to understand the match would be all-out, pretty stiff, and with no rest. Kiniski expected opponents to come up to his standards, but, as a worker, he was subtly helpful to anyone who gave 100 percent.

Terry Funk claimed if you could go one hour with Kiniski, you could go one hour with anyone in any era — now, then, and before. Kiniski was the hardest-working and best-conditioned athlete he ever met.

Standing 6'5" and weighing around 275 pounds at his peak, "Big Thunder" earned tremendous heat and manipulated every audience for maximum excitement. He rationalized his tactics by saying, "I use the rules. I don't abuse the rules."

The media, always skeptical about pro wrestling, loved Kiniski because he had one story after another for them and could talk smartly about any subject, not to mention having a legitimate background as a first-rate athlete and competitor. Dory Jr., something of Kiniski's protégé, understood why Kiniski clicked. Gene ordered Funk to stay at a good hotel, not the places where other wrestlers checked in. He told Dory always to wear a coat and tie, to dress and carry himself professionally. Kiniski did it, as Thesz had before him, and those basic guidelines worked for anyone who wanted to be regarded as a serious performer.

A good example that Sam Muchnick told me about occured when Sam entered Kiniski in a celebrity home-run contest before a Cardinals baseball game in St. Louis. He either won or finished second — depending on whose recollection you believe — but Gene did belt at least one pitch over the fence. The key, though, is what Muchnick told me happened during and after. In a group of pro football and basketball players, not to mention the baseball players and media types enjoying the show, it was Gene Kiniski the pro wrestler who was holding court. The athletes flocked to hear Kiniski telling colorful stories about *his* sport, and everyone loved it.

His interviews on wrestling shows were filibusters that made sense. Kiniski was intelligent, well read, and prepared to talk about every angle he had to sell. Gene had presence. Joe Garagiola, the original commentator on *Wrestling at the Chase*, said, "Gene had a face like a blocked punt, and he sounded like he gargled razor blades. Plus, he looked like he was eight foot tall and weighed 400 pounds. What a character!"

Kiniski was the only competitor to hold both the NWA and the AWA titles, for he knocked off Verne Gagne in 1961 before losing that honor back to Gagne. In addition, before he grabbed the NWA title, Kiniski had a series of duels with Bruno Sammartino for the WWWF laurels. Their feud began in Madison Square Garden, where Kiniski thought he had won Bruno's title, grabbed the belt, and left the ring. In the rematch, Sammartino won a Texas death match. Some NWA promoters were hesitant about turning over the NWA prize to Kiniski so soon after he had failed to topple Sammartino. Kiniski's work and reputation were so strong, however, that those concerns were for naught.

Gene Kiniski was a superstar to both rabid wrestling fans and casual followers at that point in time. He gave magazine editors more to write about. Who would win a showdown between Sammartino, Gagne, and Kiniski? Readers devoured it.

Born in Edmonton, Kiniski was a star football player in high school and learned wrestling at the local YMCA. Kiniski was a college football standout at the University of Arizona, where he also started wrestling in the off-season for promoter Rod Fenton, with whom Kiniski later became business partners. He also came under the influence of Dory Funk Sr., a cagey competitor who knew the ins and outs of the pro game. But Kiniski still had some football in his blood, and after some interest from the NFL he ended up with the Canadian Football League's Edmonton Eskimos,

Gene Kiniski abuses former champ Pat O'Connor

where he played with future pro wrestling standouts Wilbur Snyder and Joe Blanchard.

Supposedly, sideline reporters were intimidated by Kiniski because he was so intense and competitive during games. Another tale is that the coaches moved Kiniski from the offensive to the defensive side because Gene was so loud and authoritative that the quarterback had trouble calling plays in the huddle.

By that point, though, pro wrestling was providing much more income than football, plus Kiniski was having much more fun, so it was easy for him to make a career decision that turned out to be a rousing success. Soon young Kiniski was a headliner in Southern California, working with the likes of Snyder (who was also an immediate main event attraction), Warren Bockwinkel (Nick's father), Sandor Szabo, Bobo Brazil, and John Tolos. "Big Thunder" also had his first match with Thesz on November 3, 1954, in Los Angeles. In Texas, billed for a brief period as Gene Kelly, he collided with Pepper Gomez, Ray Gunkel, Duke Keomuka, and Johnny Valentine.

Somewhere in the mid 1950s Kiniski clashed with Don Leo Jonathan, an even bigger athlete at likely 6'6" and 300-plus pounds, to start a long-running rivalry. According to stories Jonathan has told, at one point in the brutal brawl he accidentally blasted Kiniski with a fist and drove Gene's teeth through his bottom lip. Blood spurted everywhere. Afterward, Jonathan felt bad and sent Kiniski a fifth of whiskey and some expensive Cuban cigars. Kiniski actually told me this story too, one quiet afternoon in the St. Louis wrestling office when Gene was in town for his last local title bout against Ric Flair in 1982. He verified the punch line. "Yeah, kid, here's the real story," Gene growled. "The next time I worked with Jonathan, I waited until we locked up and I told him the whiskey was drank [sic] and the cigars smoked. So hit me again — and harder!" And Kiniski laughed.

Typical of the true big guns of the time, Kiniski was in demand everywhere within a couple of years. He was so hot in Buffalo that a newspaper columnist noted that in 13 main events, Kiniski had drawn

163,000 fans. In his native Canada, through a wild series of wars with the legendary "Whipper" Billy Watson in Toronto and donnybrooks against Edouard Carpentier in Montreal, Kiniski became a national celebrity.

The Kiniski legend grew a little bit in the memorable flying-chair riot at Delorimier Stadium on August 7, 1957. Business was on fire in Montreal, with Kiniski involved in a dispute about a world title claim with Carpentier and another monster heel, Killer Kowalski. As Carpentier and Kowalski were battling in a best-of-three test, Kiniski came to the ring to challenge the winner. Carpentier booted Kiniski from the ring, but the explosive Kiniski grabbed a chair and hurled it at Carpentier.

Irate fans among the nearly 15,000 on hand began throwing chairs at the ring. Kiniski grabbed one and smacked Carpentier, not exactly helping the situation. Another favorite, Andre Bollet, came to aid Carpentier. Kowalski, no shrinking violet himself, started to swat at both good guys with a chair. Bollet then whacked Kiniski, who took the wrong route to the dressing room and, receiving several shots from flying chairs, had to return through the hostile crowd until police rescued him. Now that was serious heat.

By 1959, Kiniski was on a rampage throughout the Midwest and became one of the earliest stars on *Wrestling at the Chase*, which exploded onto the St. Louis scene with a cast of fabulous stars. Kiniski might have been at the top of the list, as his tag team with cocky Rip Hawk interacted perfectly with the witty Garagiola as announcer. A wild and bloody feud with "Cowboy" Bob Ellis and some thrilling bouts with NWA champion Pat O'Connor certainly helped as well.

By the time Thesz gave his personal approval to Kiniski as his successor, Kiniski had proven his mettle everywhere against everybody. And, as noted earlier, Thesz had a chosen few with whom he loved to shoot for a few minutes during matches that were worked. Kiniski was one of them because he was competitive and truly dangerous.

He first went to Japan in 1964 and instantly started a historical feud with Giant Baba, who was far more rugged and athletic in his prime than people give him credit for when they only focus on Baba's last few years. Except for Kiniski and Sammartino, Baba in those days pinned every American star who came to challenge him. In 1967, Kiniski returned as the first NWA champion in Japan since Thesz met Rikidozan a decade or more earlier. One of the most famous Japanese bouts ever was the 65-minute draw between Kiniski and Baba in blistering heat and humidity before 25,000 fans at the Osaka Baseball Stadium.

Like most champions who find that both the road and the politics offer another level of mental strain once they get the title, Kiniski was ready to step down late in 1968. His frustration boiled over at an NWA meeting where Gene was more outspoken than ever as he blasted the assembled promoters. He accused many of cheating on payoffs (Gene was not the first to make that charge) and refusing to treat the champion as a champion of a major sport. He griped that the promoters were pimps who treated talent like whores. The rant was vintage Kiniski, straight-ahead, non-stop, and as blunt as a bulldozer, except he was shooting. He owned part of the Vancouver territory so everyone realized Gene knew what he was talking about, and it hurt.

After turning over the belt to Dory Jr., Kiniski concentrated on his own promotion and toured lucrative towns as a headliner. But the divorce with his beloved wife, Marian, in 1973, and then her shocking suicide, took a chunk out of Kiniski. As gruff as Gene could be, friends like Dutch Savage knew the buzzsaw was a softie down deep. He concentrated on raising sons Kelly and Nick, opened a bar in Blaine, Washington, and stuck to wrestling in favorite towns like St. Louis, Toronto, and Portland, with the odd trek to Japan.

Like a professor, Kiniski had a story for everything and a cure for most injuries because he'd seen them all. I remember him popping Spike Huber's leg to loosen a back spasm that had Spike bent in pain. When Gene lost to Flair's figure-four leglock, he put a rock in his shoe so that he would realistically limp as he left the building after the match. Listening to a pair of rabble-rousers like Kiniski and Dick Murdoch in the dressing room was better than an evening at any comedy club.

He shook his head as WWE took over the world and his territory essentially fell apart like all the rest. Son Kelly, while a talented athlete and wrestler, wasn't cut out for the wrestling business. Nick seemed to have the gift, but an irritating try with the WWF ended with Nick saying he wouldn't do the favors that certain people wanted him to do, so — in true Kiniski fashion — he told them to stick it and went home.

Kiniski has always been undervalued, so why has he landed such a prominent position here in the final ranking of the best ever? While you could throw a blanket over numbers nine through 14, choices had to be made. Trust me. The differences are less than miniature and open to argument, but the following is what I believe.

This is where Gagne's physical and legal ownership of the title he defended works against Verne, because a good part of his case is based on that championship. How often did Verne face the WWWF and NWA champions, which Kiniski did in addition to tackling Verne himself?

Dory's NWA reign was one year longer than Kiniski's, drawing better than Gene later in the reign. Dory, however did not visit as many big towns and territories as Gene did when both were not titleholders. Before getting the belt, Kiniski had a dozen years of main events everywhere, Funk a third of that but more selectively.

Kiniski had the belt longer and drew more money than Terry, who got his loudest plaudits when he went hardcore later. But hardcore was an influential cult that didn't draw enough money to stay in business. Kiniski met the AWA and WWWF champions when that was a big deal. Neither Funk brother did the same.

The chase with Race is equally tight. Harley didn't get to the WWF until after the promotional war began and then he was slotted below the big guns. When Kiniski was there — granted, different time and circumstances — he went head to head with Sammartino. And in the AWA, Race was more often part of a tag team and not the top challenger for Gagne.

As for Frank Gotch — well, good luck mixing and measuring all those long-ago facts and accomplishments. For those who want to bump Gotch up one spot, feel free, but it seems that the overall business and pool of talent was larger and more competitive when Kiniski was in the fracas.

Over the last decade, I talked regularly with "Big Thunder," and any chat was bound to be engrossing. He was reading bundles of newspapers, swimming laps, and exercising as long as he could. If I heard classical music in the background, I knew I'd interrupted his workout session. And Gene told me often, "Wrestling fans should bow down when they drive by Kiel Auditorium, because nobody is ever going to do wrestling again like we did."

We spoke a few times late in 2009 as the end drew near and cancer started to attack him like no opponent ever had. "Big Thunder" refused to break. Nick said the old lion's brain and heart wouldn't quit; they simple refused to accept the fact that his body was breaking down around him. I can vouch for that, as Gene would entertain me by launching himself into stories of battles in the ring, disputes with promoters, and evaluations of different stars and competitors with big hearts, which he respected.

Finally, one day as the growl was going full tilt, Kiniski declared, "I've had a great life, Larry. I only have one regret. I can't go back and do it all again."

That, friends, is a regret for anyone who did, or did not, see and enjoy one of the very greatest pro wrestlers ever — Gene Kiniski. The time is here to give Kiniski what is rightfully due him.

#8 BUDDY ROGERS
The master of getting real heat

For sheer sustained heat over a long period of time, Buddy Rogers is in a class by himself. I don't just mean heat that makes noise and adds energy to a building. We're talking the most extreme heat imaginable. The heat that is actually passionate hate.

This heat isn't about "I love to hate you," as heat has often been with the most successful villains. This heat is about hating someone so much that even the most casual fan has been sucked in by the performance of the bad guy and is willing to pay good cash to see the object of loathing battered, bludgeoned, bombarded, and beaten to a pulp.

Buddy Rogers, born Herman Rohde, did that over and over. And the customers paid repeatedly. Although he took some wicked bumps and lumps, Rogers was never pounded into mush. Thus, fans had to settle for hoping he would be pinned or forced to submit, but they only got that once in a great while. Still, the serious heat Rogers generated was so strong that they kept coming back and hoping to see him put in his place.

The strutting blond was the next step up the evolutionary ladder from Gorgeous George. Much more muscular with a great physique, he was less effete, his every movement spoke arrogance, and he was surprisingly athletic. Rogers was a fabulous showman, a brilliant worker. He was completely sensitive to what every audience wanted or needed. At different points early in his career, which reportedly began in 1939, Buddy was a favorite. As he developed, however, the heel role suited his personality much better.

No rule was sacred to Rogers, and he broke them all. He was devious and vicious. He could score with a flying head scissors, a drop kick, or a high knee into the face of an opponent bouncing off the ropes, something Harley Race and then Triple H would pick up years later.

More than any other performer at the time, he was active and flew around the ring regularly.

The figure-four grapevine Rogers perfected was portrayed as a crippling hold that gained many victories for him. When Rogers was able to slither away from danger, his ring smarts infuriated the crowds. Putting on the brakes before running into a punch or a back drop from his foe, Rogers would sneer and strut about the ring in a manner much copied but seldom duplicated.

The story has always been that Rogers was not a true wrestler, not someone like Lou Thesz or Pat O'Connor. That's true, but don't forget that Herman Rohde was a policeman in a tough town before he got into wrestling and became Buddy Rogers. He was very strong and naturally nasty. He could take care of himself in most cases. A few tales circulated about opponents who had been hurt badly when Rogers took advantage of them.

Outside the ring, Rogers became adept at the politics of wrestling. His often-stated philosophy was something along the lines of "screw your friends and be nice to your enemies so that your enemies become your friends and then you can screw them too." There are many who feel this accurately depicts the backstage mentality of the business.

The heel personality he projected so well was part of Rogers' real character. Even if he wasn't a so-called real wrestler, he was a real mean guy. That true mean side made it apparent that knocking off Rogers would be no walk in the park, which made his heat grow even more. Fans picked up on it. Against almost any reasonable opponent, Rogers was one of a handful of stars who could always draw a good to excellent crowd.

Irv Muchnick, Sam's nephew and author of *Chris and Nancy*, the Benoit story, spent a couple of hours in 1985 talking with Rogers about his career. Irv thought Rogers wasn't even that aware of his gift (to draw heat). "It was just always there — unbearable, everlasting crowd tension," Irv noted, calling it "intuitive genius for controlling a crowd."

Is Buddy Rogers high up on the list of the greatest 50 wrestlers in history? Well, how high is Hulk Hogan? This is the dichotomy of pro wrestling, at least from my perspective on this project. The legitimate skilled wrestler gets extra votes, but the reality is that the business is about drawing money so the performer, regardless of his fundamental talent or toughness, must receive every bit as much credit.

To be included, the *wrestler* must be able to perform and draw money. To be included, the *performer* must be tough enough and able to draw money. Critics can snipe at Rogers and Hogan for being less than supremely talented as wrestlers, but they had more than enough talent and fire to go along with amazing gifts for connecting with the fans. Whether a boo or a cheer, it's the same thing. Like Hulk, Buddy Rogers lands well toward the top of this celebrated group.

The irony is that just as Hulk was critical to the success of Vince McMahon and the WWF in 1984, Rogers was a vital player in two major business dramas. In the late 1940s, Sam Muchnick had broken away in St. Louis from his boss and mentor, Tom Packs. The promotional war was tense, with Muchnick just hanging on. Packs eventually sold to a powerful group that included Thesz, but Muchnick helped start the National Wrestling Alliance and became tight with wily Al Haft, the impresario in Ohio. Haft was booking Rogers, and he put Sam together with Buddy. Only a couple of years earlier, Rogers had gotten over huge as an attraction for Packs, so this was a major shift.

Muchnick often told me that he didn't like Rogers personally, that Buddy was difficult to deal with, but they could do business together. "Nothing

says you have to eat dinner together to do business," Sam told me once. Rogers came to trust Muchnick, and vice versa, and it was Rogers coming in for Muchnick that turned the tide of war in St. Louis. When Rogers and Don Eagle sold out Kiel Auditorium on February 4, 1949, the momentum changed and soon the promotions merged, with Muchnick in charge.

Without Rogers, Muchnick would likely have lost the battle in St. Louis. If Sam lost, likely there would never have been a meaningful NWA. Without the NWA, pro wrestling history would not be nearly the same . . . all because of Buddy Rogers.

By 1963, Rogers was at the end of a controversial tenure as the NWA champion that had started when he took the crown from Pat O'Connor before 38,622 fans in Chicago's Comiskey Park. In what became something of a catch phrase in his interviews, after the triumph Rogers proclaimed, "To a nicer guy it couldn't have happened."

At that time, Rogers was closely allied with Vince McMahon Sr. and Toots Mondt, thus leading to many headaches for NWA president Muchnick in booking Rogers for some NWA members. Also, though Rogers' command of the psychology was better than ever, years of hard bumps and the exhausting schedule led to a few injuries that cost available dates on the champion.

The politics got testy, and Rogers' personality didn't help one bit. Most notable was the dressing-room confrontation the champ had with Big Bill Miller and Karl Gotch in Columbus, Ohio, on August 31, 1962. Regardless of who was at fault, the result was that Rogers was injured and again missed several important dates. When Buddy did work, it was often for McMahon and Mondt, for Muchnick himself, and perhaps for friends like Frank Tunney in Toronto. Muchnick realized it was time for a new champion, and the rumor mill was churning about what devious plans Vince Sr. and Mondt might have in mind. Steal the NWA title? Look into the stories of the 1920s and 1930s. It's no wonder plenty of promoters took the possibility seriously.

Lou Thesz was lured back from semi-retirement for a couple reasons. First, he was a hooker so he was a good choice in case Rogers tried something shady when they finally got in the ring together. Second, Thesz and Rogers had longstanding heat. Therefore, if he had to hurt Rogers, Thesz wouldn't hesitate. Years before, Rogers had verbally blasted "Strangler" Lewis, an all-time great and close friend of Thesz. That, along with some other shadowy tricks by Rogers, infuriated Thesz, who vowed never to do a job for Rogers again.

Please note, though, that Thesz always maintained that Rogers was the greatest performer in the history of the game. He respected Rogers for the fact that Buddy made the work look like a real test of skills and toughness, which when added to his colorful tactics made him such a great box-office attraction. Like many others, though, Lou just didn't like Buddy. At any rate, Rogers agreed to go the easy way rather than the hard way to put Thesz over and dropped the NWA laurels in Toronto on January 24, 1963.

Ah, but in a pro wrestling story, there is always another twist. McMahon and Mondt ignored the change in champions, formed the World Wide Wrestling Federation (the father of today's WWE), and proclaimed that Buddy Rogers was the champion after winning a tournament in Rio de Janeiro. Fiction plays so well in wrestling, and they needed a starting point.

On May 17, 1963, in only 47 seconds, Bruno Sammartino became the new WWWF champion by defeating Rogers in Madison Square Garden. Rogers' health had deteriorated badly at this point, as heart problems actually hospitalized him prior to the bout with Bruno.

Once again, Buddy Rogers was right in the middle at a key point in pro wrestling history. McMahon and company would have still moved on with the WWWF, but Rogers was such a huge star at the time that what he did gave credibility to the new title in critical WWWF markets, with the Northeastern media, and in the business itself. More importantly, being blown out the way Rogers was gave Bruno a jump on being the sport's freshest superstar. Buddy retired before a rematch with Bruno could be held.

Rogers knew all about being a superstar because he was regarded as such very quickly once he got rolling. It was all natural for him, perhaps one reason that promoters (a couple have claimed credit) nicknamed him

"Nature Boy." Maybe he couldn't hook a tough guy, but Rogers could surely construct an exciting match with one.

He started rolling in Texas for dapper Houston promoter Morris Sigel in the mid 1940s, became a big star in California, and then tied up with Haft and notably Fred Kohler in Chicago, where the famous Dumont televised wrestling show was produced. Rogers became one of the major standouts because the camera naturally loved this strutting blond with the finely tuned, muscular body. Throughout the 1950s, Rogers was likely the biggest heel drawing card in North America. By the end of the decade, Rogers had also been lured to the Northeast by the charming Vince Sr. and the ambitious Toots.

Records are sketchy, but it is accurate to say that if a major town had an attendance record, it was either broken or set by a match involving Rogers. From Texas to California to St. Louis, throughout Canada and along the East Coast, every promoter knew that Rogers was money in the bank. By all accounts, his success was exceeded only by his ego. Yet he also had no problem doing a job when that was what business in a particular town needed. He won, occasionally lost, and had numerous draws against every leading name in the business, including everyone of his era in the group of the 50 best ever.

Through it all, Rogers never lost one iota of heat. His influence on wrestling was so powerful that it's fair to ask whether there would have been a Ric Flair without Buddy Rogers. After years absent from the business, Rogers returned to the Carolinas when Flair was making his name and, at almost 60 years old, challenged the young stud to a "battle of the Nature Boys," which Flair won. After dabbling in managing, Rogers walked away for good.

His legacy, however, still remains an important ingredient in pro wrestling. Draw real heat, make real money. Do it for more than 20 years and join the 50 greatest pro wrestlers ever, just like Buddy Rogers.

#7 JIM LONDOS
A legendary figure who drew record crowds

Jim Londos was a colossal pro wrestling hero at a time when both the business and the country needed him. One of the greatest sportswriters ever in mainstream media drove home the point in a column for the *New York Times* when Londos died in 1975, more than 30 years after his fame peaked.

Red Smith, a Hall-of-Fame writer, wouldn't normally be expected to salute pro wrestling, but he did in praising Londos in the *Times*, of all places. He pointed out that Londos was the king in the days of the Great Depression, Prohibition, Repeal, and New Deal. When people were living hand to mouth and money was tighter than at any time in history, countless fans paid to see Londos in action, to be entertained by, as Smith aptly described, a "thickly muscled figure . . . olive oil face with gently sorrowing brown eyes." The face and figure were vitally familiar to the public long before television, which speaks volumes about Londos's ability to connect with the public.

Londos was a true superstar, a rare personality who crossed the boundaries to become a cultural icon. The country needed Londos, and a select few other sports and entertainment figures, to help weather the storms.

He was not the greatest pure wrestler by any means, although he was a tough and talented craftsman who could take care of himself. Londos *was* most assuredly a great worker, and the term was used much more within the confines of pro wrestling by the 1930s. At various times recognized as the world champion, Londos was also comfortable operating within the Machiavellian mazes of wrestling politics.

Born in Greece in 1897 and named Christopher Theophelus (or in some records Christos Thefilou), Londos immigrated to the United States after running away from home at age 13. After bouncing around looking for jobs, including working construction and posing nude for figure-drawing classes, the classically handsome Greek with the stunning physique gravitated to the carnival world. He took a job as a catcher in an acrobatic act. The boy also hung out and learned amateur wrestling at the YMCA in San Francisco, where he was then living. Christopher began wrestling in the carnival's "meet all challengers" contests and learned how to hook well enough to protect himself and to hurt rowdy opponents when necessary.

That led the rugged youngster to pro wrestling in the Pacific Northwest, where he became a solid performer with the name Jim Londos, which was allegedly a spin on famous author Jack London. Then Toots Mondt, whose name is all over wrestling's annals, spotted Londos, recognized the potential, and strapped Londos to the proverbial rocket. History was about to be made.

Londos was actually a small man, standing only 5'8" and tipping the scales around 200 pounds. Chris Jericho supporters, take note. But that low center of gravity combined with uncanny strength and huge, powerful legs made Londos more than a handful and was a wonderful story for promoters like Mondt to trumpet. Mondt loved booking Londos against ugly, bulkier rivals in a "beauty versus beast" confrontation. The "Golden Greek" would then smash his bigger opponents into defeat, often with the airplane spin he is credited with popularizing.

Some observers also think that Londos was the first, or among the first, to use what became known as the sleeper hold to record victories in 1931. In fact, Red Smith made reference to a major promotion Jack Curley put together between Londos and Ray Steele, a friend from Londos's carnival days, in New York in the early 1930s. The two combatants set up rival training camps in the mountains to get away from the New York newspapers, which covered every little item leading up to the conflict. Smith apologized that the exact details had escaped his memory, but he was certain over 40,000 fans were on hand at either Yankee Stadium or the Polo Grounds to see Londos get the victory over the rugged Steele with what was called the unconscious hold.

Fans, including the always elusive female audience, fell in love with Londos and he was a huge drawing card, particularly in the Northeast corridor where one day Bruno Sammartino would reign supreme. A great worker, Londos was always in tip-top condition, and his matches had fans cheering in delight. My late father recalled seeing Londos flatten Hans Kampfer before a capacity crowd (which would have been over 17,000 at the time) at The Arena in St. Louis.

Philadelphia promoter Ray Fabiani jumped on the Londos bandwagon; Ed White, an influential promoter in the Chicago territory, allied himself with Londos as his manager. Tom Packs in St. Louis, politically important because of his growing influence, also became a big Londos supporter. That relation soured, though, when Londos became part of an attempt to bump Packs out of St. Louis. Packs naturally stopped using Londos for a while. My late father recalled seeing Londos flatten Hans Kampfer before a capacity crowd (which would have been over 17,000 at the time) at The Arena in St. Louis.

Ah, but weren't performers, promoters, and politics such a spicy stew? Speaking of turmoil and titles, consider in retrospect how neatly Londos fit into the big picture during the 1930s. Londos won, lost, and finally regained a version of the world championship by beating Dick Shikat in 1930. But after "Strangler" Lewis dethroned Joe Stecher for another world championship in their famous 1928 struggle, Gus Sonnenberg downed

Lewis in 1929. Sonnenberg was ousted by Ed Don George in 1931. Yet Londos was being hailed as the champion too. Then Lewis beat George, before Henri DeGlane "stole" that title (with help from various promoters battling for towns and prestige behind the scenes) from Lewis in the celebrated biting disqualification. Still, in 1931, DeGlane was quickly dispatched by George. That leaves George and Londos as the champs, right?

Only one problem. Another dispute broke out between promotions in New York, a tournament was held, and Lewis beat Shikat in the finals, so "Strangler" Lewis also laid claim to being wrestling's monarch. So it was Londos, Lewis, and George with a claim to be the world champion.

But hang on. Jim Browning took that crown from Lewis in 1933. Thankfully, Londos then defeated Browning in 1934. One year later, another hot drawing card in Danno O'Mahoney topped Londos. Bless his heart — or the hearts of Mondt, Fabiani, Curley, Packs, and Paul Bowser, the promoters pulling the strings — O'Mahoney then took the measure of George supposedly, hopefully to unite everything into one championship. Is everything clear now?

And then Shikat, of all people, rebounded to beat O'Mahoney, but Shikat was whipped by Ali Baba, who was disqualified against Dave Levin but kept the title regardless until he lost to Everett Marshall. This all happened in 1936. To add to the fun, many fans ignored the championship because they so wanted to see the "dream match" between Lewis and Londos, the two biggest names since Gotch, in 1935.

Throughout this entire discord, Londos was living up to his "Golden Greek" nickname. He was indeed box-office gold, starring in front of packed houses on a regular basis. He had a superior understanding of how to take spectators on a roller-coaster ride. Often a bigger opponent the fans disliked would have Londos on the verge of defeat. He would make comebacks, only to have them stopped. Then, like a lightning bolt, Londos would pull off that one great move to capture victory against all odds. Londos trained vigorously around the back-breaking ring schedule so that he looked the part of a superstar who could survive that type of contest.

Real-life swerves for high stakes such as power and money were so delicious in those days, especially with the ever-present threat of an unexpected shoot, that no modern booker could have concocted such shenanigans. A star performer like Londos or Lewis had to stay on top of his game both physically and politically all the time to protect his rear flank.

Londos had a falling-out with Mondt, Curley, and Jack Pfeffer, yet another promotional character whom Londos hated. Mondt, sparked by dirty dealings in the O'Mahoney-Londos match, eventually double-crossed Pfeffer. At that point, Londos made a deal with rival New York promoter Rudy Dusek, and that cut Mondt and Curley out of the financial gold mine of Londos's matches. Londos's deal also caused Mondt to reopen relations with Lewis and Bowser. Yet Londos was such an overwhelming superstar that any deals had to include him. This pointed toward an inevitable showdown between Londos and Lewis, and according to most records, Londos had never yet beaten Lewis. Added to the recipe was that there had never been any love lost between the two competitors.

First, though, Ray Steele was thrust into the spotlight as Londos's policeman and had an ugly battle against Lewis in late 1932 that ended when Steele was disqualified after a mess that was allegedly part shoot, part work. Londos continued to top bills that drew serious money all over the place, while Lewis picked his spots carefully.

Finally, after alliances and partnerships came and went while deals were cut, collapsed, and were redone, it all came together: Lewis and Londos were to square off at Wrigley Field in Chicago. The public impact of their match is obvious since the event played a major part in the history of both pro wrestling giants. Jim chalked up a long-awaited triumph over "Strangler" before 35,265 fans.

His reputation among wrestling's gods thus secured, Londos made numerous trips to wrestle throughout Europe. Apparently all of his matches meant big business and a lot of money for both promoters and Londos himself. Perhaps the biggest moment came when Londos returned to his native Greece and drew what is widely agreed upon as more than 110,000 fans (or was it 60,000?) in Athens. Another 30,000 were supposedly turned away because the stadium was packed to the brim.

At the urging of Mondt — with Fabiani serving as the neutral peacemaker who reminded both parties that the goal was to make money, not fight each other — Londos took another turn on top in North America. Once more he clashed with a major cultural figure when he beat Bronko Nagurski in 1938, at which time Jim Londos claimed the world championship again. Whether Londos ever lost that rendition of the championship, which was recognized primarily by Eastern offices, is unknown. He slowed down his in-ring frolics at that point, especially during World War II, and officially retired in 1946. But in wrestling there is always a comeback, and Londos was no exception, with one match to defeat gigantic boxer-wrestler Primo Carnera in 1950.

From that point until his death, much of his time was spent working for charitable organizations, especially for Greek war orphans. He was honored by President Nixon for his many efforts in the field. Does that help answer any questions about the legacy of Jim Londos?

Now comes the difficult part, deciding exactly where Londos fits in among the greatest ever. That he must be in the upper 30 percent or so is unquestionable. Could he get over in the 2000s? No question there either. Regarding his height, consider those who have headlined for WWE. But then look at the great genetics with which Londos was blessed, and factor in how even much more spectacular he would have appeared with modern-day chemical enhancement.

Unmatched natural charisma and psychology together would create a better-built and tougher Shawn Michaels, without the personal drama. Actually, Londos's size might have worked against him more in the 1960s and 1970s. But a worker of his expertise with legitimate tough-guy skills, even if not equal to Thesz or Lewis, would have found a way into main events. Now factor in all those jumbo gates that Jim Londos drew. He had something special that was granted to only a very few.

Make the comparisons to Buddy Rogers, Verne Gagne, Harley Race, Dory Jr. and Terry Funk, Gene Kiniski, "Wild Bill" Longson, Frank Gotch, or even Stone Cold Steve Austin. Consider the pros and cons against each contender. Too close to call in some areas. Nobody said this would be easy.

But when the results are tabulated, what carries so much weight is how Jim Londos catapulted his business and himself into the public spotlight. To say he occupies a place among the 50 greatest pro wrestlers in history is not enough.

Jim Londos commands recognition in the top 10 of all time.

#6 STONE COLD STEVE AUSTIN

Stone cold at the heart of the hottest period

When it came to whipping ass, Stone Cold Steve Austin pretty much did that to the entire pro wrestling industry for the benefit of VKM's promotion. In a relatively short period of almost six years, Austin was the focal point of angles that not only played a major role in revitalizing, maybe even saving, the WWF, but also probably made Stone Cold the greatest individual generator of combined revenue from PPV buys and merchandise sales in the history of the company and the business.

Putting Austin at number six on the greatest ever might stir up some disagreement. On one hand, Austin's run on top is little more than a drop in the bucket compared to Rogers, Londos, Gagne, Kiniski, Race, and the Funks. Six years of main events versus 25 years of main events!

Yes, Stone Cold won the major championship in WWF/WWE six different times. But, all told, those six stints with the title belt only lasted 529 days. Compared to the reigns of those bunched narrowly behind him on the greatest ever roster, what Austin did as the champion seems weak on the surface. Yet that's unfair in many ways, for it is a function of what the boss wanted and the business had evolved into. Austin simply filled the role, and he did it better than most if not all who had the same opportunity.

On Austin's behalf, he had by far the biggest individual impact on one-time shows and as a money producer when put up against those squeezing him. This is unfair from the other point of view, though, because none of those on the list from Londos to Race had a national pay-per-view show on which to perform. Moreover, merchandise and gimmicks to be sold were basically non-existent. None of these greats had a giant marketing company like WWF/WWE behind them pushing, pushing, pushing.

So there is no perfect method to weigh business against business — it was simply too different for those involved.

Try wrestling skills against wrestling skills, or perhaps working ability against working ability. Austin seems to come up short there, but again, think about what pro wrestling wanted from its characters at different times. Regardless of what was required, Austin does not have the staying power on top the others had. Granted, severe injury was part of it, but *not* getting hurt is part of the genetic gift that can separate the greats from each other.

Possibly the strongest point on Austin's behalf is what he meant to the WWF/WWE in their time of need. In simple terms, McMahon's company was losing the fight against Ted Turner's WCW. While WCW was already going down the path to self-destruction, WWF had chalked up some money-losing years too. WCW was winning the television ratings war. The WWF was reeling.

Austin's character caught on like none had since Hulk Hogan (from yet another very different time period in wrestling). Stone Cold took the anti-hero, for some time a favorite drawing card in wrestling, to new levels. His personality fit as the defiant, beer-drinking roughneck who loved giving a one-fingered salute to the boss. The angle with boxing superstar Mike Tyson worked perfectly because Austin fit the role like a glove. Stone Cold's rivalry with the boss, the arrogant Mr. McMahon, was perfect for the moment. Behind closed doors, Austin navigated choppy waters. Whenever a moment arose for a spectacular performance in the ring, Austin pulled it off no matter how badly he was hurting or how much risk he had to take. As the WWF turned itself around on the back of Austin, WCW kept shooting itself in the foot.

Austin's historical significance is a trump card that bumps him slightly ahead of some very worthy competitors for the sixth position among the finest pro wrestlers of all time. The others all could point to important moments they were part of in mat history, but Austin was the star participant when the game had shrunk to only two players.

In addition, the entire soap opera occurred on the national stage for the entire world to see, or at least that portion of the world that cared about pro wrestling. Failure, or even switching sides, might well have altered what the pro wrestling scene is today. For those reasons, just as Lou Thesz slipped past Ric Flair by a hair for number one ever, Steve Austin nudges into place by a tiny margin over some mighty impressive challengers. And I get it for those who disagree.

That mercurial run for WWF is worth looking at, for it truly was amazing. These hypothetical headlines, plus a little explanation, tell the story.

Austin joins the WWF in late 1995. He was called "The Ringmaster" and was managed by Ted DiBiase, and the whole thing flopped. The idea of selling Austin or anyone as a fine classic grappler is so far from the WWF mentality then or now as to be laughable. This enterprise, however, led Austin to come up with the "Stone Cold" character all on his own, and he sold it to McMahon too.

The bible helps Austin in 1996. Stone Cold went on a roll as his new trademark finish — the stunner — caught on and he started to get some serious heat. After a victory over Jake Roberts, Austin went on a verbal rant against "The Snake," who was using a born-again Christian gimmick at the time and often quoted the Bible.

After snarling that thumping the Bible and saying prayers got Roberts nowhere, Stone Cold growled, "Austin 3:16 says I just whipped your ass!" Overnight, fans were making "Austin 3:16" signs to display at every WWF card. When the company printed that catch phrase on a T-shirt, sales went through the roof and made the WWF a fortune.

Stone Cold officially becomes the red-hot good guy at _WrestleMania XIII_ in 1997. Actually, making Austin a babyface was a no-brainer because crowds were already cheering him in duels against Bret Hart and Shawn Michaels. But the issue between Hart and Austin culminated nicely in the tricky deal of making Austin a good guy and turning Hart into a heel in the same match.

Many company insiders still feel this "I quit" showdown was one of the promotion's finest achievements. Of course, it was the perfect execution and smart psychology by Austin and Hart that made it work. This also opened the door for Austin to clash with company icons like The Undertaker and allowed the original feud to spread to include Austin against Owen Hart, Bret's brother. The bandwagon for Stone Cold was loading to capacity by then.

Real-life danger intrudes on August 3, 1997. During a heated contest with Owen Hart at the _SummerSlam_ PPV, in which Austin was to gain a victory that would move him to the very head of the WWF list, Hart messed up a tombstone piledriver that left Austin with horrendous neck damage. He was actually paralyzed for several terrifying moments in the ring. Somehow, though he was groggy, Austin was manipulated by Hart into a position to get the pin.

The brutal trauma added to the neck problem Austin was already suffering. Leading specialists warned Austin to quit wresting rather than risk paralysis or worse. Even though he stayed out of the ring, Austin was on most editions of _Raw_ because WCW was beating the WWF in the ratings and Vince needed Austin's star-power. Some of his skits strained credibility, but the company was desperate and Austin didn't want to give up his chance at superstardom.

Austin recovered and got back into action, fine-tuning what he did to protect a fragile neck. Austin kept his star soaring like a comet on the strength of his character and inventive booking, plus the right moves made at the right times. No small part of the equation was the feud

between Austin and McMahon himself, the employee who refused to buckle under pressure from the big company owner.

Mike Tyson helps Austin to a record-breaking event with *WrestleMania XIV* in 1998. Through his disputes with McMahon, enough trouble had erupted that controversial boxing great Mike Tyson was added as a "special enforcer" for the battle between Austin and then-WWF champion Shawn Michaels. At first, it looked as though Tyson was siding with Michaels and the D-Generation X crew that included Triple H. The plot drew the largest PPV audience ever at the time, and WCW was starting to feel the pressure.

Instead of aiding Michaels, Tyson made the decisive three-count for Austin and then kayoed Michaels. Austin and Tyson celebrated together, giving Austin even more of the "celebrity rub" from Iron Mike. It was also Austin's first time as the company's champion.

The WWF was on fire thanks to Austin and the new "attitude" approach of the organization. Blood, guts, and sass ruled the day. Austin's weekly dance with Vince and his family on *Raw* triggered a jump in ratings that toppled WCW from its perch, although plenty of viewers were offended when Austin threatened Vince with a gun (which turned out to be a toy). Both PPVs and house shows hit record levels as Austin, despite neck and knee problems, tackled Mick Foley, Kane, and The Undertaker. Another PPV of Austin versus Vince did more big business.

The Rock and Austin headline another record-breaker at *WrestleMania XV* in 1999. With The Rock in charge of the title and representing McMahon, the blow-off between him and Austin broke the PPV record for buys set only one year before. The question of which company — the WWF or WCW — would emerge on top was no longer in doubt.

Austin's career, however, was again in jeopardy. Late in 1999, with his neck in worse shape than ever, Austin knew surgery was inevitable. The operation in January 2000 knocked him out of that year's *Mania*, but the tide was running high for the WWF, and WCW was near the end.

Going against a lot of medical advice, Austin was back in action by the end of 2000 and locking up with Triple H, Kurt Angle, and The Rock. The magic was still there, both in person and for PPVs.

Stone Cold Steve Austin "discusses" the state of professional wrestling with Vince McMahon

Austin sets another record at *WrestleMania XVII* in 2001. Once more taking on The Rock, who brought along more than his share of magic, Austin was part of an event that became the biggest revenue-producing show in the history of pro wrestling. PPV buys plus ticket sales plus merchandise income cemented the WWF as the king of wrestling promotions.

Of course, not all of those sources were available to promotions from an earlier day. The fact was, McMahon and company perfectly utilized every tool at their disposal. And Austin and The Rock were performers of a rare breed.

But somehow everyone stumbled. While Austin got two more highly profitable *WrestleManias* (against Hulk in 2002 and one more against The Rock in 2003), as often happened in the history of the business, promoter and talent ended up on different pages. And Austin's deteriorating spine didn't help.

Although Austin balked, the booking turned him heel after the 2001 triumph. Simply put, the fans said, "No." Some things are best left unchanged, even in pro wrestling — especially if those things aren't broken. Fans wanted to cheer for Stone Cold. Business went into a steep decline. Eventually the WWF got the message and moved Austin back, but it never felt the same again.

WCW was gone, and their main stars were now part of the WWF package. The WWF missed an opportunity when a potential WCW loyalist invasion angle got royally botched up by booking too. The blame goes to Vince, for never has there been a question about who makes the final call in WWF/WWE. Austin refused to do a job as the company requested, tempers flared, and egos were bruised.

In 2003 Austin finally got the message through his thick skull that he was risking his life and mobility with every bump he took in a wrestling ring. It was time to retire. He became a visible personality with various roles in the WWE's movies and on television. Relations improved with Vince, so Austin still makes occasional visits to WWE television, hits someone with a stunner after telling them off, and floats rumors of possibly one last match. He even starred as the host of WWE's *Tough Enough* program.

The truth is, Steve Austin doesn't need one more match to secure his place in pro wrestling history. He's safe. All this from a kid who grew up following and loving Paul Boesch's classy wrestling production in Houston.

Steve Williams was an all-round athlete in high school and earned a football scholarship to North Texas State University. After using up his eligibility, Williams saw an ad for a wrestling school run by Chris Adams, who was a big name in the popular World Class promotion owned by Fritz Von Erich. The school's material promised all the fun of Houston wrestling, so Williams began training with Adams.

His pro debut came in 1989, followed shortly by a name change to Steve Austin to avoid confusion with "Dr. Death" Steve Williams, who had already achieved a degree of stardom in his own right. Adams was very high on Austin's potential. He slipped the rookie into a feisty angle where Austin and Adam's ex-wife Jeannie took on Chris and his then-wife, Toni. Though the territory based in Dallas was on its deathbed, the angle drew some people and spread Austin's name as a promising new talent. While still learning, Austin clearly had the goods to go somewhere; the question was how far. After World Class bit the dust, Austin signed with World Championship Wrestling out of Atlanta in 1991.

The newcomer got a decent push, including forming an excellent tag team with Brian Pillman. But inner-office politics came into play, a not unheard of activity in the dysfunctional WCW. Apparently some established headliners felt their status was threatened by the unpredictable Pillman and the talented, hungry Austin. Suddenly their team was split up.

A feud with Ricky Steamboat ended abruptly when Steamboat was seriously injured. Meanwhile, Hulk Hogan left the WWF and signed with WCW for a massive amount of money. Austin's progress stumbled when some incompetent booking and likely more politics left him in limbo. A torn triceps muscle put Austin on the sideline, and he was fired upon his return. In 1995, Eric Bischoff told Austin on behalf of WCW that "they" felt he was not a marketable performer. Big mistake.

After a brief time with Paul Heyman in the original Extreme Championship Wrestling, Austin signed with the WWF at the end of 1995. At ECW, Austin had worked on some character development and experimented with projecting himself in ways that would become part of the "Stone Cold" character. Although there was the early stumble in the WWF, the groundwork was in place. All Steve Austin needed was the opportunity. He got it, for which Vince McMahon should forever pat himself on the back.

Yes, it was far from the longest era of success in pro wrestling history. But what Stone Cold Steve Austin did was blow apart business records right and left while reviving a promotion that needed a shot in the arm to overcome a dangerous competitor. He was like the biggest fireworks display ever, a giant fireball crashing into an explosives factory.

And all of that made a difference in the modern history of wrestling. For that, and all the excitement he provided, Steve Austin jumps high onto the roll call of the greatest ever.

#5 BRUNO SAMMARTINO
Nobody had more power, reliability, integrity

In the mad swirl of the tornado that is pro wrestling, Bruno Sammartino stands as a sturdy paragon of what the business can be when it comes to integrity, respect, and, of course, accomplishment. His reputation has handled the ravages of time and criticism far better than some of those close to him on the totem pole.

Naturally, Vince McMahon might consider Sammartino's attributes closer to immovable stubbornness. But as Bruiser Brody once said, "You can judge the quality of a man by the strength of his enemies." Perhaps Vince isn't exactly an enemy of Bruno, but Sammartino must have done something right to aggravate someone as dominant within the industry as Vince has been. McMahon's apparent opinion on, or juggling of, history should not detract from the simple truth, though. Bruno Sammartino merits his place among the absolute best of the 50 greatest pro wrestlers in history. And he's sure as hell ahead of Jerry Lawler.

To describe Sammartino as a babyface is almost too casual. The image of Bruno has actually grown stronger over the years, to the point that even "good guy" is too weak to depict his role in pro wrestling.

Stalwart, reliable, as honest as is likely in this shady business. A picture of strength. Try using the word "hero," trite though it be, and maybe that's more truly descriptive.

How can there be any justification for WWE not inviting Sammartino into their Hall of Fame? Here is their first champion, a serious athlete who for *seven years* proudly carried the company's biggest honor — the championship belt — when those things meant something! Capacity crowds in the old WWWF territory flocked to watch Bruno lock horns with the biggest and baddest heels.

He made this championship *real* in the eyes of the public.

Does anybody think that Vince bears a grudge, either because of the business disagreements his promotion has had with Sammartino or because of the studied criticism Bruno has offered about Vince, his booking, and his business? That couldn't be part of why Vince ignores what Sammartino did for the business, and his father's business in particular. Could it? Let's all accept the obvious, shall we?

And, bluntly, Sammartino's spot in history is obvious as well.

One difference between Sammartino and the quartet of the greatest ahead of him is that Bruno did not cover as many miles in his career as Lou Thesz, Ric Flair, "Strangler" Lewis, or Hulk Hogan did. In the long run, Sammartino comparatively may not have been quite as strong nationally or internationally as they were. A few critics have called Bruno mainly a geographical superstar in the Northeast where he benefited from immigrant and ethnic populations. Questions have been raised about whether he would have drawn everywhere else as well as he did in the territory. Needless to say, those complaints have irked both Sammartino and many studious observers. Of course, has there ever been a champion who didn't get some sort of criticism?

In Sammartino's defense is the large number of major towns, all diverse, in that area. Even the smaller markets were a pretty good size. Bruno drew impressive houses everywhere. He did travel outside the WWWF boundaries, including in Japan, but there was no financial necessity to do so more often than he did. The constant travel was still

Bruno Sammartino (left) and his protégé Larry Zbyszko

a bear. And *every* superstar had some places where he drew better, or worse, than others, sometimes for reasons unknown. Plus, with mass media based in New York, which happened to be the heart of the WWWF, Sammartino was featured on the covers of national publications like Stanley Weston's *Wrestling Revue*. So Bruno was known far and wide to those wrestling followers who cared enough to find out about him.

He was as busy as the devil, a point Sam Muchnick made in the debate about having one single world champion versus more than one. In theory, Muchnick felt the sport's marketing and publicity would benefit from having one champion known everywhere. Vince Sr. and Muchnick even toyed with the idea of moving in that direction in 1965.

Yet Sam also realized that no single champion could service North America because so many cities were running regularly and were capable of producing big money gates in the 1960s and 1970s. Everyone wanted dates from the champion. As WWWF king, Sammartino usually worked every night but Sunday. The AWA titleholder generally was in action four or five nights every week. The NWA ruler in theory had one week off out of every four, but that seldom happened. In the end, the NWA ruler averaged six nights a week over the widest geographical area, and Muchnick never could satisfy the requests of all the organization members who wanted to book the champion. What if there had only been one champion to fill all those dates from NWA, WWWF, and AWA combined?

Sammartino realistically couldn't have worked any more often than he did, and he was in big towns consistently. Most importantly, perhaps, he was such a powerful performer that word about his prowess spread far and wide. Today, anyone who has dug even a little into pro wrestling's history grasps the truth about how high, give or take a few spots, Bruno should be on any top 50 study of all time.

That scheme in 1965 would have certainly added another feather to Sammartino's cap. Like all wrestling plots, though, this one is difficult to pin down fact for fact. Everyone had their own agendas, along with their own recollections of why what might have happened did not happen.

And, of all the players, only Bruno is alive today, and he may not have been privy to all the closed-door machinations.

Thesz had captured the NWA title from Buddy Rogers in 1963, the culmination of a booking battle between the Vince Sr.–Toots Mondt faction who handled Rogers and the rest of the NWA. McMahon and Mondt started the WWWF later in 1963 by awarding its title to Sammartino after Bruno beat Rogers. The new entity simply ignored what had happened between Thesz and Rogers.

Bruno was massively successful in his role, as Thesz was in his. Sometime in 1965, Muchnick on behalf of Thesz met with McMahon and Mondt about the idea of a title versus title match to unite the two championships and also generate a huge and lucrative one-time event. Apparently, the idea was that Sammartino would win, and at some yet-to-be-determined date roughly one year later, Thesz would get the favor back. Reputedly money would change hands, going from the McMahon-Mondt faction to Thesz and Muchnick.

The proposed deal eventually fell apart. According to Thesz, he turned it down because he wouldn't be paid enough and also because he didn't trust Mondt in particular to let Sammartino go through with the return match. Bruno has said he shot down the deal because it would have required him to work dates for both WWWF and NWA, which would have left him with zero days off. For all anyone knows now, maybe Sam, Senior, and/or Toots got cold feet as well.

Less known was the possibility of another Sammartino and Muchnick involvement in 1973, when Dory Funk Jr. was to drop the NWA belt to Jack Brisco but was supposedly involved in a truck accident. Some in the NWA were skeptical of what Funk and his clever father were up to.

The Brisco supporters in the organization were upset. Muchnick, who was NWA president, feared that the alliance could split over the issue as he knew not everyone was supportive of his decisions.

Since Bruno was in between WWWF title reigns at the time, Muchnick booked Sammartino in St. Louis for a series of main events. I was working for Sam, who was very careful in what he said but left me with the impression that he was sending a message to the rest of the NWA, including both sides of the Funk-Brisco issue, that Muchnick was not averse to going into business with Vince Sr. (Mondt was gone by then), establishing Sammartino as champion, and removing the hugely important St. Louis market from the NWA.

Bruno and Sam always seemed to get along wonderfully, and my guess is that Sammartino never even knew what was going through Muchnick's head during this time. The NWA solved their problems by giving that crown from Funk to Harley Race to Brisco in short order. Sammartino continued as the central player for the WWWF.

But before that controversy was resolved, Race defended the NWA title against Sammartino in St. Louis on June 15, 1973. The battle went to a grueling one-hour stalemate and left yet another tale for the ages. Race, who was not a dedicated training nut and preferred cigarettes and beer, mentioned that Sammartino, who ran and lifted weights religiously, was struggling late in the duel and had become dehydrated. Harley said that to get liquid, Sammartino was licking the sweat off Race's body whenever he could.

Needless to say, Sammartino has stated that story is baloney. Yet another tale circulated about a punishing 60-, 75-, or 90-minute draw (the length varies depending on who tells this) between Bruno and Pedro Morales on September 1, 1972, when Morales ran out of gas and became dehydrated. Guess what? Supposedly Morales had to lick the sweat off Bruno's body to get water.

The point of all this? When proud, accomplished, competitive, and stubborn men, who in the end believe their own stories the most, reconstruct controversial developments that happened years and years ago, the truth likely lies somewhere in between — if there even is a truth.

This whole scenario demonstrates without doubt how important Sammartino is in the chronicles of pro wrestling. This is why he gets to cavort with the likes of Thesz, Flair, Lewis, and Hulk at the high levels on the roll call of the greatest.

Certainly all of this was the farthest thing from the mind of the young boy whose family hid on a mountain in Italy to elude the Nazi soldiers who murdered many in Bruno's native village. His father had earlier moved to the United States to seek work and had no idea what was happening. During 14 agonizing months, Sammartino's mother would sneak into the German-occupied town, once being captured and once being shot, to get food and supplies to keep her family alive. Sammartino fought off rheumatic fever before World War II ended and then moved to Pittsburgh to join his father in 1950. Bruno was a skinny, skittish 14-year-old boy.

Then he discovered weightlifting. Natural genetics, unknown before, kicked in and by 1956 Sammartino just missed qualifying for the U.S. Olympic weightlifting team. In 1960, Bruno set the world record for a bench press by lifting 565 pounds. He was also picking up wrestling fundamentals by working out with the University of Pittsburgh mat squad in addition to doing strongman stunts at public affairs around Pittsburgh.

Renowned sportscaster Bob Prince was enthralled by Sammartino and put the powerhouse on his local television show. That caught the eye of wrestling promoter Rudy Miller, who recognized that the good-looking kid had a true-life immigrant history that would appeal to everyone, along with legitimate charisma and raw, brute strength. Ah, a perfect package for pro wrestling! His Pittsburgh debut was December 17, 1959.

Naturally, Vince Sr. saw the potential and quickly got Sammartino into his Capitol Wrestling Corporation (the forerunner of WWWF) in 1960. Bruno got headlines by slamming, supposedly the first man to do so, 640-pound Haystack Calhoun and then teaming with Argentina Rocca for a main event at New York's Madison Square Garden. A hint of Bruno's business sense was revealed as well, were in play here too, for Bruno became disenchanted with low payoffs and forgotten promises by Senior. He went to work for an opposition New York promotion run by Kola Kwariani.

That also proved disappointing, so Sammartino went back to McMahon. But he got caught in what Bruno felt was a double-booking by Senior, perhaps to get revenge for Bruno working opposition, and he was blamed for no-showing a date. This led to a suspension by the athletic commission, a powerful national entity that usually had tight ties to established promotions. Suddenly, Sammartino could not get booked anywhere, failing to find work in San Francisco, Indianapolis, and spots in between. Totally discouraged, Bruno returned to Pittsburgh and started doing construction work.

Yet he knew that he had an aptitude for pro wrestling, so Bruno spoke with fellow strongman Yukon Eric, who suggested Sammartino contact Toronto promoter Frank Tunney. Canada had no athletic commissions, Tunney liked what he saw, and Sammartino got a chance in Toronto. He learned how to promote himself and — boom! — in 1962, he got over like a million bucks. Senior decided he liked Sammartino again. Mondt was in Sammartino's corner, which was critical in helping repair the business relation.

The World Wide Wrestling Federation was born on May 17, 1963, when Sammartino defeated Buddy Rogers in only 47 seconds. Stories circulated that Rogers was in poor health anyway, and indeed he seldom worked after putting Bruno over. It was the right thing for McMahon and company to do, as Sammartino was young and hungry and would become the key to the foundation of today's WWE. From Gorilla Monsoon to Killer Kowalski, Waldo Von Erich to Johnny Valentine, Fred Blassie to "Cowboy" Bill Watts, Professor Toru Tanaka to George "The Animal" Steele, Big Bill Miller to Giant Baba, and a whole lot more, Bruno faced them all and earned tons of money for Senior's promotion. Unfortunately, a trip to Japan and a match with Antonio Inoki left hard feelings that lasted years.

By January 18, 1971, after a mind-numbing and body-pounding stint of almost eight years as champion, Sammartino stepped down by putting over Ivan Koloff in New York. In traditional WWE form, Koloff flipped the title to Pedro Morales three weeks later. Business fell off with Morales, a solid performer who lacked Bruno's overall pizzazz. Late in 1972, Senior asked Bruno back, and Bruno demanded more money along with an easier schedule.

Business is always the trump card is an old saying in pro wrestling that means money talks in the end. Thus, Stan Stasiak had a nine-day reign after dethroning Morales and then Sammartino whipped Stasiak on December 10, 1973. Again Sammartino had a fabulous run with the WWWF belt, meeting a who's who of wrestling all-stars including Koloff, Bruiser Brody, Ken Patera, Don Leo Jonathan, Nikolai Volkoff, and Ernie Ladd among others. He also survived a terrifying incident with Stan Hansen that ended with Bruno breaking his neck.

Sammartino was ready to drop the title a few times, but always was offered more money by Senior to stay. Another bump between the two came when Sammartino stood up for better pay for those on the undercard. A few years later, Sammartino discovered that even with the raises he'd gotten, he still had not been paid what McMahon originally agreed to, and the two ended up in court. But first, Sammartino handed the crown over to "Superstar" Billy Graham in Baltimore on April 30, 1977, when Bruno was "protected" by the referee missing Sammartino's foot on the rope as he was pinned.

At that point, Sammartino was in a position to choose when and where he wanted to work. Probably his best angle involved former protégé Larry Zbyszko turning on Sammartino and leading to a showdown at Shea Stadium in New York on August 9, 1980, before 36,295 fans.

Bruno retired from full-time work in 1981.

Then the wrestling world changed. Vince McMahon Jr. — okay, let's make him happy — VKM began a charge to become the preeminent national promotion at the expense of every territory. Around that time, Sammartino filed suit over the accuracy of his earnings from Vince's dad. VKM didn't need the headache, especially since his dad had died, so he forged an out-of-court settlement that included Sammartino doing television commentary for what was now the WWF, a deal that paid Bruno a lot of money for little time expended.

One motivation for Sammartino coming back to the WWF was Bruno's son, David, who was a budding pro wrestler despite his father's misgivings. The father-son angle brought Sammartino back into the ring as he teamed with David for some tag bouts, in particular against Bobby Heenan and Paul Orndorff. Even in his 50s, the senior Sammartino could still get after it.

David had problems in the WWF, and Bruno continued to reluctantly perform in the ring on a careful schedule. One point was proven quickly — Sammartino could still pack 'em in, particularly in the old WWWF territory. He had feuds with Randy Savage and Roddy Piper but finally pulled the plug on his physical involvement in 1987 after a match in which he was the tag partner of Hulk Hogan. He continued doing television commentary into 1988.

Since that time, Sammartino has not hesitated to express his unhappiness with pro wrestling in general and WWE in particular. He doesn't like the circus atmosphere, the lack of basics, the booking, or the sexual overtones, and he has often described WWE as going into the gutter. The emphasis on steroids and other performance-enhancing drugs agitate Bruno to no end. Sammartino has been unhappy with many of the standouts from his time who complained in private but said otherwise in public in order to get jobs with VKM. Some of Bruno's personal comments about both Senior and Junior have been stinging.

All told, entry into the WWE Hall of Fame would be a surprise and perhaps even a disappointment if it meant a hand-shaking, smiling reconciliation between Sammartino and VKM. That would almost surely be a work.

It is, however, no disappointment and instead an honor to proclaim how much Bruno Sammartino means to this sport with his place among the greatest pro wrestlers ever.

#4 HULK HOGAN
The face of wrestling's biggest upheaval

Every contradiction, every pro and every con, every good and every bad, every right and every wrong . . . they are all here with the placement of Hulk Hogan among the 50 greatest pro wrestlers of all time. What we love and what we hate about pro wrestling is all symbolized by Hulk Hogan.

Whether Hulk deserves to be in this company is certainly not in question. The real problem is how high, or how low, he should be. The WWE list put Hogan at number 23, which clearly was meant as a slap in his face. So much for the theory that Vince McMahon had little input into the finalized roster, for relations between VKM and Hulk were frosty at best when the results were released to the public.

Hulk is close to the top. Every argument that is made about exactly where will be tinged with passion by some and certainty by others. The evaluations and requirements are all over the board because Hogan was everywhere and nowhere at once. A pure wrestler? Well, no. A great worker? That's a stretch. A great drawing card? Not a doubt in the universe about that one. Great charisma? Why even ask. A great artist on the mic? Despite hammering home catch phrases repeatedly, he got his message across as well as anyone else ever did.

A great performer? I mentioned this to Dave Meltzer of the *Wrestling Observer* and his response was most interesting: "You had to work his one match over and over and that's it. To me, a good performer is somebody who can do something other guys couldn't do. Hogan basically did [Jerry] Lawler's match he saw [when] breaking in with less ability than Lawler, and couldn't do a complete 20-minute match even then." Harsh. But Dave does call Hulk a great gimmick performer, which is obviously true.

And Meltzer, along with virtually every one of those who have ripped some part of what Hogan did, agrees that Hulk is very close indeed to being the greatest pro wrestler in history. That clearly speaks to the strange mixture of sport, athleticism, showmanship, and melodrama that pro wrestling is. In the end, all of those ingredients have to be recognized in some form. And the areas in which Hulk outdid everyone else made him unique.

Indeed, Hulk did work the same basic bout repeatedly, but he definitely did it in great form. Without him at the helm, would the great WWF takeover that Vince McMahon Jr. implemented have succeeded? The answer to that question alone locks Hulk Hogan into the top five pro wrestlers ever.

Who would have thought that about the tall, slender teenager hanging around the matches in Tampa, Florida? Terry Bollea was a fan of Dusty Rhodes and "Superstar" Graham, whose influences are visible in the bigger-than-life personality Bollea became. He was also a decent musician. While playing in a bar band around town, he was recognized by Jack and Jerry Brisco as the big guy who attended the matches. In 1976, the Briscos put Bollea with Hiro Matsuda, a highly proficient trainer for promoter Eddie Graham. The break-in period was less than smooth for Bollea, who likely offered his own share of attitude no matter how much he has since complained about Matsuda and Graham's wrestler son, Mike.

After some rookie tests in Florida in 1977, he began a heavy weight-training and bodybuilding regimen with his buddy Ed Leslie. Bollea got a chance in the low-level Alabama circuit where he was billed as Terry Boulder and teamed with his fictional brother Ed, who later was to become Brutus Beefcake for the WWF. This was followed by a tour of duty in Memphis, where the youngster got to study the clever Lawler, making the most out of what Jerry had.

Wrestling lore is unclear, again, not an unusual situation, about how Bollea got from Memphis to the World Wide Wrestling Federation late in 1979, but nonetheless that development kicked off a chain of events that would rock wrestling. Vince McMahon Sr. liked big guys and was always looking for big heels to oppose either Bruno Sammartino or Andre the Giant and, in the case of a foe for titleholder Bob Backlund, offbeat characters. Since Vince Jr. had been a huge fan of "Superstar," he probably was taken by the kid's look as well. Thus, the heel Hulk Hogan was born.

He got to shoot a bloody angle with Andre, whom Hulk met at the semi-final on a show at Shea Stadium in New York headlined by the blazing feud between Bruno and Larry Zbyszko. The crowd of 36,295 was just the first of many gigantic gates of which Hulk would be part. Hogan quickly learned how to take the credit for everything. While the angle between Hogan and Andre certainly added to a loaded show at a huge stadium, it was the Bruno versus Zbyszko dynamic that popped the gate. Regardless, it opened many eyes to Hogan's presence, which still needed polish.

A stint with the hard-hitting New Japan operation run by Antonio Inoki was a serious aid to Hulk's development. Hogan learned to work a different style (whether he used it a lot or not in his American outings), perfected the leg drop he would use down the road, and tackled a wide variety of foes from blood-and-guts Abdullah the Butcher to technically superb Tatsumi Fujinami. He also scored what was touted as a knock-out win over Inoki and got over like a million bucks. Hulk was putting it all together.

Then in 1982 he landed a small but memorable role as a superstar wrestler working with Rocky Balboa in Sylvester Stallone's *Rocky III*. That ignited even more interest in this superman character, who began working for Verne Gagne's AWA. Hogan was originally a heel managed

George Napolitano

by John Valiant. I recall sitting with Sam Muchnick in the St. Louis office and watching a television appearance Hulk made on *The Mike Douglas Show* one morning, when, if memory serves correctly, a ring was actually constructed to display this guy from the *Rocky* movie. It was a terrific plug for the business and the AWA in particular.

Sam watched Hulk's entry, saw how the crowd reacted to him, and almost immediately told me, "That guy is a babyface. He'll get over like gangbusters that way. Verne should switch him right away." Of course, Gagne realized that pretty quickly as well. A new type of superhero was born.

Much of the Hulkamania character evolved for Hulk in the AWA. He got a chance to tussle with first-rate workers like Nick Bockwinkel, plenty of room to develop his rap on interviews, and enough freedom to make lucrative trips to Japan. When Vince Jr. secretly came calling on October 24, 1983, to get Terry Bollea's name on a contract to jump to the WWF, Hulk Hogan was ready to fly. McMahon had been in St. Louis the day before, meeting with me and KPLR-TV owner Ted Koplar to lock up Vince's takeover of the famous *Wrestling at the Chase* show's time slot to begin his march toward dominance. Due to a promotional dispute after Muchnick retired, I felt squeezed to accept the deal, but even as worried as I was about the implications for my town, I could sense that what McMahon was doing would break new ground and start the biggest war in wrestling history.

St. Louis, the home of the NWA, and Hogan, wrestling's hottest new name and an AWA star, both went to VKM in only two days.

Late on the evening of October 23, Vince told me that he had been working on landing Hogan, and it was only the first shot he would fire. McMahon was confident, burning with ideas bouncing around right and left. VKM predicted, "Hulk Hogan will be the biggest star that wrestling has ever known."

The coronation came when Hulk took the WWF crown from the Iron Sheik, who had bested Backlund only weeks earlier, on January 23, 1984, at Madison Square Garden. All of the glitz and pyrotechnics from

Classy Freddie Blassie managing his young monster — the one and only Hulk Hogan

that point on were built around the pumped-up muscles and hyped-up rhetoric of an indestructible superstar.

Hogan's matches were tailored to appeal to a comic-book mentality of good guy versus bad guy, but make no mistake. The entry before and the pose-down after were all part of the show. Hulk understood the role perfectly and played it to the hilt. The lineups were dotted with performers who had been established as stars in different areas, and the promotion hit that ever-elusive casual audience deeper than most any promotion ever had before. Likewise, the WWF mined the territories that had long histories of supporting wrestling. All told, Vince's boys, led by Hogan, drew some fantastic crowds. Even in places where they stumbled at first, the company just wore down the opposition until McMahon's garish crew was the only show in town.

The successes were many and monumental. Hulk was in the spotlight for every single one of them. A tsunami of sellouts, slick television production, hot shot booking, and unapologetic propaganda washed away the few flops the WWF had along with the territorial wrestling system.

Suffice to say, for the details would fill their own book, Hogan was the key performer on almost every show.

Where Hulk particularly stood out was in mixing with other celebrities of the time. Like "Strangler" Lewis and Lou Thesz years before him, Hogan fit in with the music, movie, and television folks who loved interacting with this garrulous blond superman. Vince expertly manipulated the media, which didn't bother to dig too deep since, after all, it was "just" pro wrestling. Whether it was Hulk's cartoon show, appearances on *Tonight* and *Saturday Night Live*, or gracing the cover of *Sports Illustrated* and *People*, all the pieces fell into place to make the industry and its stars look bigger than ever.

Naturally, the bucks followed the hype. Closed-circuit television was profitable but slowing down, pay-per-view was growing, and targeted stadium cards lured the masses. The angles with Andre, Paul Orndorff, Randy Savage, Roddy Piper, even eventually Ric Flair, and others all fed the Hulk myth-making machine. Vince's relationship with NBC honcho

Dick Ebersol (the adage about who you know, not what you know is usually correct, especially with a hot product) was no small part of it, as pro wrestling was featured in a series of selected Saturday late nights and even in prime time for a bit. In fact, on February 5, 1988, a live special drew a stupendous 15.2 rating, the largest audience ever to watch pro wrestling, for a crazy, mixed-up, successful duel involving twin referees Dave and Earl Hebner, Ted DiBiase, Andre and — who else? — Hulk.

But even the mighty can stumble, as the WWF did when the steroid scandals erupted in the early 1990s and Vince ended up on trial. It was this controversy that likely ignited the growing love-hate relationship between McMahon and Hogan. Each knew how to push the other's buttons, especially when it came to business and ego. Vince dodged a bullet in the trial, but Hulk shot himself in the foot by lying about his steroid use on the *Arsenio Hall Show*. Media attention shifted, taking the bloom off the WWF rose. Blissful, voluntary ignorance by the public about synthetic physiques changed and business went down the toilet. Vince's company was hurting financially. The door was forcefully opened, at least for a while, for some smaller, less artificial talents like Bret Hart and Shawn Michaels.

Hulk was in and out, and creative control became more of an issue between star and producer. Shock waves hit in 1994 when Hogan signed with World Championship Wrestling, Ted Turner's promotion that emerged following the collapse of Jim Crockett's operation and most of the known pro wrestling world.

Once again, Hulk was back in the limelight and his presence was the driving force of the so-called New World Order, with a bad-guy turn into Hollywood Hulk Hogan. WCW gave only lip service to drug testing, the media was paying less attention, the WWF was bouncing back a little but was vulnerable, and Hogan again was a pivotal player both in the ring and politically. Hulk got to play with a litany of major names including Lex Luger, Sting, Kevin Nash, Scott Hall, Savage again when he too jumped sides, once more Flair, and Bill Goldberg.

Hulk's own television show flopped. He was in the middle of an ego-infested booking fiasco that ended when WCW failed and was sold in 2001 to none other than Vince, who had made a scintillating comeback on the back of Stone Cold Steve Austin and a few others.

Whatever issues there were for McMahon and Hogan were overcome by the potential of making big money. Soon after some surgery to repair a body part or two, Hulk was back with Vince.

How could anyone pass up the chance to put Hulk against the new superstar Dwayne Johnson, better known as The Rock? Before more than 68,000 at Toronto's SkyDome for *WrestleMania XVIII*, Hulk put The Rock over in a battle set up for Hogan to be the bad guy, but nostalgia ruled and he was cheered for everything he did.

The stage was set for further scraps with Triple H, Kurt Angle, and Brock Lesnar. Hulk even had a match of sorts with Vince himself and emerged triumphant at the nineteenth edition of *Mania*. But politics and personality were always in the way, so Hulk left and came back and left. Somewhere in that soap opera Hogan got a chance to work with Shawn Michaels. Recognize, of course, that the matches Hogan had were paint-by-numbers renditions where the psychology and memories were so strong that fans could accept even a lesser degree of athleticism than ever before in a Hogan bout. Still, Hogan was such a commanding personality that it didn't matter to the satisfied customers. They knew what they were buying, and Hulk gave it to them.

In the midst of all this, Hogan and his family were featured in a reality series that proved too real on MTV. In the end, his wife was gone, he was remarried, his son was charged criminally and tried in civil court after a horrendous accident, and his daughter tried in vain to become a pop singer. Once admired for taking care of his money, Hogan has struggled to stay afloat financially. His body is hurting physically in most ways possible.

When he does interviews Hulk spins tales that are often so absurd that nobody can keep track of which fiction is more ridiculous and inaccurate. Luckily for Hogan, his deal with TNA has provided income, but his appearances on the show have been both good and bad. In the end, it doesn't seem to matter.

Why? Because he's Hulk Hogan. Because he represents a mesmerizing truth about pro wrestling, accept it or not.

The triumph of Hulk Hogan was, of course, the triumph of Vince McMahon. Where they took pro wrestling can never be forgotten. With Hulk as the Pied Piper, pro wrestling got out of the closet for a time and became as mainstream as it could ever be. The spectacle was cool, the "in thing" of the hour, all with Hogan posing and pumping. Vince orchestrated the strategy, got two lifetimes' worth of lucky breaks and made Hulk a household name to this very day.

Reality eventually has displayed the cracks in Hulk's façade. Broken families and broken bodies are never much fun. The business itself, bludgeoned by steroids, early deaths, and uncontrollable egos slipped closer to where it used to be for decades — a guilty pleasure enjoyed by millions who did not brag about it. Though national cable and Vince's machinations continue to give pro wrestling a presence, the impact barely leaves a trace.

Hulk Hogan is the face of that as well. For the entire roller-coaster ride, Hulk was the conductor. Good or bad, right or wrong, Hulk Hogan is the first personality most people will think of when pro wrestling is mentioned. He's not the villain. He is the story of the ages — right guy, right place, right time. Hulk is only the symbol, though he surely knows how to utilize that status. Whether some of us like it or not, the truth is clear.

He's a robust symbol, more celebrity than wrestler now. Still, Hulk Hogan must be included very close to the top among the 50 greatest pro wrestlers of all time.

#3 ED "STRANGLER" LEWIS

A rock, immovable and indestructible

If the fates were kind, wouldn't it be a joy to watch Ed "Strangler" Lewis and Lou Thesz tangle, trading holds and testing their wrestling skills against one another? Wouldn't it be thrilling to see these two great shooters attempting to take each other out?

Of course, it would be just as enthralling to watch Lewis square off with Ric Flair in a contest between two vastly different styles, each of which was the very best for its time.

It is impossible not to choose this trio as the best representatives all-around for the types of pro wrestling that thrilled millions in their eras. Figuring out who comes out on top of that little three-way dance is a challenge of titanic proportions.

Lewis represents the almost shoot-like style that was fought on the mat into the late 1920s. It was absolutely tough and hard-nosed. Lewis thrived, but he also recognized the mass audience was looking for a more wide-open spectacle. With new tactics, Lewis moved the sport in that direction as well. Flair personifies the flamboyant, outrageous, and acrobatic style that built from the mid 1900s all the way to the present.

Thesz managed over his lengthy career to incorporate enough of all the forms to earn the smallest advantage for the highest placement of all the greats.

This threesome signifies the progression of what pro wrestling is between the ropes.

But Lewis might be able to take Thesz. And Flair might be able to outmaneuver Thesz. And Lewis may have had the edge on Flair. Of course, Thesz could stretch Flair. Could Lou hook "Strangler"? Maybe. Great fun to ponder and fantasize about all the possibilities, isn't it?

Possibly the biggest stumbling block for a modern follower of pro wrestling is learning and appreciating what a true colossus of pro wrestling *the* "Strangler" Lewis is. This is about Ed Lewis, whose real name was Robert Friedrich. He borrowed the name under which he became famous from another extremely capable grappler named Evan "Strangler" Lewis. Hence, Ed "Strangler" Lewis.

Ah, what a tangled web pro wrestling can weave! Here is today's history lesson. Evan Lewis, the original "Strangler," likely was the first American version of a world champion when he combined the catch-as-catch-can title with the Greco-Roman title by beating Ernest Roeber in 1893. Evan Lewis lost that honor to Farmer Burns in 1895. The trail, twisted though it was, eventually led to the immortal Frank Gotch in 1906. By hook and by crook, the path of the championship then found its way to none other than the second "Strangler," Ed Lewis, who grabbed the throne by beating Joe Stecher on December 13, 1920.

This is the "Strangler" who now stands third on our list of the finest ever to step inside the squared circle. Lewis was wrestling professionally by the time he turned 15 years old. Once he got possession of the title, Ed Lewis was intimately involved with that honor for more than a decade. This "Strangler" was right in the middle, winning the title, losing it, and politically pushing to whom it went.

The key part was that everyone in wrestling acknowledged — they *knew* — that "Strangler" Lewis was the supreme hooker in the game, even more dangerous than a shooter. Perhaps one or two stars might have challenged Lewis, but overall everyone believed that the championship would be his any time he wanted it and could engineer the necessary confrontation. But "Strangler" was all about business, and he dropped the crown or did jobs in eye-catching fashion when that appeared to be the best decision to keep business, and money, flowing. Doesn't that speak to Lewis's ability as a worker?

Wrestling was in a down period when Lewis captured the spotlight. He quickly was elevated to the status of Babe Ruth in baseball, Jack Dempsey in boxing, and Red Grange in football as a prominent national personality and athlete.

While he had no television to perform on, Lewis had a fantastic personality and the gift of gab. Newspapers loved him. Doors that had been closed to wrestling opened when "Strangler" came to town and wanted to spin his tales. He got both himself and his business over to the general public and lit the fuse for another boom time. Mic skills, if you will. When the media types saw this bulldozer of a human in action, no questions were necessary about whether he was the real deal.

At first, Lewis found it hard to get the lucrative wrestling bookings outside his base in the Midwest. Some promoters, especially those in the East, were afraid of his real skills and feared Lewis might not go along with the finishes that were asked. Then "Strangler" hooked up with two master manipulators — first Billy Sandow and later Toots Mondt — and broke through the barriers, appearing everywhere.

The trio was also instrumental in opening up the game, speeding up the matches by instituting time limits and innovating different holds and new finishes. Mondt supposedly was the idea man, while Lewis provided a wrestler's perspective. In fact, Lewis was a prime component, actually one of if not the first to play with the concept of getting heat because of his rough tactics. He knew (*everyone* knew) what he could do if he wanted. Instead, "Strangler" chose to build the business. He worked. And wrestling was the beneficiary.

"Strangler" didn't need anyone to tell him that he had to make a local favorite look good to help ticket sales, especially if that favorite could compete to some extent for real with a hooker like Lewis.

The nickname "Strangler" even had the working connotation inside the business. Evan Lewis used a type of headlock in which he applied pressure on the opponent's carotid artery with his wrist, cutting off blood supply to the brain. Possibly considered a strangle, it was very much like the tactic many policemen have learned to defend themselves with over the years.

The move was well known to all the hookers in the business even in the late 1800s. It was also a sleeper hold, but "Strangler" surely translated as a more colorful nickname for both Evan and Ed Lewis. Ed Lewis borrowed the grip along with the nickname. He made a few alterations so the hold worked smoothly into the scheme of the action. It became part of working and is now known generally as the standard headlock. Thirty-plus years later, when Lewis was far removed from the spotlight but still training aspiring new talent, he helped one youngster develop a variation of his headlock/stranglehold and not much later "Cowboy" Bob Ellis became famous for the bulldog headlock.

Nothing, though, was standard about how Lewis dominated the business. While Joe Stecher played a major role in reviving wrestling after the scandals that followed Gotch's reign, what Lewis did with Mondt and Sandow made the most impact. Lewis and Sandow pretty much stayed aligned, but Mondt was in and out — sometimes a friend, sometimes an enemy, for Toots had his own agenda and wanted to build a personal power base in the East.

Looking down the road, of course, Mondt was a player in everything that happened even into the birth of the World Wide Wrestling Federation in 1963, when Toots was much more than an adviser for one Vince McMahon Sr. Many of the swerves and tricks that Mondt used had their start when Toots was working with "Strangler" Lewis. This business, old or new, really is tied together in many different ways.

After Lewis dethroned Stecher in 1920, the alliance of Lewis-Sandow-Mondt wanted to curry favor with the Eastern promoters, so "Strangler" graciously dropped the belt to Stanislaus Zbyszko. And then Zbyszko, who was a tough gladiator himself, gave the crown back to Lewis when it served the purpose of upping the crowd and thus the gate receipts for all involved.

The threesome had a lucrative run with Lewis again on top; the key to making money and having power was controlling the world title. That's why other promoters were always plotting to steal the crown. Therefore, it meant everything to have Lewis, the wrestler everyone felt was unbeatable, on their side.

Eventually, Lewis agreed that Sandow had a perfect performer to replace "Strangler" on top and freshen up the act, thus boosting houses again when they had cooled, in the person of a huge former football player named Wayne Munn. Lewis put Munn over, but the Eastern organization saw that as an opportunity to pounce. Playing nice, they maneuvered Munn into a booking with Zbyszko, who changed the plan by cleaning Munn's clock and taking the championship.

Zbyszko was getting older and he knew he would be in trouble if the promoters involved could manipulate him into a bout with Lewis, who was angry and wanted revenge. Zbyszko saw no reason to be a victim and quickly lost the title to Joe Stecher, who many felt might be Lewis's equal in a shoot. There was history between Stecher and Lewis dating back to 1915. But Stecher was in no rush for such a showdown unless the two simply bumped in flat, conservative matches. Both respected, perhaps feared, each other and definitely were afraid of double-crosses from referees or from other directions.

Finally in 1928 in St. Louis, Lewis got the victory over Stecher. Many accounts called the showdown a shoot, but those closer to the inside agree it was a work. Thesz, having heard all the stories from most of the players involved, figured the reason they finally got a decision was that both Lewis and Stecher were simply sick of not trusting anybody.

Swerves and cheats and backstabbings were commonplace. Wrestlers like Gus Sonnenberg, Jim Londos, Dick Shikat, and Ed Don George were all involved in such scenarios. Working like cardsharps were promoters such as Paul Bowser, Tom Packs, and Jack Pfeffer. And somehow all of it always revolved around what was "Strangler" Lewis doing, who he was aligned with, what his plans were. Everyone knew that Lewis was the man, and even the toughest of the tough were very careful not to incur his wrath before a match.

Yet even he could get tricked. In 1931, when Bowser felt that Lewis had stolen the title from him in a win over George (of course Lewis believed that Bowser had set him up to steal the crown before that), Bowser lured "Strangler" into a title defense against Henri DeGlane in, of all places, Montreal.

At that time, the wrestlers went to their dressing rooms between falls in a best-of-three duel. Each man had had a fall when DeGlane, on orders from Bowser, bit himself on the arm until he actually broke the skin and drew blood. Hiding the wound as he went back to the ring, DeGlane waited for the bell, locked up with Lewis, and then screamed that he had been bitten. The referee agreed, disqualified Lewis, and gave the championship to DeGlane. This obviously triggered another round of claims, counter-claims, and even more double-crosses around the continent.

According to Thesz, Lewis said Bowser was waiting in the dressing room with several hoodlums with baseball bats in case there was trouble. "Strangler" just laughed at Bowser, told him he could regain the title anytime he wanted to, and left the next day for a tour of Europe. All in all, Lewis had decided to slow down and smell the roses a bit.

The Montreal screwjob involving Shawn Michaels and Bret Hart in 1997 was really not much more than a grade-school play compared to the double-crosses of the 1920s and 1930s. And that's only the tip of the iceberg Lewis had to deal with.

So strong was Lewis's reputation in the 1930s that he still could draw a crowd, put on a show, and, most would claim, be next to impossible to stretch or pin. "Strangler" just picked his spots. He was in constant demand from promoters and had the ability to keep past injustices from influencing future dealings when money was to be made.

In 1934 the "dream match" between "Strangler" and Londos was put together, after one previous booking for 1932 had fallen apart and ended up with Lewis meeting Ray Steele instead. Talk about charisma and the value of anticipation. Lewis and Londos were all over the newspapers and radio in Chicago. The event reportedly drew 35,265 fans to Wrigley Field, with Londos getting the victory after nearly 50 exciting minutes. Lewis may have been past his prime, but he was still special. Historians have noted that Lewis met Londos several times before 1930, and Londos had never won.

For a complete and detailed account of the era and Lewis's starring role in it, there are two excellent sources: *National Wrestling Alliance: The Untold Story of the Monopoly That Strangled Pro Wrestling* by Tim Hornbaker and *Hooker: An Authentic Wrestler's Adventures Inside the Bizarre World of Professional Wrestling* by Lou Thesz and Kit Bauman. The volume of material is almost overwhelming, but these two books do justice to the tumultuous time and the incredible mastery Lewis had over what happened between the ropes.

After his days as an active competitor ended, Lewis became an adviser and even trainer for Thesz when Lou got started. More importantly, Thesz was a loyal friend and companion as "Strangler" wound down and Thesz assumed Ed's position at the pinnacle. Lewis's health was ebbing, all the staph infections of his era having taken their toll, and he had sadly gone blind from the dreaded trachoma caused by wrestling on the dirty mats of the time. Even at the end, though, he still had the outgoing personality and the sheer strength of presence that let everyone know how dynamic he must have been in his prime.

The three best ever represent pro wrestling in all its glory and in all its ugliness. Lou Thesz, the perfect soldier displaying some of the best skills from the eras both before and after him, had the good fortune of a firm structure in the National Wrestling Alliance and the organizational expertise of its president, Sam Muchnick.

Ric Flair survived and surpassed the crumbling remains of Muchnick's structure to fit in beautifully with the way pro wrestling was going by virtue of his energy, intensity, and personality.

"Strangler" Lewis successfully fought his way through the dishonesty and back-stabbing that was the way of professional wrestling during a disjointed period, because the people who counted knew he was the best. I smile when I realize that more than 50 years later, in different conversations, Lou Thesz, Sam Muchnick, and Verne Gagne all told me that based on sheer wrestling ability, "Strangler" Lewis was the best of all time. Pretty strong endorsements, considering the sources.

Thesz and Lewis, not surprisingly, became great friends. As fellow hookers, with Lou perhaps less willing to bend at times, they understood each other. But Lewis also had plenty in common with Flair, who was someone he never met.

What did Flair and Lewis have in common? Women! And booze. "Strangler" would have gotten it and laughed if he could have seen Flair doing promos talking about his wild times with the ladies, because "Strangler" could definitely relate. Perhaps Flair was not the extreme lover of food that Lewis was, but both enjoyed the finer things life offered. Flair and Lewis were both known as party animals. But the two still had more stamina and endurance than almost anyone they faced. Work hard and play hard, as Lou Thesz said.

Some souls simply have a gift. Lewis did, and so did Flair. And so did Thesz.

Best-selling author Janet Evanovich wrote in her novel *Full Tilt* about a character "who'd earned his nickname by perfecting the headlocks once used by the world-renowned Ed 'Strangler' Lewis, who'd begun his wrestling career in the early 1900s and was touted the greatest wrestler ever." With all due respect, if Janet Evanovich knows that "Strangler" Lewis is possibly the greatest wrestler ever, there is no excuse for any rabid wrestling fan not going to the Internet to dig up the truth about this amazing performer.

Put Ed "Strangler" Lewis at number 3 — with a bullet.

#2 RIC FLAIR

The most athletically intense performer ever

What is the difference between the greatest pro wrestler ever and his worthy adversary only one quarter of a step behind? Is it some miniscule sliver of natural talent or perhaps a microscopic quirk of personality that endures? Or is it plain and simple a roll of the dice, the choice of Lady Luck who landed where at just the correct moment?

It's a race to the wire between Lou Thesz and Ric Flair, with Ed "Strangler" Lewis closing in from the outside. And it's Thesz by the tip of his nose! But we know there will be challenges to that result.

The comparisons between Flair and Thesz can be endless and without conclusive answers. They are alike, and they are different, and both are great. Would Thesz have been on top in the 1980s and 1990s as Flair was? Well, while I doubt he'd have bleached his hair blond, a great athlete like Thesz, driven to be the best, would have found a way to succeed. Would Flair have been on top from 1937 to 1966 as Thesz was? The business was changing, with heel champions like "Wild Bill" Longson and strutting blonds like Gorgeous George and Buddy Rogers finding fame. Flair would have been innovative and hungry enough to find a way.

Could Flair have become a hooker like Thesz was? He did train with Verne Gagne, a master of scientific and legitimate moves, along with shooter Billy Robinson. Richard Fliehr, before he became Ric Flair, won the private-school state wrestling title in Minnesota and earned a scholarship to play football at the University of Minnesota.

At the same age, Thesz was a teenager working out with 30-year-old professionals who knew how to hurt foes and rather liked doing it. About the age Flair dropped out of college and became a bouncer, Thesz beat salty Everett Marshall to become the world champion.

From being a bouncer, and connecting with Ken Patera and Greg Gagne, Fliehr became Flair under the tutelage of the esteemed Verne Gagne. Even though he was a pudgy 300-pounder with dark hair when he made his debut in late 1972, certain traits were evident. The kid had natural endurance and a sense of the ring and the audience, plus he desperately wanted to succeed and was already calling himself Ric Flair.

The hair was blond and the weight was disappearing when Flair hit the ground running for promoter Jim Crockett Jr. in the Carolinas in 1974. He also got a chance to study how master of psychology Johnny Valentine worked, in addition to tangling with oodles of top hands at a time the Carolina territory was catching fire.

Tragically, on October 4, 1975, he and four other wrestlers were in the crash of a private airplane. The disaster, which killed the pilot, ended Valentine's fabled career, and Flair was told he was finished because of a broken back. But Flair returned to the ring within six months, after a torturous rehabilitation, and the "Nature Boy" really began to fire on all cylinders.

The lovely ladies that surrounded a remarkable athlete who dressed in the finest clothes and wore gaudy robes to the ring still would have meant zilch in the long run if Flair hadn't been able to deliver a great match when the bell sounded. Of course, Flair got his heat as a bad guy, but one young high school teacher explained Flair's appeal best when he said, "Yeah, we booed him, but secretly we all wanted to be like him."

As Flair himself was fond of bragging, "Talk the talk, walk the walk." Flair could walk the walk, taking scary bumps night after night against Wahoo McDaniel, Roddy Piper, Ricky Steamboat, and Jimmy Snuka. His reputation spread rapidly around the country. I pushed Sam Muchnick to bring Flair to St. Louis against the wishes of erstwhile booker Pat O'Connor (not because O'Connor didn't respect Flair as a performer, but due to internal politics — typical wrestling malarkey). Once Sam saw a tape of Flair in action, he ordered O'Connor to get dates on Flair.

Dynamite is the best way to describe Flair when he hit St. Louis in 1978. The sheer energy, whether it was a television interview or a main event against Harley Race or Ted DiBiase, just exploded in the fans' faces. Although his reputation would have spread anyway, and the NWA championship was in his destiny, Flair was firmly convinced based on the history of the business that getting to the top in St. Louis was a necessity. And Flair was in main events immediately. All the requirements for stardom were evident.

In his first St. Louis feature against Dory Funk Jr. on January 27, 1978, Flair took a horrifying backward bump over the top rope and cracked his skull on the heavy wooden ring steps. The blood was flowing from the top of Ric's head, making an excellent match even more intense. Bright red blood soaked Flair's hair and ran down his face, neck, and back.

After the card, Flair showed me where the step had gouged his scalp. The blood was still oozing more than an hour later, after a shower and a walk along freezing, snow-covered sidewalks to the nearby hotel where the wrestling office was located. But now Ric was dressed to the nines and headed for the bar, which was jammed with wrestlers and fans.

I convinced Flair to talk with Dick Muchnick, Sam's son and a doctor who also worked the matches for the athletic commission. After examining and cleaning the nasty incision, Dick agreed that Flair should have stitches. "Does that mean they have to shave some hair off?" Flair asked. Dick said yes, definitely.

"No way!" exclaimed the "Nature Boy," flipping that hair back. "Ric Flair can't have his head shaved. I got a main event in Charlotte tomorrow

night." I realized then and there that nothing short of a head-on collision with a nuclear missile would keep Flair from giving every last ounce of energy he had to fulfill the promise of his image. His reputation spread rapidly and his name was immediately tossed into the hopper as a potential NWA kingpin.

On September 17, 1981, Flair began his first of many runs as champion by beating Dusty Rhodes in Kansas City. Also jump-started was a controversial journey that will forever be part of what happened to pro wrestling when VKM eventually crushed every other promotion to become the dominant force in the business by 2001. Flair was more often than not the key performer for the forces battling McMahon. But he also spent time with Vince, thus opening another door in a career that put Flair in the ring with every single meaningful performer for nearly three decades.

Can any fan ever forget the Four Horsemen, of which Flair was the one irreplaceable Two of the greatest: a bloodied Ric Flair gets the upper hand on an equally colorful Harley Race? What about ending Harley Race's last reign as NWA champion? Remember those duels with Terry Funk, Barry Windham, and Lex Luger? Sting got the opportunity to be a major player because of the fantastic battles he had with Flair. What about Dusty Rhodes versus Ric Flair!

When the NWA collapsed, Crockett picked up the pieces and tried to fight McMahon, but he folded too. With a long history of involvement in pro wrestling, Ted Turner's television company bailed Crockett out and went head-on against McMahon as World Championship Wrestling (WCW). Executives with no wrestling understanding, fellows like Jim Herd, tried to force Flair out, claiming he was too old, not understanding he had another 10-plus years in his burning heart and unbreakable body.

Flair jumped to McMahon's promotion in 1991, when WWF booking didn't push Flair versus Hogan and missed the boat to cash in on what could have been wrestling's biggest showdown ever. Yes, the bout happened a few times but never to the extent or as successfully as it should have. Why not? Those ugly wrestling politics and runaway egos again.

Two of the greatest: a bloodied Ric Flair gets the upper hand on an equally colorful Harley Race

Yet somehow the seeds of respect had been sewn between Flair and Vince before he left the WWF, after classics with Randy Savage and Curt Hennig, and went back to WCW, which had new executives such as Eric Bischoff, with whom Flair argued constantly. Good and bad awaited there, for WCW made the usual thrill ride description of pro wrestling look mild indeed. What Flair did in the ring with names like Kevin Nash, Scott Hall, and — oh my goodness, look who was in WCW now — Randy Savage and Hulk Hogan just reinforced what a once-in-a-lifetime performer Flair was. His headaches with Bischoff were less satisfying.

When WCW produced its last television show on March 26, 2001, Flair put over Sting and provided one final interview about what had been lost with the demise of WCW. But Flair was too big to fail and by November 2001 was back with the WWF. Behind the scenes, personal problems and financial difficulties were eating Flair up, but Vince came to the rescue economically. In the ring, Flair even squared off with McMahon a couple of times. Once more Flair was in the featured mix, joining forces with Triple H, Batista, and Randy Orton, whose father Bob had been tight with Flair way back in the Carolina days.

This tenure with what was becoming WWE, however, slowed down as Flair's appearances became more hit-and-miss. He seldom got time to talk, either for fear his promos would outshine WWE's homegrown stars or that he wouldn't follow the script written for him. One of Flair's biggest strengths has always been the interview because he is so flamboyant and persuasive. But any ill feelings were set aside for Flair's classic retirement bout against Shawn Michaels at *WrestleMania XXIV* and the subsequent celebration on *Raw* on March 31, 2008. A national viewing audience saw wrestling break its fourth wall in a rare display of emotion for Flair.

Of course, retirement didn't stick. The marriage between WWE and Flair, which at this point was mainly for public relations appearances, was on the rocks. By 2010, Flair was drawing a paycheck from Total Non-Stop Action (TNA), the low-level but persistent challenger to WWE. On board with Flair at TNA was yet another great whose personal life was in shambles — Hulk. Perhaps it is now indeed time for an all-inclusive look at Ric Flair's resume.

Are there are any knocks on Flair's performing skills? First, some argue that he fell into a repetitive pattern. Second, certain critics might say that he was left a beaten, bloody mess far too often when he was champion.

That first criticism is generally invalid, for every great pro wrestler had certain moves that he did best and would have disappointed audiences if he had *not* done those things. Great football teams do what works best until another squad stops them. A Hall-of-Fame pitcher throws his sharp curveball until a hitter can hit it. Why would a pro wrestler be any different? It works, it fits for the opponent, and the crowd loves it. This is as true for Flair as it is for any member of the 50 greatest, plus they all added different maneuvers to their repertoires over time.

For a perfect example of Ric's versatility, look at June 12, 1982, when he altered what he did and how he did it to make Dick the Bruiser at the end of his career look like Dick the Bruiser 20 years earlier. Flair was a prime example of a great worker, one who also played into what an older Bruiser could still do in order to construct a terrific struggle. Similarly, a one-hour draw with Bruiser Brody on February 11, 1983, which Flair has often named as one of his all-time favorite battles, was neither a Flair match nor a Brody match. Again, two great workers put together something a little different to surprise and excite the crowd.

Flair adjusted. As he got older, he knew what worked. Thus, he made the needed changes in his repertoire to get a fan reaction, draw a crowd, or juice a television rating.

Regarding the second criticism, that as a champion Flair was left pummeled and perhaps undeserving of the belt, well, that was more often a function of what bookers and promoters wanted. Once upon a time, for instance when Lou Thesz was the champ, the trick was to win in such a closely contested manner that the challenger looked like the champion's equal. This was also true for bad guy titleholders like Longson and even Rogers, who usually were victorious in the blow-off of any feud.

Flair fell into a period where a heel champion got busted around and only through luck or rules (the dreaded "Dusty finish") survived. Over the years, Flair became too comfortable with this philosophy and rarely asked for that narrow victory that would also make the opponent get over. In my mind, what Thesz and champions like him did required more of the art, thus giving Thesz a small edge for best ever over Flair. This was through no real fault of Flair's, but rather because of how the business had changed. Nonetheless, it is a point for Thesz.

The business wasn't the only thing to leave scars on Flair's psyche. Personal problems cropped up more and more as the new century dawned. Some of Flair's idiosyncrasies started to catch up with him in the 1990s and also affected his business as a pro wrestler. Being a superstar, being a celebrity, is never easy, no matter how it looks from the outside. To some extent, we saw the potential strain on Flair in St. Louis, but we wrote it off to youthful exuberance.

In St. Louis, and elsewhere, Flair had lived the part of a "stylin', profilin', limousine ridin'" stud. What he did when the bell rang put him in league with the finest performers of the time. Away from the ring, he lived the part of athletic superstar playboy with gusto. Years ago, that became who he thought he really was. While Flair spent money right and left, a few unpaid bills came to our attention. One substantial invoice came from KPLR-TV when I produced a music video at Ric's request for his use around the horn.

Since Muchnick wouldn't allow anything to make pro wrestling look bad with as important a partner as the television station, he paid the bill immediately and then deducted the cost from Flair's next payoff in St. Louis. Ric apologized profusely to Sam, blaming an unnamed business manager for not staying current. That night, he basically worked a main event for free but still was renting the limo and living large, making sure a party was rocking after the show.

It was a trip to watch Flair be Flair, and though Muchnick loved what he brought to a card, he worried about Flair. Ric was young, Sam explained, and in love with both himself and the business. I'd already heard the stories about how many big-name wrestlers had been divorced and lost fortunes due to the stress of the business and the travel.

At one point in 1981, Muchnick invited Flair to the office for a fatherly chat. Sam told Ric some stories about past stars, not just wrestlers, and how they had lost fortunes and messed up their marriages. He explained that he understood Flair wanted to live his character, but that Flair should be smart about doing it and know when to draw the line for his own good. Sam also praised Flair for his work, predicting an unlimited future for Ric in the ring. Flair was appreciative, hugged Sam afterward, and thanked him for being in his corner.

That night Flair got a fat purse after headlining a card at Kiel Auditorium. He rode in a stretch limo to the building and picked up bar tabs for everyone at the Airport Marriott lounge after the show. Naturally, Sam and I heard about it the next day. Muchnick just shook his head. "I'll bet he spent every dime we paid him," Sam said sadly.

Long after St. Louis became just a classy footnote in pro wrestling history, Flair had demonstrated that he would always be the "Nature Boy," dressing and living the part.

It's what he wanted to be. From the time I met him, he was pretty much always Ric Flair. There's nothing wrong with that, for the most successful performers always reveal an inner part of their personality that is explosive and extravagant. Most, however, understand that the public persona isn't helpful when it comes time to go home, close the door, pay the bills, and live life.

The list of Flair's financial difficulties and personal headaches is sobering to consider. The pro wrestling life is always difficult, with many bumps in the road. Flair clearly struggled with this dichotomy, if over time he even realized it was there. As Michael Bochiccio, whose company Highspots had a frustrating business experience with Flair, told journalist Shane Ryan, "He could never separate Ric Flair from Richard Fliehr."

Selfishly, we fans ignore the difficulty this caused Fliehr and those close to him, for we want to celebrate Ric Flair, the fabulous pro wrestler, the same way we do any major sports or entertainment celebrity. The purpose of this entire book is to discover exactly where Flair and all the other true greats belong among the elite in their chosen field, not to psychoanalyze one star.

But we are remiss if we fail to acknowledge the cost and the pain that is sometimes involved when a human being reaches the summit. To know how difficult Flair's personal life has been is depressing. Perhaps we fans are part of the problem by making it easier for an individual to believe that only the time spent in the spotlight matters. It's too easy to mix up the person and the character, especially for Flair, who produced so much excitement and so many thrills.

Yet one fact is not open to argument. The adrenalin ran hottest and the heart beat fastest for "Nature Boy" Ric Flair when he stepped through the dressing-room door and that huge crowd roared. . . . That was Flair in his element, and that's why he is right there with Lou Thesz leading the pack of the 50 greatest pro wrestlers of all time.

#1 LOU THESZ
The best there ever was across the board

The best. The greatest. Number one.

How do you determine the best? At sports, music, film, art, or anything else? How do you determine the greatest for professional wrestling, especially after the propaganda machine known as World Wrestling Entertainment (WWE) tried to shove their version of the 50 greatest "sports entertainers" of all time down the public's throat?

If the job is to be done, it should be done right, without regard for pushing a company's employees or allies. Picking without prejudice the very best of the litter from a business that has existed for more than a century is challenge enough.

Now try to decide who is the greatest, the best of a mind-boggling field from 100-plus years of action.

Is number one — the best — the biggest money-maker? The most creative or athletic? The best looking? The most well known? The most outrageous? The one who lasted the longest at the highest level?

Who gets to be number one in a select group of all number ones? Who gets to be the greatest of all the greats, the best of the very best?

Making that decision, surprisingly, was not as difficult as I anticipated. Naturally, the final call was razor-close, and I recognize that a few superstars outside my selection had compelling arguments in their favor as well. But what else would anyone expect? Look first at the questions that need to be answered to determine only that position, and then consider the process used to get to that point.

Imagine trying to put together a group of 100 or so as a starting pool. Imagine narrowing down from the hundreds of superb performers in the century-plus history of pro wrestling. Now imagine trying to sort out the 50 best. Now imagine putting them in order. Now imagine picking number one, the single star who shines brighter than all the rest.

One wrestler cut across generations and genres a little bit more than anyone else did. He had a foot in a greater number of different styles and philosophies of performing pro wrestling than anyone: from hard, stiff, and crusty quasi-competition to flamboyant, strutting television performance to rowdy, rough, nearly hardcore action.

He had fewer holes in his game, fewer chinks in his armor. His athleticism and ring instinct guaranteed that he would have adapted to whatever wrestling was then, now, and everything in between. He stood out just walking to the ring. The pull was so strong. He was the *champion*, title belt or not. The intangibles of his skill and his will reside even today in rare air and he always will.

By a hair . . . with Ric Flair right on his heels . . . it's Lou Thesz.

Lou Thesz is the greatest pro wrestler in the history of the game. He is number one.

Will there be squawks and complaints and gripes? Of course. So what? Take your best shot, but come with lots of ammunition. Actual facts and, most important, depth of understanding. Make sure you grasp what wrestling was, what it is, and how it got where it is. Appreciate how many building blocks Lou Thesz put there himself. The evidence is there for those who are serious, for those who really care about the entire record of pro wrestling: Lou Thesz belongs atop the golden heap.

Once upon a time, at a critical moment in the development of the business, in the ring before an important match began in 1963, Thesz told his opponent, Buddy Rogers, "We can do this the hard way, or we can do this the easy way." Nobody would say that today. Rogers chose the easy way, and, honestly, wrestling was better for it. Thesz was willing, and able, to do it either way.

That's the stuff of legends. Looking back, it is a remnant of an era on the verge of death, if not already extinct. It was not a joke, not a scripted line for a television promo on *Raw*. Thesz was dead serious. The business of pro wrestling *still* is serious on the inside no matter what label is applied or style is utilized by its performers.

Be brave enough to take the hard way here, though, and tell the truth. Take the antidote to what WWE wants to say wrestling is and was. Use the knowledge and appreciate the complete history of pro wrestling. Celebrate it. And take the hard way and state the obvious . . . Lou Thesz is number one on a star-studded lineup. And no disrespect is aimed at anyone by that assertion.

An intimate conversation with many of the greats alive today would likely reveal that, down deep, most of them think *they* should have the elusive number one position. That's pride talking, and in almost every case it's well deserved. That pride stems from an inner hunger that cannot be satisfied, which drives or drove every performer among the best of the best of the best.

In tallying up all the pluses and minuses, taking the hard way will probably ruffle some feathers. I'll still cast my vote for Lou Thesz.

The hard facts are scattered throughout this book. But . . . as with the other pillars of pro wrestling, in particular Ric Flair, "Strangler" Lewis, Hulk Hogan, and Bruno Sammartino, merely reciting the names and numbers doesn't begin to capture the essence, the soul, of what made someone like Thesz or the others the epitome of what a great wrestling performer is.

Most importantly, Thesz made the fans believe. Lou had mastered his craft so well that his connection with the audience was intimate and real.

More than anything, especially during his many years as champion, what happened in the ring mattered because of how Thesz worked his battles. To him, credibility counted, and the huge paying audiences obviously agreed.

Thesz looked like the champion even when he wasn't the champion. There was a regal bearing in his walk, his posture, his expression. Partly by reputation, partly by performance, everyone in and out of the business knew that he was the real deal.

Of course, even those with little comprehension of wrestling's history know that Thesz was possibly the finest scientific grappler ever. Verne Gagne was right there. Kurt Angle could have been. Maybe close were Pat O'Connor and, in the mind of the casual audience at least, Wilbur Snyder. Some could nominate Dan Hodge, and perhaps Jack Brisco or Dory Funk Jr. or even Dick Hutton. But, oh, that Thesz! He had some extra quality that could be sensed throughout an auditorium — Thesz would and could hurt someone if that was what was required.

Supreme athleticism, like a hungry panther. Quick, hard takedowns. Holds that looked like they hurt because many actually did. Speedy reversals. Bone-rattling body slams. Artful flying head scissors. Various back body drops known today as suplexes. Perfect drop kicks. The Thesz press, done faster and harder than today — and isn't it amazing that WWE still allows its announcers to use that term?

Thesz's facial expressions were terrific because he always reacted perfectly at exactly the correct moment — without overdoing it. When selling for an opponent, Thesz had the touch to make a foe look even better than he was, a skill Thesz prided himself on. Suddenly a crowd could see that the great Thesz was in *trouble*, and they were shocked and would stand . . . and scream. On a comeback, fire would shoot out of Lou's eyes. He didn't punch often, but when he did — yes, they bought it.

In St. Louis on April 26, 1963, Thesz defended the National Wrestling Alliance crown against Dick the Bruiser when The Bruiser was at his peak as a monster heel. The Bruiser was a tank with a Triple H–chest and shoulders that bulged. He wrecked real wooden tables that were not gimmicked, threw chairs, fought National Football League players, busted up bars, and turned angles into what certainly looked like shoots.

And here was Thesz, the older but revered champion, trying to stop The Bruiser. Just when it looked as though The Bruiser would simply bulldoze the scientific Thesz, Lou threw some vicious punches, apparently in desperation, hitting Dick's head and opening a fresh wound from a bar fight in Detroit that had actually gotten national publicity.

The blood flowed all over The Bruiser's face. And then his chest, as Thesz — enraged — pounded and pounded and pounded The Bruiser. The champion was like a shark chomping away at a victim. The sellout crowd stood and roared as loud as a runaway freight train. They stomped on the risers. It sounded like an earthquake as Thesz, his face an angry snarl, battered The Bruiser and splattered blood all over the ring.

Finally, with The Bruiser a reeling, stunned, bloody mess, the referee stopped the bout and awarded the decision to Thesz because the monster could not continue.

The scientific genius had displayed another side of his fully developed ring personality. Just when some thought they could pigeon-hole Thesz into the sparkling scientific struggles he had with Pat O'Connor, he demonstrated a completely different approach that most fans, who were not familiar with his hard-hitting physical wars against "Wild Bill" Longson, had overlooked.

Compare all of the variety required in historic duels Thesz had with everyone from Everett Marshall to Dory Funk Jr., from Bronko Nagurski to Gene Kiniski, from "Whipper" Billy Watson to Verne Gagne, from Johnny Valentine to Fritz Von Erich, from Killer Kowalski to Don Leo Jonathan, and on and on seemingly forever. Consider how he opened up Japan for NWA champions and American stars when he put together classics against Rikidozan. Look at his meetings with Europe's biggest stars on their home turf. . . . The list is endless. Just think about all of his main events from the mid 1930s into the very early 1970s.

The man was on top of the business, as the primary champion or close to it, from 1937 until 1966. Who else lasted that long, who else dominated, especially as wrestling changed its styles even in those days, a fact many today ignore or don't know?

Radically different matches, telling different stories with different plots: Thesz painted a layer of credibility — and because of it, excitement — onto each and every one. Those who were lucky enough to have seen his magic act know that Thesz could have the crowd in the palm of his hand and make them feel as intense as he was!

As champion, Thesz always wanted to tackle the top contender for the title, often a sharp, scientific babyface challenger. And he was often in bouts in which the crowd wanted a title change. So for the good of the drama, subtly he would slide into heel mode to make the duel more emotional. A quick move without a clean break. A sneaky, nasty punch. Did Thesz really pull hair? Is he that worried about this opponent? Is the champ in trouble? A look, a scowl, a quick gasp in pain. Somehow Thesz would turn the crowd just as surely as Buddy Rogers or Freddie Blassie ever did.

Furthermore, he was a hooker (the highest level of shooter, who knows submissions and how to seriously hurt a foe) and one stride ahead of Ray Steele and maybe equal to "Strangler" Lewis. Do those even exist today, or have they all gone to Mixed Martial Arts and Ultimate Fighting? Thesz was nobody to mess with. Those few who did (Paul Boesch, Kintaro Oki, and a few others) paid a price. All of the work with first George Tragos, then Ad Santel, and finally Lewis himself helped to fit the hooker's weapons into a pro wrestling context, and it paid off for Thesz.

Could Lou Thesz work? Could he work like Ric Flair, Shawn Michaels, or Bret Hart? Is an answer even necessary? Maybe they took different paths, maybe Thesz's method for working was his own, but the destination was the same. Did he sell? Of course he did, and masterfully so. The way he sold worked because it convinced fans without diminishing their belief in his reality.

Does anyone really think that someone this athletic and this smart would not have figured out how to succeed in the wrestling world of 2012? The question, as we've explored previously, is more about how many of the 2012 standouts could dominate as Thesz did in the 1940s, 1950s, and

1960s. My general belief is that the greats of any time period would fit into the demands of another time period to be great then too. But a few — a very few — more so than others.

Politics inside wrestling has wrecked more than one career. Conversely, a few have benefited from the flow of politics and personalities. Lou Thesz, by the sheer strength of his ability and individuality, often bent politics for his advantage, not the other way around. How many others have done that? Few, very few. At the height of his power, Thesz dictated when he would be champion, when he would lose the title, who he would lose it to, and when he would come back. Even those operators, promoters, and wrestlers who disagreed could not prevail in the end.

His longest turn on the throne, a seven-year reign from essentially 1950 into 1957, may have been the most stable, least challenged run by any champion in history. This was a testament both to the National Wrestling Alliance for keeping some sort of structure in a volatile business and to Thesz himself, for everyone knew he was the guy for the position.

Did Thesz play political hardball, take advantage of predicaments, make enemies, bear grudges, manipulate as needed, shade the truth, or put himself first when necessary? Of course he did. It's the human condition, especially in an ego-driven business such as pro wrestling, with money and power up for grabs. It's also the only way to breathe in the atmosphere at the peak. Thesz did it, Ric Flair did it, "Strangler" Lewis did it, Hulk Hogan did it, and Bruno Sammartino did it, all to different degrees. Sometimes there was little choice.

If he irritated a promoter, so be it because most promoters tried to fool with the talent. The fact that he stood up, whatever the motivation, likely also benefited the talent underneath in some form. After all, when the champion drew a bigger house than normal, everyone on the show got more money than usual, including the wrestlers on the undercard. No room for softies here.

Some critics might say the lone blemish on Thesz's career could be his limited number of headline events in the New York area. But much of that was based on his total distrust of Toots Mondt, a historical manipulator who was considered the brain behind Vince McMahon Sr. Thesz thought Mondt and McMahon were crooks, worse than the other shysters who promoted. But Lou did respect the devious Toots, even if he didn't trust him. So, while he often flirted with Mondt and McMahon in a business sense, more often than not he chose a different path. Mondt's people were likely just as happy he did.

The fact that Thesz once stretched Argentina Rocca, then the pet of McMahon and Mondt (allegedly knocking Rocca cold), probably didn't help the relationship. But for Thesz, it proved a point and that was what he cared about as word spread throughout the business.

Knowing this history, I found an exchange I had with Mondt to be rather ironic. I met Mondt after he and his wife, Alma, retired and moved to her hometown of St. Louis. Muchnick often got together with Toots to trade war stories and talk about current politics. Around 1974 or 1975, I got to hear these fascinating exchanges in the office. While I usually just listened with few questions, one day the fan in me came out and I asked Mondt, "Who really was the greatest of all time, in your mind?"

Without hesitation, old Toots growled, "Lewis or Thesz. No question. Thesz or Lewis." This was his opinion despite the disagreements buried in the past. That was all "just business" to wise old owls like Muchnick and Mondt, who had seen everyone up to that day. Thesz mostly got his way in the dirty politics of pro wrestling. Ask Hulk Hogan — that's no mean accomplishment. Flair should understand, because he was often buffeted by politics and he fought constantly. The battles behind closed doors are the tough ones.

The point is that Thesz was at the top any way that position is evaluated. Some might look at this list and say that "Strangler" Lewis could not do in the ring what Ric Flair (or, for that matter, Shawn Michaels) did. But could Flair (or Michaels — well, let's be serious) do what Lewis did? Isn't that an equally valid question when taking in the entire picture?

Thesz was there for the tail end of the early era, when he earned his dangerous reputation. He could certainly do much of what Lewis did. Thesz was also there as in-ring changed and became closer to what Flair did, more wide open and acrobatic. Lou could succeed in that forum as well because he was able to fit together the puzzle pieces so that his technique worked in new circumstances.

As a pure showman, Flair would be number one. As a worker, in the critical area of connecting with the audience, Thesz was Flair's equal. He just got to the same location using a different route. And Thesz tips the scales because he was the real deal and his peers knew it. Honestly, Lewis is being underestimated in all this, no matter how diligent the effort is made to evaluate him. The passage of time is just too much; what has been lost or forgotten?

Actually, Thesz has always received one crucial vote that really counts. Ric Flair called Thesz "the greatest wrestler of all time . . . no argument about it, the all-time best. He was pro wrestling."

Those three, however, are right there, representing every facet of a fascinating business. And Lou Thesz is the one who crosses the most lines, builds the bridge, reaches over the greatest number of borders, and has the gifts to be on top at any time. His status, when correctly considered, narrowly finds a residence just above legendary.

Lou Thesz is the greatest pro wrestler of them all. He is, in fact, number one.

Acknowledgments

I worry about that guy, Michael Holmes. He's educated, bright, well rounded, and has a neat family. As editor for ECW Press, he deals with all types of writing from fiction to poetry. But he probably spends way too much time talking and working with someone like me who has been involved in and obsessed with pro wrestling. Therefore, I sincerely do thank him for nursing me through yet another lengthy project. If I have anything worthwhile to say, he encourages me to say it.

Michael's son, Logan, had a role to play as well. When I found out the seven-year-old wouldn't leave the Holmes' house without wearing his John Cena baseball cap, I realized another generation had spoken and Cena did indeed deserve to be in the top 50 of all time.

Yet another valuable resource who deserves my thanks is Dave Meltzer. Ask any question, no matter how obscure, and Dave can dig up the answer. Plus he is another sounding board off which to bounce opinions and ideas. Mel Hutnick, the best attorney in the world, is also somebody who makes this battered brain work overtime by asking how and why.

Further thanks for their time, attention, support, and thoughts go to Joe Babinsack, Doug Dahm, Matt Farmer, Steve Johnson, Irv Muchnick, Greg Oliver, Ron Plummer, and Herb Simmons. Of course, hidden in the shadows but always essential are those mysterious masked marvels who have my respect and thanks while they naturally remain anonymous.

Last but hardly least, sincere thanks to my wife, Pat, and daughter, Kelly. Pat just shakes her head, yet still takes the time to read, proof, and critique what I write. Kelly, though she lives 1,000 miles away and travels regularly, always finds time for sharp advice and eager encouragement. Sometimes I'm not sure who the kid is anymore.

Maybe that's because this wrestling disease keeps you feeling young. Thanks to every reader who feeds that passion we all share.

At ECW Press, we want you to enjoy this book in whatever format you like, whenever you like. Leave your print book at home and take the eBook to go! Purchase the print edition and receive the eBook free. Just send an email to ebook@ecwpress.com and include:

- the book title
  - the name of the store where you purchased it
    - your receipt number
    - your preference of file type: PDF or ePub?

A real person will respond to your email with your eBook attached. Thank you for supporting an independently owned publisher with your purchase!